Before Renaissance

Before Renaissance

Planning in Pittsburgh, 1889–1943

John F. Bauman and Edward K. Muller

University of Pittsburgh Press

Published by the University of Pittsburgh Press, Pittsburgh, Pa., 15260

Copyright © 2006, University of Pittsburgh Press

Manufactured in the United States of America

Printed on acid-free paper

10   9   8   7   6   5   4   3   2   1

LIBRARY OF CONGRESS CATALOGING-IN-PUBLICATION DATA

Bauman, John F., 1938–
    Before renaissance : planning in Pittsburgh, 1889-1943 / John F. Bauman
and Edward K. Muller.
        p. cm.
    Includes bibliographical references and index.
    ISBN 0-8229-4287-9 (cloth : alk. paper) — ISBN 0-8229-5930-5 (pbk. :
alk. paper)
    1. City planning—Pennsylvania—Pittsburgh—History.   2. Urban
renewal—Pennsylvania—Pittsburgh—History.   I. Muller, Edward K.
II. Title.
    HT168.P48B38 2006
    307.1´2160974886—dc22
                                        2006015730

For Barb and Kate

Contents

Illustrations

Preface

From the vantage point of 1943, the year industrialist Richard King Mellon, president of the private Pittsburgh Regional Planning Association, founded the Allegheny Conference on City Development and launched what became the nationally celebrated model for urban renaissance, wartime Pittsburgh seemingly belied any evidence of distinguished planning. Smoke enshrouded the city. The fiery furnaces of the mammoth Jones & Laughlin Steel mills lining the Monongahela River eerily illuminated the night sky. Railroads rumbled constantly through the city, automobile traffic clogged narrow city streets and roadways, and riverfronts presented a bleak, degraded landscape of untrammeled industrial and commercial activity.

Few would ever suspect that this epitome of the gritty industrial city entertained a long and illustrious history of city planning that extended well into the nineteenth century. Yet there was an amazing cast of planning luminaries whose stage from time to time was the city of Pittsburgh: Frederick Law Olmsted Jr., John C. Olmsted, Edward Bennett, Daniel Burnham, John Nolen, Charles Mulford Robinson, Harland Bartholomew, and Robert Moses. To that list this book adds Frederick Bigger, the Pittsburgh planner who, in the wake of Olmsted Jr.'s 1910 plan for Pittsburgh, kept the city near or at the center of planning history.

Indeed, our very astonishment at Pittsburgh's impressive planning past instigated this book. At the urging of planning historian David Schuyler, we first proposed to write a study similar to Greg Hise and William Deverell's *Eden by Design: The 1930 Olmsted-Bartholomew Plan for the Los Angeles Region* that would reprint the Olmsted, Bartholomew, and Moses plans for Pittsburgh while providing context, texture, and interpretation.[1] However, after a modicum of research, we discovered that the history of Pittsburgh planning far transcended the history of any particular plan. In fact, the story, as we argue, in many ways recapitulated and illuminated an important chapter of the early history of urban planning nationwide, a key segment of which Jon Peterson recently and eloquently told in his *The Birth of City Planning, 1840–1917*.[2] In the Pittsburgh story, as we tell it, the Steel City not only exemplifies the main trends of planning history but also at numerous points occupies a central role.

Unveiling Pittsburgh's important place in planning history has involved an extensive search through a fairly rich body of manuscript collections and a substantial number of published works. Many of these manuscript records, naturally, exist in Pittsburgh libraries and archives, but many are found outside Pittsburgh. We researched important collections at the Carl A. Krock Library at Cornell University, the Van Pelt Library at the University of Pennsylvania, the New York Public Library, and the Library of Congress in Washington, D.C. As the story moved into the 1930s, the Library of Congress and the National Archives and Records Center (National Archives II) at College Park, Maryland, became critical. Staff members at the National Archives II proved enormously helpful, as did Fred W. Bauman and Jeffrey M. Flannery at the Manuscript Division of the Library of Congress. Useful materials were also found in the Special Collections Department at the Case Western Reserve University Library in Cleveland, the University of Kentucky Library, and the Olmsted Associates' architectural records housed at the Frederick Law Olmsted National Historic Site in Brookline, Massachusetts. We must thank the fine staffs of all of these libraries and archives who, over the years, provided greatly appreciated assistance.

Understandably, the richest trove of data on Pittsburgh planning history resides in the city itself. Special thanks must be extended to the staff of the Pennsylvania Room (particularly Audry Iaccone) at the Carnegie Library in Pittsburgh, to the archivists and librarians at the John Heinz Pittsburgh Regional History Center, as well as to the staff of the University of Pittsburgh's Archives of Industrial Society, especially Corey Seeman and Miriam Meislik, and to the librarians at the Architectural Archives of Carnegie Mellon University, especially Martin Aurand. A great deal of the research for this book was done in the library of the Planning Department of the Pittsburgh City Planning Commission. We spent many months there poring over minute books and other volumes and documents. The always gracious Planning Department staff gave freely of their time and permitted almost unlimited use of the department copying machine. Staff members of the Allegheny County Planning Department were equally helpful. Several people with keen memories of Fred Bigger and the early days of planning in Pittsburgh consented to be interviewed. For the gracious and illuminating interviews, we thank architects John Ormsbee Simonds and Dahlen K. Ritchey and former administrators of the Pittsburgh Urban Redevelopment Authority John Robin and Robert Pease. For making the cover art available to us, we thank Judith O'Toole and Barbara Jones of the Westmoreland Museum of American Art.

For travel monies, sabbatical time, and the other financial support that made this book possible, we wish to thank California University of Pennsylvania, especially its Irene O'Brien Fund; the University of Pittsburgh; and the Muskie School of Public Service of the University of Southern Maine. In the fall and winter of 1993/1994 two articles appeared in *Pittsburgh History* dealing with the Olmsteds in Pittsburgh. In May 2002 the *Journal of Planning History* published our article, "The Planning Technician as Urban Visionary," about Frederick Bigger's planning career in Pittsburgh. We wish to thank the editors of both journals for permitting the reuse of some portions of those articles. Thanks are also due to George Thompson of the Center for American Places for advice and constant encouragement.

Any book researched over almost a decade naturally incurs a vast debt of gratitude for critical suggestions and advice, for support and encouragement. We especially thank our good friend and colleague David Schuyler for his long support and involvement in this project. David and many of those whom we acknowledge here are or have been members of the Society for City and Regional Planning History, at whose conferences over the years we have given many papers based on the research undertaken for this book. At those conferences, both at the sessions and then dining together at wonderful restaurants often scouted out by Mark Rose and Ray Mohl, as well as at other forums, we have enjoyed the friendship, comfort, and advice of the following scholars: Ray Mohl, Arleyn Levee, Kristin Szylvian, Roger Biles, Greg Hise, Alison Isenberg, Chris Silver, Howard Gillette, Jon Peterson, Eric Sandweiss, Robert Fishman, Mark Rose, and James Borchert. From the very beginning of this project, the invaluable advice and words of encouragement from Joel Tarr of Carnegie Mellon University and from Michael P. Weber, the late dean of the McAnulty College and Graduate School of Liberal Arts at Duquesne University and historian of Pittsburgh, were very deeply appreciated.

Finally, we wish to pay special tribute to the late Roy Lubove, whose 1969 study of housing, planning, and redevelopment in Pittsburgh, *Twentieth Century Pittsburgh: Government, Business and Environmental Change,* was an invaluable touchstone at many moments during our work. Likewise, we benefited from many hours of conversation with Roy during the last years of his life.[3]

Before Renaissance

CHAPTER 1

Planning and the Industrial City

ON OCTOBER 25, 1945, Pennsylvania governor Edward Martin announced that the state legislature had officially authorized the creation of a state park in the city of Pittsburgh, at the "Point," the historic confluence of the Ohio, Allegheny, and Monongahela rivers. In less than a month, Pittsburgh's political and business leadership, led by the city's banking tycoon and civic luminary Richard King Mellon, mobilized the city's planning community and leveraged the state's modest $4,000,000 park appropriation into a joint public-private tour de force hailed as the "Pittsburgh Renaissance."

Mellon's figure dominated this epic moment in Pittsburgh history. A pre–World War II stalwart of the Pittsburgh Regional Planning Association (PRPA), who as a colonel during the war headed Pennsylvania's Selective Service Administration, Mellon helped found the Allegheny Conference on Community Development in 1943.[1] After the war Republican Mellon teamed with Democratic political machine boss David Lawrence to make Pittsburgh the bellwether of American postwar city planning.

Lured by Mellon's overtures and by the state's 1947 Redevelopment Authority Act authorizing local authorities to employ eminent domain powers for urban development purposes, New York's Equitable Life Assurance Company consented to risk millions of dollars on Pittsburgh's downtown redevelopment scheme. The Mellon-Lawrence plan featured the city's sixty-acre Point, in 1947 an ugly mélange of railroad yards and seedy buildings, as the urban renaissance centerpiece. An early model showed Point State Park as part of a much broader Golden Triangle extravaganza that included the gleaming chromed steel towers of Gateway Center. Pittsburgh, once America's quintessential smoky, industrial city and branded "Hell with the Lid Off," now seized the national and international spotlight as America's premier renaissance city.

A large crowd of spectators assembled on May 18, 1950, amid the crumbling warehouses, the junk-filled rail yards, and a small cluster of moldering ancient row houses that tottered unobtrusively and tremulously in the shad-

ows of the historic Point. A giant steam crane slowly raised a one-ton wrecking ball into the air and then suddenly and violently unleashed it, crashing
it against the scarred exposed side of one withered old commercial building.
Demolition had begun. Twenty-four years, later in August 1974, surrounded
now by a gleaming showcase of Renaissance I architectural fare—the sparkling new Three Rivers Stadium; the shimmering Gateway Towers; Penn-
Lincoln Parkway; and the Fort Pitt Tunnels and Bridge—city and state officials
dedicated Point Park. Speaker after speaker at the ceremony praised the city's
history, especially the symbolic national importance of the "hallowed Point"
in the struggle for Anglo supremacy over the continent. They alluded just as
frequently to the park's key role in launching Pittsburgh's urban renaissance,
underscoring the historic role of city planning in overseeing the physical rebuilding of the urban environment.[2]

Most historians of Pittsburgh's post–World War II renaissance push the
origins of the movement to 1943 or 1945 and to planning decisions stemming
from the Lawrence-Mellon progrowth alliance. Some histories of postwar
city rebuilding trace the seeds of renewal farther back to the planning activity of the 1920s.[3] This book, however, discovers the roots of Pittsburgh's renaissance in a much earlier era, in the early decades of the twentieth century,
when a partnership of public and private leaders formed to promote modern
city planning—that is, comprehensive planning viewed as a process, and built
upon an organic concept of urban space to be managed scientifically by educated professionals. These same disciples established planning in Pittsburgh,
created a solid legal framework for planning practice, and set in motion the
machinery that produced many landmark city projects such as the Pitt Parkway, Point Park, and the Golden Triangle.

Many historians, however, see some evidence of city planning before the
advent of twentieth-century progressive reform. Planning appears in the ad
hoc development of nineteenth-century urban infrastructure. Historian Jon
Peterson argues that such uncoordinated, fragmented, "special purpose planning" of parks, sewers, streets, waterworks, and boulevards lacked any comprehensive basis. It resulted, instead, from ongoing informal conversations
among city engineers, landscape architects, city boosters, businessmen, philanthropists, politicians, and others (including members of the city's notorious
ring) about how urban space should be used to enhance the city's prosperity
and prospects. This vital conversation about the uses of urban space constantly
evolved. By the late nineteenth century, progressive reformers—that is, urban
elites and middle-class professionals, organized as good government groups,

women's clubs, neighborhood improvement associations, settlement houses, and other civic bodies, and outraged by the arrogance, cost, and sheer inefficiency of boss-controlled city building—recast that conversation into a progressive discourse about social order, good government, and the imperatives of modern science, reason, bureaucracy, and the public interest. From that progressive dialogue, not only modern city planning but also a new, but fragile, public-private partnership emerged that, after World War I, strengthened as an alliance of young professional planners and a committed proplanning business community. That structure endured until the mid-1930s when, under the extreme duress of the Great Depression, federal power and resources further enhanced the authority of planning while concomitantly energizing the private and paradoxically more activist side of the planning partnership, and catalyzed urban renaissance.[4]

Using Pittsburgh as a case study, we explore the origins, nature, and consequences of modern urban planning as it unfolded in the Steel City from the 1890s through 1943. It was amid the Great Depression and World War II, when fear of imminent deindustrialization and permanent high national unemployment mounted, that the federal government, through the Public Works Administration and the National Resources Planning Board, seized the urban planning initiative. Indeed, in 1943, as Allied expeditionary forces mobilized to strike at Hitler's fortress Europe, the federal government commanded American cities to undertake postwar planning. The order ultimately spawned the Allegheny Conference on Community Development (ACCD), the progrowth consortium of downtown lawyers, architects, university presidents, and business leaders pledged to undertake a massive physical rebirth of Pittsburgh. This study, however, focuses on the solid foundation for planning erected before Mellon, Lawrence, and the ACCD pronounced the rebirth of Pittsburgh. It probes the roots of the urban planning ethos and recounts the odyssey of that band of progressive-minded architects, landscape architects, civil engineers, lawyers, business leaders, and women reformers who, conceptualizing the city as an organic whole, sought to bring order and efficiency, as well as beauty, to the city's late-nineteenth-century and pre–World War II urban environment. Despite a myriad of obstacles to planning, political and otherwise, this modern city planning movement concretely impacted the physical shape and form of the city.[5] However, solidly rooted in conventional power structures, pre–World War II planning consistently sidestepped housing reform issues and never confronted socially sensitive urban equity issues such as race and poverty. The idealized urban neighborhood was lily white.[6]

THE ORIGINS OF CITY PLANNING

Pittsburgh's late-nineteenth- and early-twentieth-century quest for beauty and order occurred amid a broader discourse about social injustice and environmental squalor. The unprecedented economic misery and labor violence exacerbated by the depression of the 1890s catalyzed urban reform. City planning became a strategy in the reformers' arsenal to advance public good. Indeed, the idea of urban rebirth informed the 1893 World's Columbian Exposition in Chicago, which featured monumental baroque architecture arranged as a gleaming "White City" around a lagoon designed by Frederick Law Olmsted Sr. This tour de force of civic art, orchestrated by paragons of American architecture Daniel Burnham, Charles McKim, and Stanford White, among others, highlighted the power of planning, especially ensembles of great civic buildings, to engender order and stir civic virtue. In his magisterial *The Birth of City Planning in the United States, 1840–1917,* Jon Peterson acknowledges the significant role of both the fair and the subsequent 1902 McMillan Plan for Washington, D.C., for spurring the City Beautiful movement and laying the foundation for modern city planning. Peterson sees a highly receptive audience awaiting these events, the groundwork well prepared by a long history of nineteenth-century sanitary reform, park, and civic art achievements, as "antecedents" to the planning movement officially inaugurated by the National Conference on City Planning in 1909–1910.

Like historian John Reps, Peterson asserts that at the "townsite level," cities have been planned for millennia. However, none of the pioneers of modern urban planning, argues Peterson, neither John Nolen, Daniel Burnham, Charles Mulford Robinson, nor Frederick Law Olmsted Jr., regarded the early town-site plans for Philadelphia, Savannah, or Detroit as precursors of their discipline. Nor did they consider nineteenth-century park, water, sewer, and transit systems, and other special purpose planning to embrace a comprehensive perspective. Nineteenth-century urban form and the social order reflected therein were, we argue, primarily the result of a host of conscious decisions. While as Mansel Blackford and Christine Rosen have clearly explained, some nineteenth-century civic and business interests desired public works to promote economic growth and some saw park and other projects enhancing the social order, these voices of business were pluralistic, not monolithic.[7] The conversation, that is, reflected myriad discussions about how and where streets, markets, public buildings, offices, libraries, and parks should or should not be built, funded or not funded, taxed or not taxed. In this respect, writes historian John Fairfield, the American city "was in important ways 'planned' before the rise of professional city planning." But there was no larger vision of city form and little means to control city development.[8]

Sam Bass Warner espied such planning in the "weave of small patterns" comprising the texture of Boston's "streetcar suburbs" of Dorchester, Roxbury, and Jamaica Plains. The weave reflected the decisions made by a multitude of landowners and small, speculative builders about house lots, house plans, and what architectural embellishments to employ. Other historians have observed that the culture and traditions of the owner/renter occupants themselves molded the fabric of city space.[9] At a different architectural and design level, Andrew Jackson Downing's rendering for the Washington, D.C., mall, and Frederick Law Olmsted Sr.'s designs for New York City's Central Park (with Calvert Vaux) and for the Buffalo park system, as well as for early suburban communities such as Riverside, Illinois, convincingly attest to the existence of a form of civic "planning" before the discipline was professionalized in the early twentieth century.[10]

But all this planning, as Jon Peterson insists, was ad hoc, uninformed by any comprehension of the city as a whole. Peterson labels this nineteenth-century design of parks, water and sewerage-carriage systems, and subdivisions, no matter how impressive, "special purpose planning." While entailing systemic design, this special purpose planning lacked coordination or a comprehension of the physical, social, or economic complexity of the city, and therefore contributed to the accusation that cities evoked haphazard, not ordered, development.

Still, urban park plans, and the rising authority nationally of urban sanitary engineers, underscored an intense environmentalism imbuing nineteenth-century middle-class reform. Olmsted Sr., the farmer-journalist turned genius landscaper, endeavored to create within America's rising industrial cities a new naturalistic landscape able to counter the popularly perceived, morally subterranean slum world of the immigrant.[11] Architects, engineers, and ardent disciples of municipal art societies and civic associations beautified vacant lots, abominated billboards, and placed grand Beaux-Arts monuments in city parks, convinced that physical improvements, parks, boulevards, water and sewer systems, and decorative horse troughs would restore civic order and nurture the good city. However, few of these environmental reformers shared Frederick Law Olmsted Sr.'s broad vision of linked urban space. They harbored only a rudimentary idea of the city as a biological system, a matrix of interconnected neighborhoods linked by streets, thoroughfares, sewers, and other vital infrastructure.

The important figures of nineteenth-century planning engaged largely in a more specialized, narrowly conceived discourse about planning, one meant to persuade urban constituencies to vote their approval of new bond issues and thus higher taxes for expensive infrastructure. Although extensive Gilded Age park, sewer, and water projects comprised systems, and boulevards may have joined peripheral parkland into a network or necklace of accessible individual urban parks that strove to meet citywide social-psychological needs, landscape architects and city engineers, like the authors of nineteenth-century model tenements, addressed not the city as a whole but merely discrete segments of the urban fabric.[12]

Only a few nineteenth-century visionaries such as Henry George and Edward Bellamy grasped the totality of the urban environment, especially the relationship between the unequal access to land ownership and power endemic to laissez faire economies and the deteriorating quality of urban life and concomitant social disorder. However, like the vibrant social gospel movement of the era, they posited millennial, apocalyptic solutions to the problem of social injustice. Miraculously, they believed that a suddenly enlightened citizenry would enact the single tax and that religiously warmed urban hearts would beget a cooperative commonwealth. Such millennial schemes, while attracting considerable attention and support in Pittsburgh and elsewhere, seemed disconnected from the entrenched, highly individualistic, laissez faire competitive order that in reality embodied the American industrial city.[13]

Modern American city planning arrived with the progressive urban reform movement that unfolded at the turn of the century. A diverse array of engineers, architects, social workers, housers, tax reformers, and progressives, such as Olmsted Jr., cast the conversation in terms of a moral environmentalism, the power of the built environment to shape human behavior. Moreover, an aura of science and deep reverence for efficiency imbued much of this discourse. In addition, aesthetic and bureaucratic values and a dedication to professional standards drove their quest and led them to replace informal, special purpose planning with "the plan."[14]

Inspired by the triumph of the "White City," and by the subsequent 1902 McMillan Plan for Washington, D.C., in the early twentieth century progressive architects and other reformers concerned about the order and management of urban space increasingly spoke of planning as a comprehensive exercise or process leading to a plan. Accordingly, planning came to be viewed as a clearly defined body of thought, a set of teachable principles concerned with achieving order in, imposing efficiency in, and exercising disciplinary control over metropolitan space. Numerous historians have demonstrated that this impulse toward a definitive social order welled up from progressive reformers' sensibilities about the superiority of the natural to the built environment, and from gnawing middle-class fears about excrescent urban slums and the putatively dangerous, foreign-born denizens of that urban underworld.[15] In the late nineteenth century in Pittsburgh and other cities, theologians, philosophers, landscape architects, settlement house workers, engineers, and enlightened businessmen grappled with the consequences of the modern urban industrial world. They fabricated a set of principles about space, order, beauty, morality, and the primacy of science and efficiency, which by the second decade of the twentieth century had been codified into what could be called the planning ethos. The ethos not only presumed a holistic view of urban space but first and foremost embodied moral environmentalism, the belief in the socially curative, morally rehabilitative effect of a cleansed, well-ordered cityscape. Several historians have observed that this planning ideal subordinated social to aesthetic concerns. For this reason, many settlement house workers, housing reformers, and social visionaries abjured the American planning camp. Among this last group was the founder of New York's Committee on the Congestion of Population (CCP) and advocate of strict German-style land-use controls, Benjamin Marsh, who stubbornly pressed for public ownership of transit and other utilities.

While sensitive to the social implications of planning, most progressive planners steered a more conservative social and political course. The disciplinarians that we explore in this study of Pittsburgh, particularly city planner Frederick Bigger, favored substituting expert, orderly, politically neutral public authority for the mayhem of the private marketplace in shaping the urban environment. In fashioning a more attractive and efficient city, planning would create a more socially equitable and just city.[16]

Supported by businessmen, architects, lawyers, and other professionals, twentieth-century planners, including Bigger, first and foremost saw themselves as members of a craft, a discipline, owners of a body of specialized knowledge. Like followers of the Chicago School of urban sociology, they viewed the city as a mosaic of specialized, but functionally integrated, spaces. In the 1920s the Chicago School's biological/urban ecological model of city form proved a convincing explanation for the functional relationship of urban spaces, "natural areas" such as the business district, the red light district, and the ethnic enclaves such as Little Italy, Polish Hill, or Deutchtown. This view reinforced the planners' faith in environmentalism, especially their hope for restoring community to immigrant neighborhoods deemed wracked by alienation.[17]

Above all, city plans served planners and public officials as crucial templates for making reasoned decisions and for educating the public about the wisdom and the timing of proposed costly civic improvements. Significantly, during the first half of the century, these master plans were invariably privately commissioned and financed.[18]

FRAGMENTED URBAN SPACE AND THE
ROOTS OF PLANNING

Of all the late-nineteenth-century American cities, perhaps Pittsburgh most defied the progressives' ideal image of the rationally ordered metropolis. Marked by steep hills, cleaved by deep ravines and hollows, the city had long ago brashly surrendered its once verdant riverbanks to iron, steel, and glass industrialism. For most city families, acrid smoke, raining soot, and the din and deafening roar of heavy industrialism constantly assaulted the senses. A cluttered downtown of impressive public buildings, department stores, and offices clearly emerged after the Civil War, and on the urban periphery a world of middle-class gentility arose in juxtaposition to gritty, industrial suburban mill towns such as Braddock and Homestead.

Modernization and rapid urban growth brought a flood of immigrants into the industrial city and its suburban mill towns, differentiating and segregating urban and regional space. A patchwork of discrete neighborhoods unfolded, politically nurtured enclaves where ethnic loyalties trumped working-class consciousness and solidarity. Like New York's Lower East Side, Chicago's South Side, and Philadelphia's Poplar Area, Pittsburgh's Strip and Hill districts, for example, became home to a jumble of Irish, Jewish, Polish, and African American enclaves. Pittsburgh's suburban middle class viewed these regions as a moral underworld, home to the dreaded dangerous classes.[19]

A riot of telegraph and telephone lines, transit catenary, and the poles used to carry them, cluttered the air space over city streets whose surfaces were crisscrossed with the trackage of a myriad of trolley companies. Horsecars, cable cars, and trolleys vied with drays, carts, wagons, and harried pedestrians for lean space on the city's narrow streets. In the subterranean world beneath city streets lay a tangle of water, gas, and sewer lines, some lost or forgotten as rival utility companies were bankrupted or merged.[20]

Adding to this melee above and below, downtown streets already tightly packed with shops and businesses teemed with makeshift stalls and peddlers' carts. In 1895 some enterprising merchants, starved for space, hawked produce from freight cars parked on Liberty Avenue. Taprooms, saloons, brothels, and cheap theaters spiced the whole affair with moral ambiguity, which deeply affronted the hair-trigger religious sensibilities of middle-class social reformers. While industry-driven modernization intensified the civic and commercial use of urban space and spawned increasingly segregated communities, it likewise produced more highly specialized professions, organizations, and families, contributing to what historian Robert Wiebe has called the "segmented society."[21]

Political machines towered among the specialized organizations that flourished in the late-nineteenth-century city. According to historian Seymour Mandelbaum, the urban political machine may have functionally bridged the widening urban social gulfs and ethnic rifts that marked the boundaries of the fragmented metropolis. Pyramid structured with a base of ward heelers and precinct captains, the machine hierarchy ascended upward through lieutenants and to the city boss himself. Erected upon ward loyalties, it exquisitely epitomized urban segmentation.

Pittsburgh's Christopher Magee modeled his machine on New York's Tweed Ring. He emphasized public works and, rife with graft, abetted urban fragmentation. As in New York, most of the public works—sewer lines and water mains, paved streets, transit lines, and park projects—benefited the developing middle-class, tree-lined neighborhoods, where bosses harvested a fortune in inflated contracts and lucrative land speculations. This special purpose planning—despite the fact that some of it, like Pittsburgh's Schenley Park, Highland Park, and Grant Boulevard, represented signal contributions to the nineteenth-century built environment—lacked the systematic design and comprehensive features sufficient to make it modern, professional city planning. For Boss Magee and his chief cohort, William Flinn, as for his engineer and chief of public works, Edward Manning Bigelow, decision making remained ad hoc. Despite Bigelow's comprehensive approach to park and boulevard development, he never conceptualized the city as a whole. Moreover, bossism neglected absent or decaying infrastructure in poor and working-class neighborhoods. Machine politicians responded to ward demands only when politically, not socially, motivated. Although bosses "got things done," contract inflation, bribes, payoffs (boodle), and other forms of political graft proved costly; for reformers in an age of millennial religious fervor, the linkage of bossism to brothels, gambling, and the liquor evil easily entrapped public works spending with bossism in the larger deadly web of moral corruption.[22]

THE COMPLEX ORIGINS OF PROGRESSIVE
PLANNING IN PITTSBURGH

In the late nineteenth and early twentieth centuries, Pittsburgh progressives, outraged by threats of violence, smoke, and sheer ugliness, rallied to impose order on the dangerously mottled industrial city. These reformers added a new, powerful voice to the urban conversation shaping urban form and culture. They gave a face as well to the novel force of mass consumption reconfiguring urban space in the twentieth century. For elites and the "New Middle Class" retrospectively, the late-nineteenth-century urban world had appeared harrowing. Such evidence of social disorder, the imminence of Armageddon, only served to heighten their commitment to moral environmentalism. Seemingly in sympathy with middle-class aspirations, Pittsburgh's chief of Public Works, Edward Bigelow, beseeched greater control over land use. He called for coordinating new subdivisions, and, echoing Frederick Law Olmsted Sr., Bigelow lent his voice to those exhorting the need to develop large, accessible city parks. Under Bigelow, Pittsburgh, like Buffalo and Boston, undertook significant special purpose planning ventures, including the development of a magnificent park system with boulevards and a zoo. Along with Andrew Carnegie, Bigelow also laid the foundation for the city to create in the Oakland section a cultural and educational center.

However, in the face of urban disorder, some reformers seized upon more radical visionary schemes seeking to restore the simplicity of an imagined republican past. Henry George, whom many Pittsburghers embraced, espoused the single tax; others invoked Christian charity and the eschatological hope of a coming Christian commonwealth. Pittsburgh's Rev. George Hodges, like Marsh and many other reformers nationally, sought answers abroad at various French expositions or toured elsewhere in Europe and spoke excitedly about *la reform sociale,* and about British socialist housing experiments. These travelers, like Hodges, and like their many compatriots in the progressive reform movement, viewed the city as a mosaic of specialized, functionally integrated space.[23]

The environmental-reformist vision of the well-designed, park-served, and sanitary city captivated the nation's imagination in 1893 when Chicago hosted the World's Columbian Exposition. In the wake of the fair, in Pittsburgh as in hundreds of other cities, large and small, middle-class men and women enlisted in civic housekeeping, municipal art, settlement house, philanthropic housing, antismoke, and other social reform movements. Members of these movements marched with social gospelers, teetotalers, business boosters, and others in a crusade to smash the corrupt alliance of bossism, vice, and big business, and to restore democracy, civic virtue, and moral order to the city.[24]

The roots of planning in Pittsburgh, therefore, lay not only buried deep in the soil of nineteenth-century urban reform, and in an emergent professionalism imbued with science and efficiency, but also in moralism and civic righteousness, in the firm belief that the city's evil ring blocked any hope for a new moral order and the creation of a wholesome, well-scrubbed, civically righteous city. From this vibrant millennial progressivism sprang the vision of a "Greater Pittsburgh," the "city as a whole," which would embody in one glorious womb not only the economically and spiritually reborn city but also the whole region. From it, as well, came the seed of the Pittsburgh Survey, and the demand for active public intervention for social justice and against immigrant poverty and squalid tenements. And, finally, from it sprang the impetus for modern comprehensive planning.[25]

Planning historians, including those who embed the origins of planning in the nineteenth-century conversation about urban progress and city rivalry, agree that the Progressive movement launched modern, comprehensive urban planning. Historians, nevertheless, differ about the source of this early-twentieth-century planning ethos, which by 1910 had produced a host of city plans and clear evidence of a budding planning profession. Some behold this progressive planning movement more rooted in settlement house work with its passion for social work, for efficiency and professional standards, and for mapping and policing the use of urban space. Others espy business interests pursuing economic goals through planning. Some see social elites in the vanguard, seeking to rationalize and discipline urban space on behalf of social order and economic efficiency, the goal of permanence and the stabilization of urban land values made shaky by the bewildering pace of urban change. In this interpretation, the advent of zoning (New York City enacted the first American zoning ordinance in 1916) marked the triumph of business's desire to "put everything in its place." A final group of historians sees technological changes in transportation involved. Progressives disdained boss-tainted, inefficient mass transit and embraced the automobile. However, the automobile exacerbated street congestion and boosted the demand for professional planning to unclog urban arteries. Meanwhile, scientific-minded settlement house workers, physicians, housers, and architects gathered volumes of data about slum conditions, smoke, crime, and delinquency, all affirming that the sordid, overcrowded urban environment thwarted immigrant adjustment and contributed to the social and economic costs of urban life.[26]

Peterson, on the other hand, traces the origins of modern, professional city planning to social and aesthetic goals of architects, landscape architects, lawyers, and others enthralled by the promise of the Columbian Exposition and the achievement of the McMillan Commission in Washington, D.C. In the early twentieth century, pioneer planners such as Burnham, Olmsted Jr., and Robinson merged park planning and civic art toward a truly comprehensive vision of the organic city, where plans embraced the totality of the city, including its physical as well as it social, economic, and political complexity. From a detailed analysis and understanding of the multitudinous parts would come an orderly, harmonious whole captured in "the plan."[27]

But, as the Pittsburgh case illustrates, by 1910 planning's rigid focus on the plan and on planning as a complex, scientific process aimed at the more efficient management of the city left abandoned Benjamin Marsh's notion of planning as a tool for social betterment, the amelioration of insanitation, the improvement of housing, and the lessening of poverty. Marsh's had been Hodge's and the Pittsburgh Survey's dream of the planned city. Olmsted Jr.'s dethronement of Marsh at the 1910 National Conference on City Planning in Rochester, New York, held the same year that Olmsted undertook his *Main Thoroughfares* plan for Pittsburgh, not only established Olmsted's quintessential role in planning history but also sealed planning's divorce from housing until the 1930s, and confirmed the Steel City's pivotal importance in understanding the planning process and planning history. Pittsburgh became a laboratory, a testing ground for Olmsted Jr.'s theories of "Practical Planning."

The Pittsburgh plan also highlighted the importance of the public-private partnership in planning. Public-private collaboration had existed in Pittsburgh at least as early as the 1890s, when Andrew Carnegie worked in tandem with the city's Public Works director Edward Bigelow on physical and cultural improvements for the Oakland section, a verdant region where philanthropists, planners, and visionaries would later flex their imaginations about better urban form. That collaboration, like the conversation, remained loosely structured. More formally defined partnerships blossomed in the Progressive Era as a means by which businessmen, lawyers, social workers, and other elite and middle-class professionals demanded a larger role in a so-called urban conversation that, they believed, had been dominated in the nineteenth century by boodlers, ward heelers, and other political "hacks." Dedicated to the values of science and efficiency, progressives like Pittsburgh's Fred Bigger after 1915 crafted a new, purified vision of the urban polity, one that necessitated reconfiguring the metaphorical table and narrowing the conversation to the academically credentialed and enlightened few—planners, engineers, social scientists, lawyers, and their business and political elite allies. Although public-sector progressives like Bigger now occupied a prominent place in urban decision making, and in the 1920s forged strong partnerships with business-dominated organizations such as the Citizens Committee on the City Plan (CCCP), Pittsburgh illustrates that politicians like William Magee still retained the power to make the final decisions.

This seminal era of progressive-professional planning, 1910–1940, comprises the centerpiece of this study. In this era, voluntary or private planning organizations such as the CCCP worked in concert with newly formed and legally sanctioned public planning agencies to systematize and codify rules for city development. With these rules, professional planners—not political cronies or the whimsy of the marketplace—would guide the rational ordering of urban and regional space.[28]

The effort herein to probe more fully the planning experience as it unfolded in Pittsburgh discloses that during the crucial decade of the 1920s, this planning professionalism finally and firmly rooted itself in Pittsburgh. This imprinting occurred despite the host of obstacles or "frictions" or "limitations" that dogged and harried the fledgling planning profession and throughout the period obstructed efforts to implement major features of the comprehensive planning process. In fact, the obstacles to implementation enshrouded the process and obscured planning's successes. Early jurisdictional battles, the political warfare between city and suburbs, Americans' visceral distrust of government, the requirements of the automobile, and one of the greatest frictions or obstacles, the fixed nature of urban land uses and the political and social power sealing the permanence of those uses, severely addled youthful city planners such as Pittsburgh's Frederick Bigger.

It was the Olmsted Jr. and Bigger ethos of scientific, practical planning, absorbed from progressivism, that triumphed, especially the scientific survey and the collection and mapping of demographic and topographic data. The vigilant monitoring of street widths, subdivision plats, building heights and setbacks, and other building activity made "mole work" the specialty of the profession. Moreover, by the 1920s planning in Pittsburgh focused disproportionately on the details of zoning, of street alignments, of lot and arterial plans, convinced that urban order itself wrought social benefits: good streets and boulevards, and good parks and playgrounds, that is, made good people.[29]

Led by business organizations, architects, and civic bodies, prior to World War II Pittsburgh legitimized planning and made it a recognized routine public sector activity. Amid the urban economic crisis of the Great Depression, New Dealers nationalized the planning ethos and, as historian Mark Gelfand long ago demonstrated, forged a crucial urban-federal planning alliance that by the 1950s provided the massive funding for large-scale urban renewal and renaissance. In fact, as we argue in chapter 8, the federal assumption of much of the financial burden of city development, through public works, work relief, housing, and other New Deal programs, further narrowed the urban conversation. In the nineteenth and early twentieth centuries, when bonds funded development costs, the conversation had been somewhat inclusive. In the 1930s, with Washington holding the purse strings, action-oriented civic bodies such as the Pittsburgh Regional Planning Association, in partnership with city and federal officials, seized the reins of the conversation from those professional planners like Bigger, who by 1943 increasingly found themselves overwhelmed by planning details.

The jewels of Pittsburgh's historic renaissance, Point Park and Gateway Towers, which rose up from the site at the Point cleared of slums, rail yards, and warehouses, are a tribute to the strength of that partnership, but also to the limitations of city planning in prewar Pittsburgh. Indeed, this study is equally an exploration of those limitations. While Pittsburgh evidences a considerable record of planning success prior to the war, in 1943, the year this study ends, other facts, including slum housing, traffic-clogged downtown streets, unfinished projects, and stacks of dusty and dog-eared plans, attested to the durability of political fragmentation and other obstacles to planning, despite the triumph of the planning ethos nationally as well as locally. The glitzy towers that shimmered within blocks of the sullen Hill District revealed Pittsburgh planning's preference for physical over social goals. Housing issues had no place in the city's planning agenda.

Over time, however, limitations aside, Pittsburgh planning had profound consequences for the urban environment in terms of streets, bridges, and buildings, but also parks, playgrounds, and tree planting. Pittsburgh planners sought to create an accessible city, to untangle the automobile-clogged urban core, to unite the sundered parts of the fragmented metropolis and build the Greater Pittsburgh. Notwithstanding the existence of persistent social, economic, and political barriers, including chronic jurisdictional battles and other forms of fragmentation, by 1943 planners had left an important and enviable legacy.

CHAPTER 2

Ring-Led Development and Planning

DURING THE 1870s AND 1880s, Pittsburgh rumbled and roared with the awful din, smoke, and fiery energy of modern industrialization. It was the nation's epicenter for the making of modern steel rails and girders, glass, heavy industrial machinery, and other basic goods. The city's having weathered the depression of the 1870s, the *Pittsburgh Post* in 1887 described "Pittsburgh and its progress as durable as the iron and steel production. Advance without recession is practically the rule."[1] William Supplee, a visitor to the Steel City in the 1890s, gazing upon the city from the heights of Mt. Washington above the confluence of the three rivers, marveled that as "far as the eye could reach the banks of [the city's] rivers were lined with industries, while steamboats and coal fleets covered the waters."[2]

The gritty, dust-encrusted tangle of cluttered alleys and narrow, traffic-clogged streets that Supplee beheld defied any semblance of deliberative order. Beauty for many Pittsburghers lay in industrialism itself. Yet by the close of the century a host of social and political reform organizations, plus the civic and municipal art and other improvement groups that had been created, redefined beauty in social, spiritual, and architectural terms. From this emerging progressive reform tradition sprang, by 1910, modern comprehensive urban planning. The movement could not have occurred in the city unless Pittsburghers had forged some sense of civic cohesion out of the fragmented social and political space that was the industrial metropolis. This chapter looks at the contested space of the nineteenth-century industrial metropolis as the arena for city building; it examines the role of special purpose planning in that same context and traces the rise of urban reform in reaction to machine politics and to the civic and social disorder wrought by untrammeled urban industrialism.

Industrialism shaped the district's population as well as its land uses. A labor-devouring behemoth, Pittsburgh's post–Civil War industry lured a steady stream of immigrant and migrant labor from southern and eastern Europe and from the American South. The city's population grew at a steady rate—from 235,000 in 1880 to 451,500 in 1900—while its metropolitan region, Greater Pittsburgh, which included such steel-making centers as Braddock, McKeesport, and Homestead, grew from 356,000 to 775,000 people.[3]

However, severe frictions existed in this densely populated, ethnically diverse urban space, where the limits of communication technology barred the easy flow of information and threatened the development of any consensus about the common good. First- and second-generation German, Irish, and Italian (especially those from Calabria and Abruzzi) Pittsburghers clustered in industrial neighborhoods such as Lawrenceville and Bloomfield, forming intimate Old World communities woven from tight familial ties. Eastern European Jews from the Pale of Settlement and Polish, Slovak, and Hungarian immigrants founded enclaves in the often fetid courts and alleys of the city's Hill District, together with a small but steadily growing population of African American migrants. Like other cities, therefore, late-nineteenth-century Pittsburgh's social and cultural landscape unfolded as a mosaic of social worlds, a densely crowded place segregated by class, race, and ethnicity, where cultural diversity, as well as political fragmentation, was accentuated by the city's bewildering topography of hills, hollows, rivers, and deep ravines.[4]

Contested space fueled civil strife, especially where labor refused to march lockstep in the new industrial army. Meanwhile, political and social barriers, as well as obstacles posed by historically fixed land uses and by socially and spatially isolated neighborhoods, further limited effective communication and strained the process of special purpose planning. From this fragmented conversation evolved the infrastructure of streets, roads, schools, and dispensaries necessary to provide a healthy and humane environment in the highly competitive, privatistic, rapidly urbanizing world of the nineteenth century.[5]

And Pittsburgh was frenzied. The city's political ring of Christopher Magee and William Flinn, like New York's regime of William Marcy Tweed and Philadelphia's James McManus, oversaw the greatest era of economic and physical urban growth in American history. Reports on "How We Grow" regularly appeared in the Pittsburgh press. City engineer Edward Bigelow in 1887 observed that "so many business interests are being attracted [to the downtown], and so many firms have discovered the necessity for making extensions owing to the boom that has struck Pittsburgh, that it is a difficult matter to procure a [building] site in the center of the city."[6] By 1890 Pittsburgh had spawned a clearly discernible central business district, including a few modest skyscrapers. Old central neighborhoods such as elite lower Penn Avenue, once a delec-

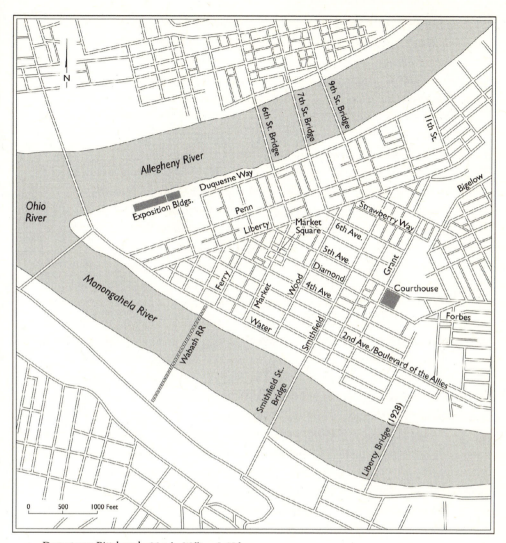

Downtown Pittsburgh. *Map by William L. Nelson*

table admixture of stately townhouses and respected professional offices anchored by the fashionable Fort Pitt Club, had surrendered their population to the city's growing East End and other suburbs such as Sewickley.[7]

Annexations, for one, impelled this spatial growth. Pittsburgh had annexed the East End suburbs in 1867 and then the South Side industrial communities in 1872, raising the city of Pittsburgh's population accordingly from 49,217 in 1860 to 156,389 by 1880. Unlike the Philadelphia and Chicago cases, where the post–Civil War suburbanization process in villages and "mainline" communities outside these cities kindled a suburban ethos hostile to annexation, in Pittsburgh early suburbanization occurred partially within the boundaries of the city. Suburban growth occurred vigorously in the city's East End, in Oakland, Shadyside, and East Liberty, verdant residential enclaves insulated from working-class homes and the smoky haze of industrialism that "soils our hands and sours our tempers." In the 1860s and 1870s horsecars ran out both Penn and Fifth avenues and made these areas increasingly accessible. Cable cars replaced horsecars in 1888, to be eclipsed two years later by electrically powered trolleys. These East End neighborhoods lured a steady stream of Pittsburgh's growing middle and upper middle class of businessmen, engineers, physicians, lawyers, and other well-educated professionals. But a fair number of skilled and semiskilled workers shared East End space, living in the smaller houses found on secondary streets.[8]

Rampant industrialization, surging immigration, and streetcar suburbanization compelled cities to make thousands of decisions about street openings and widenings, open spaces, sewers, water provision, and other sanitary, safety, and urban infrastructural issues. By 1900 this cast of nineteenth-century decision makers had collectively molded what historian Robert Fishman extols as the "Metropolitan Tradition." It bequeathed the quintessential form of the urban-industrial metropolis praised by Jane Jacobs, the dense, bustling downtown core of commercial, cultural, and government service edifices surrounded by extensive rings of factory and residential zones.[9]

Forged out of nineteenth-century urban conversations that often featured venal, corrupt ring politicians in lead roles, this decision-making process witnessed city engineers, in concert with powerful elites, undertaking impressive park, boulevard, and other public and private building developments that to this day remain centerpieces of urban design.[10] However, these urban achievements previewed rather than represented modern urban planning. As we explain in this chapter, "ring-led development," no matter how professionally guided and exquisitely designed and how pregnant with significance for the Metropolitan Tradition, drew withering fire from an emerging urban middle class inimical to inefficiency, tax conscious, highly moralistic, and, ironically, the main beneficiaries of much of this metropolitan development. In Pittsburgh after the turn of the century, with a civic center rising in Oakland and costly, haphazard ring-led development under assault, these civic-minded elites sowed the seeds of professional planning. While architects, social workers, and lawyers dominated this new planning, civil engineers like Edward Bigelow had claimed the limelight of the nineteenth-century process.

Edward M. Bigelow, director of
Public Works in the late nineteenth
century and "Father of the Parks."
Schenley Park Library and Archives Division,
Historical Society of Western Pennsylvania, Pittsburgh.

EDWARD BIGELOW AND RING-LED URBAN DEVELOPMENT

Late one evening in 1889 the young, newly appointed director of Pittsburgh's Department of Public Works, Edward Bigelow, accompanied by Richard B. Carnahan, who was Mary O'Hara Schenley's city lawyer, boarded the night train for New York and thence a steamship to London. A civil engineer who had briefly attended the Western University of Pennsylvania and was appointed city engineer in 1880, a title changed to director of Public Works in 1887, Bigelow was passionately committed to the well-being of Pittsburgh. He shared the same vision for Pittsburgh that Frederick Law Olmsted Sr. had for Boston, the vision of a "necklace" of green parks encircling the city. As director of Public Works, he extracted money from the city councils to acquire parkland adjoining the city's Herron Hill and Highland reservoirs.[11] He now coveted the Schenley family lands in Oakland for a large park. In 1889 Mary Elizabeth Schenley, heiress to the vast real estate holdings of pioneer business giant James O'Hara and widow of the British captain Edward Wyndham Harrington Schenley, had lived in London for over forty years. Yet Mary Schenley had spent her childhood on the family's 400-acre East End estate called Mt. Airy. When the city in 1869 had first attempted to acquire this Schenley acreage, tax-wary voters quashed the effort.

Made aware that Mary Schenley's Pittsburgh real estate agent was finalizing a deal to subdivide Mt. Airy into building lots, Bigelow hurried to London to persuade Schenley to reconsider her earlier offer to donate the land for a park. He succeeded. Bigelow returned to Pittsburgh with a deed for 300 acres and an option for the city to purchase another 100 acres for $125,000. On February 10, 1890, the city councils accepted the Schenley offer.[12]

Bigelow's dogged pursuit of parkland, openly but often through legerdemain, political intrigue, and even the commitment of personal resources, won him acclaim as the "Father of the Parks." Indeed, even as he obtained the land for Schenley Park, he was assembling parcels for a large park overlooking the Allegheny River, to be named Highland Park. At his death in 1916, he was lionized as "a man of stainless integrity" and of "matchless greatness," and the "embodiment of the Pittsburgh Spirit." But at the same time even his eulogizers acknowledged "the storm of abuse he had endured, his rebuffs and his many critics."[13] During his lifetime, the city in 1895 erected a statue to him near the entrance to Schenley Park. Reformers ridiculed the ceremony dedicating Bigelow's likeness, noting that at the 1895 unveiling his cousin and chief supporter, political boss Christopher Magee, had brazenly shared the dais with the honored Public Works czar. Pittsburgh's "Father of the Parks," they charged, was "married to the ring."

The city's director of Public Works wonderfully illustrates the complexity of the forces shaping the nineteenth-century city, especially the permeability of the boundary separating politics and public improvements. If any one person can be credited with most informing Pittsburgh's nineteenth-century public landscape, it is Bigelow. With respect to special purpose planning, between 1880 and 1906 his voice dominated the urban conversation. He orchestrated the provision of water, sewers, and paved streets for the booming industrial metropolis. Yet during his lifetime, he was just as often scathed as "Bigelow the Extravagant," a creature of Christopher Magee and William Flinn, the notorious Pittsburgh city bosses. Indeed, for years Bigelow unabashedly steered lucrative public works contracts for street and sewer work to Booth and Flinn, Ltd.[14] As noted, Bigelow became director of Public Works after the Pennsylvania legislature in 1887 awarded the city a new "reform" charter. Under the

1816 charter, Pittsburgh's select and common councils administered the city using standing committees. The 1887 charter proposed strengthening and centralizing power in the mayor's office by creating three administrative departments—Public Safety, Charities, and Public Works—headed by mayoral appointees. However, when the charter finally emerged from the highly politicized state legislature, the councils, not the mayor, owned the appointing power. With patronage and therefore city elections tightly managed by the Magee-Flinn machine, the ring controlled city government. The Democratic *Pittsburgh Post* branded it the "Mageesburgh Charter" and proclaimed that Pittsburgh had been "given over to the boss." The same *Post* article cited the Upperman bill, which authorized second-class cities such as Pittsburgh to provide for improvement of streets, lanes, alleys, highways, sewers, and sidewalks, and required "plans" for streets. For Magee and Flinn, the new charter and the Upperman bill set the table for a veritable banquet of lucrative public works.[15]

Magee and Flinn pursued a progrowth agenda not unlike that followed by other big-city ringleaders. Nineteenth-century bosses confronted a cacophony of divergent class and ethnic voices. Using patronage, payoffs, favors, and raw political power, they mediated or bridged the contested boundaries of socially and ethnically fragmented urban space. In 1879 Magee emerged as a powerful force in Pittsburgh's and in the state's Republican political organization. Yet Magee had never served an apprenticeship in smoke-filled city saloons or bathhouses like Chicago's colorful duo, John Coughlin and Hinky Dink Kenna. From an old Pittsburgh family, boss Magee doubled as a respected city businessman, a partner in the late 1870s of the Pennsylvania Tube Works, and owner of the *Pittsburgh Times*. In 1879 he combined forces with William Flinn, partner in the contracting firm of Booth and Flinn, Ltd., a member of the city's Fire Board, and a Pittsburgh ward boss deeply enmeshed in Allegheny County politics. The merger produced Pittsburgh's ring, an organization closely allied not only with city contractors but also with banks holding city funds, traction tycoons such as the Mellons, and railroad powers such as the Pennsylvania Railroad, as well as liquor and vice interests. Labor hated the ring, not only because of its intimacy with industrial moguls like the Mellons but also, argues Francis Couvares, because by transforming local labor leaders into professional party hacks, or "bummers," it subverted labor solidarity and co-opted labor's power to shape a working-class social and political milieu.

Magee and Flinn consolidated power by using their political organizational skills to nominate and elect to the city's select and common councils "cheap and dependable men." Ring vassals included blood relations as well as bartenders, brothel owners, and liquor dealers, whose link to the liquor trade and other vices subjected them to the magisterial system and therefore even to tighter ring control. Through a network of ward-level organizations, the ring invidiously infiltrated crucial "centers of plebeian sociability" such as neighborhood boat clubs, union halls, and, of course, saloons. It further tightened its grip at both the city and county levels by controlling the rich patronage derived from the ring's power over police and fire department appointments and over late-nineteenth-century city building.[16]

Pittsburgh's political machine, like those in other cities, thrived on public works. Bossism and infrastructure building coalesced in the nineteenth century, making the machine a leading force in city development. Ring suzerainty superimposed over the fragmented, neighborhood-controlled government of the post–Civil War city a centralized, boss-dominated system capable of taming the hurly-burly provincial democracy of the city councils and paving and illuminating crude streets, building parks, and laying modern sanitary sewers and water mains, which Jon Peterson labels "special purpose planning." None of these projects reflected a broad, comprehensive view of the city. Instead, they responded politically to the machine's ward-heeling agenda and, as well, to pressures from businessmen and other elites anxious about Pittsburgh's stature in the hierarchy of successful cities. A competent engineer, Bigelow drew the specifications for these modern streets and sewers, assuring that those contractors favored by the ring, mainly the firm of Booth and Flinn, benefited; but the traction and real estate interests of Christopher Magee also benefited from free use of the paved streets and from daily escalating land values.[17]

Under the reign of Magee and Flinn, Pittsburgh undertook a massive "continuous" public improvement program. In addition to the new and improved streets, sewers, and water mains, ring-led development included free bridges, boulevards, and large parks. These actions reflected, as noted, a larger conversation involving booster organizations such as Pittsburgh's young Chamber of Commerce about progress, urban health and welfare, modern infrastructure, and the need for Pittsburgh to remain competitive in a nation of urban marketplaces increasingly linked together by a network of steel rails. At the height of the "Metropolitan Age" in the 1890s, bridges, parks, and boulevards mushroomed in cities from Seattle, Cincinnati, and St. Louis, to Providence, Boston, and New York. Pittsburgh newspapers and the *Annual Report of the Department of Public Works* resonated with words and phrases such as "modern," "the trend of improvements," "wonderful changes," "professional municipal policy," "public works of the greatest magnitude," and "a veritable rebuild-ing of the city's plant anew."[18]

Engineer Bigelow's familial ties with the ring did not render him any less a disciple of efficiency. No longer were workers "unfit for any manual labor . . . turned over to the chief of the DPW [Department of Public Works] to [be] . . . put . . . to work on the streets."[19] Prior to the 1870s Pittsburgh had lacked any topographical studies, and its Byzantine sewer system defied both engineering logic and the city's hilly topography. Bigelow's Engineering and Survey Division purportedly undertook a modern topographic survey and utilized scientific data to resewer the city and repave city streets. Between 1888 and 1899 the department laid 190 miles of new sewers, graded 94 miles of city streets, and repaired 22 miles of streets with asphalt and 55 miles with block stone, most cut from Flinn's own Ligonier quarries.[20]

But while urban political machines like Flynn and Magee's modernized city infrastructure and, for many citizens, provided a healthier and safer urban environment, this progress proved not only uncoordinated but terribly uneven. Progress scintillated in the heart of Pittsburgh's downtown, where in the 1880s and 1890s many new, modern buildings arose, including numerous impressive banks, a post office, and architect Henry Hobson Richardson's Allegheny County courthouse. However, as historians Christine Rosen and S. J. Kleinberg have made clear in their studies of industrial Baltimore and Pittsburgh, respectively, machine bosses often spurned working-class and immigrant districts, where votes were controlled and voters were placated with jobs and other personal favors, not sewers and clean water. Indeed, the bosses' actions served actually to widen the social and economic chasm between middle- and working-class Pittsburgh.[21]

Under ring rule, Pittsburgh's downtown burgeoned; even so, it was the East End neighborhoods of Oakland, Shadyside, Homewood, and Highland Park that experienced the greatest growth. "The old wards of our city," wrote Bigelow in 1890, "are very rapidly being turned into manufacturing sites and thereby forcing the residents thereof to locate in the East End in outer wards. Having once established their homes there, they very naturally and very properly ask [for] such streets and sewer improvements as well as water supplies as will make their lives accessible and healthful."[22] It was this growing East End, shielded from the grit and soot of industrialism and home to many of the city's industrial elites, including George Westinghouse, Henry Clay Frick, Henry J. Heinz, William Larimer Mellon, and Magee himself, that the bosses endeavored to keep free from dust and dirt; supply with clear, plentiful water; and make accessible by modern mass transit. This unmerited liberation reflected not only an elite embrace of the vaunted "Pittsburgh Spirit," a theme touted by Magee as well as the Chamber of Commerce and other boosters, but also Magee's private quest for profits from lucrative East End traction and real estate investments.

Bordering the main line of the Pennsylvania Railroad, and as early as 1859 served by horsecars, the East End communities attracted a steady stream of home seekers. A few years after the city had annexed the region in 1867, the state legislature through the Penn Avenue Act created "Improvement Districts" in the East End overseen by street commissioners elected by property owners. These commissioners identified streets to be paved and chose the surface material and the paving contractors. They also apportioned the dollar amount to be assessed residential abutters. Before the state supreme court in 1879 declared the Penn Avenue Act unconstitutional, many parts of the East End enjoyed improved streets. Still, after 1879 paving East End streets and providing fashionable, well-lit carriageways continued to preoccupy Department of Public Works engineers.[23]

Good streets provided the solid surfaces for mass transit, which in turn also made the district highly appealing for middle-class Pittsburghers seeking a safe, wholesome, unpolluted environment for intensive Victorian family life. As early as 1860 several horsecar lines served the area. Magee personally invested heavily in these traction lines, exploiting his political power to secure franchises and special advantages for his transit companies. He owned the Central Traction line down Fifth Avenue and by 1888 the Duquesne Traction Company, the first cable transit in Pittsburgh. In the early 1890s Pittsburgh traction companies switched from cable to trolley technology. At the same time, Magee dueled with Philadelphia traction magnate A. B. Widener for control of Pittsburgh's rail transportation. Magee triumphed, merging all six East End lines into the Consolidated Traction Company.[24]

Good transit, sewers, modern plumbing, and solid street surfaces further enhanced the healthfulness and attractiveness of the East End, multiplying the wealth of real estate speculators such as Magee. Before 1888, noted Edward Bigelow in the Department of Public Works 1895 *Annual Report:*

Not a foot of sewer pipe [existed] in the East End. Nor was there a street paved which people could travel with any degree of safety. You know the condition of Penn, Fifth, Ellsworth, Frankstown, and the other avenues, and you know the many miles of streets that have been repaved [by the city] as well as the number of miles that have been repaved with improved pavements upon petition and at the voluntary expense of the property holders. Therein, I mention the East End, especially, as the great growing section.

The working-class South Side, added Bigelow almost apologetically, "[has] been proportionally well cared for."[25]

Developers of lots in Shadyside and Oakland cashed in on the panache of East End real estate. Many, such as the Beechwood Improvement Company and Sadler and Martin, installed water pipe systems as part of their lot development plans, and then awaited passage of city ordinances reimbursing them for the cost.[26] Indoor plumbing especially appealed to East End home seekers. A considerable portion of the 38,762,000 gallons of water pumped from the Highland Park reservoir in 1891 (up 48 percent from the 20,280,000 gallons pumped in 1883) served affluent East End homeowners blessed with indoor plumbing and expansive lawns.[27]

Magee, like many fellow East End residents who basked in new improvements, regarded the region as a garden spot safe from the dangerous immigrant hordes who inhabited Pittsburgh's Hill District, Polish Hill, and other industrial neighborhoods. That was certainly on Andrew Carnegie's mind when, accompanied by Mayor Henry Gourley, James Scott (chairman of the Carnegie Library Building Committee), H. Kirke Porter, and David McCargo, among others, he toured sites for his gift of a library to the Steel City. The steel tycoon favored the East End, where open space permitted "plenty of ground around the buildings, both for ornament's sake and to give room for the inevitable growth of the buildings as the population increases and other donations are made to the library." Carnegie had in mind not only the library but other buildings, such as a music hall. Atop Herron Hill, Carnegie halted the group. He impishly denied that he was Moses leading his guests to the mountaintop; yet, like Moses, with his arm raised, Carnegie directed the delegation's eyes toward his chosen site. He let Scott explain the choice. "Do you see yonder?" Scott pointed to the southeast.

That is Oakland. You see how thickly it is built up. Over there, beyond is Schenley Park. Look at Bloomfield and Bellefield down here, how compactly they are populated; and see how those new houses are lying around you. I want you to bear in mind that nearly all this building has been done within the last ten years. Mr. Porter says that most of it has been done within three years. This is where the center of the population of the city will be, and that before very long. The city is growing at an astonishing rate, and you can see this is the only direction in which it can grow. Out in this direction is where the central library should be located.

This, then, was Carnegie's chosen site, accessible by transit, "where people," added the steel baron, "will congregate." Moreover, the site abutted the planned ten-acre grand portal to Schenley Park, which Pittsburgh optioned to buy.[28]

Clearly, Bigelow's parks and boulevards and other modern improvements were by design making the East End the residential centerpiece of nineteenth-century Pittsburgh. While Magee nurtured the typical booster's gilded view of the city, of a streamlined modern city, its paved streets, parks, and boulevards gleaming amid the whir and haze of industrial progress, engineer-trained Bigelow forged a much more empirically based vision of progressive Pittsburgh. In addition to words such as "progress," "modern," and "technical expertise," his verbal arsenal included, as well, "planning" and "systems." In the independence afforded him by the 1887 charter, Bigelow espied the resources and power to put his stamp on urban form.

Historians exploring Bigelow's role in Pittsburgh history and the source of his inspiration have pointed to several other factors: the City Beautiful and "back to nature" movements, and the late-nineteenth-century fear of social unrest. City Beautiful, as a term, argues Peterson, gained currency after 1900, not before. In the social unrest scenario, the specter of middle-class America "standing at Armageddon" spurred a search for order and a quest for social control.[29] Bigelow's vision for city parks embraced all of these elements and more. He operated as the quintessential professional municipal engineer who, like landscape architect Frederick Law Olmsted Sr., professed to transcend the whirligig of nineteenth-century politics. He guided the urban conversation about needed urban improvements and persuaded a tax-wary public to support one bond issue after another.[30] Bigelow likewise centralized the administration of public works, hired experts, and introduced "metropolitan methods to meet the emergence of rapid [urban] development."[31] These "modern" methods, as suggested, involved systematic planning. He protested the haphazard, individualistic, and speculative platting of new subdivisions, which ignored the "impact one subdivision plan might have on another adjoining plan," and in 1890 he boldly urged that "all plans conform to a general plan of the city affecting the district in which the property may be." However, Bigelow's interest in planning did not translate into planning practice. His orientation remained fixed on projects, not the creation of a plan.[32] Such a plan materialized only in Bigelow's imagination. Planning in Pittsburgh for parks, as a case in point, remained "special purpose." And here a vision did unfold.

Bigelow's park vision was democratic as well as scientific. While his program of sewer and street installations served the East End more than the South Side, Lawrenceville, or Herron Hill, his centerpiece of verdant parks, where the natural landscape was ennobled by design and linked to other bucolic places by spacious boulevards, encompassed all classes. It was an aesthetic and social ethic shared by other nineteenth-century civic improvement enthusi-asts. Bigelow, like Frederick Law Olmsted Sr. and the Harrisburg photogra-pher, naturalist, and later American Civic Association president J. Horace Mc-Farland, believed that large landscaped parks could introduce civic values into the dark, smoky industrial cities and make urban living more civilized, hu-mane, and rewarding. "It is noticeable," explained Bigelow in his 1891 report, "and creditable alike to the city and the people, that with such immense mul-titudes as have gathered from time to time in these resorts (city parks) few, if any arrests have been necessary, this showing that if the beauties of nature, enhanced by art, have not of themselves a moral effect, they are at least en-joyed by a good and reputable class of people, for whose benefit and enjoyment no stone should be left unturned."[33]

Pittsburgh's director of Public Works situated the romantic park at the center of an intensive discussion about city life and its future held mainly in elite parlors. Nineteenth-century British and American writers and landscape architects from essayist and social thinker John Ruskin to Andrew Jackson Downing and Frederick Law Olmsted Sr. had built a solid foundation of so-cial and aesthetic theory about the value of urban green spaces. Parks served as the lungs of the city in the battle against pestilence and disease; moreover, they were democratic spaces and acted as a civilizing tool in the war against chaos and civil disorder. Verdant space spiritually and physically uplifted the downtrodden and, like libraries and the Young Men's Christian Association (YMCA), provided an alternative to the saloon. "[City] Parks [like Schenley and Highland] have for their chief motive," wrote Bigelow in language remi-niscent of Olmsted, "the elevation of the people." They "give to the toiler . . . an opportunity for relaxation and recreation and confer moral and physical ben-efits."[34]

Bigelow's vision centered mainly upon his two giant pleasure gardens, Schenley and Highland parks. Here nature was artistically configured under the supervision of landscape architect William Falconer to present a natural-istic landscape of forested hillsides and picturesque ravines. At the same time, quite formal landscaping in some portions of the parks sought to impress visi-tors. By 1900 the public entered Highland Park through a monumental neo-classical portal, which Bigelow had erected in a manner consistent with the thinking of the 1890s civic art and nascent City Beautiful movements. In ad-dition to the landscaping features, the parks embodied the then fashionable recreational and educational pursuits common to parks across the nation. Pic-nic areas and shelters, lakes for skating and boating, special programs such as

Fourth of July patriotic festivities, a botanical conservatory (the gift of Carnegie's friend Henry Phipps), and a zoological garden (a $100,000 embellishment donated by Christopher Magee) appealed to a broad social spectrum of visitors. The bulk of facilities, however, catered mainly to the resources and interests of the middle and upper middle classes. Bridle trails, twenty-foot-wide driving ovals for the entertainment of carriage owners, a golf course, baseball diamonds, polo grounds, and tennis courts drew patrons in particular from the well-heeled neighborhoods of the East End.[35]

Although these "pleasures" favored the elite, Bigelow emphasized "accessibility" for all, particularly the working class for whom park air would engender not only delight but also moral and social-psychological benefits. Not all East End residents fully embraced the director's thinking. Bigelow had launched his park-building campaign in 1889 with Mary Schenley's donation, but not before he had successfully overcome stiff opposition from East Liberty homeowners who feared that his plans for Highland Park invited the "riff raff."[36] "Access," in fact, preoccupied the park director. A primary element of Bigelow's park "planning" included a network of free bridges, boulevards, and low-fare transit availing his parks (especially Schenley Park) to Bloomfield's Germans and Italians or the Hill District's varied immigrant population. Moreover, during the 1890s Magee and Flinn, like Bigelow, fought assiduously to free the Monongahela River of toll bridges—for political and financial profit. Building a toll-free Twenty-second Street bridge increased access for South Side ironworkers and steelworkers, while at the same time, through lowered costs, directly benefited Magee's Manchester Traction Company, which ran its transit vehicles across the river into Old Birmingham.[37] But accessibility extended beyond free bridges. Beechwood Boulevard snaked

A bird's-eye view of Schenley Park, circa 1900. The Carnegie Library is at the left. *Carnegie Library of Pittsburgh.*

across the East End, connecting Highland and Schenley parks, while Grant (later Bigelow) Boulevard led from the downtown, skirting Herron Hill and passing through Bellefield to Schenley Park. Bigelow closely monitored the social composition of park visitors and reported on the orderliness and good behavior of the Pittsburgh working classes, especially on the Fourth of July, a day, proclaimed the Public Works director, when "every resident of Pittsburgh can bring his family to the celebration in Schenley Park by the most direct route without passing a toll gate."[38]

That Pittsburgh in 1895 hailed Bigelow as both "Bigelow the Extravagant" and the "Father of the Parks" indicates the deep anxiety that many tax-conscious citizens harbored not only for his ring connections but also for the costliness of his ventures. Bigelow had secured at little public cost vast acres of land for park purposes and at no apparent municipal cost both Magee's zoological gardens at Highland Park and Henry Phipps's conservatory. Meanwhile, taxpayers absorbed a hefty $900,000 bill to enlarge Highland Park, plus a substantial expense for expanding, landscaping, and embellishing Schenley Park.[39] Most of this money came from public coffers, specifically the 1895 bond issue for improvements to Schenley and Highland parks. These funds enabled the Public Works director to fully utilize cheap Citizens Relief Committee labor. The committee oversaw a city emergency jobs program created amid the depression of 1892.[40]

Throughout the late nineteenth century, Bigelow commanded a special place in the urban conversation. Supported by the Chamber of Commerce, he imagined his great peoples' parks rivaling those of New York and Philadelphia. He praised the practicality and efficiency of his boulevards and free bridges, and he declared Pittsburgh "one of the very best lighted cities in the World." Yet the term "extravagant" clung to him like a shroud, placing the efficient engineer Bigelow at the center of the crusade against the ring and political corruption in Pittsburgh. Ironically, his opposition came mainly from the upper and middle classes, the putative beneficiaries of Bigelow's driving ovals, golf courses, and polo grounds, facilities rarely if ever used by immigrant, working-class Pittsburghers.[41]

THE FRICTIONS AND LIMITATIONS OF NINETEENTH-CENTURY RING-LED DEVELOPMENT

Although ring payoffs and other forms of graft helped forge cohesion amid increasing nineteenth-century urban fragmentation, the urban machine derived its power from that very fragmentation, from the precinct and ward captains enmeshed in the polyglot diversity of city neighborhoods. It therefore lacked the moral force to orchestrate a conversation about, or a vision of, the city as a whole. The ring-led conversation spawned a rival discourse that easily degenerated into squabbling about excessive taxes, the cost of graft, and the unevenness of services. Despite the many physical achievements of ring-led development—the courthouse, fire stations, parks, sewers, and paved streets—reformers perceived this largesse as not only morally corrupt and costly but, alas, as sorely inadequate. Lincoln Steffens's exposé of Pittsburgh's Flinn-Magee machine, "Pittsburgh: A City Ashamed," revealed the awful cost of rigged contracts, franchise giveaways, and other forms of graft. Director Bigelow's Department of Public Works may have openly advertised for contractors to undertake such giant projects as Pittsburgh's Negley Run and Thirty-third Street sewers, but when the bids were opened, disclosed Steffens, Booth and Flinn were too often named the lowest "acceptable" bidders. Moreover, to the consternation of the ring's East End opponents, particularly councilman Samuel Warmcastle, the final bid ($293,559 for the Thirty-third Street sewer) exceeded by over 100 percent the estimated cost ($138,000) of the project. Despite the outrage, councils obediently approved the contract. That project costs so vastly exceeded estimates invariably resulted in city taxpayers, as opposed to abutters, paying the entire cost of the improvements.[42]

The actual price tag of ring-led development proved even higher. While expensive rigged bidding benefited the East End and the ring-favored traction magnates and real estate tycoons who operated there, a large part of the city suffered little or no services. In the Hill District and other poor or working-class neighborhoods where decent housing was scarce and where most residents in the late nineteenth century were either European immigrants or African Americans, landlords refused to connect their decrepit tenements to water lines, sewers, or electricity.[43] As late as 1907 large sections of the city such as the Saw Mill Run area suffered from a lack of sewers and running water. Residents there hand-carried water to their houses from common courtyard hydrants. Lodgers in many of Pittsburgh's dank cellar and courtyard dwellings did the same. In the sordid flats opposite Union Station, one water hydrant supplied thirteen houses.[44]

Nor did Bigelow's beautifully paved, immaculately manicured, and well-lit Beechwood and Grant boulevards reflect the general condition of streets and roadways elsewhere in late-nineteenth-century Pittsburgh. City streets excavated for resurfacing or for installing streetcar tracks or conduit for cable cars remained muddy quagmires for months. Often the deep trenching for conduit installations ruptured old sewer lines, and the disgorged stench conjured up old fears of "effluvia-caused epidemics." "The streets in Pittsburgh are in horrible shape," a Penn Avenue physician angrily reported in 1888. The outraged practitioner suspected a link between street work and the incidence of cholera. Another doctor charged that "these [street] excavations must necessarily be deleterious to the health of the people in a crowded city. When the ground is broken it takes time to settle and noxious odors ooze up between the cobble stones."[45]

Pittsburghers also charged that ring-favored traction companies—some owned by Magee himself—"have almost unlimited privileges." They cited the blocks of Penn Avenue from Eleventh to Eighteenth streets that were "so torn up by street railway construction to forbid vehicles of every sort and where the sidewalks were so obstructed as to disgust pedestrians."[46]

City dwellers not inconvenienced by muddy, impassable streets or threatened by the foul stench of exposed sewers bewailed the sheer inadequacy of Pittsburgh's water supply. Some, especially temperance crusaders, denounced the absence of free drinking fountains in the central city, which tempted strollers to quench midsummer thirsts at the corner saloon. Others voiced more serious grievances.[47] Small and rotten pipes in the downtown periodically burst, rendering the central city without any water for personal, business, or fire-protection purposes. Elsewhere in the city defective pipes and deficient pressure kept water barely trickling at faucets. The Reverend Father John Murphy, president of Holy Ghost College (later Duquesne University), complained in 1888 that dwellers living on the narrow streets and alleys of the bluff above Second Avenue had suffered from a short supply of water for fifteen years.[48]

In 1889 a severe outbreak of typhoid fever on the South Side suddenly riveted the city's attention more on the quality of city water than its quantity. For years, South Siders raged that Pittsburghers allowed a private ring-protected concern, the Duquesne Water Company, to crassly serve South Side neighbors. Councils in 1889 had bestowed a thirty-year franchise on the Duquesne Water Company, which competed side by side with the city-owned water supply. Ringleaders pleaded that the city was helpless to meet the area's rising demand. Indeed, in 1889 the city's Bureau of Water Supply, faced with limited capacity, called for modernizing the giant steam engines at its Brilliant Station, which raised water from the Allegheny River.[49] In truth, neither the Allegheny River nor the Monongahela River provided safe water for the city or the Duquesne Water Company.[50]

Finally, there was the downtown itself. Despite its architectural master-

A muddy street and old houses near the moldering Exposition Hall located at Pittsburgh's derelict Point, circa 1900. *Library and Archives Division, Historical Society of Western Pennsylvania, Pittsburgh.*

pieces such as Richardson's courthouse, Pittsburgh's nineteenth-century downtown of narrow streets and alleys, like the urban cores of Cleveland, Philadelphia, Boston, and other cities, groveled in filth and confronted appalling traffic congestion. Freight trains of the Pennsylvania Railroad belched acrid smoke and rumbled and screeched down the center of Liberty Avenue, a major city corridor. The steep grade of Grant's Hill, known as the Fifth Avenue "hump," made reaching the courthouse for horsecars, as well as for heavily laden drays, wagons, and carriages, daunting. Hazardous grade crossings abounded, where railroads, trolleys, carriages, and wagons, bent on perilous collision courses, met at intersections.[51]

Businessmen owning property in or adjoining the Fifth Avenue and Grant Street district pushed for what became an important example of late-nineteenth-century special purpose planning: the proposal to have the hump leveled by fifteen feet, the cut dimension recommended by courthouse architect Richardson. The row in 1888 over who would pay the estimated $450,000 cost of the cut (it rose to $3,000,000 by 1898) not only put city ringleader Christopher Magee at the center of the debate, but it also illuminated one of the chief "frictions" of nineteenth-century urban development: the deeply entrenched historic pattern of urban land use and the towering legal and financial barriers facing any effort to alter the existing built environment. If laying conduit proved disruptive, the specter of excavating millions of tons of earth verged on the apocalyptic.[52] The hump cut exposed another long-standing urban "friction": the nineteenth-century practice of assessing abutters for the cost or damages caused by improvements. Bigelow, who favored the costly hump cut, blamed the city's inaction on the "perniciousness of a few property owners," who while abutting the proposed cut, were not positively affected.

A decade later, in 1898, the same controversy still delayed the project. Its now much steeper cost assured that the entire city, not individual abutters, would ultimately bear the cost. That realization turned East End and South Side businessmen into strident enemies of an improvement that, as they saw it, disproportionately benefited downtown competitors and at their expense. Anti-ring Pittsburghers chimed in that Magee's Pittsburgh Traction Company, with tracks on Grant Street, stood to profit handsomely from city-paid damages. The whole "hump cut scheme," critics charged, amounted to ring boodle. "Let those whose property was damaged be reimbursed by those who benefit," stormed the anti-ring *Post*. Needless to say, the hump at the turn of the century remained uncut. Other projects seeking to ease congestion and improve traffic circulation such as the widening of Diamond Street faced similar barriers involving equity. Opponents of the Diamond Street project believed that the city's high estimates of damages assured that taxpayers, not the beneficiary abutters, would pay the project's cost. Moreover, widening Diamond Street entailed demolishing a number of the "most substantial buildings in the city . . . just to benefit some with businesses above Fifth and Smithfield." Again, those demurring espied "some [Magee-led] street railway scheme behind it."[53]

The shift from outright rancor toward a more reasoned discussion about vital urban improvements in some cases awaited the building of a scientific consensus. By the late 1880s the new bacteriological sciences more and more convincingly implicated Pittsburgh's foul water in epidemic disease. But on this issue civil engineer Bigelow blocked progress. Despite exhortations from Pittsburgh's business and scientific communities, Bigelow stubbornly held that modern bacteriological evidence did not prove that the city's riverine water sources carried typhoid. Bigelow, who worked mainly to increase the volume of water supplied to Pittsburgh's East End suburbs, lobbied for bigger and better pumps and larger reservoirs. The 1889 South Side typhoid epidemic provoked the Pittsburgh Engineering Society, in concert with the Chamber of Commerce, to create an elite-studded, twenty-nine-member Joint Committee on Water Supply. The committee's findings condemned the city's water supply and recommended a slow sand filtration system modeled on Lawrence, Massachusetts. Andrew Carnegie even donated money to construct a model filtration system that the Joint Committee erected on the grounds of the First Unitarian Church on Craig Street near Fifth Avenue.[54] Such political pressure, compounded by the mayoral election of 1896, in which filtered water was the central issue, forced the councils to establish that year the Pittsburgh Filtration Commission, which included Chancellor William Holland of the Western University of Pennsylvania (later renamed the University of Pittsburgh), Bigelow, Warmcastle, and Flinn. Among the experts it employed were Pittsburgh engineer Morris Knowles and MIT hydrologist William T. Sedgwick.[55] Bigelow had long protested that building a filtration plant would cause the city's bonded debt to skyrocket and raise the tax levy by at least 7 percent. Expert analysis, he admonished, "had failed to discover a single typhoid fever germ in our Allegheny River water, although the same experts had no difficulty whatever in discovering and identifying for our committee an abundance of typhoid bacteria at Lawrence, Massachusetts."[56] Undaunted, the commission's 1899 report recommended slow sand filtration. Bigelow at last relented, ultimately becoming a staunch proponent for constructing a filtration plant, to be located in Aspinwall, opposite the Brilliant Pumping Station and the Highland Park reservoir. Again and again politics intruded, delaying completion of the plant until 1907.[57]

In fact, politics towered among the "frictions" distracting the debate and thwarting progress on Pittsburgh improvements.[58] That the machine usually rebuffed the entreaties of working-class neighborhoods, except for a haphazardly developed playground here or an isolated water hydrant there; that it favored the East End; and that graft escalated the cost of all ring-led improvements profoundly impacted nineteenth-century urban form. Moreover, state Republican boss Matthew Stanley Quay's unremitting challenge to the power of Pittsburgh bosses rendered the city machine especially vulnerable to the opposition of East End reformers and their anti-vice, low-tax platform. As a result, until 1900 "progress" for these city reformers would be cast more in millennial/

evangelical terms, not in the scientific and bureaucratic jargon of the pioneer planning movement.

Portrayed by its enemies as monolithic and invincible, Pittsburgh's Republican Magee-Flinn political machine in reality stood perpetually on guard, mending walls, tending or "healing" constituencies, and girding itself against attacks from "moral watchdogs," from "goo-goo" reformers from within the party, and from the power of rival state machines from without.[59] Magee and Flinn waged a thirteen-year-long battle against Quay.[60]

The 1889 election for delegates to the new County Executive Committee marked a key event in the long Magee-Quay warfare, and one crucial to the urban conversation. Determined to rid himself of Magee, Quay dispatched his lieutenants to Pittsburgh with instructions to champion the anti-ring cause of East Ender Samuel Warmcastle, a reformer battling Bigelow and ring extravagance. Pittsburgh's ring countered with "Home Rule" as a battle cry. Magee and Flinn branded Quay as a "outside dictator" and assigned ring loyalists such as Bigelow to line up votes in rebellious outposts such as the cantankerous Fifth District of the East End. Magee's "Home Rule" strategy worked. Victorious, the millionaire Magee swiftly announced his retirement from politics, but only temporarily.[61]

The internecine 1889 "Home Rule" battle had produced a short-lived truce between the Magee-Flinn and Quay camps. Quay conceded to Flinn and Magee control over Pittsburgh politics. This meant, in the words of the *Philadelphia Press,* that "the thousands of dollars annually to Flinn, whose success as a contractor depended upon his political 'pull' in the city [of Pittsburgh], remained intact." Then "in return [for] a fair share of the patronage of that office [the postmastership]," Magee and Flinn promised to cease opposing Quay's choices for city postmasters and to refrain from making trouble in Harrisburg.[62]

Such harmony lasted very briefly. Newspaper exposés in 1890 revealing Quay's criminal plundering of the state treasury fueled Magee's determination to destroy his powerful adversary. In retaliation, Quay continued to back Pittsburgh's anti-ring reform movement, which favored civil service reform and advocated the uniform valuation of property.[63]

The Quay-Magee warfare over patronage control and political ambition not only demonstrated the limits and the vulnerabilities of the ring but also bared the ring's reliance on ward healing, the placating of narrow constituencies, and the nineteenth-century political basis for fragmented special purpose planning. While the ring prided itself on its ability to get things done on a citywide scale, political expediency habitually forced it not to address city-wide goals, but—as noted earlier—to satisfy the particular ad hoc wishes and whims of city neighborhoods. For example, South Side residents in 1897 protested any further bond issues for improvements until they got $250,000 for a hilltop park, $500,000 for a boulevard, and $150,000 for a public square.[64] Building a park for the South Side, fielding the myriad complaints about street openings and water supply, and managing and negotiating the politics of street widenings and street cleaning, such ward-healing activities reinforced the costly reality of ring-led development and eclipsed Bigelow's wider vision of a metropolitan, "organic" city. It left planning a dim hope, but one that city reformers would avidly seize.[65]

REFORM

Pittsburgh's politically opportunistic reform movement rooted itself in a moral outrage roiling beneath the steamy surface of post–Civil War industrialism and urbanization. Its stern, traditional brand of Scotch-Irish Calvinism reflected the evangelistic form preached before the Civil War by Rev. Charles Grandison Finney and afterward by revivalists such as Dwight Moody and Josiah Strong that nourished a deep distrust of opulence, which reinforced latent republican fears about wealth corrupting politics. Among many evangelical Presbyterians, anxieties about the moral degeneracy of urban-industrial society stiffened resistance to modernism and, long before Pittsburgh progressives triumphed in 1906, mobilized city reformers to do battle against the ring.[66] Reformers, concerned about urban fragmentation and its relationship to what they viewed as the haphazardness and cost of ring-led urban growth, sought to seize leadership of the urban conversation from the bosses and, Bigelow's engineering credentials notwithstanding, base city improvement decisions on science, expertise, and bureaucratic efficiency, not politics. Within Pittsburgh, their ideas and actions ultimately fostered the establishment of planning in the twentieth century as a profession and discipline.

In contrast to those optimistic vanguards of urban progress such as Magee and Bigelow, many of these antimodernist, moral reformers viewed the city as a "menace" to be subdued. Indeed, a number of historians have detected this substrata of moral evangelicalism underlying much of the discourse about progressive reform and the urban future.[67] Throughout the 1880s and 1890s, evangelical Protestants in Pittsburgh waged holy war against the vice, crime, and the general disorderliness of the industrial city. Pittsburgh's Law and Order League used spies to ferret out and arrest not only prostitutes but also apple vendors, roller coaster operators, bartenders, and other violators of the Sabbath. Law and Order League agitation produced the 1888 Brooks Law closing two out of every three city saloons. A holy crusade in 1892 padlocked all city brothels, which during Mayor Henry Gourley's administration (1890–1893) had boldly operated under ring protection, and forced homeless city prostitutes to seek nightly shelter in city jails.[68]

By the 1890s much of that moral outrage focused on the ring. Evangelically minded reformers closely identified the ring with saloons, crime, vice, and the other evils of urban life, such as smoke pollution, foul water, and typhoid fever.[69] Fear of incipient labor violence, of an impending battle of Armageddon arraying hordes of anarchist-led immigrant workers against the bastions of capitalism, compounded this popular apprehension of a moral breakdown and fueled the conviction that society had lost its vitality as well as its moral fiber. With the carnage of the 1877 railroad strike still etched on many minds, and headlines about anarchists and bombings in Chicago's Haymarket still aflame, word of the 1892 battle of Homestead stunned middle-class Pittsburghers convinced that "inferior races" from eastern Europe threatened to extinguish the residue of moral culture and decency left in the Steel City. Such fears helped catalyze the city's quest for order.[70]

In early-twentieth-century Pittsburgh, this strain of moral outrage infused the political rhetoric of reform mayoral candidates like George Guthrie and culminated in Guthrie's 1906 election. However, in the 1890s other forces also propelled reform in Pittsburgh, including a civic consciousness awakened to the importance of beauty and to a healthy, orderly, and more permanent environment. The modern Pittsburgh, wrote Erasmus Wilson in his 1898 *Standard History of Pittsburgh*, "no longer accepts as a compliment . . . [that] Pittsburghers work as hard as their ancestors." Pittsburghers today, asserted Wilson, "are more intelligent, because they find time for some leisure, and in their leisure they have turned their attention to music, science and art, universities, hospitals, parks, conservatories, and boulevards."[71]

Among the growing body of the new middle class who flocked to the city's East End, the young lawyers, engineers, and college-bred managers—spawned by the mushrooming corporate capitalism, cosmopolitanism, and a heightened refinement of taste—steadily replaced the dour culture of nineteenth-century Presbyterianism.[72] The gospel of hard work, the bedrock doctrine of Pittsburgh Calvinism, a theology still preached to the working class by Carnegie, Frick, and other industrialists, steadily yielded to newer doctrines such as "muscular Christianity," which espoused healthfulness and the usefulness of play, sport, and recreation. Bigelow's emphasis on parks, golf courses, and carriage ovals neatly fit this new mood.[73] So did the new interest arising among the elite in erecting splendid architecturally exquisite mansions along Fifth and Penn avenues or in the lush western suburb of Sewickley Heights, estates magnificently landscaped by nationally renowned firms such as the Olmsted Associates. More flamboyant colonial revival, Tudor, and chateauesque styles replaced the darker Queen Anne shingle styles. Frick's chateau-style mansion, "Clayton," and Henry J. Heinz's "Greenlawn" reflected the city elites' rejection of staid, unadorned architecture. Having once spurned luxury, the "modern" elite now embraced an emerging cosmopolitanism that exalted consumption and craved beauty.[74]

This embrace of beauty reflected a growing acceptance of environmentalism, a key element of the late-nineteenth-century urban conversation nascent earlier in Bigelow's park movement. It taught that a positive relationship existed between the use of urban space and human behavior, that enlightened humans can socially engineer a better, safer, healthier, and more productive society. Environmentalism occupied a central place in the settlement house movement that originated in England's Toynbee Hall and was transplanted to America by Chicago's Graham Taylor and Jane Addams, and thence to Pittsburgh by the Reverend George Hodges, rector of Shadyside's Calvary Episcopal Church. Hodges, like Taylor and Addams, had sojourned in England and on the Continent, where he absorbed the social thought current among European reformers.[75]

In the 1890s Hodges and his moral reform ideas galvanized Calvary's laymen and vestrymen, including future Pittsburgh mayor George Guthrie, Orphans Court judge Joseph Buffington, and H. D. W. English, head of the Berkshire Insurance Company and president of the Chamber of Commerce. Hodges made Calvary a "linchpin" in the movement binding social reform to the planning idea in Pittsburgh.[76] He preached the "social gospel" to his elite parishioners, who included Henry Clay Frick. Christian theology, expounded Hodges, must be transformed into effective social action, that is "from creed to deed." His stinging sermons denounced the immoral consequences of unfettered industrial capitalism, the low wages, inhumane work conditions, bad housing, insanitation, corrupt politics, and vice that destroyed men and women for profit. Pittsburgh's ring posed both a moral and a practical barrier to reform because, in Hodge's view, it peopled municipal offices with venal, inefficient men. In Hodges's New Jerusalem, a righteous, educated citizenry would banish vice and administer city government on "moral principles."[77]

In 1893, joined by his parishioner H. D. W. English, Hodges founded Kingsley House, a settlement located at Seventeenth and Penn avenues, in the industrial, saloon-infested Twelfth Ward. Four years later, with Frick's generous support, Kingsley House moved to Bedford Avenue and Fulton Street amid the dense immigrant and African American enclaves of the city's Hill District.[78] Modeled on London's Toynbee Hall, Kingsley House, like Jane Addams's Hull House in Chicago, not only investigated social problems (such as the proliferation of neighborhood saloons) but also attempted to address the health and other social needs of the city's poor.[79] Kingsley House, like settlements across urban America, strove to ameliorate the physical environment of the industrial city. It was therefore integral to the emergence of planning in the city. Settlements from the start engaged in neighborhood reconstruction, believing, as Graham Taylor argued, that in well-designed neighborhoods, "it was easier to live right and harder to go wrong." Kingsley House, with other organizations such as the Pittsburgh Playground Association, pressed for good housing and neighborhood playgrounds. In fact, the Men's Patriotic Guild of Pittsburgh First Unitarian church, comprised of some of the same men who taught night classes at Kingsley House, in 1895 changed its name to the Citizens' League and spearheaded the city's water filtration movement.[80]

By 1895 Hodges and his fellow social environmentalists marched abreast in a growing army of reformers bent on cleansing the city both morally and physically. Two organizations, the Chamber of Commerce and the Civic Club of Allegheny County, also trudged with Hodges in the vanguard. In his study of businessmen and the foundations of planning in Seattle; Portland, Oregon; Oakland; and San Francisco, Mansel Blackford emphasizes that urban entrepreneurs seized upon planning as a tool to stabilize the urban environment. Founded in 1887, Pittsburgh's Chamber of Commerce, guided in the 1890s by Calvary's H. D. W. English, early became a prime force in Pittsburgh opposed to "civic ugliness" and dedicated to civic improvement. For business organizations such as the Chamber, Greater Pittsburgh, as an economically powerful, highly industrialized metropolitan area, could afford neither the incubus of black, lung-searing smoke, nor high typhoid rates. Such wretched images buttressed the city's mean reputation for physical and social squalor, images that, for business' sake, the Chamber toiled to expunge. Under English, the Chamber vigorously campaigned for park improvements, for water filtration, and for clean government.[81]

While Kingsley House operated with a male-dominated board of directors, women such as Kate Everest directed and staffed many of settlement's activities. Women, however, were equally if not much more prominent in another reform organization, the Civic Club of Allegheny County (CCAC) founded in 1895.[82] Like Hodges's settlement house movement, Pittsburgh's CCAC deplored the city's execrable moral and physical environment and proclaimed the need for expert, not ring-led, development. A joint reform effort uniting the elite Twentieth Century Club and the Women's Health Protective Association, the CCAC sought to promote civic betterment through "better municipal government, improved social conditions, increased educational opportunity, and a more beautiful city in which to live."[83] The CCAC's specific projects underscored the organization's emphasis on moral environmentalism. But its stress on the environment and the transformational power of civic beauty places the CCAC firmly among the civic improvement organizations that Peterson saw as precursors to the City Beautiful movement and planning. The CCAC not only built and operated bathhouses in the Hill District, Soho, and other poor, working-class neighborhoods, but it also campaigned for parks and playgrounds "where children learn to respect authority, to recognize the rights of others and observe the principle of playing fair."[84] Likewise, it battled for tenement house reform, smoke abatement, an antiexpectoration ordinance, a municipal hospital, a tuberculosis pavilion, and a city tree commission. Led from 1895 to 1907 by the dynamic Kate McKnight and social elite Elizabeth Thaw, the CCAC rose as one of Pittsburgh's most important reform organizations. Its reform agenda, including its Children's League of Good Citizenship, underscored the central goal of Pittsburgh reform to remake the sordid industrial city—Pittsburgh as a whole—into the scrubbed, safe, and sanitary world then unfolding in the city's East End. While the word "planning" never appeared in CCAC literature prior to 1906, the comprehensiveness of the organization's "civic betterment" agenda; its sensitivity to aesthetic concerns, tree planting, parks, and smoke control; and its educational programs and interest in research and data collecting made the CCAC an important landmark in the early history of Pittsburgh planning.[85]

However, in the reformers' minds, before Pittsburgh could become a moral, orderly planned environment, its corrupt ring government had to be vanquished. This meant installing the "right men" in municipal government offices. Oliver McClintock and George Guthrie fit perfectly the nineteenth-century profile of the "best men." Guthrie, an East End scion of one of Pittsburgh's best families and a member of Hodges's Calvary Episcopal Church, practiced law. McClintock, a Pittsburgh merchant, Presbyterian elder, and a trustee of the Western Pennsylvania (Presbyterian) Seminary, cofounded

Shadyside Academy and served as a director of the CCAC. Both men denounced the moral and political degradation of urban industrialism and made the ring a special object of their scorn. In their view, the city's 1887 charter had saddled Pittsburgh with the Magee-Flinn tyranny. Despotic, ring-appointed department heads such as Bigelow undertook outrageously costly projects that mainly served the interests of greedy bosses. Ring-selected property viewers ruthlessly assessed legally helpless residents and businessmen alike. Therefore, oppressed middle-class taxpayers bore the heavy burden of ring excesses.[86]

Railing against ring-bloated taxes and unfair assessments, a citizens' movement took root in the East End as early as 1893, which proved strong enough to help elect anti-ring Democratic mayor Bernard McKenna.[87] In late 1895, buoyed by the CCAC, and by the advent of the National Municipal League, McClintock and his band of East End reformers founded the Citizens Municipal League. In February 1896 the League ran George Guthrie for mayor. Guthrie lost that year, but only by 1,000 votes, and mainly because Republican orators such as Congressman John Dalzell instilled fear that a local party defeat would weaken the chance to elect Republican William McKinley president in the fall and dash the opportunity to reinstitute the high protective tariff Dalzell deemed so vital to Pittsburgh's prosperity.[88]

Guthrie's defeat further galvanized the reform mood in Pittsburgh. News of charter reform proposals regularly appeared in the Pittsburgh press in 1897 and 1898. Indeed, the *Pittsburgh Post* touted a "wave of reform."[89] Meanwhile, both Quay and Bigelow faced serious political trouble. The U.S. Senate refused Quay his seat in Congress; as for Bigelow, Boss Flinn ordered the city councils to fire him for his sudden audacity in refusing to steer city contracts to favored ring enterprises.[90]

Bigelow's firing unleashed several years of political chaos in Pittsburgh culminating in the "ripper" bill, which abolished the mayor's office in the city and replaced it with a recorder post empowered to appoint city department chiefs, and Magee's death in 1901. By crippling the ring, the political turmoil fortified the city's reform movement and begat the Voters' League, which pledged to ferret out corruption and to realize the vision of a morally and environmentally purified Pittsburgh. This was an embryonic planning vision conceived in the 1890s in the city's East End region of Oakland. It was the vision of a civically reborn, monumentally beautified, and efficiently governed city that flourished as part of the progressive reform movement alive in early-twentieth-century urban America.[91]

THE OAKLAND CIVIC VISION

The Oakland vision beheld an educational and cultural center adjoining Schenley Park. Edward Bigelow and Andrew Carnegie led this development. As noted earlier, by acquiring through donation and purchase 400 acres of undeveloped land from Mary Schenley in 1889 and by assiduously fashioning it throughout the decade into a grand urban park, Bigelow had enlisted his new Schenley Park in the reformers' crusade to ameliorate the social ills of industrial Pittsburgh. In the following year Carnegie offered Pittsburgh a gift of $1,000,000 to establish an institution containing a public library, art galleries, and meeting rooms for learned societies, if the city provided the land and maintenance. He agreed to a site for the library and institute adjacent to Schenley Park in Oakland. Propounding his notion of "scientific philosophy," Carnegie argued that men who acquired great wealth had the responsibility to further civilization's progress, in part by helping people to improve themselves. Already celebrated for its industrial prowess, smoky Pittsburgh was ready, in his opinion, to excel in the arts and sciences, to become renowned for more than its iron and steel mills. Carnegie's quest for a more civilized Pittsburgh nicely complemented Bigelow's social aspirations for his parks and middle-class reformers' goal to make the city a more cosmopolitan and environmentally sustainable place.[92]

Despite voluminous surviving records concerning Carnegie, no document indicates that he and Bigelow actually held, or discussed, a vision for Oakland prior to 1893. Presumably, these two principal participants must have exchanged views during both the selection of a site and the city's donation of land for the institute. We know that the two men were more than passing acquaintances. For example, Bigelow felt comfortable enough to visit Carnegie's palatial Fifth Avenue New York City home in December 1893 on behalf of the Citizens' Relief Committee to beseech a sizable donation for mitigating the depression's devastating impact on Pittsburgh's workers and their families.[93] At the dedication of his library and museum complex in 1895, Carnegie paid tribute to Bigelow for acquiring and then beautifying the Oakland site.[94]

Who else may have participated in discussions about Oakland with Bigelow and/or Carnegie is equally unclear. However, other civic leaders such as William Holland, Carnegie's childhood friend and longtime partner Henry Phipps, and Christopher Magee revealed by their actions support for a vision of Oakland that, in architectural historian Franklin Toker's words, made the place "a shimmering alter ego" to the sooty, commercial, and industrial downtown. For example, Carnegie credited Holland for pointing out the importance of the Oakland site for his institute, and in 1893 Henry Phipps erected there a large botanical conservatory, "the first permanent demonstration of a large-scale enclosed botanical garden in the United States." Phipps's garden sat on parkland only a short distance from the site of Carnegie's library, then under construction.[95]

Although Carnegie and Bigelow in 1889–1890 laid the foundation for Oakland to become the heart of Pittsburgh's cultural life, the vision of Oakland as such a civic center most likely did not emerge until 1893, the year of the World's Columbian Exposition in Chicago. The fair seized the imagination of Pittsburgh's elite. It received unprecedented acclaim the summer and fall of 1893 at the moment Bigelow's park, Carnegie's institute, and Phipps's conservatory were taking shape. Like Americans across the country, Pittsburghers traveled in large numbers to Chicago to see the pristine "White City," the epitome of electrically lit (by Pittsburgh's George Westinghouse) and radiant urban modernity. The Chamber of Commerce exhorted Pittsburghers to visit the fair and ran special trains to Chicago. Pittsburgh newspapers reported page after page of detail about the fair with its glistening lagoon and fountains, arrangement of monumental buildings in a Court of Honor, neoclassical architecture, and ornamental sculpture. The fair intensified public interest both nationally and locally in civic art, in landscape architecture, and in municipal improvements. In December 1893, after the fair had closed, the *Pittsburgh Bulletin* observed that "Pittsburg[h] was the country's workshop and little else, and its people seemed averse to laying aside their overalls and working garb, and devoting time to the cultivation of their higher, beauty-loving natures. But the Columbian year finds more manifestations of the existence of this awakened feeling, in the homes of the busy middle class, than could be noted in the abodes of the rich, twenty years ago."[96]

Historian William Wilson has argued that "when nonprofessional interest in civic design and municipal improvement grew in the late 1890s, it did not look to the fair." On the contrary, Pittsburghers, and especially Bigelow and Carnegie, seemed uplifted by the World's Columbian Exposition and in the remaining years of the century worked to create a more expansive civic center of education and culture in Oakland.[97] The ever-practical Bigelow was so impressed with the fair that he arranged for the purchase and shipment of six railroad cars of the exposition's exotic plants for Phipps's new botanical conservatory. William Holland, a social friend of Phipps's as well as a good friend of and adviser to Carnegie, had spent a week at the Chicago fair site erecting an exhibit of his university.[98] Carnegie himself hailed the World's Columbian Exposition for its patriotic and environmental achievements. The fair, he wrote in an essay on it in an 1894 issue of *Engineering Magazine,* exposed Americans not only to foreign cultures but also to people from different parts of the United States. In the temperate comportment of the masses, in the swelling of national pride, and in the display of American industry and arts, the fair furthered the cause of national unity and pride, and reflected the "Triumph of Democracy" to this Scotsman who had immigrated a half century earlier and made his fortune in his adopted country. In this respect, the fair complemented one of Bigelow's goals for Schenley Park. Moreover, and most significant for the development of Oakland, Carnegie applauded architect and chief of the exposition's construction Daniel Burnham for the efficacy of his comprehensive plan for both buildings and grounds as well as for the beauty deriving from the fair's order, symmetry, and Beaux-Arts architecture. The visitor's first view of the scene "will be the last to fade from his recollection," Carnegie wrote. Impressed by the high quality of American painting and sculpture at the fair, he nonetheless emphasized the enduring influence of the civic art of the fairgrounds: "After every work of art, every ponderous engine, every invention, everything that proved the cunning brain and hand of man, has faded away, the general effect of the purely artistic triumph attained by the buildings and their environment will remain, vividly defined in the memory and recorded there unmixed with baser matter."[99]

Carnegie profusely lauded the public spirit of Chicago. Those who attended the World's Columbian Exposition, he remarked, now saw the city as a "very modern community." Carnegie proclaimed that Chicago should serve as a model of "salutary civic pride" for other cities, a model he wanted to bring to Pittsburgh.[100] At the dedication of his magnificent library and cultural institution in 1895, Carnegie and other speakers made clear that the library, music hall, art galleries, and museum, along with the park and conservatory, were meant to broaden the horizons and elevate the ideals of the industrial city's residents through the "influences of the beautiful and the good in nature, art, and letters." A couple of years later, Carnegie took satisfaction in the changes he espied. He wrote:

"The civilized world will take note of the fact that our Dear Old Smoky Pittsburgh ... has entered upon the path to higher things. ... As for myself, I am amazed at what has been accomplished. I had prepared myself for years of waiting for the Harvest—even for disappointment. I had not ventured to estimate at its value the mass of latent desire for the things of the spirit which lay inert in the hearts of our fellow citizens of the industrial hive, which needed only the awakening touch.[101]

In 1897 Carnegie traveled to London with Chancellor Holland to urge Mary Schenley to sell more of her land in Oakland, this time to the Western University of Pennsylvania for its relocation from Allegheny City (this adjacent city was a separate municipality until 1907). With close ties to Carnegie, the city's elite, and Oakland itself, the chancellor undoubtedly understood that his institution of higher learning would make a superb addition to this emerging civic complex. Before assuming leadership of the university, Holland from 1874 to 1891 had been minister of Oakland's Bellefield Presbyterian Church. He had married into an elite Pittsburgh family, the Moorheads, and after 1894 lived in a comfortable home across Bellefield Street from his former congregation and only one block north of, to use Holland's words, Carnegie's "magnificent gift" to the city. Holland likewise maintained close ties with the East End reformers. He not only wrote the final report in 1899 for the commission investigating typhoid and the city's water supply, but he also received a personal invitation from George Guthrie to join the Kingsley House Association. Holland and his family enjoyed a summer retreat in the Allegheny Mountains near Cresson, not far from where Carnegie also maintained a vacation home. The two men often dined together at a local inn and strolled through the woods, during which walks the scientifically inclined Holland identified for his older friend types of regional flora and fauna. In the early 1890s Carnegie turned to Holland, a world-renowned butterfly collector and authority, to establish a learned society, an academy of arts and sciences, that would meet in the new institute. Moreover, Holland advised Carnegie concerning the formation of his fledgling Oakland cultural complex and in the press defended the steel tycoon's management plan for these institutions against the views of "the head of the ring." Carnegie respected and trusted Holland and had a close enough relationship with him that he appointed Holland to boards overseeing his institute's activities. In 1898 Carnegie made Holland the complex's second director.[102]

When Holland became chancellor of the Western University of Pennsylvania in 1891, he immediately recognized the limitations of the school's cramped, isolated location in Allegheny City for its access to students and for the physical expansion of a rapidly growing institution. Since Carnegie was a trustee of the university, it seems likely that Holland and the canny Scotsman would have discussed the advantages of relocating the campus to Oakland, which would also further broaden the vision of the area as an educational and cultural center. The board of trustees agreed to such a move in 1896, and the two men approached Mary Schenley the following year without success. Schenley's willingness to donate and sell land, often with the urging of her agent in Pittsburgh, William A. Herron, remained crucial for the development of Oakland in the 1890s. Sales of small amounts of land to the city rounded out city park plans. She donated the site for the Western Pennsylvania School for Blind Children, which opened in 1894 only two blocks north of the rising Carnegie Institute. Persistent requests by the chancellor extracted an agreement from Schenley in 1898 to sell to the university ten acres of undeveloped land across Forbes Avenue from the Carnegie Music Hall entrance; but Holland failed to raise the purchase money and the deal collapsed. He resigned his chancellorship in 1901 to focus on his leadership of the Carnegie Institute without having accomplished the relocation of the university to Oakland.[103]

Notwithstanding Carnegie's role in approaching Mary Schenley on behalf of the university, his lukewarm financial support harmed Holland's efforts to raise money for the purchase of the Oakland site. Carnegie rejected Holland's request for a donation for the venture. It seems Carnegie hoped that other wealthy Pittsburghers would support the university. He was more interested in establishing practical technical schools for the training of skilled craftsmen in Pittsburgh. When he announced his intention in 1900 to establish the Carnegie Technical Schools, boss Christopher Magee found thirty-two acres, part of which he owned, adjacent to Schenley Park and across Junction Hollow from Carnegie's expanding institute. While his actions delayed the move of the Western University of Pennsylvania to Oakland, Carnegie had succeeded in adding to the area's educational resources. In 1903 Henry Hornbostel won the architectural competition to design the campus of the Carnegie Technical Schools, and he arranged the buildings in a manner reflective of the Chicago world's fair's Court of Honor, although it was Thomas Jefferson's plan for the University of Virginia that more profoundly inspired his plan. The school opened in 1906.[104]

While Holland negotiated in vain with Mary Schenley, Bigelow acted to enhance Pittsburgh's emerging cultural center. In 1895 he enticed New York sculptor Guiseppe Moretti to help beautify Highland and Schenley parks with his art, much like sculpture had adorned the "White City" in Chicago.[105] As noted earlier, Bigelow implemented his idea of accessible, interconnected parks, in the fashion of Boston's "Emerald Necklace," by constructing a boulevard from downtown to the Oakland entrance of Schenley Park and another one from the park's opposite end northward to Highland Park. Bigelow also acquired more acreage from Mary Schenley for the Oakland entrance to the park, and in 1898 he built a handsome stone arched bridge over St. Pierre's Ravine that trended southward from the front of the Carnegie Library. This bridge completed a romantically designed approach by connecting Grant Boulevard (then under construction) to the Schenley Bridge, which spanned Junction Hollow and led directly into the park. At the same time, Bigelow and the city agreed to provide land for Carnegie's proposed expansion of his institute.[106]

Bigelow and Carnegie orchestrated this first decade of the Oakland civic center development. Toward the end of that decade, in 1898, Franklin A. Nicola, the man who would become the center's guiding hand, initially made his presence felt. Nicola, a land developer from Cleveland who had recently moved to Pittsburgh, purchased from the city three acres that had been part of Mary Schenley's holdings. The parcel was situated strategically between Oakland's main thoroughfares of Fifth and Forbes avenues and diagonally adjacent from the Carnegie Institute. He then organized the Bellefield Corporation to develop a fashionable, ten-story hotel on this key site. Additionally, he invited the nation's leading landscape architecture firm, the Olmsted Associates, to prepare a plan for the hotel grounds, which would also make a smooth and appropriate transition to the Schenley Park entrance. As if coordinating his work with Nicola, and there is no reason to suppose he was not, Bigelow also contacted the Olmsted firm to consider a plan for the entrance to the park.[107]

Local historians usually attribute the conception of Oakland as a civic center to Nicola, especially because of his prominent role in promoting and developing the idea in the first decade of the twentieth century. However, as a businessman relatively new to the city but with strong ties to the city's business community and the Magee-Flinn political machine, Nicola may have simply seen the opportunity to capitalize on the emerging cultural and educational center and the potential of the considerable acreage that Mary Schenley still retained in Oakland. At the Schenley Hotel's grand opening ball in 1898, Carnegie joined the other fifty stockholders and many more of the city's elite in celebrating this newest addition to Oakland. Whatever Nicola's role in envisioning Oakland's future, the roster of the Bellefield Corporation's stockholders indicates that the vision of Oakland as the city's civic center enjoyed deep and broad political support. In addition to Carnegie, Schenley, Nicola, and the city's most prominent businessmen, such as George Westinghouse, Henry J. Heinz, Henry Phipps, and A. W. Mellon, reform leader and mayoral candidate George Guthrie was an investor alongside his machine opponents Christopher Magee, William Flinn, and William Magee, who would play an important role in the emergence of planning in the next decade. Thus the development of Oakland as an educational and cultural center enjoyed bipartisan support, unlike many other proposals for municipal development at the time.[108]

By the end of 1900 Carnegie had endowed Oakland with two major institutions, and as architectural historian Toker has written, he had signaled "to other industrial leaders to endow the area with buildings of such magnificence that it might create a new Pittsburgh free from the stigma of the old."[109] Simultaneously, Edward Bigelow, with the blessing of his political benefactor Christopher Magee, had fashioned a major urban park and worked to enhance the Oakland area around his park through land acquisitions and donations, boulevards and bridge construction, and cooperation with Carnegie's philanthropic endeavors. Charles Mulford Robinson, a pioneer and leading proponent of city beauty and planning, recognized that amid this city—more familiar than most with the typical haphazard urban development—there was a vision behind Oakland, if not actual formal planning. In 1906 he wrote that "a very interesting educational and cultural center is developing at the portal of the East End. It is one of the few examples in this country of consciously directed growth, though it should be added that it has its limitations in the fact that as yet that growth has not had professional direction, and seems still vague and uncertain as to the general scheme."[110]

Robinson did not explicitly recognize, however, that the efforts of men of power, means, and public spirit, as he put it, to nurture a great civic center also involved the cooperation of political leaders and public officials who shared the vision. Even at this early stage, several years before the idea of city planning as a municipal responsibility achieved consensus in the public conversation, public and private cooperation in shaping city space took place and advanced the notion of not relying entirely on the vicissitudes of the private market for development of important civic areas. If conscious development through the even minimally coordinated efforts of private and public leaders worked in Oakland, why could not such partnership be effective in improving Pittsburgh's congested, dirty downtown and other important environmental problems?

"PLANNING" IN THE RING-LED ERA

Planning as a formal, deliberative exercise—that is, an expert-led conversation about the urban environment viewed comprehensively—built upon the excitement of the Chicago world's fair, the apotheosis of the planning principles of Chicago in the McMillan Commission's plan for Washington, D.C., and the surging reform impulse that was progressivism. In Pittsburgh, progressive planning awaited the civic groundswell following the election of reform mayor George Guthrie. Prior to 1906, amid ring-led development, Bigelow fathered a magnificent park system and made it accessible via designed parkways, free bridges, and boulevards. The Department of Public Work's Bureau of Surveys undertook topographical surveys and collected other data, laid miles of sewers and water lines, and with the help of outside consultants built a large-scale slow sand filtration system. More significant, Oakland not only served as the gateway to the city's East End suburbs, and to Schenley Park, but it was also already unfolding as a civic center, a model of civic consciousness, of redeemed civic virtue, and of the possibilities of consciously planned public space.

But to the reformers' chagrin, Pittsburgh's ring in 1905, although weakened, still sat at the head of the conversation. The ring derived its power from the city's fragmented neighborhoods, not the city as a whole. While Bigelow in the nineteenth century had salted his reports with references to planning, the systematic coordination of projects, and appeals for control of lot subdivisions, his actions (for example, steering contracts to Booth and Flinn, Ltd.), his imperial (some say "tyrannical") manipulation of property viewers' assessments and court awards, his favoring of East End development over less-affluent working-class neighborhoods, and his complicity in ring-owned traction deals commandeering city streets for private profit impugned the depth of his commitment to planning. So did the freight trains clogging main thoroughfares such as Liberty Avenue, muddy excavated streets, soot-filled skies, and the brash billboards advertising Beeman's Gum and other products, which cluttered city streets and intersections, even the streetscape opposite Carnegie Hall in Oakland. Such visual disfigurement mocked Bigelow's proclamation of progress and demeaned the city's reputation nationally.[111]

Pittsburgh, in fact, experienced a heightened interest in positive environmentalism amid the labor violence and mass joblessness attending the economic depression of the 1890s. Middle-class reformers moved by the travails of labor—the low wages, sordid living conditions, rising tuberculosis and typhoid fever rates, and other hazards of working-class life—supported parks and playgrounds, the civic tableau of Oakland, and the settlement house movement. They swelled the ranks of the women-dominated CCAC. But prior to 1900 most of these reformers, such as Oliver McClintock and George Guthrie, saw the city's redemption more in terms of moral than physical renewal, and they saw the ring as a satanic force insidiously destroying the moral life of the city. McClintock portrayed Pittsburghers as overtaxed and demoralized, victimized by Bigelow's tyrannical assessments and by Booth and Flinn's shoddy street and sewer work, and prostrate before the feudal oppression of a "government of bosses." Branding Pittsburgh's ring "a reproach," the Chamber of

Commerce, like McClintock and Guthrie, deemed its destruction "a vital necessity."[112]

Therefore, although settlement people like George Hodges and the civic reformers of the CCAC promoted physical improvements such as smoke control, parks, playgrounds, and housing betterment, and while in 1899 Oakland's emerging civic center and projects such as Grant Boulevard attested to the existence of an important, albeit fledgling, civic improvement movement, it was not until the early twentieth century that the Pittsburgh discourse, the so-called urban conversation, blossomed into an exercise that might be called modern planning. In 1903 the Pittsburgh Architectural Club (also called the Pittsburgh chapter of the American Institute of Architects), organized in 1899, mindful of the sheer ugliness of the downtown district and of the need "for developing a sense of the beauty of all things," launched a competition "for improving the water front, and the betterment of present conditions in the interesting location we call the point with its present dilapidated houses and unsightly exposition building."[113]

The competition produced "idealistic," mainly baroque, designs for a remodeled "triangle," but it whetted the appetite of civic leaders for physical reform, for the ideas of Rochester architect Charles Mulford Robinson, Chicago's Daniel Burnham, and Boston's Frederick Law Olmsted Jr., whose landscape designs already adorned the lavish estates of Henry J. Heinz, Elizabeth Thaw, and William Larimer Mellon. Upon Magee's death in 1901, and with Flinn hobbled by Thomas Bigelow's "ripper" bill, the city in the early 1900s turned at least somewhat away from its obsession with moral reform and toward moral environmentalism, toward building the beautiful city.[114]

CHAPTER 3

If Ever a City Needed the Definite Plan

WITH THE ELECTION of their candidate, George Guthrie, as mayor of Pittsburgh in 1906, the city's reformers had finally broken through the Republican political machine's grip on the executive office. They were now positioned to advance the many projects for civic betterment, which they had been pushing for more than a decade. Beginning around 1890, as explained in chapter 2, a number of religious and civic groups advocated an array of reform measures. Amid the clamor for ending governmental corruption, eradicating vice, lowering taxes, mitigating poverty, and other reforms, organizations such as the Civic Club of Allegheny County (CCAC), the Chamber of Commerce, and the Pittsburgh Architectural Club, inspired by the Chicago World's Columbian Exposition in 1893, recognized the importance of improving public spaces, infrastructure, housing, and the environment for uplifting the city's moral condition and enhancing its economic prospects. The development of Pittsburgh's two major municipal parks and the cultural and educational center coalescing around Andrew Carnegie's gift of a library, natural history museum, art gallery, and music hall complex in the 1890s generated a sense of optimism. However, specific reform proposals for smoke abatement, water filtration, better workers' housing, more playgrounds, improvement of the historic Point area at the junction of the three rivers, and city-suburb consolidation, dubbed a Greater Pittsburgh, encountered strong opposition from vociferous lower taxation proponents, self-interested business leaders, and ideological opponents of public sector involvement in private property matters.

Despite the diversity of interests promoting civic improvements and of ideological stances regarding the proper relationship between the public and private realms, the lively urban conversation in Pittsburgh that ensued after 1900 enabled reformers to forge a consensus on both the wisdom of planning and what specifically should be done. Additionally, the conversation itself served to create the political will to get it done. After more than a decade of organization, study, and advocacy, often informed by national experts and associations, Pittsburgh's reformers in the early 1900s believed they were finally making headway against the obstacles they faced. While rarely noted explicitly during the early years of reform, the idea of city planning took hold after the turn of the century. And Guthrie's election brightened prospects that the reformers would effect significant changes. The public conversation intensified, and planning became an important theme; indeed, within three years after Guthrie's election the reformers embarked on the development of a city plan.

REFORM'S ENVIRONMENTAL AGENDA

By the time Guthrie took office in 1906, reformers had promoted several projects for improving the environmental and health conditions of the city. Many organizations such as the Voters' League or the Pittsburgh Municipal League pursued specific agendas, but the CCAC, formed in 1895, and the older Chamber of Commerce addressed the widest array of issues across the reform spectrum. The mostly elite and upper-middle-class women of the CCAC believed environmental reforms that created a cleaner, healthier, and more efficient and attractive city would in turn provide a morally uplifting influence on the citizenry, especially the immigrant population. In the initial years of the new century, CCAC members pressed tirelessly for public baths, playgrounds, public gardens, neighborhood parks, waste incineration, smoke abatement, model tenements, housing codes, a subway, and water filtration. The CCCA opposed the indiscriminate siting of billboards, particularly on the region's steep hillsides, and pushed for a division of forestry to plant trees throughout the city. This environmental agenda, of course, complemented the CCAC's active involvement in political and vice reforms.[1]

While not spearheads of reform like some of the CCAC's settlement workers, Steel City businessmen, as historian Robert Wiebe earlier observed, swelled the ranks of reformers. Although coming from the same social, often socially prominent, strata of professional and business households as the CCAC, Chamber of Commerce members more directly represented the interests of business. The Chamber considered itself a clearinghouse for municipal issues, established committees to study specific problems, cooperated with sympathetic organizations like the CCAC, prepared legislation for the city councils or state government to consider, and worked to create favorable public sentiment for its projects. Prominent on the Chamber's agenda were projects like the Greater Pittsburgh movement, which through the proposed consolidation of Allegheny City and surrounding suburbs with the city of Pittsburgh, purported to create a more efficient urban entity and elevate the city's national stature. The Chamber emphasized transportation improvements such as a tunnel to spur development of the adjacent South Hills suburban area, the removal of tolls from bridges, better mass transit, and enhanced commercial navigation on the region's waterways. With reformers holding some leadership positions in the Chamber, the body also promoted water, sewage, housing, smoke, and recreational reform proposals similar to those advocated by the CCAC.[2]

Although these proposed environmental reforms mainly involved building infrastructure, the aesthetics of public space design increasingly loomed in importance. Whether voiced as earlier by the director of the Department of Public Works, Edward Bigelow, in his vision for the city's major parks or as later by the CCAC in its proposal for a city forestry division, among local reformers the philosophy and language of Olmstedian urban park advocates circulated in tandem with the newer ideas of the City Beautiful movement. Inspired by the Chicago world's fair and by visions of civic art and neighborhood improvement, the City Beautiful movement between 1901 and 1902 burst full bloom onto the American urban scene. According to Jon Peterson, "full scale City Beautiful planning" embodied civic centers, gateway railroad stations, grand boulevards, belt parkways and park systems, and public playgrounds. To commemorate the centenary of the planning of Washington, D.C., in 1901 Congressman James McMillan, in concert with the American Institute of Architects (AIA), impaneled a committee of professional architects to restore the capital to its beauty captured in L'Enfant's original 1801 plan for the city. In January 1902 the McMillan Commission, which included Daniel Burnham, Charles McKim, and Frederick Olmsted Jr., displayed their finished plan in the Corcoran Gallery. The plan that in Peterson's words combined the civic vision of large-scale ensemble planning captured in the Chicago fair with the older tradition of park planning excited national acclaim catalyzing the City Beautiful movement.

Pittsburgh well knew the McMillan Commission's Burnham and the allure of the City Beautiful. Not only had Burnham designed the elegant Frick Building, which in 1901 arose on the city's prominent Grant Street, but also in the same year he had designed the city's grand Pennsylvania Station. As a gateway terminal, Penn Station stood as a central feature of City Beautiful planning. To underscore the centrality of the movement for Pittsburghers, just hours from the city in the state's capital, Harrisburg, Horace McFarland unfolded a City Beautiful extravaganza. The AIA had spearheaded the McMillan Commission's celebrated Washington, D.C., plan. Likewise in the Steel City, the local architects championed City Beautiful design. The Pittsburgh Architectural Club promoted good design through annual exhibitions and a yearbook. In

1900 it supported the idea of a municipal art commission to advise on the design of streets, public buildings, and other places of interest, noting that there was need for "developing a sense of the beautiful in all things ... [because] progress consists not so much in material prosperity as in spiritual and mental advancement." In that same year the club held a competition for a plan of the downtown district in order to "arouse public interest," even if the "schemes are too idealistic to meet the full approval of those within whose power it lies to better the present conditions." The club declared its intention to examine in the coming year specific parts of such a plan, particularly the waterfronts, the Point, and the removal of the "hump," the hill on the eastern edge of downtown that caused traffic congestion and acted as a barrier to development.[3]

Five years later the Architectural Club held another competition to design a downtown civic center and, based on the entrees, presented a plan for one in its annual publication. The club's plan featured a public square surrounded by mu-

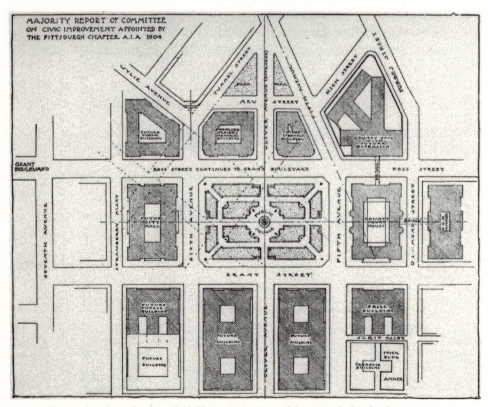

The Pittsburgh Architectural Club's 1905 City Beautiful–inspired plan for downtown Pittsburgh. *Carnegie Library of Pittsburgh.*

nicipal buildings next to Henry Hobson Richardson's Allegheny County court-house. It was to be both a breathing spot amid the dense development of down-town and an opportunity to display inspiring, monumental civic buildings. As part of the proposal, the local architects again made a plea for beauty. "Men need beauty precisely as they need fresh air and clear skies. To condemn them to live among ugly surroundings, under skies blackened with smoke, is to deaden their sensibility to the beautiful and to rob their lives of one great element of inter-est and dignity." They also warned of the dangers of bad planning. "For it must not be forgotten that bad city planning produces bad building, and bad building and bad planning combined induce dirt and disease, and thus like loss of char-acter in an individual, the breaking down of the laws of health and decency go hand in hand with the evils of a bad scheme."[4] The Architectural Club's foray ex-plicitly aligned planning with the moral environmentalism of the city's reform-ers. Collectively, the environmental reform recommendations of the CCAC, the transportation proposals of the Chamber of Commerce, and the design schemes of the Architectural Club, "civic improvements" as they were called, formed the core of the conversation about urban beautification. Yet, as elsewhere in urban America, these civic designs, often based upon an urban ideal, no matter how scintillating, existed outside of any broad planning framework or any process for comprehending and reshaping the city as a whole.

A CONSENSUS TO PLAN

With George Guthrie in office, reformers knew they had not just a mayor sympathetic to their cause, but also a man who had long fought side by side with them. Guthrie was a socially prominent lawyer and communicant of Cal-vary Episcopal, the church at the center of reform. Over the years he had bat-tled the political machine and advocated civil service and city charter reforms. As mayor, he would not achieve as much as he and his supporters hoped be-cause he lacked the support of the machine-dominated city councils, but he did preside over some administrative reforms, the completion of the water fil-tration plant, the enactment of a smoke-abatement ordinance, and the removal of the railroad tracks from Liberty Avenue in downtown. With the annexation of several adjacent municipalities and Allegheny City, he had partially fulfilled the progressive dream of a Greater Pittsburgh. However, the mayor's embrace of the Pittsburgh Survey may have been his greatest contribution to the ad-vancement of civic improvements, especially planning.[5]

Only a month before Guthrie took office, the chief probation officer of the Allegheny County Juvenile Court invited the editors of the *Charities and the*

Mayor George W. Guthrie,
Pittsburgh progressive mayor in
1909 who created the Pittsburgh
Civic Commission. *Carnegie Library
of Pittsburgh.*

Commons, Edward Devine and Paul Underwood Kellogg, to conduct a social
survey of Pittsburgh. With a warm reception by the mayor and endorsements
(as well as some financial support) from the CCAC, the Chamber of Commerce, and others in the local reform community, they agreed to the challenge. Funded generously by the Russell Sage Foundation, Kellogg headquartered the Pittsburgh Survey in Kingsley House in the city's teeming central
immigrant district. He orchestrated a wide-ranging investigation of working
conditions, housing, health, the environment, political administration, and
numerous other problems. Even before the results were serialized in the *Charities and the Commons* in early 1909, Kellogg and his investigators had exposed
the dreadful social consequences of what they viewed as the region's spectacular industrial development and weak sense of civic responsibility. They blamed
the social injustices and environmental degradation on the undemocratic and
corrupt rule of the Republican political machine, the extreme political fragmentation of too many municipalities, the excessive embrace of individualism at the expense of civic consciousness, the unchallenged power of corpora-

tions that repressed effective union organization, and the uncaring policies of absentee-owned corporations, noting especially J. P. Morgan's newly formed United States Steel Corporation.[6] Historian John Ingham has argued that the emphasis on the role of absentee ownership deliberately deflected responsibility for Pittsburgh's problems from local elites, many of whom actively participated in or supported reform organizations and endorsed the Survey itself.[7] Indeed, the Survey's analysis and recommendations underscored city reformers' positions and recommendations, although Kellogg's attack on corporate labor policies and working conditions did not sit well with the business community. In fact, reports of the Survey in the local and national press stung Pittsburgh's pride. Local boosters and even some reformers denounced it for being too focused on the worst examples and for neglecting positive public and private sector accomplishments in civic improvement. Some city defenders asserted that conditions in Pittsburgh were no worse than in other large cities, and sometimes even better.[8]

Despite its challenge to civic pride, the Survey team's presence excited the local reform community and encouraged city progressives to intensify their efforts. Reform fervor led the Chamber of Commerce to host a joint meeting of the National Municipal League and the American Civic Association in November 1908, billed as the Sixteenth National Conference for Good Government. The *Pittsburgh Post* proclaimed on the eve of the meeting that "it is fortunate that at this meeting we are to have the report of the Pittsburgh Survey. This survey represents true courage on the part of Pittsburgh. No progress can possibly be made in civic betterment of any American city until the citizens of that city know the true conditions and have these conditions presented without fear and without favor."[9] The conference featured an exhibit at the Carnegie Institute entitled "A Practical Study of Municipal Government and Civic Improvement." Organized through the cooperation of several local groups, it displayed graphically the findings of the Pittsburgh Survey, and presented Benjamin Marsh's influential exhibit on the population congestion of New York City. Using maps and charts, the Survey's exhibit excoriated Pittsburgh's deplorable workers' housing, its inadequate water treatment system, and the prevalence of industrial accidents. The most striking aspect of the exhibit was "a frieze of small silhouettes three inches apart stretching in line around both ends and one side of the large hall . . . over 250 feet in length. The figures represented 622 persons, the death-toll from typhoid fever in Greater Pittsburgh during the previous year."[10]

The Survey's emphasis on the "scientific" investigation of local conditions and the marshaling of facts appealed to the city's progressive reformers.

H. D. W. English, owner of a successful insurance company and president of the Chamber of Commerce, praised the Survey at the conference, stating, "There has been nothing about the Survey . . . of that yellow [journalism] order that we sometimes get in our papers. These have been cold facts given us about our conditions here in Pittsburgh . . . that we may look at ourselves and know ourselves as we are." He then exhorted fellow businessmen, engineers, and manufacturers to solve the city's problems. In the Chamber's 1907 and 1908 annual reports, he noted with satisfaction the awakening of the members to the need for civic involvement. "Pittsburgh," he claimed, "should be a model city. Perhaps, no city in the world contains the same amount of engineering, professional and business skills." Summarizing his message, English unsheathed his fondest phrase, "a city to be distinctly great commercially must be great civicly [sic]."[11]

Pittsburgh reformers had heeded English's prescription. The CCAC, in cooperation with the Chamber of Commerce and other groups, for example, finally had achieved the systematization of charity with the formation of the Associated Charities in 1907. A year later, the Voters' League's investigation of political corruption produced arrests and later the convictions of more than a dozen Pittsburgh bankers and councilmen. With continued success in fighting corruption during the subsequent few years, reformers celebrated the city's great "victory for civic righteousness" in 1910 with a giant downtown rally featuring ex-president, and celebrated champion of progressive reform, Theodore Roosevelt.[12]

English's optimism also reflected progress on several environmental projects in 1906 and 1907. The Chamber initiated a study of sewage issues, and, with the cooperation of the CCAC, shepherded a smoke abatement ordinance through the city councils. In recognition of the Chamber's role in drafting and passing this legislation, the city asked it to name the head of the new Division of Smoke Inspection. Further, the CCAC and the Chamber successfully pressured the city in 1906 to budget for more housing inspectors and then succeeded in getting even more inspectors approved during the next few years. The Chamber and CCAC also initiated studies aimed at controlling the unsightly billboards that pockmarked the city's landscape. Although both the new smoke control ordinance and housing legislation failed to solve the problems, at the time of passage reformers thought that they were at last making progress to improve Pittsburgh's debased environment.[13]

The conversation in 1906 and 1907 still included concern for the design and use of public space. In 1906 the CCAC endorsed the local chapter of the AIA's plan for a downtown civic center. The following year, the CCAC praised the city's creation of Arsenal Park from the grounds of the federal government's former Allegheny Arsenal, a proposal the club had initiated and promoted for several years. In that same year, 1907, the Carnegie Institute and the Architectural Club hosted a three-week graphic presentation of "Pittsburg[h]: A City Beautiful." The exhibit featured traffic recommendations to enhance access to downtown and a grand civic center, much along the lines of the earlier proposal. A baroque plaza would provide a "proper setting" for the Richardson courthouse and other public and semipublic buildings. The civic center, reported the *Pittsburgh Dispatch*, would create "a pleasing effect which always attends a combination of order and usefulness." The Architectural Club also advocated a scheme for the rearrangement of streets in Oakland to accommodate more efficiently the unfolding educational and cultural district centered on the earlier development of Schenley Park and the Carnegie Institute. To further the conversation on design plans, the Arts Society of Pittsburgh held a free public meeting at the Carnegie Institute during the exhibit, at which Cleveland's noted progressive reformer Frederick Howe presented a lantern slide lecture on municipal improvements featuring "the schemes of other cities and also the possibilities of Pittsburg[h]." This exhibit culminated seven years of advocating good designs for public spaces by the Architectural Club.[14]

Visitors to the 1907 exhibit at the Carnegie Institute could not help but notice that the educational and cultural center in Oakland was undergoing a second, and what would turn out to be a massive, phase of development. Whereas Bigelow and Carnegie had dominated the center's emergence in the 1890s, businessman Franklin F. Nicola provided the creative energy after the turn of the century. Nicola illustrated how the entrepreneurial vision of what historian Marc Weiss called the "community builder" could give breadth and form to the City Beautiful. Indeed, Pittsburgh's pièce de résistance Oakland civic center took its penultimate form under Pittsburgh's premier community builder, Nicola. Because Nicola envisioned Oakland as a palette, a totality, a plan that encompassed a civic ensemble, and residential as well commercial components, he incorporated vital elements of comprehensiveness into his planning.

Oakland's two early visionaries remained supportive during this new phase; but inspired by City Beautiful plans such as Burnham's 1903 plan for a civic center in Cleveland, Nicola, formerly of that Lake Erie city, envisioned this large district as "a model city," as "the city's social, educational, club, and best residence center."[15] Years later local architectural historian James Van Trump observed that "his [Nicola's] spirit brooded over the entire Oakland district until his death."[16]

Public and philanthropic cooperation engineered Oakland's initial flowering in the 1890s. Under Nicola, commercial and philanthropic efforts prevailed. With the purchase of a large tract of undeveloped, surprisingly rural, land within Oakland, Nicola planned a massive development, building on the foundation that Bigelow and Carnegie had erected. As a developer, Nicola operated on a much larger scale than traditional nineteenth-century builders did. He was, in the words of Weiss, "a community builder [who] designs, engineers, finances, develops, and sells an urban environment using as the primary raw material rural, undeveloped land."[17] While he needed the cooperation of public officials and civic leaders in realizing his plans, he eschewed the guiding hand of a professional planner, as Charles Mulford Robinson astutely observed in 1909.[18]

When Mary Schenley died in November 1903, considerable undeveloped property in Pittsburgh passed into her estate. In 1905 the three American executors of the estate sold 103 of prime Oakland acres, the undeveloped Schenley Farms land immediately north of the Carnegie Institute, to Nicola and his associates.[19] Since the completion of the Schenley Hotel in 1898, a project that Nicola directed, Carnegie's proposals for vastly expanding his institute (tripling its size) and for building technical schools were taking shape, and three new churches punctuated Oakland's skyline. During these years, Nicola must have busily prepared for the possibility of this new development. Only days after his purchase, the *Pittsburgh Dispatch* reported that the property would be converted "into one of the garden spots of the country," and that several "leading" institutions would soon call the area home, including the Western University of Pittsburgh (University of Pittsburgh).[20] Indeed, the university purchased a hilly 45-acre site from Nicola, and with his financial aid Chancellor Samuel B. McCormick launched an architectural design competition for the university's new campus.[21]

Nicola convinced other institutions to embrace his vision as well. Allegheny County purchased a key block in 1906 for the erection its Soldiers' and Sailors' Memorial Hall. As a founding member, along with his brothers, Nicola persuaded the new Pittsburgh Athletic Association to erect its grand Beaux-Arts clubhouse across the street from it.[22] In 1908 he induced his friend Barney Dreyfus, owner of the Pittsburgh Pirates, to purchase a seven-acre site across St. Pierre's Ravine from the Carnegie Library for a new baseball park. Dreyfus chose Nicola's firm, the Schenley Farms Company, to build the ballpark, Forbes Field, while the Oakland impresario's younger brother, Oliver Nicola, headed the general contracting company that actually put it up.[23] Besides these ma-

Aerial view of Oakland in 1923, the city's epitome of City Beautiful planning, showing the University of Pittsburgh, Nicola's Schenley Hotel, the Soldiers' and Sailors' Memorial Hall, the Pittsburgh Athletic Club, and, in the foreground, the new Schenley Park entrance. *Aerial Photographs of Pittsburgh, Archives Service Center, University of Pittsburgh.*

jor institutions, six more clubs and social societies, as well as three additional churches, erected new facilities by 1915 in Nicola's emerging civic center.[24]

Nicola also planned a residential neighborhood to round out his community. He set aside the northeast corner of the property for homes, subdivided it into ninety-six lots, and with carefully fashioned building standards and deed covenants promoted an upscale, quality residential quarter. He invested heavily in extensive grading and landscaping, and embellished the neighborhood with shade trees and planted shrubs for an "uniform park effect." He required setbacks from the streets, wiring buried underground, and invested heavily in a massive stone retaining wall. Finally, Nicola tied together the educational, institutional, and residential elements of his development by extending Grant Boulevard (soon to be renamed Bigelow Boulevard) on a jagged course through his development from its terminus at the northeast corner of Schenley Farms to St. Pierre's Ravine at the entrance of Schenley Park and the Carnegie Library.[25]

As a community builder, Nicola not only promoted his Oakland project to residential buyers and various institutions for the profit of his Schenley Farms Company, but he also planned it in the context of the city as a whole. This refreshingly novel approach employed a broader view than that of the typical real estate speculator.[26] Nicola's promotion of a civic center with schools, churches, and private clubs built upon both the earlier Bigelow-Carnegie vision of an educational and cultural complex and the ongoing rapid expansion of the middle- and upper-class East End neighborhoods. Besides his interest in profitability, Nicola had identified a need of the city and an opportunity to grace industrial Pittsburgh with a distinguished City Beautiful civic center. As a former Clevelander, Nicola would have been familiar with Burnham's 1903 dramatic civic center in the lakefront city. Within two years he imported the idea to Pittsburgh. Only six years later, in 1911, the nationally recognized architectural critic Montgomery Schuyler heralded the accomplishment in a 1911 article entitled "The Building of Pittsburgh." He exclaimed:

This [civic center] it has attained in fact in a fuller measure than it has been attained in any other American city. . . . The panorama which one sees looking northward from Schenley Park comprises and combines the social and civic functions which are elsewhere scattered. . . . There is no other "civic center" in this country to be compared with this, excepting possibly Copley Square . . . already the architectural excellence and the architectural impressiveness of this real civic center suffice to strike the stranger with admiring astonishment and to foster a just pride on the part of the Pittsburgher.[27]

Schuyler, like Charles Mulford Robinson before him, recognized that private and philanthropic efforts had created the Oakland civic center. A combination of public, semipublic, and private spaces, Oakland emanated from the visions of several powerful men—Bigelow, Carnegie, and Nicola—and the propitious availability of undeveloped property within the region of the city where the civic center could be shaped.[28] With the exception of Bigelow's grand public park and the work of architect Henry Hornbostel, who designed buildings for Carnegie's Institute of Technology, the new campus of the University of Pittsburgh, and several other key Oakland civic buildings, the privately predisposed industrial elite saw little need for professional expertise to guide the development of the raw land.[29] In contrast, through the means of the urban conversation, these same elites and many reformers increasingly came to believe that the built-up central city, in particular the downtown where their business interests often lay, required modern city planning to create the desired efficient, healthful, and aesthetic urban environment.

THE DAWN OF COMPREHENSIVE PLANNING

Events in 1907 and 1908 propelled Pittsburgh's age of progressive reform. Two crises in 1907 raised fears about the city's economic prospects and intensified the sentiment in favor of environmental reform and planning for the central city. A damaging flood on March 15 halted train service, shut down many mills, and put thousands of workers temporarily out of work. The flood covered an estimated 53 percent of downtown and dirtied most of the rest of the central business district with "back water from sewers and ground flow." Floods were a "constant menace" for Pittsburgh, but they had been getting more disruptive and costly in recent years as a result of rapid urban development and continued logging in the mountainous watersheds of the rivers.[30] Then, compounding the insult, a national financial panic hit Pittsburgh businesses very hard in the fall, devastating the city's stock exchange, which never recovered from the blow.[31]

In the wake of these two events, civic leaders took action. Alarmed at the costs to business, the Chamber of Commerce in February 1908 appointed a Flood Commission under the leadership of industrialist Henry J. Heinz and the ever-present H. D. W. English to study the flooding problem and propose both prevention and protection measures.[32] In October of the same year the city staged a sesquicentennial celebration that, fortuitously, coincided with the headlined arrests of several city businessmen accused of political graft and corruption. Both heightened the mood of civic jubilation. Festivities associated with the sesquicentennial climaxed with the laying of two cornerstones, one for Soldiers' and Sailors' Memorial Hall and the other for the first building of the University of Pittsburgh's new campus, both situated in Oakland.[33]

Pittsburgh's 150th year, 1908, proved to be pivotal for planning in the city. Support from the reform mayor; confirmation of the extent of the city's problems from an outside, scientific investigation; the momentum of recent reform successes; and concern for the economy culminated in November 1908 with a declaration of the need for planning and action toward actually undertaking the first city plan. The joint meeting of the National Municipal League and the American Civic Association in mid-November provided the venue. Mayor Guthrie welcomed the conventioneers to Pittsburgh, and in the course of the proceedings offered a rationale for planning coupled with a plea for more power for cities to control development:

What we are we owe to our city. The value of our property is only great because of the congestion brought here . . . because of the protection which the city gives to it. . . . Now, is it absurd under such a situation that a man should be permitted to do something with his property which is destructive to the best interests of the whole community? . . . The mere responsibility of the individual is something that he answers for to a higher power than the city; but his responsibility to the city . . . imposes on him a responsibility for which he should be legally answerable to the city. . . . Let the city have its rights . . . to move forward freely to the highest development which [it] can obtain.[34]

While agreeing with Guthrie on the need for planning, Chamber of Commerce president English stressed that the city's civic organizations, not government, should manage the planning tool. Drawing on the Chamber's recent successes, and its long-held progressive suspicions of local politicians and excessive governmental power, he opined that the "men who make up the membership of a commercial organization, . . . engaged in voluntary work," and acting "apart from the municipal government and administration" can best bring the expert knowledge to solve civic problems. In his view, municipal governments were not inclined to act on long-term goals, but businessmen were. English averred,

municipalities . . . are not capable of looking very far into the future and seeing benefits from money expended today which will come back, perhaps, to our children. Such things as better housing conditions, better transportation facilities, better care of the children of the streets and better sanitary conditions, the granting of franchises viewed in a broad way, sometimes look too advanced to the ordinary legislator, but it is not difficult to show to the thoughtful business man that all this counts, even counts from the dollars-and-cents point of view, let alone the matter of civic pride.

By participating in committees and developing recommendations for city government, English went on, businessmen would also be more apt to gain confidence in the administrative branch of city government and thus provide the cooperation between municipal legislatures and civic organizations essential for progress. Thus English, the leading voice of the private sector in the public conversation, acknowledged the need for long-range planning, although he was clearly not convinced that government would undertake the task.[35]

All of these resounding declarations of the city's ability to rectify the social and physical problems described in the Survey set the stage for dramatic action. Buoyed by the rhetoric, Robert A. Woods, director of Boston's South End Settlement House and a participant in the Survey, envisioned Pittsburgh replacing Chicago as a model of civic improvement. The World's Columbian Exposition, he pointed out, had overcome the scorn heaped upon Chicago for its social problems and brought it the nation's respect for its social progress. "Pittsburgh succeeded Chicago as the chosen example of the cynics," he con-

tinued. "Pittsburgh is earnestly, and with that unparalleled Pittsburgh productive instinct, taking to heart these large plans for associated and public enterprise through which alone . . . a twentieth century city's prosperity goes hand
in hand with its honor."[36]

With his three-year term nearing its end, and unable to succeed himself,
Mayor Guthrie fully intended to make Pittsburgh the model of civic betterment, which Robert Woods and English predicted. He did not want to let the
momentum of 1908 dissipate. In view of the improbability that the state legislature would grant new powers to the city in the near future, Guthrie adopted
English's vision of reform. At the closing session of the joint meetings, the
mayor announced that he would appoint a commission "to take charge and
make history and remove from existence many and perhaps all evils which
have been pointed out to us by our kindly friends. . . . Those of you who belong
to Pittsburgh and those who are our guests . . . will join me in gratification
at the knowledge that the lessons which we have received during this week
will not be fruitless."[37] He proudly named English to chair the commission.
In January 1909, less than two months after the joint meetings had adjourned,
Guthrie appointed the Pittsburgh Civic Commission (PCC) of eighteen business and professional men and charged it "to plan and promote improvements
in civic and industrial conditions which effect the health, convenience, education and general welfare of the Pittsburgh industrial district." The new PCC
had an advisory board chaired by Mayor Guthrie and comprised of national
progressive reform luminaries, such as New York's Robert W. De Forest, Chicago's Graham Taylor (associate editor of the *Charities and the Commons*),
Boston's Robert Woods, and the *Survey*'s Paul Kellogg. The advisory board
also included one of the nation's leading proponents of city planning, Daniel
H. Burnham, who had willed the Columbian Exposition into existence, mas-
terminded the 1902 McMillan Plan for Washington, D.C., and was at the time
engaged in his benchmark plan for Chicago.[38]

The PCC believed that the Pittsburgh Survey provided the factual foundation
for civic improvements. It formed fourteen committees to study specific issues
and prepare recommendations for improvement. The committees covered most
of the issues already part of the reformers' agenda, including the environmental
concerns of sanitation and public hygiene, cleaning up and beautifying streets
as well as private premises, adequate housing, and municipal art and design.
There were also separate committees to study rapid transit and city planning.
The PCC charged another committee, the Ward Organization, with creating favorable public opinion for its proposals through civic education in each ward,

coordination with other organizations, and cooperation with public officials. These topics and approaches copied the work of the CCAC and the Chamber of Commerce. The PCC, therefore, embodied the progressives' vision of a voluntary group of business and professional leaders developing plans for civic betterment based on the "scientific" investigation of experts and working with public officials to carry them out. A key element of its agenda was city planning.[39]

In the February 1909 issue of *Charities and the Commons*, in which the results of the Pittsburgh Survey were published, and only one month after the PCC's formation, Charles Mulford Robinson advocated planning for Pittsburgh by just such a group as the PCC.[40] In ending his article, entitled "Civic Improvement Possibilities of Pittsburgh," Robinson wrote, "The final word, which has to do with the needs of the whole community, hardly requires saying. It is a plea for comprehensive planning. Surely, if ever a city needed the definite plan that an outside commission could make for it, it is Pittsburgh."[41] Robinson clearly meant to support what was already in motion. Most of the design issues he addressed, as well as some others, had been part of the city's urban conversation since early in the decade. And almost certainly, in his short visit to the city, he gleaned the elements for his proposals from this conversation.

Robinson's essay was not so much a plan for the city as an overview of what needed to be done—almost an outline for a plan. Beginning with the downtown, he urged solving traffic congestion by removing the infamous hump, reconfiguring trolley patterns, installing a subway, widening some streets, and opening new approaches to principal arteries. His proposal for unsnarling the traffic at the Point was impractical, but it underscored the landmark's potential as a park. He called for improving the river wharves and described the desirability of landscaping the river frontage into parkland. He also advocated architecturally aesthetic treatments for buildings located on the small triangles created by streets intersecting at acute angles. Finally, Robinson supported the concept of a civic center for the downtown, though he believed that the Architectural Club's plan was not ambitious enough.[42]

Casting his gaze beyond downtown, Robinson exhorted the city to rehabilitate its slum districts, housing, playgrounds, parks, and bathing facilities. He praised Oakland as a rare example of "consciously directed growth," and supported the architects' plan for rearranging and widening Oakland's streets. He proposed a broad parkway from the downtown civic center to Oakland, which would accommodate all forms of traffic and be "democratic in its benefit" by offering access for the residents of the poor central neighborhoods through which it would traverse. "There is no park," Robinson observed, "so popular as a great street." This scheme linked the proposed civic center in downtown to the city's flowering educational and cultural district with a monumental, City Beautiful–style corridor that, he believed, would spark a rejuvenation of adjacent poor neighborhoods. Finally, Robinson stressed the importance of preserving the natural beauty of the city's suburbs, adding more recreational parks, and landscaping in places some of the steep hillsides for the contemplation of nature.[43]

The public conversation about environmental reform in Pittsburgh had begun in the 1890s amid the various reform concerns of several organizations. Believing that environmental reforms of, for example, water, air, and housing quality would improve the health, productivity, and moral condition of the general public, as well as the city's image and business prospects, the CCAC and the Chamber of Commerce studied the problems, proposed solutions, and attempted to effect appropriate legislation. In 1900 the local chapter of the AIA injected design considerations of public spaces into the conversation. Inspired by the City Beautiful movement, the architects argued that good design nurtured a city's spirit. At this point, the notion of city planning became part of the conversation, although it was clearly subordinate to the specific issues of environmental reform. Through lectures, exhibits, meetings, mutual support of each other's ideas, and outright cooperation, these groups kept several projects in the public's eye during the next six years, even though governmental approval did not follow.

The election of a reform mayor in 1906 and the presence of the Pittsburgh Survey team a year later altered the political climate. The Republican machine's control of both city councils created serious obstacles to the reformers' agenda, but they began to achieve some victories with, for example, the addition of more housing inspectors and the passage of a smoke abatement ordinance. Under the leadership of reformer H. D. W. English, the Chamber of Commerce increasingly accepted the necessity of imposing some public control over urban space. Thus the Chamber slowly started to accept the wisdom of some long-term planning for flood prevention, transportation, public spaces, and housing. The formation of the PCC in January 1909 indicated that the city's leading civic agencies had reached a consensus on the desirability of city planning.

THE PITTSBURGH CIVIC COMMISSION FINDS ITS PLANNER

Robinson, like Burnham, Nolen, and Olmsted Jr., stood in the vanguard of early-twentieth-century planners whose work in Washington, D.C., Chicago, St. Louis, and San Francisco during the 1905–1909 national craze for city plans carried them inexorably away from the City Beautiful and toward the more practical realm of modern, comprehensive planning. Simultaneously, another group of planners, more concerned about factory and housing conditions, immigrant lives, and social justice, critiqued the City Beautiful movement from the different vantage point of social progressivism. Numerous sociological tours of Europe to expositions and other events convinced progressives such as Thomas Adams, Florence Kelly, Frederick Howe, and Benjamin Marsh that while, in America, planning advanced real estate and corporate agendas, in England, Germany, France, and other European states with modern, "planned" sunlit working-class suburbs like Letchworth, Welywn, and Port Sunlight, it benefited ordinary people. Following the European example, American social progressives generally favored government intervention to mitigate social wrongs. City Beautiful planning, they protested, ignored the greatest civic evil: fetid tenement housing and congested slums. Several historians have noted the indifference of American planning to the "housing problem." On the contrary, rooted in the environmentalism of civic art and in the City Beautiful movement, professional architect-planners such as Nolen believed that attractive, well-designed urban places, with suburban land made accessible by mass transit, relieved congestion and bettered housing. Robinson, in fact, juxtaposed the "sociological" discipline of housing to the civic art of city planning. Planners, moreover, deferred to the housing movement itself, to Lawrence Veiller's campaign for stricter tenement laws, and to the work of housing philanthropists such as Elgin R. L. Gould and the model tenement movement. Therefore, to cite housing historian Peter Marcuse, while housing and city planning were linked from the earliest days of modern planning in Europe, "contrary to all expectations, the city planning movement in its early days, as it moved from intellectual crusade to practical influence, contributed very little to the solution of the housing problems of the ill-housed, and perhaps actually worsened it."[44]

In 1909 Benjamin Marsh had determined to alter that fate. To promote his social progressive vision of a European-style planning movement, Marsh in 1909 convened in Washington, D.C., the first National Conference on City Planning, and brought with him to the capital his graphic modular display of the social and physical horrors of New York City tenement life. Pittsburgh reformer and secretary of the PCC Allen T. Burns turned to this critical conference in search of a planner for Pittsburgh. Like Chicago; St. Louis; San Diego; Columbia, South Carolina; New Haven, Connecticut; and San Francisco, "Pittsburgh," Robinson had exhorted, "needed a city plan." The formation of the PCC in January

1909 indicated that the city's leading civic agencies agreed, and Burns traveled to Washington, D.C., in May to find the right person for the job.

Reiterating the propositions of Guthrie, Robinson, and others, Burns told the social workers, housers, lawyers, and architects at the conference that Pittsburgh needed "a city plan comprehending as many, in fact more, of all the fundamental features in city life than any plan yet made in America."[45] With Burns in the audience, Frederick Law Olmsted Jr. spoke at the keynote session. The thirty-nine-year-old landscape architect was a partner with his stepbrother, John C. Olmsted, in Olmsted Associates, the thriving successor to their father's preeminent firm. His apprenticeship at the Chicago world's fair in 1893 had introduced him to planning, and he gained a distinguished reputation in the emerging field for his work in 1901 on the U.S. Senate Park Commission. The commission members had visited the great European capital cities as part of their preparations, and while Olmsted Jr. conceived of the impressive regional park system portion of the plan, he soon became renowned for city planning. In 1907, for example, he launched a study of New Haven, later published in 1910, and shortly authored another plan for Rochester, New York, published a year later. As he rose to address this historic conference on city planning in America, the peripatetic Olmsted had just returned from "some months of hurried travel in Europe devoted to the study of urban planning."[46]

In 1909, at the moment of Olmsted's address, America's embryonic city planning movement existed in a twilight realm somewhere between the architectural world visible in the building of urban parks, tree-lined Haussmanesque boulevards, and Beaux-Arts civic centers, and the civic engineering sphere responsible for sewers, waterworks, and street design. Olmsted's recent European tour had compelled him to rethink the future development of American cities. In his speech, he praised Europe's "conscious and organized public effort at city planning," which he found particularly evident in its design of wide streets and main thoroughfares. Americans, he noted, had long recognized the "deficiency in their main thoroughfares, whether resulting from a wholly unregulated natural growth of local streets, or from . . . a mechanical standardizing plan such as has so often prevailed both in English and American towns." He espied the advent of "a far broader, deeper, wiser attitude than that which merely set as an arbitrary minimum of street widths and establishes a mechanical method of agglomerating block after block." This new attitude, asserted Olmsted, recognizes that "the ultimate purpose of city planning is not to provide facilities for certain architectural effects, but is to direct the physical development of the city by every means of control within the power of the municipality in such a manner that the ordinary citizen will be able to live and labor under conditions as favorable to health, happiness and productive efficiency as his means will permit."[47]

In his speech, studded with references to French, Swiss, and German land use practices and law, Olmsted elevated the nascent art of city planning to a higher scientific realm. He proposed a process whereby cities might escape the "hapless fatalism" that perpetuated social and physical ugliness, and move planning beyond the mere dabbling with beauty. Planning, exhorted Olmsted, must integrate beauty with practicality.

Olmsted had come to Washington, D.C., in 1909 determined to outmaneuver Marsh and to rescue his fledgling modern planning profession from the contamination of social progressivism. As Olmsted saw it, comprehensive planners viewed urban space organically. Streets, boulevards, parkways, waterways, and rail lines functioned as arterial networks, facilitating access to commerce, industry, and residential space. Using currently tabulated data, maps, surveys, assessment records, and other information, planners over time scientifically managed the flow of goods, people, and urban well-being. In this objectified system, data, not sentiment, ruled.

Olmsted enthralled the Pittsburgh delegation. Burns and the PCC had found their planner. Pittsburgh's practical-minded elites had first encountered the Olmsteds not as planners but as landscape architects for their homes and engaged the firm for some larger landscaping projects such as the Schenley Hotel in Oakland and the upgrading of Allegheny Cemetery, the city's aging, grand, "rural" cemetery. They were comfortable with the Olmsteds and trusted their aesthetic judgment in private landscaping matters.[48] Now they discovered another forte of the Olmsted firm: planning the "City Practical."

On behalf of the PCC, on June 9, 1909, Burns invited Olmsted to visit the city and consider devising "a complete plan for the whole Pittsburgh industrial district." Olmsted may very well have seen Pittsburgh as the perfect opportunity to demonstrate his vision of useful, modern, comprehensive city planning. Without hesitation, Olmsted agreed to assemble a team of experts who would undertake "a preliminary examination of the situation" and prepare a report on the "means of bringing about a more orderly and systematically planned development of the controllable physical features of the Pittsburgh Industrial District." Olmsted enlisted the noted transit expert Bion J. Arnold and hydraulics engineer and designer of San Francisco's Hetchy-Hetchy and New York's Catskill water systems, John R. Freeman. Olmsted visited the city

Frederick Law Olmsted Jr. at Palos Verdes, circa 1925. *National Park Service, Frederick Law Olmsted National Historical Site.*

in the summer and fall, interviewing local officials and "experts," and carried on a lively correspondence with Burns.[49]

In mid-December Olmsted forwarded to the PCC his report on the "method of procedure" to prepare a city plan that included evaluation of major thoroughfares, mass transportation, sewers, and water supply for the entire industrial district. It also presented the need for a thorough study of the city's freight-handling facilities, parks and playgrounds, local passenger railway service, flood control on the waterfronts, smoke abatement, and public control of private property development. Finally, the report outlined the data required for the investigation of these various issues, and ended by urging the addition of a separate report on revising the city's building code. Consistent with most city planning agendas nationwide, which tended to discount the redeeming of aging inner-city neighborhoods with their tenements and boardinghouses, in favor of the perceived greater potential of the city periphery, the PCC narrowed Olmsted's focus for the final plan to the downtown district, main thoroughfares, and a few specific topics. Burns requested that he study the "design of a thoroughfare system [to include] the outlying suburban district . . . where open country is being converted into streets and lots" because "it is those localities that prompt action will secure the greatest ultimate economies in proportion to the immediate effort expended." In apparent cooperation between the city administration and the PCC, a moment of good feeling that would not last for long, Burns reported that the new mayor, William Magee, had retained Bion Arnold to study the electric and steam railroads and Allen Hazen of New York to investigate the sewer system. Further, as Olmsted wished, the mayor indicated his intention to appoint a commission to examine the city's building code and to engage Freeman to report on the water system as well.[50]

FREDERICK LAW OLMSTED JR.'S PLAN FOR PITTSBURGH

Frederick Law Olmsted Jr.'s vision of city planning transcended the limited charge presented by the PCC. He viewed the modern city as a mosaic of functioning parts, "a complex of interrelated systems."[51] Social and economic efficiency derived from the rational integration of steam and electric railways, streets, thoroughfares, sewers, water systems, housing, markets, and public buildings into an organic unity that encompassed the urban core as well as the expanding suburban periphery. Along with other urban progressives of the day, he believed that congested and ill-paved streets, haphazard development, typhoid-laden water supplies, substandard housing, inadequate access to parks and playgrounds, and a host of other urban ills placed a costly burden on residents, consumers, manufacturers, and retail business owners. City planning, Olmsted promised, would provide "intelligent control and guidance of the entire physical growth and alteration of cities." He defined the planner's task as being "the rearrangement and improvement of what had been unwisely done [in the past and] . . . the wise and economical layout of what still remains to be done." Broadly, the planner also had to address "the distribution and treatment of public spaces" as well as private development "in so far as it is practicable for the community to control or influence such development." However, since "the transportation system . . . makes the modern city possible," the planner had to start with the means of circulation. Efficient arterial highways, railroads, and mass transportation facilitated commerce and communications, and thereby enriched the city. The emphasis on scientific methodology and practical factors, which, argued Harold J. Howland in the *Outlook* magazine, Pittsburgh's industrialists embraced, did not foreclose for Olmsted attention to beauty. Unfortunately, bemoaned Olmsted, planners "had not always made it clear that . . . in a well ordered municipal life, civic beauty should be as clearly the by-product of utility as individuals' happiness should be a by-product of healthy living. Civic beauty in its most healthy and normal development is the nearly inevitable by-product of the most absolute civic utility, of efficiency and fitness."[52]

Even though Olmsted believed a city plan should encompass all the elements that Freeman, Arnold, and he had outlined in their preliminary report, he plunged with gusto into the more limited study of main thoroughfares and the downtown requested by the PCC. Olmsted recognized that Pittsburgh presented an ideal opportunity for an architect-planner like himself, who aspired to position the youthful modern planning profession in the vanguard of modern progressivism. After all, Olmsted's invitation stemmed from the city's progressive fervor and the Pittsburgh Survey, which in a flourish of publications for a national audience was detailing the city's social, political, and physical problems and among other actions called for a city plan. Moreover, Survey director Paul Kellogg, together with such prominent urban progressives as Robert A. Woods, Graham Taylor, and Robert W. De Forest, sat on the PCC's advisory board. What better city than Pittsburgh, the archetypal befouled industrial metropolis, to show off planning's wares?

Olmsted wasted no time undertaking the Pittsburgh plan. He contracted with the PCC to spend at least six days a month in the city, and assigned Edward C. Whiting from his Brookline office to oversee the daily operations in Pittsburgh. By January 4, 1910, only days after the PCC accepted the preliminary report, Whiting opened the Pittsburgh office and began collecting data. However, Olmsted's and Whiting's quest for information on parks, streets, property assessments, and even something as mundane as the square area of suburban communities encountered one obstacle after another. In April the chief engineer of the Pittsburgh Flood Commission, George Lehman, confirmed what Olmsted had already discovered: there was a serious dearth of city survey data available for planning. Lehman apprised Olmsted "that the city does not even possess reliable ordinary street maps." Replying to Lehman, Olmsted suggested that an exhibit be prepared for Mayor Magee exposing the "inaccurate, inconsistent and incomplete" state of current survey data. In his final plan, Olmsted informed Pittsburghers that he considered nothing of greater or of more "vital import to every taxpaying citizen of the present and future city . . . [than] making comprehensive and accurate topographical maps. It is only on the basis of such maps that all municipal engineering, and indeed much other work directly managed by the City, can be planned and carried out with proper economy and efficiency." Such maps, concluded Olmsted, "are absolutely essential to an intelligent planning or control which will avoid the heavy penalties that follow haphazard city growth, especially in a such a hilly region."[53] Although Magee tried to remedy this situation, the creation and updating of accurate survey maps remained an ongoing burden for city planners during the next several decades.

During the course of the year-long planning process, Whiting collected reams of demographic, economic, traffic, engineering, and other information on Pittsburgh and its surrounding communities, as well as useful comparative data on European and other American cities. Basic questions about the form and use of urban space drove the firm's search for information. How are streets used? How do street grades and widths affect the intensity of street use? Can street size and design be related to property values? Wherever possible, the firm sought out local experts and officials and tried to cooperate with ongoing studies such as that of the Flood Commission. Some city departments and bureaus, especially the Department of Public Works, were suspicious of this unofficial, "outside" planning effort and refused to cooperate.[54]

Olmsted argued that several perennial themes of the decade-long conversation on bettering Pittsburgh, such as the need for a downtown civic center and restoring the historic Point, still required in-depth study. Despite the tight one-year deadline for the completion of his plan, he tackled these special issues with surprising thoroughness. Perhaps the most unusual study involved the request, eventually to become a demand, by the federal government to alter the piers and raise the heights of the bridges over the Allegheny River in order to facilitate commercial navigation. Olmsted gathered information—locally, nationally, and internationally—on riverboats, river navigation, bridge construction, bridge traffic, and the impact of bridge ramps on land consumption and use. He compared the local situation with the experiences of similar-sized European cities—Lyon, France, for example—and concluded that since traffic demands on the bridges far outweighed river usage, the heights of bridges should be only modestly raised so as not impede traffic between downtown and the North Side. And typically he cautioned that final decisions needed to await the recommendations of the Flood Commission, a federal investigation of riverboat design, and the local studies of mass transit and street-level changes near the rivers. Olmsted presented the bridge study as a separate thirty-two page appendix at the end of the final plan.[55] The fate of the Allegheny River bridges was not decided until the 1920s, when new ones were finally erected.

Mayor Magee's desire to move ahead on specific projects without waiting for the PCC's plan forced Olmsted and Whiting to plunge precipitously into some issues and offer advice on others, often before they deemed it desirable. Magee had built his early 1909 mayoral campaign on a prodevelopment platform and packaged a series of projects into a bond issue. Although the PCC, not the city, had engaged Olmsted and also sought his opinions on these bond issue improvements, Olmsted needed the mayor's cooperation in order to prepare his plan, and therefore responded promptly to the mayor's inquiries.

No sooner had Whiting settled at his Pittsburgh desk than Magee requested the firm's opinion concerning the replacement of the historic produce market at Market Square. Olmsted rejected the current proposals for either rebuilding a market there, locating a new city hall at the square, or even erecting an eighteen-story office tower with the two lower floors reserved for the market. After consulting with market operators in other cities, he recommended in his final report another site for the market near Penn and Liberty avenues, which had more space and railroad service.[56] Three weeks later, in mid-January, the mayor asked Olmsted to present his view of two other long-standing and hotly debated topics: removal of the hump on the eastern edge of downtown and the filling of St. Pierre's Ravine in Oakland, allowing for a more formal treatment of the entrance to Schenley Park. In the case of the hump cut, Olmsted advanced specific recommendations on the proper depth of the cut and street widenings. For St. Pierre's Ravine, however, assuming the mind of a modern comprehensive planner, he reverted to his standard modus operandi, placing the problem in the larger picture and counseling a comprehensive study of the issue, particularly with reference to extant plans. Olmsted advised that any final design for the Schenley Park entrance await completion of plans for Oakland's streets and a new thoroughfare in Junction Hollow. Treatment of the entrance, he cautioned, also involved aesthetic concerns with respect to the Carnegie Institute and plans for the new baseball park. He urged officials to allow sufficient time for further study because making the ravine into a grand plaza would be a "radical change" of an already adopted plan (that is, Bigelow's work in 1898), and such a decision should always be based on "conclusive arguments" that the new design would be "so much finer." Ultimately, a court injunction against the bond issue delayed Magee's improvements, providing Olmsted time to complete his investigations of specific topics and insert his findings into the final plan.[57]

For the most part, Olmsted's completed plan, entitled *Pittsburgh: Main Thoroughfares and the Down Town District: Improvements Necessary to Meet the City's Present and Future Needs*, did deal narrowly, as the title suggested, with "remodeling in the downtown district and improvement of main traffic routes between the heart of the city and the outlying districts." His recommendations for widened streets, a new tunnel, and broad boulevards linking the East End and South Hills suburbs to the downtown; for functional and accessible waterfronts; and for systematically preparing and updating municipal maps and other vital planning data embodied the essence of the "City Practical." Indeed, Olmsted spent eleven pages, or 8 percent of the report, on the technical aspects of widening old streets in order to accommodate the great variety of vehicles now part of urban life.[58] As if to underscore the city's practical focus, Bion Arnold also issued his study in 1910 under the title *Report on the Pittsburgh Transportation Problem*. Commissioned a year earlier by Mayor Magee, Arnold, like Olmsted, worked rapidly and advanced several recommendations for improved mass transportation service, including better integration of extant facilities and the construction of a subway system. The report sparked considerable discussion of the deteriorating state of the region's transit service, but no consensus formed around a plan of action during the following decade.[59]

As in other large fin de siècle cities, traffic congestion already jammed Pittsburgh's downtown streets. This problem commanded Olmsted's main attention, just as it did Robinson's and Burnham's in their planning work. According to Olmsted, "an isolated and limited business district like that of Pittsburgh, made up almost wholly of narrow streets and connected with the rest of the city by a series of bridges and of bridge-like gaps in the hills which wall it in . . . [demands] a wide circuit street connecting these outlets together, so that not all the travel is forced to filter through the midst of the business district." In a proposal that would set the city's planning agenda for a quarter century, he proposed to use Water Street along the Monongahela River and Duquesne Way along the Allegheny River as part of an inner loop that would circulate traffic around the business district and thereby off downtown streets. Olmsted also recommended widening several streets within downtown, particularly the principal arteries of Fifth, Forbes, and Penn avenues; improving the connection of Grant (Bigelow) Boulevard to the downtown grid; and building a new, high-level parkway along the Monongahela hillside (later built as the Boulevard of the Allies), all to improve access to the rapidly developing East End of the city. The modern street plan of downtown Pittsburgh and the city's main arterial routes are indebted to the plan.[60]

Yet nearly half of the plan addressed traffic improvements beyond the downtown and even beyond the city boundaries, providing an outline of highway building for the county for decades to come. Olmsted advanced eighty recommendations for street, bridge, and tunnel projects that "would, even if it were possible to implement them at once, impose an altogether unreasonable financial burden." He urged the city and county to tackle some of these urgent issues before costs and other difficulties increased markedly.[61]

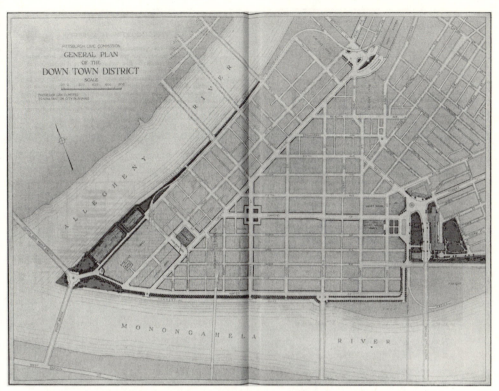

Olmsted Jr.'s "General Plan of the Down Town District" showing Water Street and Duquesne Way as part of an inner loop, principal and minor arteries, Market Square, and the civic center (darkened area on right). Frederick Law Olmsted, *Pittsburgh Main Thoroughfares and the Down Town District; Improvements Necessary to Meet the City's Present and Future Needs* (Pittsburgh: Pittsburgh Civic Commission, 1911). *Archives Service Center, University of Pittsburgh.*

A number of the proposals for "outlying thoroughfares" had long been under serious consideration. For example, Olmsted weighed in on the controversy surrounding the South Hills tunnel and bridge project. Two proposals for such a tunnel faced Olmsted. Former city Public Works director and, in 1910, consulting engineer to Allegheny County Edward Bigelow allied himself with a group of South Hills residential land developers who favored a low tunnel through the escarpment, which would empty traffic into the Saw Mill Run Valley. Frank Gosser of the South Hills Board of Trade backed the high tunnel route. Persuaded by Gosser, Olmsted adopted the shorter 2,000-foot-long higher tunnel, believing, as Gosser did, that it afforded greater and easier access to the already developed South Hills region. Ultimately Bigelow and the

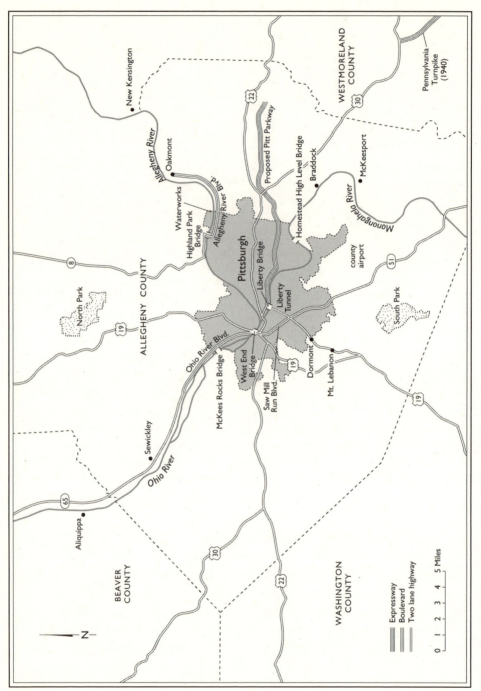

Pittsburgh and Allegheny County. *Map by William L. Nelson.*

real estate developers triumphed, and the 6,000-foot-long lower tunnel—now called the Liberty Tubes—was driven through the hill in the 1920s.[62]

Controversies aside, Olmsted's *Main Thoroughfares* plan highlighted the South Hills Tunnel and Bridge (now the Liberty Bridge) as the southern gateway to a proposed civic center in downtown. His endorsement of another long-discussed improvement for Pittsburgh confirmed the enduring vitality of the City Beautiful idea. No matter how "practical" they imagined themselves, civic leaders in 1910 favored a magnificent downtown civic center. For businessmen boosters of the progressive stripe, cathedral-like civic centers visually proclaimed the victory of civic virtue over the demons of excessive immigration, political corruption, civic indifference, and social problems. Olmsted treated the civic center as a necessary, albeit not indispensable, part of the downtown urban fabric. It fit as much into his scheme for traffic articulation as into his plans for a new city hall, another topic under current consideration. Keenly sensitive to landscape considerations, Olmsted identified an unlikely site for the center—a dreary, billboard-defiled freight yard located at the foot of the bluff occupied by the Holy Ghost College, now Duquesne University. According to Whiting, Olmsted found the rugged spot "eminently characteristic" of the hilly city, and additionally, wrote Olmsted in the report, it is serendipitously "flanked on the northwest by the noble and distinguished architecture of the courthouse and jail—masterpiece of Richardson, priceless examples of the work of one of the few great artists America has yet produced." In imitation of Princes Street in Edinburgh, Scotland, or Park Avenue in New York City, Olmsted proposed that "the central area of low ground, occupied by the railroad, be decked over at about the level of Fifth Avenue, and that a great public square with gardens be laid out," modeled after the celebrated public gardens of Europe. About this great square Olmsted would assemble the city's proposed new public buildings. On the east side of the square, "as though terraced on the hillside," explained Olmsted,

would be the principal municipal building culminating in a tower which would spring from the highest level at Bluff Street, where the playground of the Holy Ghost College could be utilized as a park. The ground enclosing the square would be completed by another building at the north with frontage on Forbes Street, Fifth Avenue, and Sixth Avenue, and by a low building on the south serving to screen the factories and freight yards beyond Second Avenue but leaving open the view of the opposite hills. Also along the east side of the square with its imperial formal gardens and "ascending gently from Forbes Street," would run the grand approach to the new South Hills Bridge across the Monongahela River.[63]

Recommending a design for the new city hall proved harder. After reject-ing Edward Bennett's (of Burnham and Bennett) design as too expensive and finding that another architectural authority, Cass Gilbert, was not available, Olmsted and PCC Planning Committee chairman T. E. Billquist settled upon Wilhelm Bernhard, an architect on Olmsted's Brookline staff. Already at work on the waterfront part of the plan, Bernhard added the city hall assignment to his workload. In mulling over a style for Pittsburgh's civic center, Olmsted, Whiting, and Bernhard shunned the baroque architectural motif fashionable

Arnold W. Brunner's and Frederick Law Olmsted Jr.'s rendering of a towering, grand Pittsburgh civic center facing a formal plaza at the approach to the proposed Liberty Bridge. Frederick Law Olmsted, *Pittsburgh Main Thoroughfares and the Down Town District; Improvements Necessary to Meet the City's Present and Future Needs* (Pittsburgh: Pittsburgh Civic Commission, 1911). *Archives Service Center, University of Pittsburgh.*

nationally for civic center designs. Bernhard explained in quite unflattering terms that such ornate architecture "does not appeal to me here, as the disgusting atmosphere of Pittsburgh . . . obliterates all smaller details." Whiting concurred, writing to Bernhard that "a picturesque and happy arrangement of building masses without a faithful adherence to any well defined classical style will lead to the most appropriate and harmonious results. The irregular and picturesque arrangement of buildings does not call for any nicely balanced, refined beaux arts architecture." Pittsburgh, as Olmsted so clearly implied in his report, was not, after all, Paris. Finally, Olmsted engaged New York architect Arnold W. Brunner—who was active in planning for such cities as Cleveland; Rochester, New York; and Grand Rapids, Michigan—to prepare a rough draft of a municipal building, from which they worked up a final impressive rendering for the civic center.[64]

Just as he would turn the mottle of railroad yards, industrial sheds, and billboards plastering the hillside of the gritty civic center site into something functional and beautiful, Olmsted proposed the transformation of Pittsburgh's equally defiled riverfronts. He assailed Pittsburgh's Monongahela wharf as "ineffective and primitive." Pittsburgh draymen in 1910 still hauled goods up and down the city's ancient quays. Meanwhile, modern riverfront facilities in Paris, Lyon, Frankfurt, and Berlin served as both "useful and attractive" models. Olmsted lashed out at the "shortsightedness and wasteful commercialism of . . . late nineteenth century" America. Europeans were aesthetically more sensitive, charged Olmsted, and combined their working quays with parks and promenades. On the other hand, Americans, believing falsely that economic and useful things were normally ugly, "disregarde[d] what might have been the aesthetic by-product of economic improvement."[65]

Coordinating with the Flood Commission, Olmsted proposed to widen Water Street and Duquesne Way into tree-lined riverfront parkways useful for traffic but also "for pedestrians to walk and sit under pleasant conditions, where they can watch the water and the life upon it, where they can enjoy the breadth of outlook and the sight of the open sky and the opposite bank and the reflections in the stream." Olmsted contended that such tree-shaded walks along the commercial streets in Paris, Lyon, and dozens of European cities added greatly to the "comeliness of the city itself, the health and happiness of the people and their loyalty and local pride." He added that

Pittsburgh has an unusual opportunity to secure this incidental value for recreation in the treatment of its riverfront . . . [because] immediately across the Monongahela are the high and rugged hillsides of Mt. Washington and Duquesne Heights, and below these

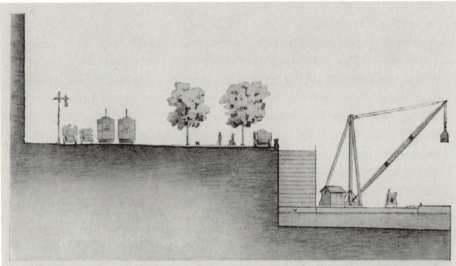

Alternative section for the water front, suggesting a floating commercial quay that would rise and fall with the river. Large cranes could transfer freight directly from the boats to trucks at the street level. At certain places roadways would cut through the promenade to provide access to ramps leading down to the quays and to provide places for freight trucks to stand while being loaded and unloaded.

A page from Frederick Law Olmsted Jr.'s 1911 *Main Thoroughfare's* report detailing proposed improvements to the city's riverfront quays. Frederick Law Olmsted, *Pittsburgh Main Thoroughfares and the Down Town District; Improvements Necessary to Meet the City's Present and Future Needs* (Pittsburgh: Pittsburgh Civic Commission, 1911). *Archives Service Center, University of Pittsburgh.*

are the lesser but still striking hills along the Ohio from the West End to McKees Rocks. The outlook over the river with its various activities to these hills immediately beyond, would be notable in any part of the world.[66]

Citing Europe again, but ignoring the reality that by 1900 railroad transportation in Pittsburgh had already rendered the city's wharves obsolete for most commercial purposes, Olmsted pressed the city to redesign its waterfront to accommodate both recreation and commerce, as European cities had done. In addition to widening Water Street and Duquesne Way, he recommended a masonry commercial quay, accessible, as in Berlin, from the street by inclined ramps "of reasonable gradient, parallel with the river... and equipped with power cranes for direct loading and unloading between steamers or barges, tied up at the quay, and wagons upon it." Floating land stages reached by gangplanks and bridges would aid the movement of cargo from ship to shore.[67] In the years after 1910 Pittsburgh's decision makers prudently balked at these elaborate plans for commercially revitalizing the waterfront, but unfortunately they also failed to grasp the value of the pedestrian promenade and public space, which Olmsted had also proposed.

Olmsted's imagination soared to almost mystical heights as he pondered the significance of Pittsburgh's Point. In terms of traffic circulation, the Point joined the two streets of his waterfront improvement, and therefore presented a practical problem. He seized upon the monumental significance of the Point as a historical and geographical location, even though in 1910 the tangle of rail yards, warehouses, and tenements all but obscured the hallowed remnants of Fort Pitt and the blockhouse and a view of the beginning of the Ohio River. In *Main Thoroughfares*, he affirmed the belief that at the Point, "all the most inspiring associations of the city are chiefly concentrated. Poetically, this spot, at the meeting of the rivers, stands for Pittsburgh."[68] Earlier in August Olmsted had suggested to Whiting that "I think the end of the point ought to have a pointed form projecting beyond and below whatever high level concourse may be designed for the bridge."[69] At the same time, he understood that the inevitable location of two high traffic bridges at the Point encumbered the fashioning of a proper monument to this historically and geographically significant site. Always mindful of the relationship of the parts to the whole, he cautioned that it was

essential that the whole Point be regarded as one single monument, that no pains be spared in bringing the best artistic skill to bear in working out the details of the plan, and the general plan, when thus worked out, shall really determine the construction of all the parts. At any time conditions may arise, as in regard to one of the bridges, for which the general plan does not exactly provide; but, if so, the plan should be adapted as a *whole* to meet the new conditions, so that work may still proceed in accordance with the complete plan. Never can a single feature of The Point safely be designed independent of the rest, if worthy results are to be obtained. And what is true of this great monumental feature is true in large measure of all public improvements in relation to a comprehensive plan.[70]

With this prescient statement, Olmsted put his finger on both the problem that stymied several future designers of Point proposals and led to some astonishing concepts, most notably Frank Lloyd Wright's outlandish beehive/ziggurat solution, and the key to the eventual solution that Ralph E. Griswold and Charles M. Stotz advanced for Point State Park in the 1940s.[71]

Although the PCC confined Olmsted to examining the downtown and main highways, he always considered public lands to be an essential part of a comprehensive city plan. In addition to special sections on the Allegheny River bridges, topographic surveys, and the market as well as the public land proposals for downtown, Olmsted included a twenty-one-page section in the final report titled "Parks and Recreational Facilities." Despite Pittsburgh's notorious reputation for dreadful smoke pollution, he thought that--in the spirit of City Beautiful enthusiasts—the region's hilly topography offered "unrivaled . . . natural opportunities" for parks, scenic parkways, and picturesque landscapes. The city of Pittsburgh had begun to take advantage of the hills and valleys with its parks initiative of the 1890s, but Allegheny County had yet to act. In the special section on parks, Olmsted proposed an ambitious program more as a guideline than a blueprint for future action. He deplored the neglect and abuse of the city's hillsides. "In far too many cases they [hillsides] are apt to be wholly uncared for and to become shabby, dirty, and altogether unsightly, depreciating adjacent property, and contributing largely to the slatternly conditions." He urged the city to "assume the burden of maintaining the land in a decent and attractive condition, converting it from a public nuisance into a park asset of positive value to the public." Drawing again on European precedents, he recommended the creation of walkways, terraces, overlooks with benches, and even alternative ways of laying out roadways where slope grades permitted.[72]

Olmsted highlighted two particularly egregious situations. In Mt. Washington, the steep bluff opposite downtown on the south shore of the Monongahela River, he saw the opportunity for people to enjoy the "grandeur" of the city's "mighty landscapes." Formerly known as Coal Hill, Mt. Washington was "now largely an unfruitful waste, a place of raw gullies and slides mingled with some painful advertising signs." He implored that it "be protected from defacement and its earthy portions . . . be reclothed with the beauty of foliage."[73] Grant Boulevard presented Olmsted with a similarly neglected case. In the 1890s Edward Bigelow had developed Grant Boulevard along the steep hillside overlooking the Allegheny Valley as both a major arterial from downtown to the East End and a parkway to his new Schenley Park. Olmsted agreed with Bigelow's concept of the boulevard as a link to the park, but he lamented that it is "a boulevard by courtesy . . . [lacking] even room for shade trees; it is a mere street, in all appearances." Further, barren, eroded hillsides above and below it were both dangerous and an "eyesore." He proposed turning the boulevard into a real parkway by widening the route and adding both a planting strip and accompanying "tree-shaded promenades" and "overlook terraces." Landscaping, retaining walls, and terracing would solve the problems of the hillsides. In subsequent years, Grant Boulevard was widened, hillsides protected, and overlooks provided, though not always with the care for design that Olmsted envisioned.[74]

Having been asked during preparation of the plan about the entrance to

Schenley Park, Olmsted gave special attention to that important site in Oakland in the final report. After considerable discussion with Whiting during the year, he published two plans for the entrance. One retained the picturesque topography of St. Pierre's Ravine and the graceful stone-arched bridge that crossed it, providing an informal entrance to the park. The other design filled in the ravine, buried the bridge, and imagined a grouping of public buildings around the resulting plaza. It also shifted Grant Boulevard to a "more direct and dignified approach," and projected terraces at the south end for looking into the park. Despite its being a "radical change in [the] park design already established," Olmsted favored the more formal scheme. Both proposals involved specific adjustments to extant streets and recognized the importance of the adjoining Junction Hollow for a major roadway around the rapidly growing Oakland area. Unlike much of the rest of the plan, the specificity of these two plans comprised more of a blueprint than a guiding framework. Perhaps this was because the entrance to the park had been part of the urban conversation for ten years, and existing designs were already on the mayor's desk. Nevertheless, the Schenley Park entrance, or Schenley Plaza as it soon became known, remained a subject of planning during the next half dozen years.[75]

As the Olmsted firm had done in several cities over the years, young Olmsted, like his father, treated parks in a comprehensive and regional context. His report drew special attention to the need for providing adequate recreational opportunities for "wage-earning families," because of the "influence of their health and vigor upon the efficiency of the coming generation," and "because they, least of all, have energy and opportunity to seek out healthful recreation at a distance." He first recommended the creation of neighborhood parks within a quarter to a half mile of every family, comprising altogether at least 5 percent of the city's total area. At the same time, the city and county working together should provide rural parks that are spacious and secluded from adjacent lands. These parks, while more remote from the homes of working-class families, would offer a salubrious contrast to urban conditions, which such families could enjoy on weekends and holidays. He identified seventeen "Special Park Opportunities" from local parks and playgrounds to larger parkways and rural parks.[76]

Clearly Olmsted's report had an impact on the shaping of twentieth-century Pittsburgh. As a key figure in the emerging American planning profession, he affirmed not only the legitimacy and priority status of many projects long part of the urban conversation but also the legitimacy and necessity of city planning itself for Pittsburgh. His report addressed projects such as the widening of Fifth, Sixth, and Forbes avenues; the building of the South Hills Bridge and

Tunnel; Schenley Plaza; and the hump cut, all of which came to fruition before or shortly after World War I, though not always in the form he would have approved. Other proposals, such as the improvement of Grant Boulevard or the designing of the Point, took many more years before being implemented in some form. Some worthy ideas, such as the downtown civic center or the waterfront promenades, and some not so worthy ones, such as the construction of elaborate new quays, never materialized. *Main Thoroughfares,* as Olmsted noted in the introduction, combined the need to advise on pending issues with the goal of providing a guiding framework for decades of development to come. However, constrained in its focus and prepared in only a year's time without adequate data, the report did not purport to be a fully comprehensive plan. Such a planning effort would have to be the primary mission of a public planning entity that Olmsted knew Mayor Magee was interested in pursuing with the state legislature. At the very least, Olmsted's Pittsburgh plan demonstrated a deliberate movement by the young profession's most illustrious member away from the City Beautiful and Marsh's social progressivism and toward "practical" comprehensive planning.

MAYORAL POLITICS AND THE PLAN'S RECEPTION

The PCC published *Main Thoroughfares* in March 1911. Articles about the report appeared in Pittsburgh newspapers as well as in the *Outlook* and *Survey* magazines.[77] But given the city reformers' initial great expectations, the report should have attracted greater attention than it did. Its tepid reception in Pittsburgh forecast the report's failure to become the beacon for the city's future development that reformers had originally hoped.

From the outset, Olmsted's plan was embroiled in a Progressive Era battle royal between the PCC and new mayor William Magee. Magee was the nephew of Christopher Magee, the powerful Republican political boss whom the reformers had fought bitterly until his death in 1901. The younger Magee had attended public schools, trained in law, and rose to be district attorney before becoming a city councilman. In 1901 he was appointed to serve out his uncle's term in the state senate. When in January 1909 he won the right to be the Republican's mayoral candidate against the Guthrie-endorsed Civic Party reform candidate William H. Stevenson, he was already at the relatively young age of thirty-six an experienced politician and head of the city and county Republican Party. Despite this familial and political lineage, Magee was reportedly not closely allied with the older machine elements of the Republican Party. Indeed, sensing the voters' dissatisfaction with corruption, particularly in the wake of the recent indict-

William Addison Magee
(1873–1938), mayor of Pittsburgh,
1909–1914 and 1922–1926, whose
progressive instincts made him a
strong proponent of city planning.
Carnegie Library of Pittsburgh.

ments of councilmen for graft, he led a revolt within the party against the machine leaders, and came to the electorate in 1909 as a man of integrity, an expert in municipal government, and a practical politician who believed in the efficacy of partisanship and the art of compromise.[78] Conveniently ignoring the Republican city councils' hostility to reform, he charged the Guthrie administration with both inexperience and an idealism that, while laudable, proved ineffective. Magee proclaimed that "the result of three years of reform has demonstrated conclusively that while a mayor may do no wrong, he at the same time may do no good." He ran on a prodevelopment platform that included the removal of the hump, the widening of key city streets, and the improvement of riverfronts. Unlike his more elitist reform opponent, Magee campaigned vigorously in working-class wards and won the mid-February election with an impressive margin that also retained Republican majorities in both councils.[79]

Understandably, the Guthrie-appointed PCC had viscerally opposed Magee, whom it viewed as the standard-bearer for the Republican machine and a political opportunist. The reformers believed Magee's development program pandered to civic boosterism and ward politics instead of upholding the principle of comprehensive planning as advocated by Olmsted. It was a battle for the heart of the comprehensive plan. The PCC was just getting organized in early 1909 and still discussing planning issues when the new mayor took office on April 4. Magee rapidly cobbled together a number of politically appealing special purpose projects into a hefty bond issue of $6,775,000, which included filtered water for the North Side, buying private bridges and freeing them of tolls, and building new playgrounds, streets, and bridges. Pittsburghers approved the bond issue in November; by the time Olmsted had agreed to prepare a city plan at the end of 1909, the city, particularly the Department of Public Works, was drafting plans for Magee's cornucopia of projects.[80]

Magee, however, did not ignore the PCC's planning effort; indeed, he regularly asked for Olmsted's advice on several issues during 1910. But unwilling to share the political limelight, Magee did not wait for the reformer's plan. The confrontation between the PCC and the mayor over his improvement package erupted when, at the instigation of a taxpayer's lawsuit, the state supreme court voided the bond issue referendum of 1909 and enjoined the city from further implementing it. Magee vowed to resubmit the issue to the electorate in November 1910. A week after the supreme court defeat, he sought Olmsted's opinion on several projects so that he might more effectively bundle together his city improvements for a new referendum on a revised bond issue. Olmsted responded promptly and at length, and Magee moved forward expeditiously, adding more projects to the original bond issue and thereby increasing the price tag to $10,305,000. This revised bond issue included money for a new city hall, a new bridge at the Point over the Allegheny River, and a tuberculosis hospital. The councils complied with the mayor's wishes and passed the ordinance for a new referendum at the end of September. The battle with the PCC heated up.[81]

Campaigning to defeat Magee's bond issue, the PCC's Allen Burns pressured Olmsted to finish his plan quickly. Delay, Burns wrote Olmsted, meant "losing for us the opportunity to secure funds and influence improvements." Lacking Olmsted's plan, the PCC engaged two civil engineers to examine each proposal of the bond issue on its merits as well as the adequacy of the city's cost estimate. The PCC also charged that Magee's "pernicious" grouping of so many projects in one bond issue was a ploy to pass unworthy projects on the coattails of worthy ones. Moreover, the commission wondered how citizens could trust an administration that was so extravagant and had two cabinet members under indictment, including Joseph G. Armstrong, the director of the Department of Public Works. H. D. W. English even unrealistically registered disgust with Magee's refusal to allow a private civic organization to monitor public expenditures as they unfolded.[82]

Mayor Magee countered with a vigorous campaign in defense of his bond issue. The city, he averred, had been without adequate improvements for nearly ten years, resulting in only "modest growth." An investment in improvements would increase tax valuations and hence grow city revenues. Thus, reasoned Magee, the city could eventually lower taxes. Moreover, a vote in favor of improvements was one "in favor of efficiency and progress in government." As the confrontation grew more torrid, Magee bitterly accused the PCC of not acting in good faith when it asked for access to the city's plans and estimates for each project. PCC members, he charged, had their minds already made up, and acted purely on political motives in attacking his administration. He noted that the Chamber of Commerce had voted in favor of the bond issue, rejecting its own subcommittee's negative report submitted by English and Guthrie. Finally, Magee claimed that the PCC suppressed its own engineers' report because it supported his improvement plan. In rebuttal, the PCC wondered if Magee had actually read the report, for the report supported only half of the ordinances and found that neither the sewer nor the city hall proposals fit into the larger plans advanced by John Freeman and Olmsted.[83]

Magee's politically astute approach of packaging projects into the bond issue, which served almost every section of the city, overwhelmingly carried the vote in the November election. Department of Public Works director Armstrong was prepared to initiate the projects, as soon as the bond issue funds became available. Under his administration, new bridges, such as the impressive Bloomfield Bridge, a span soaring high over the deep ravine through which the Pennsylvania Railroad ran, connected neighborhoods formerly remote from each other. Filtered water was extended to many more parts of the city, and streets were straightened, widened, and paved. Magee agreed to join the county in constructing a new municipal office building. More land was added to the parks, and the Shade Tree Commission during its four years of existence planted over 7,000 trees along city streets and operated a large nursery where it nurtured another 5,000 trees for eventual transplantation. While in order to justify many of these projects, Magee might have been able to refer his critics to Olmsted's *Main Thoroughfares,* he could not as easily explain the Department of Public Works's action of dumping truckloads of fill into St. Pierre's Ravine at the Oakland entrance to Schenley Park. Gradually, the once-graceful 1898 stone bridge that arched the ravine disappeared under the rising mound of dirt and debris. Meanwhile, despite Olmsted's two proposed designs for the site, no plan for the important park entrance had been adopted.[84]

If St. Pierre's Ravine represented the negative side of city departments acting without either public consensus or a formal comprehensive plan emerging from the public conversation, then the hump cut reflected a successful outcome of such a discussion and process of consensus building. The severe grade of the hump on the eastern edge of downtown impeded the smooth flow of traffic to the rapidly growing East End communities and inhibited investment in "high-class retail trade and offices."[85] The cut had been discussed since at least the 1890s, and in 1906 Mayor Guthrie ranked its removal a priority. Three years later Mayor Magee beseeched Olmsted for advice on the project in order to press the councils for action. In his *Main Thoroughfares*, Olmsted had scorned the Bureau of Surveys's existing plan for the hump as inadequate and recommended a deeper cut in order to facilitate the use of Forbes, Fifth, and Sixth avenues as primary east-west arteries and to accommodate increased north-south traffic resulting from the proposed South Hills Bridge and Tunnel. Faced with the legal complexity and expense of cutting down Grant's Hill, Magee had left the project out of his successful bond issue. However, in 1912 the council passed a special bond issue to cover the $3,000,000 expense, and work began immediately removing the hill. The project covered twenty acres, parts of eight streets, cuts as much as sixteen feet deep, and the demolition of many buildings. It involved the waiver of damages by most property owners and the reconstruction of infrastructure by several public service corporations. In lowering Grant Street and Fifth Avenue, the cut forced the reconfiguration of the ground floors of Richardson's Allegheny County courthouse masterpiece, as well as that of the office tower designed by Daniel Burnham for Henry Clay Frick. Frick, now residing in New York City, had stubbornly refused to give a waiver for damages to his properties until he was assured that other major property owners had also consented. The cut did permit the widening of key streets leading into downtown. The Department of Public Works used fill from the cut to raise the level of streets in flood-prone areas near the rivers. Remarkably, the hump cut was completed in a year, despite the enormous scale and expense of the project.[86]

By the time Olmsted completed his plan and saw it published in March 1911, Magee's improvement program was well under way. Traffic engineer John P. Fox wrote Olmsted that he hoped the Brookline planner could have restrained "the Civic Commission [PCC] on the bond issue." It seemed to Fox that, as a result of its confrontation with the mayor, the "influence of the commission is just about ended, as far as public improvements go."[87] The public's atten-

The "hump cut," showing the massive sixteen-foot lowering of Grant's Hill at Fifth and Grant streets between Henry Hobson Richardson's county courthouse and the Frick Building. *The Helen Clay Frick Foundation Archives, Archives Service Center, University of Pittsburgh.*

tion had moved on to charter reform, corruption prosecutions, and other issues. City newspapers reviewed the plan more as a contribution to the literature than as a guide for the city's future development. They praised Olmsted's talent and imagination, while dismissing his plan as "too costly" and "fit for a capital city, not Pittsburgh." Magee lamented that a plan with so many recommendations but without "more study of the financial means of accomplishing them" would lead to inaction and become "an excuse for indifference."[88]

THE INITIAL TRYING YEARS OF CITY PLANNING

Although Magee successfully outflanked the PCC with an improvement program that the commission scorned as the antithesis of scientific city planning, he had not renounced planning for Pittsburgh. Nor had he severed his relations with Olmsted. In fact, he acted quickly to establish planning in the public sector. In view of both the decade-long conversation among civic groups and political officials, culminating in the preparation of *Main Thoroughfares*, and the dalliance between the mayor and Olmsted, it is clear that Magee had ample opportunity to consider the wisdom, pragmatically and politically, of planning for his city. In October 1910 Magee wrote an article for the *Pittsburgh Post* in which he spelled out his "plan for development." The article voiced his advocacy of the bond issue, but it went much further. He called for projects that both stimulated "material prosperity" and the "moral development, education of the people, and the beautifying of the city itself." The mayor emphasized smoke abatement, solution of the street railway problem, restoration of hillside vegetation, planting of trees along streets, construction of a canal to Lake Erie, consolidation of suburban municipalities into a Greater Pittsburgh, and a "city plan" for that larger entity. None of these proposals had appeared in the bond issue. Further evidence of Magee's interest in planning may be inferred from his taking seriously Olmsted's plea for proper survey maps. Just weeks before *Main Thoroughfares* appeared, Magee interviewed a man recommended by Olmsted to direct a topographical survey of Pittsburgh.[89]

The mayor's opponents, including many reformers, might have cynically attributed Magee's embrace of planning simply to politics. In this view, planning could not have been important to him, for he had pushed through the bond issue without waiting for the PCC's plan, which was only weeks from completion. Skeptics might even have seen politics underlying Magee's March 1911 (the month Olmsted's plan was published) submission of bills to the state legislature for authorization of planning, public art, and forestry commissions. The Chamber of Commerce, which had supported Magee's bond issue, hosted a local conference in January 1911 on city beautification. With representatives from the major civic groups, the conference discussed several issues highlighted in *Main Thoroughfares* and called for legislation to prohibit the undue proliferation of billboards and to enlarge the powers of the Shade Tree Commission.[90] The cynics might suspect that Magee, as a successful practical politician, had wasted little time in getting ahead of the momentum for establishing such commissions, sparked by Olmsted's report and the Chamber's conference.

These critical views of Magee's motivation for advocating planning probably miss the sincerity of his effort. In March 1911, only days after its publication, Magee wrote Olmsted to express his pleasure with the *Main Thoroughfares* report and inform him of his submission of legislation for the creation of a planning commission. In response, Olmsted urged the mayor to attend the Third National Conference on City Planning in Philadelphia. In December 1911, six months after the successful passage of the planning legislation, Magee sent a fifteen-page "Message to City Planning Commission," in which he outlined his view of planning. Although the message reiterated positions he had expressed in previous statements, it was a remarkably thorough and informed statement that made the case not only for planning but also for increasing local powers over land use, even more than the 1911 legislation permitted, in order to make comprehensive planning more effective.[91]

Magee had evidently given a good deal of thought to the subject. He wrote that the rise of public concern for creating healthy, safe, efficient, and prosperous communities would always encounter conflicts of different perspectives and interests. These laudable goals could only be achieved "in the highest degree," he ventured, "by the preparation of constructive plans comprehensive in scope." Planning had to be conducted by an independent body in order to negotiate the "conflict between the expediency of the moment and that abstract conception of the future." Moreover, as an independent body, it could "bring about a co-relations of effort on the part of large numbers of public officials independent of each other" and call on the many active and influential civic groups. An effective comprehensive plan had to "harmonize" the interests of the city, surrounding municipalities, and the territory to be developed in the future. Accordingly, he argued here and elsewhere for the consolidation of county municipalities with the city. Because the county commissioners dismissed his earlier proposals to this effect as "impractical," he went on to advocate the creation of a special metropolitan district. In order to influence and in some cases control development, Magee also argued for the expansion of municipal powers. Always the practical politician, however, the mayor acknowledged the ever-present financial obstacles to implementing improvements put forth under a comprehensive plan. For this problem, he proposed the creation of "betterment districts," wherein those who most benefited from an improvement would pay their fair share through special assessments or even tolls as direct users. In this manner, he reasoned, more improvements would become self-supporting and therefore more likely to be built.[92]

Mayor William Magee, who for reformers had embodied the return to ring politics, implemented some of the progressives' most cherished proposals. With the help of influential civic groups, he guided through the state legislature both charter reform that restructured the city's legislative bodies and new public agencies that established the foundation for planning by the public sector. And he intended to support these initiatives during the remaining years of his mayoralty term. Although city reformers remained skeptical, Magee fought the type of uncoordinated special purpose projects that historically were the usual order of city business. In 1911 he advanced an ambitious series of proposals to address the issues of planning and beautification long embraced by civic groups and eloquently advocated by Olmsted. Some of these proposals met stiff resistance. The city council denied his request to fund the much-needed topographic survey essential for planning. His proposals to incorporate the Shade Tree Commission into a Forestry Commission with power over "open spaces," and girded to exercise "the right of eminent domain," and to consolidate forty municipalities with Pittsburgh into a single entity both failed to gain state approval. While Magee argued vociferously that a Greater Pittsburgh would allow the efficient planning of critical infrastructure, suburban politicians saw a more imperial motive that threatened to raise local taxes and destroy their autonomy.[93]

If Magee failed to obtain these important parts of his program, each corresponding with an Olmsted recommendation, and each purporting to augment a planning capability for city government, he did in 1911 achieve two important successes in the state's authorization of a City Planning Commission and an Art Commission. Despite Olmsted's and Magee's philosophical statements to the contrary, the creation of these two bodies seemed to underscore the separation of beautification from practical planning. In the short term, the separation served to advance the cause of planning during its darkest days; however, over the long run it may have allowed the planning commission to concentrate on practical matters without an adequate sense of responsibility for aesthetic considerations.[94]

State law created a Department of City Planning under the control of a City Planning Commission (CPC). The mayor appointed the commission's nine members, who served without compensation. The law empowered the commission to prepare a plan, but not enforce it, for Pittsburgh and an area extending three miles beyond the city limits. It could make recommendations to the city council on proposed highways, bridges, tunnels, railways, parks, playgrounds, public buildings, and other public works, as well as prepare maps of the city. The reports backing these planning recommendations were to be available to the public. In short, the commission's actions were to be transparent, but only advisory. It possessed only one regulatory power; the commission passed judgment on all new lot plans within the city limits. In order to carry out its mission, the CPC could employ personnel to staff the Department of City Planning. The council, however, had to appropriate the funds for its operation.[95]

The act authorizing the Art Commission created a second nine-member body appointed by the mayor, seven members of which comprised a sculptor, painter, three architects, and two laypersons. The mayor and director of Public Works completed the commission's membership. Commission members also served without pay, but they, too, could hire a staff, depending on funding by the council. The Art Commission had to approve the acquisition, alteration, and demolition of all public art "intended for ornament or commemoration," as well as approve the design of public buildings and facilities. Since the act intended "to secure . . . as may be reasonably practicable, the free light, air and prospect of the streets and open spaces—and prevent the obstruction of the same by unsightly structures," the commission could both propose regulations to the city council and approve of the actions of public service corporations, which affected public streets and spaces. Also like the CPC, it could advise private property owners, but lacked power to enforce compliance with its recommendations.[96]

Following passage of his November 1910 bond issue and the May 1911 legislation founding the CPC and the Art Commission, Magee had the city astir constructing projects under discussion for years. Further, in fulfillment of progressive goals, he had positioned city government to guide and influence future urban development. The decade-long conversation about physical development, environmental reform, and beautification had finally borne fruit. While the Department of Public Works drew up plans and dispatched construction crews to build bridges, widen streets, and reengineer topography, the mayor appointed the members of his new commissions, gave them budgets, and urged then to get busy planning the city's future development.

In 1912 both the CPC and the Art Commission were at work with Mayor Magee's support. The mayor appointed to the CPC a mix of prominent businessmen, public officials, and engineers, but he also appointed William Flinn, the contractor who for years led the notorious Republican machine. Flinn's election as CPC chair surely alarmed the reformers and confirmed their worst suspicions about the mayor's real intentions. However, Flinn resigned within two months. The CPC soon warmed to its task by organizing itself into six broad subcommittees ranging in focus from land transportation and river improvements to smoke abatement and water and sewage issues. Through 1913, the commission met more than sixty times, submitted numerous reports to the city council on specific projects, passed judgment on several lot plans, and discussed numerous public projects from the design of the waterfronts and a civic center to hillside reforestation, antibillboard legislation, and the proposed Monongahela Boulevard to the East End, all part of the general conversation and embedded in the Olmsted plan.[97]

At the same time, the CPC deliberated over what its proper role should be. It sent members to national conferences and asked Olmsted for advice. At one meeting with the mayor, the city council, the director of Public Works, and the CPC, Olmsted urged all city departments to report their projects to the commission as early as possible in order that it could suitably influence the outcome. Olmsted also advocated legislation that would allow the CPC to act as a planning body for suburban districts, which Magee undoubtedly supported but which had little prospect of success in Harrisburg. Most important, Olmsted warned the CPC against becoming "overwhelmed" in trying to oversee all minor "plans" before the city council. True to his vision of modern comprehensive planning, he saw the commission's primary value residing in its "large, broad, far-sighted view of the City's requirements and of the general drift and tendency of its current decisions." It was the signal virtue of the CPC, observed Olmsted, that it collected a wide range of information, which it "digested . . . [and] studied in a more leisurely, patient and comprehensive manner." This unique capability among city administrative agencies permitted its judicious evaluation of the future. Unfortunately, Olmsted's concern over the crush of debilitating minutiae in everyday planning responsibilities would prove to be prescient.[98]

From its inception, the CPC pursued the preparation of a comprehensive city plan. Propounding Olmstedian views of the importance of avoiding haphazard growth and planning for "generations" to come, not just a few years in the future, the CPC undertook the "preliminaries and general fundamentals" necessary to erect the basis for a "city plan." The commission saw itself as "the clearinghouse of all civic effort" and as the body "to suggest how each particular line of work may best be carried out with relation to the general good." Nonetheless, it still cautiously reigned in expectations by adopting Magee's financial and practical concerns. The CPC reported that "it will be a modest plan compared to the expansive flights of some of our sister cities and is based chiefly on the ideal of cold practicability and the furnishing of a maximum benefit at a minimum of cost." Further, the CPC assured the city council that after careful evaluation of improvements with respect to the plan, it would propose "as recommendations for the consideration of Council only those projects of which there appears to be a reasonable prospect of accomplishment in the near future. . . . All other improvements passed upon by the Commission will be submitted as additions to the City Plan." Looking to the future, the CPC referred to the experience of Germany and recently New York City in advocating the state legislature to confer upon it the power of zoning for the "nature and size of buildings." Although the commission lamented the slow pace of its work on the plan due to "limited funds" and "a small force," it still predicted "much progress toward the completion of the Pittsburgh Plan in the coming year."[99]

Those hopes were soon dashed. Politics and budgetary constraints conspired to eviscerate the commission. Legally unable to succeed himself as mayor, Magee turned over his office on January 5, 1914, to his political enemy, newly elected Joseph G. Armstrong. Armstrong boasted working-class origins. A native Pittsburgher, he left school to become a skilled glassblower and was active in the Knights of Labor. Labor activism led to his election to the city council and later to four years as coroner. Magee appointed him director of Public Works, whereupon Armstrong eventually faced charges of malfeasance in office. Although a five-month investigation by the city council cleared him in late 1912, his relations with Magee soured; the mayor, after questioning Armstrong's good faith and loyalty, dismissed Armstrong in October 1913. The city council, however, supported Armstrong, and apparently the voters did as well.[100]

As director of the Department of Public Works in 1910, Armstrong had been uncomfortable with Olmsted's preparation of a city plan for the PCC. With Magee's complicity, he basically ignored Olmsted's endeavor and instructed his staff to proceed with planning the projects packaged into Magee's bond issue. Elected mayor in 1914, Armstrong all but dismantled a planning commission that he may have perceived as impeding the Department of Public Work's ability to carry out its ordinary responsibilities for street openings. In his annual report for 1914, the new mayor noted that the national financial panic forced the city to concentrate on repairing existing infrastructure rather than undertaking new development. Pointing to the city's budgetary weakness, he eliminated the Department of City Planning's staffing except for the secretary-engineer, who was transferred to the Department of Public Works. Unable to continue work on the city plan and other future improvements, the CPC was reduced to the routine approval of lot plans, the sole province over which it had legal power. In 1915 the CPC did not even file an annual report.[101]

Mayor Armstrong did not seek a similar reduction of the Art Commission, perhaps because it faithfully reported each year how little it cost the city. A companion agency to the CPC, the Art Commission managed to keep alive the faint embers of municipal planning during the next five years. In 1912 Magee had appointed the Art Commission's initial members, prominent local architects A. B. Harlow, A. B. Orth, and H. K. McGoodwin, who was also dean of the School of Applied Design at the Carnegie Technical Schools. Magee added politically powerful businessman W. L. Mellon; John W. Beatty, director of Fine Arts at the Carnegie Institute; and, as required by statute, a painter, John W. Alexander, and a sculptor, Hermon A. MacNeil, both residents of New York City. The commission reviewed designs for bridge portals, monuments, fountains, lampposts, and public buildings such as fire-engine houses and hospitals. It prepared reports on current design issues such as a memorial to the sunken battleship *Maine* and advocated city actions like the city's purchase of land on undeveloped hillsides for overlooks and along bridge approaches to plant as screens. Toward the end of its second year, November 1913, it hired an assistant secretary, a young architect named Frederick Bigger, to coordinate with other city departments, lecture to the public, and amass a reference library. The lack of cooperation by other city departments nettled the Art Commission, which finally badgered the city council to order city departments to refer their projects to it. The council's edict produced feeble results, but the appointment of Bigger proved significant for the history of planning in Pittsburgh.[102]

The Art Commission, nevertheless, endured and scored some modest victories. It tackled two long-standing major design issues in its early years, which had also been part of Olmsted's plan and involved important planning problems. The commission engaged Chicago planner and Daniel Burnham's former partner Edward H. Bennett in 1913 to prepare a design for the Point and adjacent waterfronts. Submitted in 1914 and passed along to the city council with the commission's eager endorsement, Bennett's report proposed a small park at the Point and widened avenues paralleling the rivers, including promenades. It wrestled with the problems of approaches to the bridges and flood control, which had concerned Olmsted.[103] While this plan initially was met with enthusiasm by city political leaders, it soon died. Another commission foray into the thicket of the entrance to Schenley Park did eventually have success. After much discussion, the commission held a national competition for an entrance design in 1915, which attracted forty-four plans and 3,000 visitors to an exhibition of them. The winning plan by Philadelphia architects H. Bartol Register and Horace Weils Sellers shared many features with Olmsted's earlier plaza plan. After some tinkering with the design and fixing the location of the related and much-discussed Mary Schenley Memorial Fountain, the commission obtained the city council's approval of its plan in 1917. An amended version of it was completed in 1923, nearly twenty-five years after Edward Bigelow first asked Olmsted Associates to look into the issue.[104]

The Art Commission's new assistant secretary, Frederick Bigger, spearheaded the body's growing advocacy of city planning. In 1915 the commission reported that it had offered twenty-seven lectures on civic art and city planning. It also noted that a proposed war memorial in Oakland awaited a plan for Oakland, but no such plan was available. Two years later, in 1917, the

Schenley Plaza, part of the Schenley Park entrance (circa 1936). The plaza was completed in 1923, nearly twenty-five years after Edward Bigelow asked the Olmsted Associates to "look into the issue." *Pittsburgh City Photographer Collection, Archives Service Center, University of Pittsburgh.*

Art Commission met with the enfeebled CPC to discuss the Schenley Plaza plan. The next year the Art Commission assumed the role of official clearing-house for city improvement plans, which the CPC had seen for itself, in arguing the benefits of good design for the proposed replacement bridges over the Allegheny River before the mayor, council, Allegheny County commissioners, city engineer, Department of Public Works, the CCAC, the local chapter of the AIA, and even the newspapers. Its frustration with the CPC's inability to produce a city plan intensified when normal activities were suspended during World War I. In 1917 the Art Commission confessed that presently its "effort has been to hold the ground already gained and . . . prepare for accelerated activity after the war." It averred that comprehensive planning was fundamental to "the work an art commission is called upon to do," and urged that enabling bills be resubmitted to the state legislature to allow Pittsburgh to write districting and zoning regulations. In 1918 the increasingly important Art Commission still deplored the lack of a plan: "It does not seem as if the City can much longer postpone . . . comprehensive planning for the present or for the future."[105]

WHITHER PLANNING?

The election of George Guthrie as mayor in 1906 had excited the optimism of city reformers. With access to the power of city government, progressive-minded Pittsburghers hoped to implement long-discussed environmental, health, social, political, and beautification plans as part of the city's urban conversation. Although this conversation had previously lacked consensus on the need for formal city planning, by the end of Guthrie's term in 1909 such a consensus existed. As one of his last acts, Guthrie appointed a voluntary organization of civic leaders, the PCC, charged with developing solutions to the city's many problems. Consistent with an emerging consensus, the PCC identified the importance of planning and engaged the nationally prominent landscape architect and city planner Frederick Law Olmsted Jr. to prepare a city plan, albeit one restricted to the metropolis's main highways and the downtown.

Politics, however, threatened to marginalize this nascent planning initiative after Republican William Magee succeeded Guthrie as mayor. Even though he was elected on a prodevelopment platform that featured numerous infrastructural improvements, Magee, feared reformers, presaged the return to power of the old Republican machine. His program, they charged, embodied the same old piecemeal package of projects and flaunted the need for careful, "scientific" planning. Such fears proved unfounded. While Magee successfully pursued his bond issue, he at the same time invited Olmsted's counsel, professed a belief in planning, pushed through the state legislature the authorizing acts for both the CPC and Art Commission, and supported the work of these new bodies. Unfortunately, his successor, Joseph Armstrong, left the CPC without the means to fulfill its mission. The planning impetus that had emerged with optimism during a decade of reform conversation and advocacy seemingly ended in 1914 with the decision of a hostile politician. In October 1918, the Municipal Planning Committee of the CCAC, chaired by Frederick Bigger, issued a special bulletin, entitled *Comprehensive City Planning for Pittsburgh*, which once again made the case for planning in words reminiscent of the conversation a decade earlier.[106] It might have seemed as if the previous ten years had not happened.

Despite the moribund state of comprehensive planning in Pittsburgh as the new century's second decade drew to a close, progress in planning had been achieved. To begin with, planning had been formally established as part of city government. Although Armstrong had weakened the CPC, he had not eliminated it. Civic groups, including the Chamber of Commerce, no longer doubted the efficacy of planning and advocated the rejuvenation of comprehensive planning by city government. Further, the agenda, recommendations, and planning philosophy eloquently advanced by Olmsted remained part of the urban conversation among civic leaders and many public officials. The Art Commission, for example, managed to get the city council to approve a plan for the entrance to Schenley Park. Major highway improvements had been completed, and many issues, such as the Monongahela Boulevard, hillside restoration, the topographic survey, and even improved low-income housing, were under active consideration. Of course, other proposals, such as a downtown civic center or waterfront parkways and promenades, were fading rapidly from the conversation.

Civic organizations had brought planning to the forefront of public discussion, but implementation depended on the action of public officials. Politicians eventually established planning, just as they also diminished its influence. It appeared that, once again, civic groups would have to force public officials to take action. Now, however, the formal machinery for planning was already in place, as was the voice of a committed, local expert busy among civic leaders promoting the advantages of renewed planning. Since traffic, transit, environmental, housing, land use, and recreational problems had not been solved during these years of business as usual, the elites were prepared to respond favorably once again to the persuasive arguments of Frederick Bigger and the civic groups.

CHAPTER 4

The Rebirth of Planning in
Post–World War I Pittsburgh

AFTER WORLD WAR I modern, comprehensive professional planning would flourish again in Pittsburgh. Still youthful, even ungainly at first, planning in Pittsburgh and in the region gained greater stature and authority during the 1920s. City business and civic elites embraced planning as an essential element of the modern urban economy. New elite-based planning organizations, principally the Citizens Committee on the City Plan (CCCP), arose, and new luminaries in the world of Pittsburgh planning emerged, namely Frederick Bigger.

During the 1920s, a powerful coalition of public and private sector business and civic leaders transformed the progressive planning impulse into an ethos. The ideas of planning visionaries and professionals such as Charles Mulford Robinson, Frederick Law Olmsted Jr., John Nolen, and Pittsburgh's Frederick Bigger were in many instances during the 1920s etched into state and local ordinances overseen by fledgling, but often effective, planning commissions, departments, and zoning boards, which increasingly exercised statutory authority over the shaping of urban space. However, legal authority and actual power are not always the same thing. Politics, as both Olmsted and Bigger understood, constituted a vital interposing force. For planning to be forged into a vision or an effective discipline, citizens had to be educated about planning, and planners often failed as teachers, leaving the actualization of planning dreams unrealized and the language of the conversation garbled rather than clarified.

Unfulfilled dreams notwithstanding, an in-depth look at Pittsburgh's planning history reveals the importance of the 1920s as a landmark epoch. During the flapper decade, a fledgling Pittsburgh City Planning Commission (CPC) and the department it oversaw staked out professional and bureaucratic territory separate and distinct from the realm of city engineering and public works. As in other cities, these planning agencies erected a solid administrative framework amid a decade of serious urban conversation about the role of the automobile, new subdivision controls, zoning, and regional growth. In doing so, they helped shape the contours of urban development.

These successes contradict the traditional interpretation of American city planning in the 1920s. Historians of planning have generally disparaged the achievements of planning during the so-called normalcy decade. Eyewitness accounts in 1929 documenting Pittsburgh's still traffic-clogged streets, sooty skies, and ramshackle housing convinced one historian that "it was evident that American architects and planners had failed."[1] Other, more generous histories of planning during the 1920s rehearse somewhat routinely the saga of the three great decade-long initiatives: zoning, the master plan, and regional planning. None, they insist, warranted much praise. Throughout urban America, according to the critiques, zoning ordinances faced deeply entrenched patterns of land use and an avalanche of disabling appeals, and master plans—generally produced by outside consultants—proved too costly to execute and languished on dusty planning department shelves. Regional planning for Philadelphia and New York, including visionary, European-inspired new town designs such as those drawn by architects Clarence Stein, Henry Wright, and Clarence Perry, offered eloquent, but generally too costly, alternatives to the traffic-congested, slum-ridden reality of the modern metropolis.[2]

But historians who blithely dismiss 1920s planning as impractical and ineffectual ignore two important facts. First, in Pittsburgh and other cities, a robust restructured national and increasingly international urban economy transformed radial-centered central business districts from gritty, deafening industrial hubs into modern centers for the delivery of a host of financial, corporate management, retail, medical, legal, and other business and professional services. In the new mass-consumption, mass-communications society of telephones, radios, and movies, marketing professionals hitched consumer product identities to cities, thus enlisting architecture and urban design together with the radio and movie media in the cause of mass advertising. By 1931, for example, Pittsburgh's skyline proclaimed Pittsburgh the home of Mellon's (Gulf) petroleum wealth, as much as Chicago's hailed Woolworth's and New York City honored Chrysler.[3]

In fact, Henry Ford's triumph—the ubiquitous assembly line–produced, gasoline-powered automobile—posed an enormous challenge to what by 1920 already appeared to be inadequate urban form. Historians Scott Bottles and Marc Foster contend that flapper-era planners toiled mightily, but vainly, to retrofit the pre-twentieth-century big city to accommodate the automobile. Fledgling planning departments worked with traffic engineers to design wider streets and wrangled endlessly over meeting the demand for parking as well as determining the appropriate size and location of private garages and commercial gasoline and service stations. They also grappled with speculative large-scale real estate developers who, during the 1920s, aggressively platted subdivisions on formerly inaccessible urban and suburban tracts.[4]

Although the "new metropolitan form" of the city had already evolved by the turn of the century, during the 1920s places such as Pittsburgh experienced considerable spatial and economic change. While the congruent metropolitan form of a downtown core ringed by streetcar-accessible neighborhoods, industrial corridors, and more distant satellite towns remained intact by 1930, automobility spawned a burgeoning new suburban world on the city's urban fringe. The Herculean challenge of efficiently and effectively linking this expanding metropolitan world to the old city proved time consuming and confounding.

Second, the new planning "profession" fully emerged in the aftermath of the Great War. Once in 1909 a mere loose federation of architects, landscape designers, engineers, and lawyers, planners in the 1920s assiduously cultivated a professional identity. By 1929 that identity had greatly solidified. This evolving planning professionalism itself constituted a force shaping Pittsburgh in the 1920s. Engaged day to day in "mole" activities, as historian William H. Wilson called them, approving lot plans, assembling data, preparing topographical surveys, usually within the Spartan surroundings of municipal offices, city planners identified a body of specialized knowledge, molded professional standards, and created a strong self-consciousness and sense of identity. This youthful planning profession shunned any particular political or capitalistic agenda; furthermore, it may actually have restrained pell-mell city building. As John Fairfield, Paul Boyer, and Richard Foglesong have observed, elite-led planning deliberately interposed an undemocratic, "disciplinary" layer in the city-building process. In the name of protecting threatened urban land values, it invited government intervention and directly challenged America's sanctification of individualism by restraining the unfettered use of private property. By 1930 planners in Pittsburgh had successfully institutionalized that planning process.[5]

Several factors illuminate the vitality of the planning ethos in Pittsburgh during the 1920s. First, by the end of World War I Pittsburgh's reform-minded business class fully invoked what historian James Fairfield has called a "New Discipline." Moored in progressivism, Pittsburgh's proplanning businessmen, engineers, lawyers, and architects believed that ecological forces shaped the city; that urban problems such as traffic congestion, housing blight, and epidemic disease, while intractable, could at least be managed if not overcome;

and that credentialed, scientific-minded experts should control urban decision making. Second, as noted earlier, planning in Pittsburgh before World
War I had involved public and private sector collaboration. A cadre of Pittsburgh business and professional elites shared a mutual interest in urban
public improvements and either as individuals such as Andrew Carnegie or
Franklin Nicola or through organizations such as the Pittsburgh Civic Commission (PCC) collaborated, and at times fought, with the "public" realm of
city and county departments and commissions. During the 1920s, these same
Pittsburgh business and civic leaders rekindled their zeal for bureaucratic solutions and social and environmental control, and they pioneered the use of
the public partnerships wherein private and public sector planners and proplanning politicians worked in tandem with influential civic organizations.
They subscribed to "expert" planning with the same vigor that they displayed
for Frederick W. Taylor's theories of scientific management and for the "Americanization" movements that endeavored to regularize, or make predictable,
the bewildering social and economic forces, national and international, that
governed the complex new modern mass-production/mass-consumption urban economy. In many ways business leaders viewed city planning as an extension of traditional civic boosterism. Taming urban space, like countering
unionism, quelling labor violence, and harnessing the mercurial business cy-
cles, assured the primacy of Pittsburgh in the highly competitive urban hierarchy and produced general urban prosperity.[6]

FRED BIGGER, WAR BONDS, AND THE PLANNING ETHOS

On the eve of World War I, Pittsburgh's faith in the redemptive powers of
planning had survived mainly among the members of the Civic Club of Allegheny County (CCAC) and the Art Commission, not within the chambers of its
almost moribund CPC. On taking office in 1914, Mayor Joseph G. Armstrong,
a glassblower and Public Works director, harbored deep suspicions about the
kind of formal planning espoused by Frederick Law Olmsted Jr. and the 1911
CPC. He had forged close ties to both labor and the William Flinn political
machine and entertained city plans of his own for a public works extravaganza.
In the tradition of the "plebian" city, Armstrong viewed public works as providing city jobs, not the chance to redesign the urban environment. Moreover, his
administration faced the immediacy of economic recession as well as the prospect of world war. He "reorganized" the CPC and, in the "name of economy
and convenience," relegated it to a tiny office within the Department of Public
Works. There between 1914 and 1918, Secretary-Engineer William A. Gelston

juggled both public works and planning. Neither of Gelston's duties relieved what Charles Mulford Robinson in 1908 had assailed as Pittsburgh's utter lack of beauty.[7]

Under the city's 1911 charter, the Pittsburgh Art Commission oversaw "City Beautification," approving proposals for new public statuary and other streetscape improvements and exploring ways to adorn such notoriously ugly but potentially spectacular vistas as the Point. At the same time the Art Commission in November 1913 hired Chicago architect Edward H. Bennett to design a scheme for the city's historic Point, it appointed thirty-three-year-old architect Frederick Bigger to serve as its assistant secretary. The latter move may very likely have formally launched Bigger's extraordinary planning career in Pittsburgh.[8]

Born in smoky Pittsburgh in 1881 and a graduate of the University of Pennsylvania's School of Architecture, prior to 1913 Bigger worked professionally in both Seattle and Philadelphia, two cities where a young impressionable architect might easily have witnessed and experienced firsthand the artistry and euphoria of City Beautiful planning. In any case, Bigger in 1913 returned to his birthplace convinced that this gritty patrimony could likewise be beautified if only comprehensive planning prevailed. Bound on a mission, and using the Art Commission for his bully pulpit, Bigger in 1915 embarked on a crusade to revive comprehensive planning in Pittsburgh. In fact, he thrust himself into the vortex of the urban conversation that also included exhortations on city planning by both the Voters' League and the CCAC.[9] In "Municipal Improvement," the first of a series of articles published in the *Pittsburgh Post,* Bigger emphasized that the solution to practical urban problems such as traffic congestion, trash-littered play areas, and moldering slums involved doses of both the practical and the beautiful. Beauty and economy derived from good planning, contended Bigger. Indeed, he regarded planning as "an asset of incalculable value to the city," because "in the absence of planning city bond issues [would] tax our progeny for improvements which have ceased to exist and will have been replaced long after the bonds have matured." Haphazard and piecemeal urban development, Bigger's bête noire, spawned a litany of evils: "unhealthy crowding, . . . the inadequacy of the main thoroughfares and of many minor ones, . . . the lack of or inconvenience of access to adequate breathing spaces for the healthy recreation of the people, . . . the lack of trees, grass, . . . and the almost overwhelming lack of beauty everywhere."[10]

In the vein of Frederick Law Olmsted Jr., Bigger beseeched the city to plan comprehensively, that is, to precede action on public improvements and on all

Frederick Bigger, architect and town planner. *Carnegie Library of Pittsburgh.*

land use decisions by carefully considering how such decisions "will affect various parts of the city and the various aspects of the life of the citizens." A plan, asserted Bigger, represented "concrete evidence" that such thoughtful consideration about the implication of urban form for the work, recreation, and residential life of the city's people had been dutifully rendered. "Just how practical or feasible such a map or plan will prove," reasoned Bigger, "depended upon how thorough the considerations of the various subjects has been." Bigger, like Olmsted before him, believed that comprehensive planning exceeded in breadth and scope the knowledge and talents of any one discipline such as engineering, architecture, or landscaping. To his thinking, planning drew as much upon sociology and aesthetics as upon engineering. His 1915 article bemoaned that Pittsburgh lacked an organization, whether an art commission or a planning commission, capable of effective scientific, comprehensive planning. Like George Guthrie and Allen Burns had a decade earlier, Bigger implored Pittsburghers who had the improvement and beautification of the city at heart to become interested in planning, acquire knowledge of the subject, and become active in public or semipublic organizations where their interest and knowledge would be of value.[11]

Bigger may have misread the strength of the sentiment for planning, which gestated beneath the surface of wartime boosterism in Pittsburgh. During the Progressive Era, organizations such as the CCAC and the elite-oriented PCC had fashioned a workable foundation for planning. Nationally, World War I firmed up planning's stature, especially among city businessmen who from the beginning championed the discipline. While the war shattered the progressives' idealism and religious fervor, it exalted those practical, scientific progressive values relished by business. Wartime mobilization and industrial regimentation especially validated the ideal of bureaucratic efficiency, which had infused the progressive plans of Frederick Law Olmsted Jr. The wartime housing and town-planning ventures of the U.S. Emergency Fleet Corporation and U.S. Housing Corporation, including Yorkship Garden Village in Camden, New Jersey, employed highly esteemed architect/planners such as Olmsted, John Nolen, and Frederick Ackerman. These model worker communities not only set an important precedent for government intervention in the housing marketplace but also enhanced town planning's appeal as a "practical" means of building socially and economically useful worker communities that would improve labor productivity, satisfaction, and efficiency. Before the armistice ended World War I in 1918, self-described architect and town planner Bigger had left the Art Commission "to do war work," very likely reconnaissance for either the U.S. Emergency Fleet Corporation or the U.S. Housing Corporation. Government housing, like the wartime experiments with industrial management and economic controls, glorified the goals of civic order and economic stability, together with the idea of the cooperative state and the need for trade association collaboration.[12]

World War I rejuvenated Pittsburgh's industrial economy, which had suffered extensively in the economic recession in 1914–1915. Big wartime orders for steel products, glass, and coal dispelled the economic gloom of the prewar years. Boosters hailed Pittsburgh as the "Arsenal of Democracy" and lauded the city's extraordinary feat in far exceeding its quota in all four wartime citywide bond drives. Led by a dedicated corps of upper-middle-class women hailed as the "Mothers of Democracy," Pittsburgh's matronly bond sellers tirelessly canvassed the city in 1918, neighborhood by neighborhood, door to door, and raised $164,000,000 in bond subscriptions, despite peace talks in Europe and an influenza pandemic that overwhelmed both city hospitals and mortuaries.[13] Fueled by torchlight parades and other patriotic pageantry calculated to submerge eth-nic and racial differences and excite Americanism, these bond drives ignited a "Pittsburgh first," "Pittsburgh forever" spirit, a spirit easily translated into fab-ulous city-betterment language. When church bells throughout the city tolled victory in November 1918, many of the ecstatic throng parading through the smoky, gritty streets of Pittsburgh believed that the city sat on the threshold of unparalleled greatness.[14]

Sadly, other events, which became clearer in the months following the war's end, dampened the euphoria. Wartime and postwar labor shortages and a vio-lent steel strike in 1919 diminished the resurgent confidence in the primacy of Pittsburgh industrialism, as did census figures confirming another dreaded decline in the city's vaunted position as one of America's largest cities. De-spite continued absolute growth, the news in 1919 that Pittsburgh had slipped from the eighth to the ninth most populous city, behind rivals such as Cleve-land and Detroit, startled city boosters. In the words of *Pittsburgh First,* the Chamber of Commerce's new official publication whose very name evoked the lingering ecstasy of the wartime Liberty Bond drives, the census facts "augur ominously for this community's future."[15] Recognizing that the metropolitan area ranked fifth in the nation, but fearing the city being "relegated to the mi-nors," Pittsburgh business elites reignited the prewar campaign for a Greater Pittsburgh, the merger of the city and its Allegheny County conurbation into metropolitan Pittsburgh. "The prosperity of the city and its industries," ex-horted the Chamber, "and of all the peoples, those in the suburbs as well as the city depend upon the growth and material advancement of the great mu-nicipality." The Chamber echoed as well the Pennsylvania Department of La-bor's cry for public works projects to employ the thousands of ex-doughboys looking for civilian jobs.[16]

The Chamber of Commerce predicated its postwar vision of the scintillating planned city upon a collateral goal of achieving industrial harmony and over-coming worker militancy. While embracing planned spatial order, business no longer trusted that environmental reform alone would produce a tractable work-force, especially after the violent labor-management clashes of 1919. Labor strife gripped postwar urban-industrial American silencing mills nationwide, includ-ing Chicago, Cleveland, and Pittsburgh. Convinced that "foreign," "Bolshevik" ideas had fomented the violence that exploded in the 1919 steel strike and that urban immigrant enclaves nurtured un-American values and behaviors, plant managers during the 1920s suddenly reversed their time-honored divide-and-conquer policy that split workers along ethnic lines. In its place, Pittsburgh industrialists erected a regime of worker education aimed at obliterating ethnic-American culture. Fashioned largely by the Chamber of Commerce's Inter-Racial Council, the program communicated "American ideas" to foreign-born workers in six different languages. The Inter-Racial Council hosted numerous Americanization activities, including "What is Americanism?" essay contests, language classes, reading programs, even a "toast to soap." Hopefully, explained the Chamber, these Americanization programs and the many others sponsored by the Young Men's Christian Association (YMCA) and Young Women's Christian Association (YWCA) and by city settlement houses would "allay the discontent which is so largely the result of misunderstandings of and between the racial elements that comprise our population."[17]

But odes to soap, essay contests, and the encouragement of library use hardly comprised the extent of corporate America's quest for industrial harmony in the 1920s. In her landmark study of Chicago industrialism and ethnic workers in the 1920s and 1930s, Lisbeth Cohen demonstrated that business' Americanization drive involved a large-scale effort to "restructure interpersonal relations" within as well as outside the mill gates.[18] The campaign extended to urban form itself. A *Pittsburgh First* article beseeched the city to better its worker housing if it hoped "to preserve the prosperity and growth of the district, as against other industrial centers . . . and combat labor shortages and industrial unrest." The same issue preached that "to stimulate our industries and commerce, increase our property values and municipal income and benefit all classes through the general welfare," Pittsburgh must promote a progressive policy of civic improvements, the lack of which "has driven many of our best working people to other cities and caused grave dissatisfaction among our workers." "Art" and "beauty," proclaimed the city's Chamber of Commerce, are the "best cure for Bolshevism."[19]

A REAWAKENED PLANNING MOVEMENT

Pittsburgh's planning movement reawakened in 1918 amid the final bloody weeks of the October Argonne offensive that was the climax of the Great War in Europe. Months earlier, in April, newly elected mayor Edward V. Babcock, president of Babcock Lumber Company and long active in Pittsburgh civic issues, had foreshadowed the new era by reconstituting the city's languishing CPC. Anticipating victory in Europe, but fearing a postwar recession, Babcock lifted the two-year-old ban on public projects. Next he joined his business associates in the Chamber of Commerce in busily drafting a massive postwar, jobs-creating city improvement program, one dazzlingly packaged for voter approval in a bond referendum; its centerpiece was Babcock's pet project, a downtown subway loop.[20] Mindful—as his predecessor Joseph G. Armstrong apparently was not—that the city's 1911 charter assigned the CPC a critical deliberative role in shaping all ordinances and bills relating to "any street, boulevard, parkway, park, playground or other public grounds . . . tunnel or subway," Babcock on April 19, 1918, exercised his prerogative and reappointed the CPC. Hoping to bridge the seemingly implacable differences between the Department of Public Works and the CPC, Babcock selected former mayor Armstrong to chair the resurrected body. Unlike the feckless prewar body that Armstrong had brashly stripped of power and personnel, Babcock's commission occupied a more secure position in city government. The city council appropriated over $5,000 for the new commission, which in 1918 and 1919 met weekly in the mayor's office.[21]

However, despite being politically and legally fortified, the city planning conversation that prevailed under the auspices of Babcock and his Armstrong-chaired commission preserved the "project" mentality inherited from its historical alignment with civil engineering, architecture, and public works. Little of Frederick Law Olmsted Jr.'s admonition to treat planning as process, or of the Art Commission's Frederick Bigger's plea for "comprehensiveness," marked its operation. Indeed, the city's Bureau of Engineering, located within the Department of Public Works, generated the lists of improvement projects, which drove the commission's 1918 agenda. Together with Babcock, the chief engineer of the Department of Public Works attended every CPC meeting.[22] Typically, most of the 1918 CPC meetings addressed mundane development issues, approving or disapproving proposals for subdivision plans, street gradings, and street widenings.

Mayor Babcock's grand 1919 city improvement bond issue visibly underscored the new CPC's traditional subservience to the Department of Public Works. The city's Bureau of Engineering generated the "List of Improvements," which featured long-standing projects favored by business organizations such as the Water District and Lower Downtown Triangle Improvement Association (TIA). But the bond items especially reflected Babcock's and the Chamber of Commerce's urgent priority to solve the city's traffic congestion problem.[23] Among the seventeen improvements packaged together in the bond issue approved by city voters on July 8, 1919, most addressed streets and transit. These included the mayor's $6,000,000 downtown subway proposal and two other key projects found in Olmsted's *Main Thoroughfares* plan—the widening, grading, and paving of major sections of Second Avenue, Diamond Street, and West Carson Street, and the building of a "new . . . Monongahela Boulevard Route" to Oakland and East Liberty. Babcock's bond issue also called for construction of the Mt. Washington Roadway, which in conjunction with improvements to Brownsville Avenue and Carson Street, constituted a second boulevard system. A jubilant prodevelopment Chamber of Commerce postulated that "no scheme of improvements ever contemplated by the city of Pittsburgh is more widespread in its benefits . . . [and] promises greater relief to traffic problems than [these] . . . two new boulevard systems."[24]

No matter how exciting, these grand proposals for large-scale bridge, highway, subway, and other bond-funded public improvements deeply troubled the youthful new breed of professional city planners such as Frederick Bigger. Mayor William Magee had recognized the regional implications of urban development and in 1911 had lobbied to give the new CPC jurisdiction over suburban growth.[25] Bigger questioned the metropolitan implications of improvement items, and how they fit into any broad regional plan. Regional jurisdictional problems had plagued progressive-minded civic leaders since the turn of the century and incited the perennial call for metropolitan government. The city of Pittsburgh in the 1920s comprised just one of a myriad of competing regional political jurisdictions that vied for scarce tax dollars and harbored often conflicting visions of the urban future. Foremost among these jurisdictions was Allegheny County itself. While all of the grading, widening, and other road-building projects in Babcock's mammoth proposal, including the $6,000,000 item for a downtown subway, fell within the jurisdiction of the city of Pittsburgh, many of the other projects in the 1919 list that ranked high on both the CPC's docket and on the Chamber's "desire list"—the South Hills Bridge project improvement, for example—breeched city boundaries and involved county government.[26]

Allegheny County in 1918 had announced the creation of its own planning commission. The county, however, subordinated the commission's role to the construction department of its Department of Public Works, on which it relied for all technical aid and advice. Not only was the Allegheny County Planning Commission (ACPC) primarily an engineering office, it was also deeply enmeshed in politics. County political infighting delayed the appointment of commission members until 1924.[27]

From the outset, the CPC and ACPC viewed each other as rivals. The CPC recognized that in the absence of metropolitan government, the host of bridge, highway, and other joint city-county projects invited a structured city-county dialogue. The urban conversation, that is, should be widened to encompass the region. Initially, joint city and county planning discussions occurred in-formally, usually in the form of requests by the county for city collaboration on such projects as the Sixteenth and Forty-eighth Street bridges and the pro-posed South Hills Bridge and Tunnel. Conveniently, Babcock turned the coun-ty's requests over to the young planning commission, which in turn invited the county commissioners to meet, together with "their engineers."[28] Without a comprehensive planning process, Allegheny County could only participate in these discussions on a project-by-project basis.

This lack of comprehensiveness was a serious problem. According to the modern tenets of planning espoused by the members of the National Con-ference on City Planning, city betterment schemes must abjure the designa-tion "projects," and instead highway, street, bridge, park, and improvement projects should be systematically and scientifically programmed as part of a comprehensive planning "process." But the seventeen enumerated improve-ments, no matter how patently crucial to perceived city progress, smacked of the kind of special purpose projects that professional planners detested. A he-roic Pittsburgh that had triumphed in one wartime Liberty Bond drive after another, and was now poised to defend its touted industrial supremacy against all postwar challengers, deserved modern comprehensive planning. More-over, such planning should be managed and display the same scientific rigor unveiled in the city's wartime bond drives, food conservation programs, and munitions production.[29]

Many historians of planning see the end of World War I ushering in a "New Urban Discipline." For a city to be good, wholesome, and prosperous, averred Pittsburgh's Chamber of Commerce, it must also be "a place where workers who operate the plants . . . enjoy health, happiness and physical fitness and en-hanced worker efficiency."[30] The war had underscored the benefits of such sci-entific and bureaucratic values espoused earlier by progressives such as Fre-derick Law Olmsted Jr. The reawakening of the planning movement and the exuberant endorsement of planning by the city's Chamber of Commerce at-tested to how vigorously business and professional classes sought a rationally ordered city. This new consensus, the outcome of a renewed urban conver-sation and shaped as much by business elites as by young architect/planners such as Frederick Bigger, condemned the legacy of past haphazard, speculative patterns of city development for the horrendous traffic congestion, the jerry-built slums, and consumptive children that imperiled urban life. "We are a small town people," exhorted the Pittsburgh Chamber of Commerce's George Wallace. "We grew up on a farm where there is no necessity for community action. We have [now] learned that recreation is a necessity not a luxury. To accomplish desired results we must act on some well thought out coordinated plan. No one would question the advisability of a mill plan. No one builds anything without a plan."[31]

Unrestrained speculative development had despoiled the city; enlightened capitalism wedded to modern principles of industrial management and guided by professional planners would reclaim it. Planning technicians of the 1920s rejected social justice appeals, "single tax" miracles, and evocations of a Christian Commonwealth. The New Jerusalem would not arise from the ashes of Armageddon, but from zoning, comprehensive planning, and vigilantly regulated space. Redeeming city life demanded efficient administration and regulatory control not only over subdivision plans, street openings, and street widenings but also over the profusion of gasoline stations and garages, automobile showrooms, and neighborhood movie theaters.[32]

THE BIRTH OF THE CITIZENS COMMITTEE ON THE CITY PLAN

Energized by war-born patriotism, by Babcock's boldness, and by Bigger's indefatigability, the conversation about Pittsburgh and the future of the city's built environment had significantly quickened in the fall of 1918. Championing Pittsburgh as the City Beautiful and City Practical, the CCAC, through its Municipal Planning Committee, now wasted little time making known its plans for a new post–World War I city "that will give greater comfort, safety, health, convenience, utility and add to all these beauty." Toward that end, the CCAC in mid-November 1918 prepared a zoning bill and, echoing Bigger's 1915 appeal, challenged Pittsburgh civic elites to match their cohorts in Chicago by sponsoring a new city plan. Olmsted's 1911 plan, sponsored by the Pittsburgh Civic Commission (PCC), had never been officially adopted and was limited by the PCC in its scope. As a result, the Municipal Planning Committee summoned "Pittsburghers who had enough pride in the City and enough good will in his [sic] heart and enough dollars in the bank to put up the expense that the work may go ahead."[33]

Anticipating the CCAC's call by over a month, Bigger in early October 1918 perambulated the Fourth Avenue and Grant Street sanctuaries of Pittsburgh's corporate aristocracy, exhorting business support for a plan envisioning the future magnificent city possible through comprehensive city planning. On October 26, 1918, at Bigger's behest, three of Pittsburgh's most illustrious civic and business leaders—banker and financier Richard Beatty Mellon;

Charles D. Armstrong, president of Armstrong Cork; and James D. Hailman, a prominent city engineer and apostle of planning—met in the boardroom of the downtown Mellon National Bank, where they compiled a list of about seventy prominent citizens to whom they dispatched an "urgent invitation" to "meet for consultation with a few persons interested in the industrial and civic progress of Pittsburgh."[34] Three days later, Bigger's civic troika, joined by business luminaries such as J. H. Lockhart, Albert J. Logan, William Larimer Mellon, Henry Buhl, Hamilton Stewart, William H. Robinson, D. P. Black, Grant McCargo, W. L. Clause, and Wilson S. Arbuthnot, founded the CCCP. The group pledged itself to secure for Pittsburgh "the benefits of scientific and comprehensive planning leading to systematic progress along predetermined lines . . . such as is now being applied elsewhere." Real planning, exclaimed the newly formed CCCP, would "control . . . [the city] development both industrially and socially."[35]

Only a month after the 1918 armistice had ended warfare in Europe and America's expeditionary force began returning, the CCCP mobilized to plan Pittsburgh. It formed a nine-member Executive Committee headed by Armstrong and including R. B. Mellon; Howard Heinz; department store magnates Henry May and Edgar J. Kaufmann; George Davison, president of Gulf Oil; Roy Hunt of Alcoa; and Wilson Arbuthnot, who was president of a large wholesale dry goods business and long active in local progressive initiatives. Mellon heir and Pittsburgh Republican Party chieftain William Larimer Mellon headed the CCCP's finance committee; Frederick Bigger took the lone salaried position of executive secretary. Through late 1918 and into 1919, the CCCP Executive Committee met variously in Mellon's Fifth Avenue mansion, in Bigger's old Art Commission office in the City-County Building, and in temporary quarters in Mellon's downtown bank.[36] Once ample funding had been secured from board member pledges, Bigger moved the committee into permanent offices on the sixth floor of the First National Bank on Fourth Avenue.[37]

Fred Bigger's energy and verve infused the CCCP. An unmarried, quintessential professional dedicated to Pittsburgh planning, Bigger endowed the voluntary organization with intellectual zeal, a steady devotion to bureaucratic detail, and the mantle of scientific efficiency. However, a serious problem arises from interpreting this "New Urban Discipline" too rigidly as the activity of molelike technicians singularly engaged in making master plans or in zoning. Bigger's professional life, in fact, belies too easily characterizing him as a planning mole, for he just as easily qualified as a "skylark," to borrow historian William H. Wilson's terminology. Wilson divided early planners into "moles" (realists) or "skylarks" (utopians). Realists abjured the "unpractical" City Beautiful movement, embraced free enterprise, and planned for the existing city. According to Wilson, zoning "towered among . . . [their] greatest achievements." "Skylarks," on the other hand, "dreamed," in Wilson's words, "of new and better cities and societies." These planners decried the degrading commercial-industrial city and saw urban decentralization and regional settlements as the pattern of the future.[38] Frederick Bigger, who dominated Pittsburgh planning in the 1920s and 1930s, defied any such simple categorization. For example, Bigger, who tirelessly espoused comprehensive planning, firmly believed in zoning, and burrowed with the best moles into the morass of planning detail, was the very same person who believed fervently in the town planning ideas of Ebenezer Howard, and in 1923 joined Clarence Stein, Henry Wright, and Lewis Mumford as charter members of the skylarkian Regional Planning Association of America (RPAA). As the next chapter explains, Bigger in the 1920s regularly visited New York to intellectualize with Mumford, Stein, Wright, Fred Ackerman, Robert Kohn, and the other members of the RPAA about greenbelt towns and the new age of urban reconstruction. During the 1930s, Bigger became chief planner for building the New Deal's first greenbelt town.[39]

However, during the 1920s no one espoused a greater faith in comprehensive planning than Frederick Bigger, and perhaps none proffered a greater vision of planning's promise, a promise captured in his favorite phrase, the "accessible city." Bigger, in fact, imagined a planned urban region, decongested, uncluttered, and deslummed, with a healthy managed downtown of office towers, small shops, and department stores, surrounded by sparkling, well-planned urban neighborhoods uncontaminated by industry, warehouses, and gasoline stations, and located near parks and playgrounds, which were easily accessible to mill workers as well as mill managers either by foot, by highways, or by public transit. These would be socially inclusive, aesthetically attractive, and affordable neighborhoods where land use would be publicly controlled for the public good. Bigger preached Platonic elitism, not republican equality. His vision of the new city, the new metropolis, assumed an intellectual or planning aristocracy aligned with and empowered by a benevolent, albeit self-interested, urban elite that in concert with planners would redesign the industrial city.[40]

Vision aside, throughout his long city planning career Bigger functioned primarily as an adviser, a coordinator, and an expediter, rarely wielding the draftsman's pen, preferring instead to guide and assist the planning impulses of others. Few would have suspected the sheer passion for visionary planning ideas that smoldered within this bespectacled, thin-framed, thirtyish man who in 1918 orchestrated the resurgence of modern planning in Pittsburgh.

Advised by Bigger, the CCCP proclaimed a singular lofty goal: "To create the City Plan and further . . . city planning in all its aspects in the Pittsburgh District." Bigger estimated the cost of a city plan at between $150,000 and $200,000, and proposed a fund-raising strategy mimicking the wartime bond drives. The CCCP solicited monies through an annual subscription campaign, aimed at the Pittsburgh civic and business elite. Subscribers automatically became members.[41]

In its early publications the CCCP enthroned expertise. It likewise glorified planning as process and extolled the importance of scientific surveys and the acquisition of topographical data, all vital aspects of planning avidly espoused by Olmsted Jr. In concert with the professional planning cohorts, Bigger and the CCCP viewed the city organically, and thus proscribed isolated, uncoordinated projects. Good planning fully embraced the organic nature of the city; it strove to link city parks, playgrounds, waterways, sewage disposal, housing, food-distribution facilities, and the other parts of the city into a living whole. Properly planned, cities promoted industrial growth and improved housing conditions and abetted the conservation and enhancement of city property values.

Likewise, the CCCP, in typically progressive fashion, abjured politics. City planning, vowed the CCCP, "will not be a matter of political controversy. Any problem arising will require technical competence rather than political partisanship."[42] At the same time, the CCCP as a voluntary agency forged close links with the public sector. Public and private cooperation and collaboration had characterized the city's successful wartime efforts, and it epitomized the planning effort of the 1920s. CCCP policy pledged the organization to assist city and county planners, "securing expert advice for them wherever possible."[43] The committee confined itself to advising and assisting. Zoning, for example, deeply concerned the CCCP; the organization studied and endorsed the CCAC's proposed 1918 zoning ordinance, paid to have it reprinted and distributed citywide, and lobbied state legislators to pass zoning enabling legislation.[44] Meanwhile, it reserved the politically volatile task of drafting zoning ordinances and maps to the city.

Following what it revered as the Chicago model, the CCCP viewed its exalted mission to be production of the city plan itself. It plainly saw the need for the voluntary sector to prepare the city plan. At the same time, the CCCP recognized the critical importance of the CPC's eminent domain and police powers to outlaw nuisances and to secure public health, safety, and welfare.[45] Professional planners realized that only public sector agencies wielded the crucial enforcement powers and legal authority to police rampant speculation and impose order on unruly land use patterns. The CCCP, in fact, lobbied Harrisburg to broaden those legal powers to include the right of excess condemnation, the ability of the city (and planners), that is, to take land through eminent domain proceedings exceeding that deemed necessary to remedy nuisances or promote the public welfare.

From the beginning, the CCCP openly strove to make the planning commission and itself as much as possible alter egos. In truth, their personalities meshed from the very beginning when on December 11, 1918, James D. Hailman, a member of the CPC but "speaking on behalf of the CCCP," asked the CPC to meet with the CCCP to discuss common interests. A year later the CCCP and the CPC formalized their relationship by establishing "official cooperation."[46] The CCCP confirmed this informal amalgamation when, in 1923, it changed its by-laws to create six ex-officio directors that included the head of the city's Department of Public Works, the school board president, the CPC chair, the ACPC chair, and the presidents of both the Chamber of Commerce and the CCAC.[47]

Circumstances, as we shall see, greatly facilitated public and private cooperation in planning. As Hailman had done, Howard Heinz, Albert Logan, George Davison, and Wilson Arbuthnot served not only as founding members of the CCCP, but they also exerted considerable influence as prominent figures on the municipal affairs committees of the Chamber of Commerce. All harbored a keen, vested interest in zoning, downtown traffic control, harbor improvement, transit, housing, and other city planning issues. Likewise, the CCCP deliberately plotted to make both the CPC and the ACPC philosophically images of itself. Toward that end, the CCCP cajoled and, when necessary, flexed its political muscle to have mayors and county commissioners appoint CCCP members to the two commissions. On the whole, it enjoyed considerable success, particularly with the city. Generally, the CCCP placed anywhere from four to six of its members, including, of course, Bigger, on the nine-member CPC. Consequently, it is fair to say that during the 1920s, the directorates of the region's public and private/voluntary sector planning agencies exquisitely interlocked, connecting the CPC and the ACPC directly to the larger urban conversation and making them sounding boards for the planning

goals and ambitions of Pittsburgh's civic and business leadership.[48] Throughout the 1920s, James D. Hailman, the first president of the CCCP and a staunch
Chamber of Commerce member, sat on the CPC. Hailman served before Bigger's appointment as the first executive secretary of the CCCP. Similarly, U. N.
Arthur, the chief engineer of the ACPC, worked closely with the CCCP and
the Chamber. Other bulwarks of the CCCP, R. B. Mellon and Howard Heinz,
heir of the Heinz food empire and a director in 1919 of the Pittsburgh Chamber of Commerce, served during the decade on the ACPC.[49]

The Joint Planning Conference (JPC), first created in 1922, endeavored to
formally modulate the flow of conversation between the CPC, the ACPC, and
the CCCP. Frederick Bigger, then secretary of both the CCCP and the CPC, assumed the secretaryship of the JPC, which espoused metropolitanism, "act[ed]
as a clearing house and board of review," and strove to "harmonize" the planning activities of all three major planning bodies. Alas, the activity of the JPC
came in fits and starts, and by 1929 the body existed in name only.[50]

The shortcomings of the JPC aside, during the 1920s the CCCP and the CPC
meshed beautifully. Either Bigger or Hailman faithfully represented the committee's viewpoints at every commission meeting, and the commission members rarely demurred. When, for example, in 1922 the commission considered a
communication from the CCCP objecting to a proposed street-widening plan
for Manchester Avenue and urging the CPC to join them in opposing the plan,
Hailman moved and Bigger seconded that "this commission concurs with the
Citizens Committee in suggesting to the mayor that Manchester Avenue be
made a six (6) lane thoroughfare."[51]

While the elite composition of the CCCP enhanced the civic stature and
moral authority of the CPC, Bigger delivered impeccable professionalism and
a worthy record of achievement. However, Bigger himself conceded that the
CCCP's primary task of comprehensive planning consumed time not easily spared by urban professionals and businessmen. "It is difficult to get my
[CCCP] committee together," Bigger wrote to the planner John Nolen in 1919,
"as they are all busy men with large interests requiring their attention."[52] Despite its affluent membership, raising funds for the costly work of planning
preoccupied the organization. The CCCP cheered in 1920 when told that the
city would continue to "generously support" the CPC; increased public funding of the CPC lightened the CCCP's burden of such expenditures.[53] Meanwhile, the CCCP pursued its job of comprehensive planning. While CCCP finance committeemen Arbuthnot, William Larimer Mellon, Richard Beatty
Mellon, and Hamilton Stewart tabulated the latest pledges of monetary sup-

port for the fledgling voluntary planning body, Bigger pondered ideas for urban park, community, and arterial highway systems floated earlier in his 1915–1917 articles. Ultimately, he outlined a three-pronged planning program for Pittsburgh involving surveys of city housing, industry, and recreation.

The widely acclaimed Chicago model of comprehensive planning dictated that the committee retain a distinguished technical consultant to provide the expertise that Daniel Burnham had supplied Chicago. A subcommittee of the CCCP headed by Hailman submitted three names: John Nolen, Edward Bennett, and Harlan Bartholomew. On March 10, 1919, Bigger mailed a letter to Nolen's Harvard Square office in Boston asking the renowned town planner, fresh from his service with the U.S. Emergency Fleet Corporation in World War I, to submit "the conditions and terms under which . . . [Nolen] might be willing to make a housing survey or consult with local people on such a survey." Nolen had recently completed a similar survey for Bridgeport, Connecticut.[54]

Bigger moved faster than Nolen responded. By early April 1919 Bigger had scrapped his three-pronged survey idea and drafted instead a detailed "Outline of Work for Comprehensive Plans of Pittsburgh and Contiguous Districts," which he estimated would cost $302,000. The task involved three stages: the examination of existing conditions, an analysis and study of plans, and the formulation of specific recommendations. In stage one, technicians gathered extensive data for the preparation of eighteen maps describing street railways, streets and roads, housing, playgrounds, and other existing conditions. Analyzing these map data would produce comprehensive plans for major streets, transportation lines, waterfront development, housing, industrial development, and, of course, zoning. Bigger projected a five-year process, which included publicity, public education, and the employment of an outside consultant, all in close collaboration with the city and county planning agencies.[55]

Nolen found Bigger's "Outline of Work" to be impressive, remarking that it showed "a grasp of principles both to the survey and the preparation of the city plan." At Bigger's invitation, Nolen visited Pittsburgh to consult with the CCCP on both the "analytical report" and on the city bond issue. Like Chicago's Edward Bennett, another candidate for the planning job, Nolen in 1919 boasted an eminent national planning reputation. But the CCCP chose neither Nolen nor Bennett. Instead, at the rate of $250 a day, plus expenses, for work to consume at least three days per month, it chose the young St. Louis engineer/ city planner Harland Bartholomew, who had recently won praise for his work on that city's first zoning ordinance. Bigger had suggested Bartholomew's name in his "Outline," calling him a new star in the zoning field. Pittsburgh required Bartholomew to utilize both his planning and his zoning talents. Indeed, most planners in the 1920s considered the two inextricably linked.[56]

ZONING THE STEEL CITY

As in other American cities in the early 1920s, Pittsburgh's progressive business and civic leadership embraced zoning, not as a substitute for city planning, but as a necessary part of comprehensive planning. Zoning, defined as the legally enforceable division or mapping of the city into height, use, and space coverage districts, originated in Bismarckian Germany, where planners hoped to produce the "healthy city" by regulating the use, price, and supply of urban land.[57] American planners such as Benjamin Marsh and Frederick Law Olmsted Jr. praised the orderliness and disciplined growth of German towns; but no American city actually adopted zoning until July 25, 1916, when New York City unveiled its first ordinance. Conceived, promoted, and drafted into law by lawyer and planning evangelist Edward M. Bassett, head of New York's Height of Building Commission, the city's districting scheme sought to thwart the block-by-block advance of forty- and sixty-story, air- and light-choking skyscrapers. Pressed by New York's Fifth Avenue Association, the 1916 zoning resolution also aspired to check the steady encroachment of garment factories and lofts into the carriage trade district and to preserve Fifth Avenue's carefully cultivated elite residential and commercial image.[58]

Despite the shortcomings of New York's ordinance—it was hardly comprehensive, it failed to restrict building heights, and it did not provide incentives to upgrade commercial or industrial districts—Edward Bassett and New York City gained national fame together as, respectively, the czar and epitome of zoning. Progressives in Pittsburgh and other cities, where seemingly dizzying building heights and mushrooming automobile garages, service stations, and laundries aggravated downtown congestion and threatened utter mayhem in an already mottled city, seized the idea of urban-environmental reform via legal mandate.[59]

As early as 1915 the Municipal Planning Committee had attempted to lock zoning into a new comprehensive building code. These civic reformers in Pittsburgh, as elsewhere, embraced zoning originally as a tool for positive urban-environmental change, not as a means to stabilize commercial or suburban real estate values.[60] The CCAC's ardor for zoning arose from a historic concern for tuberculosis, typhoid, and other epidemic diseases ravaging Pittsburgh's less fortunate. These plagues, argued the CCAC, resulted from "the overcrowding of people in . . . [tenements], and the ensuing physical and moral un-wholesomeness . . . [of] unkempt neighborhoods."[61] Zoning fashioned on New York City's ordinance would not only relieve congestion but, in the CCAC's words, overcome the "vast economic and social waste which is entailed in our present heterogeneous and inadequate method of building on land."[62] Like the Pittsburgh Taxation League, another enraptured apostle of zoning, the CCAC also believed that districting would protect middle-class East End residential areas from the encroachment of apartments, auto showrooms, gasoline stations, polluting industries, and other tawdry land uses, and thereby stabilize real estate values.[63]

In 1917 the CCAC took the first step toward a zoned Pittsburgh. That year, after consulting with Bassett, the Municipal Planning Committee, assisted by New York's Lawson Purdy, drafted a zoning enabling act for submission to the Pennsylvania legislature. The Municipal Planning Committee incorporated into its bill the recommendations of the Taxation Study Committee, which displayed an equal passion for zoning legislation.[64] Not until the spring of 1919 did the Pittsburgh CPC approve the final draft of the zoning bill. Shortly afterward, Pennsylvania joined nine other states in passing an enabling act authorizing zoning in cities of the second class. The act empowered city planning commissions

to recommend the boundaries of districts and the appropriate regulations and restrictions imposed therein . . . [and] to regulate and limit the height and bulk of buildings hereafter erected or altered, and, for these purposes, to divide the city into districts, of such number, shape and area as it may deem best suited to the purpose . . . [and] to regulate and determine the area of yards, courts, and other open spaces in connection with buildings . . . [as well as] restrict the location of trades and industries.

Finally, the law established the procedure for amending the ordinance, by creating a three-person Board of Appeals, one member of which would come from the CPC.[65]

Zoning ipso facto elevated the role of the public planner, making zoning, according to one historian, a "key factor in the development of the planning profession." Bassett, who was dedicated to the professionalization of urban planning, believed that zoning's affinity for technical minutiae—devising a complex hierarchy of graded land uses and, district by district, prescribing and justifying in precise language the permissible and proscribed activities within each zone—bathed planners in the aura of scientific expertise.[66]

Simultaneously, zoning further loosened planning's already tenuous identification with social reform and deepened lay support for the profession. Pittsburgh's Chamber of Commerce, like the CCCP and CCAC, vigorously championed the idea. Zoning complemented businesses' postwar infatuation with economic regularization and efficiency as well as reformers' goals of the centralization of decision making in municipal government. Further, zoning fit with ongoing and parallel interests for regional planning and cooperation. Proposed 1926 state legislation for a metropolitan district included a provision for a district board to regulate land use.[67] Fordism, as some called it, the achievement of ultimate efficiency by the technical mastery of every facet of the human social and economic sphere, appealed equally to corporate realty interests, the "Community Builders," to use historian Marc Weiss's term, for whom zoning, like restrictive covenants and deed restrictions, protected the exclusivity of the large-scale subdivision plats sprouting up in the 1920s in places such as suburban Pittsburgh's Mount Lebanon. Finally, zoning buttressed comprehensive planning. By scientifically mapping and differentiating land uses, it impartially grappled with the politically inscrutable and legally Byzantine land use issues that arose during the decade, including skyscraper development, downtown congestion, the proliferation of automobile garages, warehouse and industrial expansion, and the mushrooming of gasoline stations.[68]

Bigger's 1919 "Outline" had assigned zoning a priority. In fact, together with solving traffic congestion, winning passage of state enabling legislation to permit the CPC to undertake zoning in Pittsburgh had topped the CCCP's 1919 planning agenda. "By fixing the character of the various districts of the city," stated the CCCP's Armstrong, zoning simplified the ordering of urban form, prescribing in advance the requirements for street widths, street railway lines, transportation facilities, and the like. Armstrong acclaimed zoning as the "essential" first part of the city plan.[69]

Accordingly, between 1919 and 1923 the CCCP worked closely with the CPC to undertake the zoning process. The committee had chosen its chief consultant, Bartholomew, as much for his experience with zoning as for his city planning credentials. On October 13, 1919, only six days after his appointment by the CCCP, the St. Louis engineer/planner appeared before the CPC, meeting in Mayor Babcock's office, where he outlined and described the first steps and the personnel required for zoning Pittsburgh.[70] Two weeks later, on October 27, the commission created a Bureau of Zoning and Districting, which, led by Pittsburgh's Department of City Planning chief engineer U. N. Arthur, in the spring of 1921 launched the survey and mapping of city "Use Districts."[71] For the next several years, Bartholomew frequently attended CPC meetings, fielding questions, examining and approving maps, and okaying draft ordinances.[72]

Repair garages and gasoline stations like those pictured here at Forbes and Shady avenues in Squirrel Hill mushroomed in residential neighborhoods, convincing the CCCP that to preserve order, zoning was imperative. *Pittsburgh City Photographer Collection, Archives Service Center, University of Pittsburgh.*

During the years 1920–1922, preparing the zoning ordinance preoccupied the CPC, whose often-wearying agendas brimmed monotonously with garage, building height, street-widening, and subdivision applications. To lighten its burden, in mid-1921 the commission pigeonholed all further applications for industrial land uses that it deemed incompatible with the draft ordinance.[73] Zoning understandably headed the list of topics discussed at the 1921 annual National Conference on City Planning hosted by Pittsburgh at the William Penn Hotel. At the conference, the City Planning Department's U. N. Arthur, and commission member James Clark joined Bassett for a roundtable discussion of zoning focusing on Pittsburgh's progress.[74]

Although absent from the roundtable, both Bigger and Morris Knowles, a nationally known consulting engineer, just as eagerly endorsed zoning, but for housing reasons. Knowles, like the CCCP's Armstrong, believed that zoning, together with street and transit plans, addressed the city's housing problem by opening less expensive fringe land for development and diminishing crowding in central city neighborhoods. Districting, argued Knowles, "provide[d] sufficient light and air, for healthful and pleasant working conditions and for living conditions in congested neighborhoods." It benefited "public safety and morals, . . . prevent[ed] the overcrowding of tenement districts and . . . provide[d] that measure of privacy necessary for the development of decent homelike surroundings." Zoning champions especially pounded the overcrowding theme; the dangers of sunless, airless streets; and the moral and social benefits of urban decongestion.[75]

Zoning, therefore, dominated much of the urban conversation during the 1920s. But both zoning and city plan preparations demanded population statistics, social and economic data, topographical maps, and other information that ten years earlier Olmsted had found missing in Pittsburgh. Bigger, Bartholomew, and Knowles spent most of their time and resources in 1919 and 1920 compiling these data. Amid the data gathering, mapping, and assessment of the city's improvement needs, a city election in 1922 returned William Magee to the mayor's office. Magee kept the CPC fixed on zoning. He promptly appointed several new members to the commission, including the architect, town planner, and now zoning enthusiast Bigger, and also Knowles, a board member of both Pittsburgh's Chamber of Commerce and of Secretary of Commerce Herbert Hoover's Advisory Committee on Zoning. At its June 13, 1922, meeting the commission elected Knowles chair and Bigger secretary.[76]

With Bartholomew's technical help and Bigger's dedication and supervisory skills, Pittsburgh produced a comprehensive zoning ordinance and districting maps covering every square inch of city space. The ordinance created five use districts: heavy industrial, light industrial, commercial, residential "A" (single-family dwellings only), and residential "B" (duplexes and apartment dwellings). It also regulated the intensity of development on lots within these use districts. In addition to isolating obnoxious or dangerous industrial land uses such as acid manufactures, dye works, and animal-rendering plants, the ordinance dealt with such politically and aesthetically sensitive automobile-related issues as billboards and garages. To combat central city traffic congestion and forestall looming skyscraper canyons from robbing downtown streets of air and light, the ordinance established a tall building zone limiting office heights to 265 feet; it furthermore stipulated that with setbacks, towers could soar to unrestricted heights.[77]

Pittsburgh's 1923 zoning law, like others of the era, attempted to immaculately arrange urban space by conceptually seeing it as a household. In Constance Perrin's words, it sought "to put everything in its place." In fact, the idea of the "well-ordered household" dominated prozoning rhetoric. *Progress*, the monthly publication of the CCCP, featured cartoonist Cy Hungerford, who deftly satirized Pittsburgh's muddled abodes, where, he wryly observed, a piano was plunked down in the kitchen, a bathtub squatted in the parlor, a scraggly pile of laundry dried in the second-floor bedroom, and the garage was perched in the attic.[78]

As Pittsburgh planners neared completion of the proposed zoning ordinance in the fall of 1922, Bigger readied the CPC for the contentious political phase of selling the ordinance to a skeptical citizenry. He forthwith summoned Edward Bassett to advise him on strategy. As required, the commission submitted in January 1923 the draft ordinance to the city council, which in conjunction with the CPC proceeded to hold nightly public hearings at the courthouse, the Carnegie Library in Oakland, the South Side Market House, and a host of other public venues.[79] CCCP monies enabled the commission to print and widely circulate copies of the draft ordinance. While business leaders applauded the aims of the CPC's ordinance, individual companies often feared that zoning threatened present and future expansion plans.[80] To allay fears, the commission orchestrated an elaborate publicity campaign, which included a dinner for newspaper editors, public exhibits, and lantern slide lectures in neighborhood movie houses.[81]

Nevertheless, serious opposition persisted. Zoning's most vitriolic enemies in Pittsburgh, such as Senator David Reed and W. T. Mossman, represented trust companies, realtors, and owners of sizable parcels of downtown property such as the estate of Jones & Laughlin Steel Company founder B. F. Jones. Speaking for a large bloc of Pittsburgh businessmen and women as well as trust and realty interests, Reed and Mossman attacked the constitutionality of zoning, especially its threat to individual property. Reed stretched the objectionableness of zoning to the breaking point. Zoning discriminated against propertyless working-class families, argued Reed, by outlawing or restricting boardinghouses and limiting space for "modest" homes, that is, slum housing.[82]

The bitterest enemies of zoning in Pittsburgh discharged their heaviest broadsides at height restrictions. Building heights, insisted Reed, "should be regulated only by the [natural] economics governing buildings. In our opinion no modern office building or properly equipped hotel can or will be built in the city after the passage of the ordinance."[83] Local architects feared that severe height restrictions, as propounded by Bigger, would stifle creativity.

Reed's political prominence notwithstanding, opposition to zoning fizzled in the face of substantial support for districting led by the Chamber of Commerce, the CCAC, the local chapter of the American Institute of Architects (AIA), and the CCCP. Proponents of the ordinance quashed Reed's individual liberties case by simply countering that the law created a Zoning Board of Appeals, which provided a permanent forum for litigating and correcting any problems caused by the ordinance.[84]

The city council voted approval of the ordinance on July 30, 1923, thus setting firmly in place one anchor of the heralded twin moorings of city planning. Approval of zoning hardly ended the CPC's deep involvement with zoning. Enacting zoning inaugurated a lengthy, labor-intensive process of appeals, hearings, and adjustments that, to Bigger's and others' chagrin, preoccupied the commission throughout the decade.

THE PITTSBURGH PLAN

While zoning enthusiasts engaged in the urban conversation preached that districting would relieve population congestion and improve urban housing conditions by limiting densities, they never viewed zoning as a panacea. Instead, by providing an important instrument for orderly growth, zoning, they urged, served the ultimate goal of comprehensive planning; the plan itself, not zoning, fixed the critical coordinates for that growth.[85]

Bigger understood that the state legislature had narrowed Pittsburgh's immediate postwar planning agenda when it empowered the CPC to perform two carefully defined, time-consuming tasks: first, in 1911 approving subdivision plans, and, second, in 1919 creating the zoning ordinance. The ACPC, not given statutory life until 1923, oversaw subdivision platting as well as numerous roadway openings and widenings in the bevy of townships and boroughs located in the metropolitan region beyond the city. Thus, as Bigger declared in his 1915 and 1917 articles, the lofty mission of producing modern comprehensive plans to guide future urban development devolved upon the private sector, that is, Pittsburgh's CCCP.

Under Bigger's tutelage, the CCCP savored its job. Committee members, as noted, touted the model for creating a city plan developed in 1907 by Chicago's Commercial Club, which had engaged Daniel Burnham and Edward Bennett to redesign the Windy City. Pittsburgh's civic elites strove to relate planning to the "life of the city . . . , to make it a product of the best wisdom, technical talent, of Pittsburgh business and professional men." Bigger and the CCCP Executive Committee created nine subcommittees covering such vital urban planning issues as major street plans, recreation planning, legislative priorities, public transit, waterways, and freight terminals. More than sixty of the city's leading businessmen, lawyers, architects, and other civic leaders, many active in the Chamber of Commerce, served on these committees.[86]

Bigger, assisted by advertising executive George Ketchum, engineer Winters Haydock, and consultant Harland Bartholomew, spearheaded the planning effort. During the years 1920–1923, staff members and the subcommittees on playgrounds, parks, transit, and major streets plans met regularly for hours at a time, studying maps and statistical data collected by CCCP technical staff. Subcommittees worked closely not only with Bigger, Bartholomew, and other staff experts but also with civic and business organizations such as the Chamber of Commerce and the CCAC, and with public agencies, namely the CPC. This lengthy and arduous process, a new aspect of the urban conversation, one projected in Bigger's 1919 "Outline of Work," resulted in six reports issued by the CCCP between 1921 and 1923; collectively the reports constituted the *Pittsburgh Plan*.[87]

No reason exists to doubt the CCCP's claim that the finished plan represented the tireless dedication and fervent devotion of Pittsburgh's business and professional elite. However, both Bigger and Armstrong conceded that the busy schedules of prominent business executives such as George Davison, Edgar J. Kaufmann, R. B. Mellon, and William Larimer Mellon limited their involvement. Technical staff personnel, including Bigger and Bartholomew, conducted the extensive research and analyses and produced the hefty reports that these technicians were forced to vigorously defend before each of the CCCP's six committees. Therefore, the reports generally reflected the special knowledge and expertise of key staff persons such as Bigger on parks, recreation, and streets; William Hudson of Bartholomew Associates on waterways and railroads; and Haydock on transit matters. Some reports, namely the major street and transit plans, patently owed homage to earlier planning studies, especially Frederick Law Olmsted Jr.'s 1911 *Main Thoroughfares* plan.[88]

In any case, the completed city plan that CCCP president Charles Armstrong formally announced in 1923 fulfilled the planning committee's ambitious goal to produce a framework for all future city development and civic betterment. Possibly still haunted by the Pittsburgh Survey's indictment of the city's scabrous social and physical environment, Armstrong brandished the newly finished plan as hard evidence that "our city is not as hopelessly backward as some might think."[89]

The six reports dealt essentially with three main issues: recreation (playgrounds and parks), transportation (transit, railroads, and waterways), and, reflecting Bigger's interests in mobility or urban accessibility, the *Major Street* plan. *Pittsburgh Playgrounds,* the first installment of the plan, appeared in June 1920, over three years before its companion report on parks arrived on the planners' shelf. The committee expedited the playground report in order to influence how the city spent the $831,000 earmarked for recreation in Babcock's 1919 bond issue. The CCCP considered the playground study, together with the *Parks* report, to be a recreation plan. Bigger's thinking imbued both reports, especially the parks study, which contained the fullest expression of the architect/town planner's vision of the accessible city. Bigger's progressive urban environmentalism is clearly evident in the playground study. Progressives like Bigger emphasized the importance of play and the "play instinct." Constructive play or physical education emerged in progressive thought as the ideal arena for teaching citizenship, a field of battle in the crusade against crime and delinquency. Playgrounds, therefore, nurtured the physical, mental, and moral development of the child. Settlement houses, public schools, and that bastion of the social gospel, the urban church, had long embraced the playground as a vital part of the community fabric. "Here in the playground," wrote Bert Smyers of the Pittsburgh Chamber of Commerce's Committee on Public Education, "the child learns to be unselfish, to respect the rights of others and to appreciate co-operation—the greatest lessons of life."

> Give the boy a place to play,
> Let him have his youthful fun!
> Rob him now, and you may pay
> When some greater ill is done![90]

In 1896, pressed by the newly formed CCAC, Pittsburgh had opened its first playground. Four years later the city announced a citywide recreation plan, and in 1915 it created a Bureau of Recreation that absorbed the Pittsburgh Playground Association founded in 1906. But despite the city's Bureau of Recreation, by 1920 Pittsburgh's recreation program languished. It drew scathing rebukes from planners like Frederick Bigger who saw little progress. At a time when the automobile rendered city streets "the playground of first resort for most city youth, dangerous and unusable, in many areas of the city, particularly [in] poor, high delinquency areas such as the Hill District," Bigger charged that "alleys and tiny rubbish strewn lots served as the prime play areas."[91]

In typical progressive parlance, the CCCP report addressed the "Play-

ground Problem." Brimming with the verbiage of scientific efficiency, it recommended a "unified" citywide playground and recreation program linked to
a system of parks and boulevards. The report vented Bigger's and the CCCP's
outrage at what planners decried as the city's past "haphazard," politically
driven mode of playground development. Bigger denounced the city for its
"hodgepodge" of isolated and unsupervised "lots" bereft of equipment and located without reference to other recreational opportunities. CCCP researchers
unearthed scant information—maps or other data—indicating any rationale
for the location or the design of existing recreation facilities; in fact, the city
seemed unaware that it actually owned one particular park site located on the
grounds of the historic U.S. Arsenal in the city's Lawrenceville section. Playgrounds frequently hugged the ungraded slopes of steep hillsides, sites totally
unsuitable for popular neighborhood baseball diamonds. Void of indoor facilities, swimming pools, or shallow ponds for ice skating, most city parks and
grounds in 1920 operated seasonally, not year round.[92]

The report exhorted Pittsburgh to select park and playground sites "not according to selfish [political] interests," but according to need. For every Pittsburgh district, it scientifically calculated the severity of need for recreation,
and it urged city officials to adopt its precisely mapped program for the systematic development of playgrounds. Bigger's program analyzed the age, gen-
der, and racial composition of the city neighborhoods and, using the data,
designed a citywide system of accessible junior and senior playground and
athletic and community center facilities.[93]

The Chamber of Commerce, the CCAC, the Pittsburgh Central Labor
Council, the Allied Boards of Trades, and the Pittsburgh Chapter of the AIA
all endorsed the recreation plan, and the CCCP expected prompt action by the
city council. Goaded by the CCCP, the city council at the very least consulted
the report in expending the $831,000 bond appropriation for recreation; but
this hardly placated the reformers. When the bond funds dwindled in 1920,
the CCCP, joined by the Chamber and the CCAC, drafted revised recommendations. In January 1922, with proplanning mayor William Magee serving in
office for a second time, but with less than $31,000 left in the playground till,
the CCCP intensified its campaign, haranguing the city council for its continued "piecemeal, haphazard" management of the city's playground program.[94]

Meanwhile, five other CCCP subcommittees sculpted individual segments
of the city plan, including the plan for city parks. In its *Playgrounds* report,
the CCCP had balanced equal portions of progressive outrage and scientific
empiricism; undiluted vision making ruled in the commission's 1923 report on

parks. As opposed to "utmost efficiency," the *Parks* report forcefully articulated Bigger's social philosophy of the good, well-planned city. It borrowed elements from English civil–servant–turned–urban visionary Ebenezer Howard's "Garden City," as well as from architect Clarence Perry's concept of the neighborhood unit. But it also reflected Olmsted Sr.'s nineteenth-century masterpiece, the "Emerald Necklace," the shimmering ring of romantically planned parks encircling the city of Boston. In that Olmstedian vein, Bigger's park plan espoused the reformist theory that combining beauty with enhanced accessibility would harmoniously unify the physically, socially, and economically fragmented parts of the city.[95]

Like the *Playgrounds* report, the *Parks* report offered recommendations. It urged topographical surveys of undeveloped park tracts, notably the Frick, Mt. Washington, and Sheraden park sites. It espoused the development of neighborhood parks and community centers as advocated in the *Playgrounds* report. It pleaded for new pedestrian-accessible entrances to Schenley, Highland, and McKinley parks, together with the development of downtown waterfront parks, a city boulevard system, and the Saw Mill Run Parkway.

Bigger proceeded to weave these recommendations into a holistic vision of an urban community, where workers emotionally numbed and demoralized by the monotony of regimented industrial workplaces and housed in crowded, uncomely neighborhoods found in city parks wholesome environments able to divert the mind and to spiritually and physically reinvigorate the body. Bigger anchored much of his faith in urban parks in the nineteenth-century writing and works of landscape architect Andrew Jackson Downing as well as those of the older Olmsted. Bigger contended that humans, like plants, thrived in fresh air and sunlight; moreover, parks served not only as natural but democratic spaces where the immigrant poor mingled with the upper classes and learned what it meant to be an American.

Embracing the progressive parks credo, Bigger wrote that "open spaces [were] the city's lungs . . . [and] as the city grows the need to provide such open spaces becomes more frequent and urgent." For Bigger, Pittsburgh epitomized the urgency. Early-twentieth-century immigration and urban growth spawned unprecedented racial and ethnic diversity in the Steel City. Bigger cited the 1920 census, which revealed half of the city's population either foreign born or the offspring of foreign-born parents. In harmony with Olmsted Sr., Ebenezer Howard, Lewis Mumford, and the RPAA, Bigger in the 1920s viewed open space as abetting social and moral stability. "A proper development of municipal recreation," argued Bigger in his 1923 *Parks* report, very much like Edward

Bigelow had earlier in the annual reports of the Department of Public Works, "should assist, almost more than any other activity, in the orderly assimilation of these diverse [immigrant] elements into the fabric of good citizenship and stable Americanism." Cities like Pittsburgh, admonished Bigger, offered immigrants an alluring smorgasbord of leisure-time activities, some wholesome, some not. Accessible, attractive parks, boulevards, and recreational areas countered the perceived evils of pool halls and dance halls and other commercial amusement places, while paying economic returns in public health, contentment, efficiency in the workplace, and better citizenship.[96]

Bigger incorporated this economic and social rationale for parks and playgrounds into his vision of urban community. Verdant park drives and boulevards and elaborate park entrances enhanced both the beauty and the accessibility of urban recreation. Architecturally pleasing shelters, comfort stations, and food stands strengthened the social and aesthetic quality of city parks. Bigger's grand scheme included small as well as large parks. As Olmsted Jr. did a decade earlier, he saw small parklets providing landscape and architectural treatment at street intersections and on craggy hillsides.[97] His vision closely resembled Clarence Perry's school-centered, "community cell/neighborhood unit" concept, which hypothesized an intimate community design restoring the face-to-face social relationships abraded in the maelstrom of nineteenth-century industrialism. Public schools and libraries, along with city parks, playgrounds, and community centers, formed the nucleus for revitalized civic life. Designed by architects "as worthy examples of civic art," public schools and libraries clustered around a park, public square, or commons, making this "the hub of community life and an incubator of social value ... knitting together diverse elements of the population." Development along such lines, pleaded Bigger, "should appeal to those who fear either an excessive 'paternalism' or excessive 'socialism' in the growing centralization of control."[98]

Other features of Bigger's park plan further attested to his strong commitment to social and aesthetic as well as practical goals. His plan for the downtown waterfront rejected the popular contemporary idea of transforming the city's decaying Monongahela and Duquesne riverfront quays, once a clamorous, churning sea of commercial activity, into parking lots. "Human needs," he wrote, "are greater. The majority of workers in the business district do not own automobiles." He, for one, did not own a car in 1923; nor did he ever learn to drive. Therefore, Bigger believed that the recreational needs of downtown workers demanded primary attention. In a manner reminiscent of Olmsted Jr.'s earlier recommendations, he proposed making those high-profile riverfront areas flanking each of the city's downtown bridges into modest but "attractive rest parks." Bigger pictured these parklets trimmed with flowers and planted with shrubs and trees.[99]

Tree plantings and flowerbeds likewise embellished Bigger's proposed fifty-four-foot-wide Saw Mill Run Parkway, as they did his plan for a complete boulevard and parkway system that he imagined to be separate from the city's major street plan. These beautification projects, as well as his design for a public forest and an outlying boulevard system (an "Emerald Necklace" for Pittsburgh), link Bigger in some important ways to the landscape architecture tradition of the Olmsteds and Charles Mulford Robinson.[100]

Throughout the six-volume comprehensive *Pittsburgh Plan,* Bigger, Bartholomew, and their cohort of technician assistants reflected the then-current seminal ideas of University of Chicago urban sociologists Robert Park and Ernest Burgess, who viewed the city as a biological system. In their anatomical lexicon, streets, thoroughfares, and highways functioned as the vital arteries and veins of the city. The biological language underscored the heightened importance of urban traffic problems. Major arteries or thoroughfares carried through traffic; streets and avenues bore local traffic. This traffic orientation, as historian Clay McShane observes, obliterated the ancient social function of streets. Once, at the dawn of mass automobility in 1911, Olmsted Jr. imagined Paris and Lyon, France, with their quayside pedestrian walks, as possible models for the future of waterfront cities like Pittsburgh. Although Bigger injected riverfront parklets into his 1923 *Parks* report, by 1921 the idea of café life and idle strolling as alternative uses for city streets faded from most planners' views. For Pittsburgh and other cities, economic survival now hinged on relieving traffic congestion.[101]

Bigger's trademark thinking appeared just as indelibly in the CCCP's *Major Street* plan, unveiled in September 1921, as it had in the *Parks* plan. Here Pittsburgh's master planner foreswore much of the eloquence and vision lavished two years later in the *Parks* document. The *Major Street* plan (explained in greater detail in chapter 5) attacked a vital and eminently practical issue; it sought to create a "general circulatory system, to secure the uniform flow and diffusion of traffic."[102] Bigger and the CCCP stressed that Pittsburgh must integrate its streets and thoroughfares into a complete, coordinated system before the city attained the enviable distinction of having a major street system.[103]

While traffic-clogged streets obsessed city planners, the CCCP recognized that an effective city plan must also coordinate the city's major street system with its transit and rail transportation lines. The rest of the *Pittsburgh Plan,* therefore, explored city transportation, including waterway, railroad, and transit systems. This part of the urban conversation excluded all but the initiated. Here the CCCP gave the engineers free rein. Indeed, the *Transit* report epitomized engineering practicality and economy, and focused, for example, on the advantages and disadvantages of subway and elevated systems. The report spurned earlier reformist arguments for improved trolley service that linked low-cost rail transportation to decongestion, better housing, and freer access to parks and fresh air. In fact, it never mentioned lower fares, better service, or the public ownership of traction. Instead, it endorsed replacing cumbersome downtown surface cars with a subway system, funds for which had been voted in the 1919 bond referendum.[104]

Economy, not reform, also justified planned railroad improvements contained in the 1923 *Railroad* report. Since 1850 railroad terminals, freight yards, and rights-of-way deleteriously affected downtown land use patterns. In Pittsburgh, as in almost every American city, railroad terminals and their ramshackle shed appendages blocked commercial and major street expansion, while numerous at-grade railroad crossings posed a constant danger to pedestrians and automobiles and exacerbated traffic congestion. At the time of the report, the Pennsylvania Railroad was at last relocating its giant freight terminal, which had long obstructed traffic flow at the north end of Grant Street, creating the notorious Grant Street jog. The *Railroad* report, like the *Transit* report, both principally authored by Winters Haydock, entreated Pennsylvania Railroad executives to proceed with plans for diverting through rail traffic away from the downtown and for constructing a two-tiered enlargement of Pennsylvania Station.

However, the plan debunked the highly touted union station idea that enjoyed popular acclaim in other cities. Since suburban residents accounted for over half of all railroad passengers arriving daily into downtown Pittsburgh, and since 72 percent of these commuters traveled on Pennsylvania Railroad trains, the report considered the city's existing Daniel Burnham–designed Pennsylvania Station the logical hub and recommended that the Pittsburgh and Lake Erie and Pittsburgh and West Virginia lines cooperate with the Pennsylvania Railroad by sharing a common terminal facility.[105]

In *Waterways,* the sixth and final report of the *Pittsburgh Plan*, William Hudson, the Harland Bartholomew staff, and the committee members muted Bigger's earnest appeal that the city beautify its riverfronts. The briefest of the six reports, *Waterways* was the most adamantly pragmatic of the eminently practical *Pittsburgh Plan*. For years traffic on Pittsburgh's three rivers had been declining, and with the revenue loss arose a defiant clamor to take action to revive the region's waterway commerce, including canalizing the Ohio River and building a water route from nearby Beaver, Pennsylvania, to Lake Erie, thus keeping Pittsburgh competitive with the iron and steel industry gravitating to Gary, Indiana, and Cleveland. Pittsburgh planners, however, focused more on waterfront use than on waterways development. *Waterways* highlighted the city's uncomely quays as industrial and commercial assets for loading and unloading coal, sand, oil, and other products, and downplayed their potential as recreational and scenic areas. The tenor of Hudson's report contrasted starkly with the blithe community-centered vision embedded in Bigger's *Parks,* and amplified the commercial rootedness of most 1920s planning. For Hudson, who authored much of the *Waterways* report, "navigation interests ha[d] a prior right to the use of those portions of the City's waterfront which can be advantageously used for water transportation," and, he pronounced that "no encroachments should be permitted thereon which will interfere with such activities."[106]

FAIT ACCOMPLIS

The CCCP formally unveiled its six-volume *Pittsburgh Plan* on June 1, 1923. Euphoria about the future of planning reigned. At a banquet celebrating the event attended by prominent Pittsburgh business leaders, illustrious city professionals, city and state officials, and other dignitaries, including representatives of a host of city civic organizations, Charles D. Armstrong and Mayor Magee, joined by the chairpersons of all five of the CCCP subcommittees, outlined and praised the plan and the planning ethos in Pittsburgh. Armstrong's keynote address recited the improvement priorities, the subway loops, the Boulevard of the Allies extension to Schenley Park, the Grant Street widening, Liberty Bridge, and Saw Mill Run Parkway, and he applauded the more than 200 business leaders and professionals who unselfishly contributed their scarce time and talents to the planning process. But, Armstrong added, his kudos to the private sector should never serve to diminish the importance of the planning experts involved in the plan, "for without professional city planning," he explained, "I doubt any city plan worthy of the name could be prepared."[107]

The CCCP, however, considered all the money, time, and effort on planning wasted without public support. It regarded public education as critical to planning's success. A real triumph meant spreading the planning ethos citywide. As Arthur Hallam exclaimed when pleading for the *Major Street* plan, it must become "more than a paper plan . . . so that in [the] future no important street [or park, or playground, or transit line] will be undertaken without reference to the program set forth by the committee."[108] The CCCP undertook an educational campaign, orchestrated by Pittsburgh advertising genius Howard Ketchum, to marshal broad popular backing for its plan and win official endorsement from the city council. In addition to the publication and widespread circulation of the committee's newsletter, *Progress,* members delivered hundreds of lectures at public schools, colleges, churches, club meetings, and numerous other forums. Junior Civic Club volunteers fanned out across the city knocking on doors and delivering pamphlets explaining the city plan. Organizations such as the Pittsburgh chapter of the AIA, the CCAC, and the Chamber of Commerce forwarded to the CPC resolutions on behalf of the *Playgrounds* and *Major Street* plans. In 1923 the city council and the CPC officially endorsed both plans.[109]

Bigger and the CCCP were justifiably giddy about planning's prospects in 1923. Pittsburgh possessed both zoning and a city plan. Moreover, the city now boasted a planning infrastructure that consisted of a reinvigorated CPC led by the progressive, quintessential planning technician Frederick Bigger. The city was committed to planning professionalism and dedicated to the central goal of comprehensive planning expounded by Bigger as early as 1915. Although Allegheny County in 1923 still lodged planning within the county's Department of Public Works and still reflected an engineering mentality, a planning department finally existed there, too; and through a CCCP-created JPC, the city and the county endeavored to plan cooperatively.

Firmly supporting this urban planning venture in the 1920s stood such powerful Pittsburgh elite-dominated agencies as the Chamber of Commerce, the CCAC, and the CCCP. Planning attracted city business leaders who were convinced that comprehensive planning, together with scientific management and the "Americanization" of the immigrant labor pool, promised a new era of economic and social stability. Fortified by this civic support, assured that planning was both structurally and legally secure, and flourishing a six-volume city plan, Pittsburgh planners in 1923 seemed poised to finally and fully tame the undisciplined metropolis.

But, as the next chapters disclose, the youthful, often exuberant planning profession shared not one but several visions of the urban future. Moreover, huge obstacles limited the ability of even the most ambitious planner to remake the industrial city.

CHAPTER 5

Planning and Professionalism in the 1920s

CHARLES D. ARMSTRONG, Frederick Bigger, James D. Hailman, and the other exultant Pittsburghers who attended the Citizens Committee on the City Plan's (CCCP) 1923 banquet honoring the committee's six-volume *Pittsburgh Plan* truly savored the golden moment. No sooner, however, were the tables cleared and cigars lit (Bigger preferred a pipe) than the revelers confronted the disconcerting reality that the organization (and its newly formed corporate parent, the Municipal Planning Association) had achieved the sole purpose for its founding; Pittsburgh was now zoned and boasted a newly minted comprehensive city plan. In closing his speech that warm June evening, and fully anticipating the crisis, Armstrong firmly announced that if, for no other reason, vigilance alone warranted that the planning association exist for at least another year. One year later, after printing its July 1924 issue, *Progress,* the organization's upbeat newsletter, ceased publication, proclaiming that "planning [has] taken hold in Pittsburgh and its environs." The CCCP itself, while not disbanding, suspended further activity.[1]

The planning that took hold in Pittsburgh in 1924 had a dual personality. Reflecting the disposition of the city's planning maestro, Frederick Bigger, planning practice in the Steel City possessed a strong practical side; but faithful to Bigger's competing temperament, it also had a visionary bent. This chapter explores the achievements of professional-led planning in Pittsburgh as it unfolded in the 1920s. Because of Bigger, planning in Pittsburgh possessed this somewhat Manichaean character—practical, but streaked with vision. In Pittsburgh, as throughout urban America, political reality usually militated against the adoption of more radical, European-inspired planning schemes such as England's garden cities. Bigger, as this chapter explains, harbored the dream of garden cities especially as propounded in the 1920s by Lewis Mumford, Clarence Stein, and the Regional Planning Association of America (RPAA). But in Bigger's practical view, this social vision of carefully planned residential communities and satellite towns was best nurtured through deliberate adherence to comprehensive planning, and through patient enforcement of land use edicts. Therefore, in concert with the city's business community, which embraced planning as a tool to restore order to the tangled fabric of urban space, under Bigger, Pittsburgh planners in the 1920s wrestled with the details of zoning, the enforcement of subdivision ordinances, and the retrofitting of the city and its region for the automobile. Just as tirelessly, planners worked to solidify the legal foundations for the institution of city and county planning.

Out of this mix of vision and practicalism emerged by 1929 a professionalized, legally and institutionally secure planning tradition committed to comprehensive planning. Although the City Planning Commission (CPC) and Allegheny County Planning Commission (ACPC) differed somewhat, structurally and philosophically, both shared the same unwavering commitment to ordered space. And both by the end of the decade claimed an estimable record of accomplishment.

SKYLARKS IN THE SMOKEY CITY

Fred Bigger's dominant place in Pittsburgh's planning community kept the visionary face of planning alive in the city despite the ascension of practicalism. A vision different from either the City Beautiful or the City Practical had emerged in late-nineteenth-century England. This broader, comprehensive vision turned from the practicalist's obsession with lot plans, street widths, and building heights, to fathom the relationship of ordered space to human social well-being. What configuration of housing, parks, workplace location, and street and thoroughfare design, asked visionaries, best promoted community cohesion and happiness? Among professional planners, the vision usually glowed rather than radiated. Visionary planning in places like Pittsburgh frequently manifested itself in little more than dedication to the comprehensive plan. This was far from Ebenezer Howard's *Tomorrow: A Peaceful Path to Real Reform* (1898), which envisioned a whole new urban structure sharply divergent from the densely settled pattern of commercialized, industrialized London. In *Tomorrow* (reissued in 1902 as *Garden Cities of Tomorrow*), Howard unveiled his design for a decongested London surrounded by planned satellite towns each in turn protected from unplanned, speculative urban development by the inclusion of a lush, parklike greenbelt. By 1919, thanks to Howard and his devoted and energetic disciples Raymond Unwin, Barry Parker, and Thomas Adams, several garden cities arose on the London periphery, including Letchworth in Hertfordshire near Oxford, and Welwyn. In America, Forest Hills Gardens in Queens,

New York, and Garden City on Long Island derived from the swift transatlantic migration of the garden city idea.

Howard's vision intrigued the Scottish biologist and urban theorist Patrick Geddes and his American disciple, Lewis Mumford. Both Geddes and Mumford deplored what they viewed as the biologically dysfunctional, antihuman form of the congested, modern industrial city. They hypothesized the dawn of a new era of ecologically sound urban regions where the virtues of town and country were mutually harmonized. Mumford, and the group of young architects/planners and philosophers who in the 1920s joined his intellectual excursion into the realm of urban reconstruction, believed that modern technology, especially the liberating force of the dynamo and the sprawling regional electrical grid systems, fostered the emergence of a new, vibrant urban culture vastly different from the brutalizing patterns of human existence plaguing modern urban industrial civilization. Mumford's intellectual and technical basis for this hypothesized reconstruction of American urban life lay in what he called the "fourth migration." The three preceding migrations, lectured Mumford, had settled the American frontier and peopled both its factory towns and its teeming immigrant cities. The "fourth migration" triggered by the automobile and powered by behemoth dynamos and giant electrical transmission lines made possible a new decentralized urban form of satellite communities buffered by belts of greenery, where socially constructive, cooperative human values might flourish. Here, indeed, was a different conversation, one purveying the vision of a reconstructed, more civilized and communal urban life, and one seemingly rejected by the rank-and-file "practical" planners.[2] Significantly, both planning tendencies, the visionary and the practical, existed side by side in Pittsburgh during the 1920s and contributed to solidify planning professionalism in the city.

By 1919 Bigger, the moving force behind planning in Pittsburgh, no longer managed the activities of the Art Commission. A year earlier, during the waning hours of World War I, he had departed the commission "to do government war work."[3] It can be strongly inferred, while not confirmed, that Bigger's "war work" involved local reconnaissance for either the U.S. Housing Corporation or the Emergency Fleet Corporation. During this same era Bigger had entered the national debate on planning. In 1914 he was elected to membership in the American Institute of Architects (AIA) and promptly chaired the institute's Committee on Municipal Improvements and City Planning, the so-called Community Planning Committee earlier chaired by Henry Wright and Clarence Stein. At the 1917 National Conference on City Planning in Kansas

City, Missouri, Bigger shared the table at a discussion on the appropriate relationship between municipal art and planning commissions with J. Horace
McFarland, Frederick Law Olmsted Jr., John Nolen, and Alfred Bettmann,
among others. Among these stellar figures in planning history, whom Bigger
counted as acquaintances, Stein, Wright, Benton MacKaye, Tracy Augur, and
Frederick Ackerman, all future members of the landmark RPAA, had worked
with Robert Kohn and Frederick Law Olmsted Jr. on America's seminal experiment with federally built (wartime) housing. Bigger was also reportedly
one of the fifty-two charter members of the American City Planning Institute,
established in 1917.[4]

Bigger's thinking about the city and its predicament had matured enormously during his first years in Pittsburgh, 1914–1918. Originally a spokesper-
son for the City Beautiful, he had burgeoned into an articulate and strenuous
advocate for comprehensive planning and at the same time emerged a master
of the technical skills and the administrative and bureaucratic knowledge necessary to constructively manage urban planning.[5] Moreover, in the 1920s he
midwifed the birth of the CCCP and helped prepare its six-volume, comprehensive, yet practical plan endorsed by the business elite.

Still, on one Friday in April 1923, this same technical expert, who daily immersed himself in the bureaucratic details and politics of Pittsburgh planning, hastily packed his suitcase, boarded the eastbound express for New York
City, and spent a long weekend dreaming better cities with Lewis Mumford,
Clarence Stein, Fred Ackerman, Robert Kohn, and Henry Wright as a charter
member of the RPAA. Historians Roy Lubove and Carl Sussman, and Mumford himself, trace the roots of the RPAA back to Charles Whitaker and the
World War I government housing initiative. Indeed, Bigger's probable involvement with the other RPAA charter members in the war housing venture and
his mingling with the same individuals through his AIA and American City
Planning Institute activities led to his invitation to the organization's initial
meeting. None of Bigger's writings prior to 1923 explored the organic nexus
between urban and rural areas, mused about the dynamic impact of technology on urban form, projected a new regional basis for urban civilization, or
even faintly broached Mumford's idea of a "fourth migration." Nevertheless,
Bigger found solid common ground with his RPAA colleagues in vigorously
opposing "piecemeal" planning and in disdaining the "realists'" capitulation
to economic constraints. Unquestionably, by 1923 Bigger's comprehensive urban perspective embraced the urban region and its topographical features. As
his part of the urban conversation in Pittsburgh, he linked traffic, population

congestion, and speculatively inflated land values to the urban housing problem, and he imagined a culturally homogenous "accessible city," ideas that recommended him to the RPAA as a kindred intellectual spirit.[6]

No matter how great or small, Bigger's involvement in the RPAA is significant. As Carl Sussman argues, membership in the somewhat exclusive, loosely organized "society of friends" never exceeded twenty-five. Yet this handful of architects, foresters, economists, sociologists, and other academic types influenced American thought and policy making, especially during the 1930s. If Bigger can be better known by the company that he kept, it was distinguished. In addition to Mumford, Wright, and Stein, over the ten years that the RPAA existed, 1923–1933, the circle of friends included forester, philosopher, and author Benton MacKaye; the economist Stuart Chase; architects Russell Van Nest Black, Robert Kohn, and Tracy Augur; and the noted housers Edith Elmer Wood and Catherine Bauer, leading figures in the garden city movement of the 1920s and the modern housing initiatives of the 1930s.

Bigger's introduction to this group may, as noted, date to his war housing work in 1918. Perhaps it came through his AIA connection. Historians credit both Whitaker and Stein with assembling the group. Stein had formed a modern planning atelier in 1918. Whitaker edited the *Journal of the American Institute of Architects*, which published some of Mumford's first articles, and in 1923 he convened in New York City the initial meeting of the group attended by Bigger.

This tiny band of planning intellectuals exalted the potential of both modern technology for realizing visionary communitarian housing and the town planning schemes of Ebenezer Howard and Raymond Unwin. Yet with the exception of Fred Ackerman, whose philosophical blend of Fabian and Guild Socialism imparted a distinctive and often harsh strain of anticapitalism to his thinking, the RPAA abjured radicalism. Albeit not "radical," this merry band of communitarians nevertheless rejected the prevailing Harding-Coolidge-Hoover "business as usual" mood of the 1920s. Member Stuart Chase casually labeled the group as "mildly socialistic." At the very least, argues Sussman, they were "willing to abandon large areas of the free market in favor of a planned economy."[7]

Sussman's encapsulation of RPAA political views aptly fits Bigger, although he was decidedly not a core member of the RPAA clique. Most studies of the organization identify Bigger only as a charter member. However, Bigger's affair with the RPAA was hardly casual. Although it is impossible to place him with any regularity at the "informal" lunch and dinner gatherings in New

York City or at the weekend discussions at the Hudson Guild Farm in Net-cong, New Jersey, where MacKaye attempted to revive Appalachian folk danc-ing, Carl Feiss fondly recalls Bigger's presence at RPAA sessions in Stein's at-elier on the top floor of the famous Dakota apartment house opposite Central Park.[8] By 1924 Bigger corresponded with "My Dear Mumford" about bringing the Scottish biologist-philosopher-planner Patrick Geddes's "Cities Exhibit" to Pittsburgh, and established a long and close friendship with Russell Van Nest Black and Clarence Stein. Throughout the remaining three decades of his professional life, Bigger retained his interest in the communitarian principles and alternative urban forms advocated by his RPAA colleagues. In his 1923 *Parks* report for the CCCP, he had expressed his view, at about the same time the RPAA was established, that small parks around which neighborhood in-stitutions like schools and libraries clustered would help revitalize civic life. Bigger's social vision also included a concern for housing reform, and he par-ticipated in the national conferences on slums and low-income housing dur-ing the 1930s. Like his colleagues at the RPAA, he envisioned one of the so-lutions to the housing issue to be better-designed communities. Through his relationship with Stein and Wright in the 1920s, he was undoubtedly famil-iar with their path-breaking community and town planning designs for Sun-nyside Gardens on Long Island and Radburn in New Jersey. In 1930 Bigger tried his hand at community planning when he submitted a design for the Buhl Foundation's proposed housing project in Pittsburgh's Mt. Washington neighborhood. Although his entry was not selected, indeed Stein and Wright won the commission with their innovative residential community known as Chatham Village, a few years later Bigger was appointed the chief planner for the Roosevelt administration's Greenbelt Town program, which planned four communities and built three of them on the periphery of Washington, D.C., Cincinnati, and Milwaukee. These visionary ideas nurtured by the RPAA, by John Nolen and others, kept planners in Pittsburgh and elsewhere aware of the higher social or community-building purposes of the profession.[9]

For Bigger and for many professional urban planners in the 1920s, behind the trenches where planners drafted lot plans and the details of zoning maps lay a larger, joyous world to be built of better cities with thriving, healthy communities. In fact, during the 1920s the lot approval process, zoning ap-peals, and other mole work, which mired Pittsburgh's Planning Department in seemingly routine matters, rarely eclipsed the agency's ardor for general or visionary planning. This vision making radiated most brilliantly from Bigger's *Parks* and *Major Street* reports, and it resonated throughout the decade in the

CPC's public and private discourse. Mayor William Magee galvanized the city's general planning effort in 1924 when he commanded the CPC to prepare a program of city development. The city council seconded Magee's action by approving in early 1925 a $50,000 expenditure for the "Preparation of General Plans and Estimating the Cost of the Major Street Plan in the Business District Recommended by the Citizens Committee on the City Plan." The $50,000 catalyzed the general planning effort and further elevated Bigger's stature in city planning.[10] One month later the commission formally acknowledged the director's extraordinary role in city planning, especially his "efficient and effective service in the preparation of the recent zoning ordinance and other executive service for the Planning Commission." "Bigger," proclaimed the commission, "has been the active agent in the stimulation of . . . [the CCCP's] major street plans." Therefore

the City Planning Commission for the purpose of effectively carrying on the work which has been given it and for the better undertaking of its responsibilities, does hereby designate its Secretary, Frederick Bigger, under the general direction of the Chairman of the Commission, to act as an executive officer of the Commission and of the agencies and work of the Commission, particularly referring to the newly assigned work, and [that] the entire staff of the Commission shall be under his direction to allot the men as may be directed by the Secretary and the Chairman of the Commission.[11]

The "newly assigned work," which Bigger now directed, referred to the Inter-District Traffic Circuit, whose centerpiece, the Liberty Crosstown Thoroughfare, would not be completed until the 1970s. But the vision of a crosstown expressway, embedded in the commission's *Major Street* report, took root and form under Bigger in the 1920s. In his mind, a crosstown expressway formed part of a vital regional highway system, bypassing the downtown and connecting the South Hills and the North Side via the Liberty Bridge. Throughout the 1920s, Bigger complained that there was simply not enough time for city planners to complete the comprehensive plan.[12]

Nor did Bigger's *Parks* report unnecessarily languish from disuse. During the late 1920s, the CPC undertook topographic and other planning studies for the Nine Mile Run Valley recreation area, for a public golf course bordering the city's waterworks in Aspinwall, and for beautifying and enhancing accessibility to Schenley Park.[13] Despite the obsession with technology and assembly line efficiency marking the 1920s, the urban beautification theme rife in the parks study enjoyed enormous attention. Although the city's Department of Public Works had dumped city shade tree work on the Planning Department, the commission took the tree-planting job seriously and integrated it into general planning as a beautification tool. It rehabilitated the Shade Tree Division's ramshackle nursery facility and purchased thousands of seedlings, including catalpas, red oaks, American elms, Norway maples, and European lindens. Taking seriously Olmsted Jr.'s 1911 observation that Pittsburgh's rivers and Mt. Washington rivaled the haunting mountain valley setting of such alluring European cities as Berne and Lyon in beauty, the commission purchased fourteen acres of scarred and denuded hillside land contiguous to the Mt. Washington Roadway (under construction in 1927) and launched an ambitious tree-planting project. Elsewhere, aided by the May-Stern Company and in alliance with the Art Commission, the Department of City Planning's shade tree workers toiled for months attempting to transform the Boulevard of the Allies into the Champs-Elysées.[14]

THE COUNTY'S VISION

Through Bigger and his role during the 1920s on Allegheny County's Major Highway Plan Committee, visionary planning helped shape the Pittsburgh region's ambitious highway planning program. Ironically, county planning seemed an unlikely host for visionary planning. As implied, by the 1920s not one, but actually two public planning bodies operated in the Pittsburgh region, the CPC legally established in 1911 and the ACPC founded in 1918. The 1911 law, explained earlier, gave the CPC specific jurisdiction over lot plans only; in 1919 the state expanded that body's authority to include preparing and overseeing the city's zoning ordinance. Otherwise, as in most cities, the CPC in the early 1920s exercised mainly recommendatory powers. Still, the CPC possessed the legal authority to make important decisions affecting urban space (the power to approve lot plans and to zone). And through its Department of City Planning, replete with its own budget and reporting directly to the Pittsburgh City Council, the CPC had the political freedom to do just that.[15]

The ACPC, on the other hand, originally possessed only recommendatory powers. Between 1911 and 1923, the agency lacked even legal status, being simply an advisory board lodged in the county's Department of Public Works. Convinced that the county required a major highway plan to complement the city's *Major Street* plan, the CCCP between 1921 and 1922 lobbied Harrisburg to create a legally constituted county planning commission able to develop a county road plan as well as approve township subdivision plans. The CCCP succeeded in 1923; however, the ACPC awaited independent status until the 1930s. Before that, it operated as an appendage of the Engineering Division of the county's Department of Pubic Works.[16] For most of the 1920s, the ACPC, with its robust staff of bridge and road surveyors, was headquartered on several floors of the Old City Hall building, where it stored its transits and other surveying tools in the basement.[17] With bridge building and major highway and tunnel projects ranking high in 1922 on both county and city agendas, including Mayor Magee's, the CCCP recognized the importance of coordinating the activities of the two commissions. Accordingly, in November 1922 representatives of the CPC, the ACPC, and the CCCP created a "voluntary" Joint Planning Conference (JPC), which met frequently between 1923 and 1925, but less often in the later 1920s.[18]

Despite some similarities, important philosophical differences distinguished the ACPC from the CPC. Chaired by John F. Bell and guided by such loyal commissioners as Charles E. Armstrong, Richard Beatty Mellon, Henry P. Haas, and Howard Heinz, the ACPC closely resembled in elite composition its city counterpart. Its driving force, Secretary William Gelston, a civil engineer, exuded professionalism; but the county's Planning Department toiled in the shadows of the county Department of Public Works. That vassalage status stirred a penumbra of doubt among city professionals not only about county planning's independence but about the seriousness of its commitment to comprehensive planning. Even with the JPC, those doubts thwarted the real city-county planning cooperation necessary to expedite the numerous critical joint planning projects such as the Liberty Bridge and the Saw Mill Run Parkway.[19]

County actions in the middle of the decade may have momentarily allayed the CPC's misgivings about the county's cooperation. Two former Pittsburgh mayors undertook large infrastructure improvement programs when they became county commissioners. Joseph Armstrong, elected commissioner in 1923, and Edward V. Babcock, elected in 1927, each promoted successful bond issues for constructing the bridges and highways desperately needed to accommodate the burgeoning automobile and truck traffic of the county's industrial and suburban residential communities. Moreover, in this period the county purchased thousands of acres for, and began development of, two large parks that became known, appropriately, as North Park and South Park. Armstrong's successful bond issue of April 1924 targeted $29,000,000 for highways, bridges, a tunnel (the Armstrong Tunnel connecting the South Tenth Street Bridge on the city's south side with Forbes Avenue), and a much discussed new county office building. After centralizing existing separate bureaus, including roads, bridges, automobiles, and architecture, among others, under the Department of Public Works, the county commissioners charged their new superdepartment with developing a comprehensive transportation plan. The reorganization strengthening the Department of Public Works left the newly chartered ACPC nominally independent by reporting directly to the county commissioners, but with most of its staff ensconced within Public Works. Although Pennsylvania's governor Gifford Pinchot upgraded state roads that penetrated the county, the spread of industry and population since the 1890s demanded the creation of a system of highways that facilitated commuting to and from Pittsburgh by automobile, allowed cross-county traffic to bypass the city, and expedited rapidly growing trucking. Such a system, however, had to adapt to the preexisting network of wagon roads, tackle the engineering challenges of the county's difficult topography, and not lose sight of the total costs.[20]

The Department of Public Works produced a remarkable countywide plan called the Major Highway Plan, often touted as the Ultimate Highway System Plan. Public Works set up a Plan Study Committee dominated by its own staff members and including Frederick Bigger, who advised the body. No member of the ACPC participated. At this moment at least, the presence of Bigger seemed to signal both the intent to plan comprehensively and cooperation between the county and the city. Completed in early 1925 after only seven months of deliberations, the plan reflected what Robert Fishman calls the "metropolitan tradition" in American planning by maintaining the centrality of downtown Pittsburgh in the region while encouraging the decentralization of population and industry with a proposed elaborate system of highways throughout the rural or less-developed periphery. Indeed, the weblike highway scheme of radials and belt loops bears a striking resemblance to the highway plan proposed four years later in the Regional Plan of New York and Its Environs, which many historians consider the apogee of metropolitanist planning.[21] Comprehensive in spatial coverage and anticipating growth for decades into the future, the county's plan must have excited the visionary impulses of Bigger.

The county's Major Highway Plan addressed the desired goals of alleviating congestion in the region's primary center and the suburbs. It recognized three classes of highways. Six riverside highways would provide major—that is, boulevard—access of "unbroken continuity" through the principal river valleys of the region. These boulevards would both move traffic of the industrial towns to and from Pittsburgh and bypass Pittsburgh via bridges at key intersecting points. Approximately twenty radial highways would reach out "spoke-like from Pittsburgh to the county boundary." The new radials anticipated mostly improving existing roads by straightening out curves, widening narrow lanes, and extensive grading, all for automobiles and increased volumes of traffic. The third class of roads revealed the vision of two "circuit," or "belt," highways, inner and outer loops that would connect the river and radial highways. This Ultimate Highway System would require dozens of bridges, including major structures to span the three rivers and largest tributary valleys, and many smaller ones over streams, creeks, and narrow hollows. Officially adopting this plan in the winter of 1925, the county had apparently taken an important step toward embracing the world of professional planning, despite the relatively weak position of the ACPC in the organization of county government.[22]

Politics, however, trumped the good intentions of the Major Highway Plan, influencing each year which elements of the plan were actually constructed.

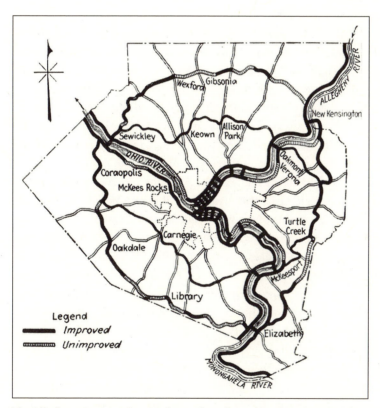

The Allegheny County Major Highway Plan of 1925. The plan created what was called the "Ultimate Highway System." *"Allegheny County Develops Ultimate Highway System Plan,"* Engineering News-Record 99, no. 15 (1927): 581.

The county Department of Public Works essentially used the ACPC for a stamp of approval, submitting construction schedules each year only weeks before surveys and road work had to begin for a successful construction season. Although ACPC members who were part-time, unpaid, and without much support staff generally approved the plans, the county commissioners who had final authority often overruled dissent on specific elements of the scheduled projects. Thus many highway projects and small bridges reflected political considerations rather than the guiding framework of the Major Highway Plan.[23]

Before bitter conflict within the Republican Party diminished construction progress in the early 1930s, the county succeeded in significantly upgrading its highway network, including several boulevards, and erecting a number of bridges, impressive both from architectural and engineering standpoints. The successful bond issue of 1928 extended this ambitious highway and bridge construction period under, at least theoretically, the still official countywide plan. The Democrats, after wresting power from the emaciated Republican machine in the second half of the 1930s, parlayed New Deal funds into completing more of the Ultimate Highway System. New highways such as the Ohio River Boulevard and the picturesque Allegheny River Boulevard, complete with scenic river overlooks, whisked traffic through the river valleys. The improved radial roads in tributary stream valleys encouraged residential suburban growth away from the traditional development areas located in the principal river valleys. Even some parts of the circumferential loops were built.

More remarkable than the highway development, however, was the bridge construction of the late 1920s and 1930s. Several of the more than 100 small and large bridges erected in these years added to the Pittsburgh region's renown for bridge design, engineering, and construction. The West End (1932) and McKees Rocks (1931) bridges over the Ohio River allowed traffic to bypass downtown, while the Three Sisters bridges over the Allegheny River (1926–1928), the Liberty Bridge (1927), and even the South Tenth Street Bridge (1933) from the South Side crossed directly into the downtown. Numerous other bridges, especially the Highland Park Bridge, the Westinghouse Memorial Bridge, and a few between steel towns of the Monongahela Valley such as the Homestead High Level and the Rankin bridges, completed the county building campaign.[24]

The county Department of Public Works, led by the aspirations and politics of the county commissioners, orchestrated the campaign. Although the original 1924 bond issue was attacked for the failure to consult adequately with the various interested agencies in the city and county, as well as with the

U.S. Army Corps of Engineers, the Department of Public Works did produce a grand scheme that contained the elements of a master plan to guide the transportation development. Because many of the projects, especially bridges, were in the city and because many highways connected to the city street plan, the county's penchant to often ignore its own Major Highway Plan strained relations with the CPC, which for a fleeting moment in the mid-1920s exuded an unusual sense of cooperation.

MOLE WORK

While Bigger occasionally cavorted with Lewis Mumford, Clarence Stein, and a few mildly "socialistic friends" in New Jersey, and while streaks of vision tinged planning ideology and illumined the planned Pittsburgh region landscape, to the joy of the city's business elite, Pittsburgh planning remained firmly grounded in Olmstedian practicality. Prominent city businessmen in Pittsburgh, as elsewhere in urban America, had overseen planning's birth in the city, and in 1923 it was Pittsburgh's business and civic elites who rightfully celebrated the success of planning in the city. In the early-twentieth-century struggle between tradition and modernity, between science and quackery, between "root, hog, or die" individualism and environmental mastery and control, and between haphazard and planned urban growth, business now stood tightly united with progressivism.

Indeed, business found the planning ethos that emerged in the 1920s quite palatable. This emergent culture of planning easily comported with the ethos of scientific management, economic regularization, and labor paternalism that pervaded mainstream corporate boardrooms during the 1920s. While still steeped in progressivism, planning in the 1920s had seemingly shed its zeal for social reform, especially the goal of engineering urban space to achieve greater social justice. Technical planners of the 1920s such as St. Louis's Harland Bartholomew and Pittsburgh's Fred Bigger prescribed zoning and comprehensive planning as a rational approach to urban development, as a sensible way to impose order on the chaotic mélange of streets and tortuous alleys that blocked the smooth flow of modern urban commerce. Business hailed planning's new scientific-bureaucratic bent. Influenced by the Chicago School of sociology where social scientists such as Robert Park, Ernest Burgess, Lewis Wirth, and Charles Merriam emphasized the immutability of the natural forces that shaped the complex, socially heterogeneous urban environment, planners in the 1920s contended that cities could be managed and regulated, but not structurally altered. Most practical planners readily admitted the social implications of regulating building heights, zoning, and reconfiguring transit routes; but they denied any power to use government to restructure the urban organism into a "Model of Christian Charity."[25]

Meanwhile, Bigger, like most planners, minded the details and never allowed his weekend vision making to impair his ability to assume a practical and solidly technical demeanor during the weekdays. Nor did his interest in community planning diminish his ardor for strong, corporately backed private sector planning that buttressed and defended the goals of the public sector. Out of this blend of diverse ideas and the energy derived from strong civic support for professional planning, Pittsburgh by the end of the decade built a public planning edifice that served as a model of city planning. And this edifice survived the revenue deprivation of the Great Depression and proved receptive to federal planning initiatives, including public housing.

Planning, to be sure, was one sector of government activity that during the ruggedly individualistic "New Era" won enthusiastic support from the city's business and professional leadership. And with Bigger, James D. Hailman, and Morris Knowles ensconced on the CPC, Howard Heinz presiding over county planning, and the JPC mediating intergovernmental planning decisions, private monitoring of public planning decisions effectively existed with or without an active watchdog agency.

Despite or because of this unqualified business support for planning and the new disciplinary order, public planning flourished in Pittsburgh during the 1920s. Yet unlike in Daniel Burnham's Chicago, widely envied for its parks, boulevards, and diagonal arteries, planners in Pittsburgh during the decade left a fairly modest physical legacy. Pittsburgh's monument to planning was less visible; it was sculpted ploddingly, but carefully, and only fully emerged at the end of the decade as the institutionalized edifice of city planning. Professionally, bureaucratically, and legally, Pittsburgh's CPC by 1929 had attained stature, legitimacy, and, most important, authority.

With Bigger at its helm, the CPC claimed the moral and scientific high ground in Pittsburgh's ongoing urban conversation about the centrality of comprehensive planning in all future decision making about boulevard expansion; the location of traffic arterials, park entrances, and civic centers; and other critical uses of urban space. As an agency, by 1923 it had existed longer than the ACPC; it was independent, and after 1922 the CPC had benefited from the tireless, unselfish service and leadership of Frederick Bigger. Albeit a modest, self-effacing personality, the nationally known Bigger served the commission as its in-house expert. First at Pittsburgh's Art Commission and then in the CPC, he had imbibed the heady wine of the City Beautiful movement and then plunged into the new realm of specialized knowledge called professional urban planning. It was a body of knowledge, a set of principles and values that he himself was helping codify. By 1923 a core of planning knowledge existed in the form of zoning ordinances, technical treatises, published articles, university courses, volumes of city plans such as Pittsburgh's six-part plan, and the proceedings of the National Conference on City Planning. Collectively, this corpus of plans, ordinances, articles, and other documents constituted the ethos, the curriculum, the scriptural foundation for planning certification, identity, and professionalism.[26]

Under Bigger's and James D. Hailman's leadership, the CPC forged a solid, self-confident professional urban planning organization that by the end of the 1920s ranked among the best in the United States. Its role in producing the 1923 city zoning ordinance and its position as the guardian and enforcer of the city plan elevated the commission's status and maneuvered it into the spotlight at the moment when the entire city desired and expected action on public improvements. Indeed, in 1923 several key items of the 1919 bond issue, including the subway system, the Boulevard of the Allies extension to Schenley Park, and the Liberty Bridge, remained unfinished. One year later Mayor Magee pressed for a new bond issue and entrusted the CPC with the complete study and planning for all the bond issue projects to be presented for the public's approval. This stance contrasted markedly with his 1910 bond issue, which for political reasons packaged improvements for rapid approval before Frederick Law Olmsted Jr. could complete his plan for the Pittsburgh Civic Commission. Magee, like the CCCP, a rabid backer of planning, now acknowledged that "successful preparation of [such] a study and plan . . . would probably involve enlarging the personnel among the city's engineering staff, and that an effective work arrangement between the Department of Public Works and the Planning Commission is essential."[27]

Although key members of the CPC in the 1920s spoke for vested city interests—Albert H. Burchfield for the Joseph Horne department store and other downtown retailers; A. J. Kelly and L. W. Monteverde for real estate; George S. Davison, James M. Clark, and E. W. Mudge for the Gulf Oil Corporation and the city's corporate establishment—others such as Bigger, Hailman, and Knowles steadfastly and rigorously promulgated the gospel of progressivism, that efficient, socially responsible urban development required a comprehensive viewpoint based upon the assembling and analysis of facts. This hardly obscured the conservative bent of planning conversationalists in the 1920s who strove to replace political expediency in land use decisions with scientific efficiency. Nor did it alter their determination to stabilize and protect established urban real estate values and achieve the most orderly and profitable uses of urban space. Planning historian Mansel Blackford contends that businessmen historically espoused professional planning because orderly urban growth addressed long-standing Chamber of Commerce concerns about traffic flow, congestion, urban blight, and the need to protect and strengthen residential neighborhoods.[28] Bolstered by this consensus, Pittsburgh's nine-member CPC and its Planning Department flourished in the 1920s. Accordingly, the CPC broadened its domain and, in turn, the Planning Department experienced significant increases in staff and budget. At first the commission's domain encompassed only zoning and jurisdiction over street, alley, and sidewalk widenings and openings, plus oversight of all plans of lots. Standing committees, including one for legislation, existed for each area. However, after the commission endorsed the CCCP's *Major Street* plan and Magee had ordered it to plan for the 1924 bond issue, the CPC created a new special standing committee, the General Plans Committee, headed for most of the decade by Bigger. Next to the Committee on Zoning, the General Plans Committee ranked highest in esteem; invariably either Knowles, Hailman, or Bigger, or all three, served on both of these key committees. The commission added three more standing committees during the course of the 1920s, one on procedures and publications, a committee on street names, and when in February 1927 Public Works transferred its shade tree work to the CPC, a Shade Tree Committee.[29]

Of the nine planning commission members, only the executive secretary, Bigger, earned a salary. Most of the commission's swelling budget funded the City Planning Department's growing staff, mounting supplies, and space demands. These rising costs and demands reflected the department's enlarged responsibilities after 1924 for making surveys of proposed major downtown street improvements and for its huge ongoing topographical mapping project. By 1928 major street planning alone occupied the full time of two staff members.[30]

Engineers continued to play key roles in city planning departments nationwide. U. N. Arthur, the department's chief engineer, headed a corps of engineers, draftsmen, and surveyors that by 1926 employed over seventy-five people full- and part-time. Not until 1928 did the staff for the first time include a "city planner" position, budgeted at an annual salary of $4,500. The commission's total budget, which in 1922 had been $55,000, soared to $185,000 in 1928, including $4,000 for an executive secretary, that is, Bigger's salary. Compare that with the 1928 county planning budget of only $52,240.[31]

Although engineers such as Hailman and Knowles continued to be prominent in the world of planning, Bigger and his commission professionals worked assiduously to separate and distinguish planning from engineering and public works. Professional planners believed that, being immersed in the quotidian world of the material and physical sciences, in mechanics, and in slide rules and logarithms, engineers reasoned project by project, one street and one bridge at a time, not comprehensively. Engineers ideally executed projects only after planners had assured that the project's site and design conformed to the city plan. Bigger's insistence that a "planner" be hired in the department underscored this concern.[32] The commission's determination to define itself and its work apart from public works, and its drive to professionally divorce itself from engineering, originated as early as 1921 when it sponsored the annual meeting of the National Conference on City Planning. After 1921, at the invitation of either Flavel Shurtleff of the National Conference on City Planning or John Nolen of the American City Planning Institute, the commission faithfully dispatched Bigger, Hailman, Arthur, or Knowles to these national meetings held in Baltimore; Fort Worth, Texas; Detroit; and other cities. In 1923 the commission carted three large sections of its zone map to exhibit at the fifteenth annual meeting of the National Conference on City Planning in Philadelphia.[33] Bigger made the Pittsburgh CPC a charter member in 1926 of the Pennsylvania Association of Planning Commissions, and three years later Knowles addressed the association on "Making a Regional Plan Effective."[34]

The CPC proudly flaunted its *Major Street* plan and other general planning work. These were the headlined activities that kept it fully engaged as a leading voice in the urban conversation and thus a critical voice in shaping the modern city. Ironically, it committed most of its budget and staff time to what historian William H. Wilson branded, perhaps unfairly, as "mole" activities. In Pittsburgh, as in other American cities, mole work involved the laborious procedure of studying and approving subdivision or lot plans; surveying and accepting plans for street openings and widenings, sidewalk installations, and other public works; conducting the topographical mapping of every square inch of Pittsburgh land; and dealing with the constant stream of appeals for zoning variances.[35]

Zoning work consumed endless department time. Individuals, businessmen and women, and venerable institutions alike requested the city to rezone lots from residential to industrial, or, in the case of the University of Pittsburgh, begged to exceed the city's height limits for architect Charles Z. Klauder's projected fifty-two-story design of the university's Cathedral of Learning.

(The Cathedral of Learning finally topped out at forty-two stories, or 525 feet.) These entreaties regularly bombarded the Pittsburgh City Council, which forthwith referred them to the Zoning Commission's Board of Appeals.[36] The CPC staff, however, was forced to investigate each appeal and recommend approval or disapproval. Although an ardent friend of zoning, Bigger resented this burden. Only three months after passage of the Pittsburgh zoning ordinance in 1923, Bigger complained that zoning issues deflected the commission's attention away from the real task of planning, and that during that time "the commission's staff had served the Board of Appeals to the detriment of the Commission." Significantly, in 1911 "practical-minded" Frederick Law Olmsted Jr. had warned the young city planning profession that it must take the broad view and not get bogged down in planning minutiae.[37]

But zoning comprised merely one of the commission's "routine matters." Both the CPC and ACPC staffs worked with city Department of Public Works engineers to approve city ordinances opening, widening, and fixing the widths of roadways such as the Boulevard of the Allies and adjoining sidewalks; the department also established the grades of myriad streets and roadways, and dedicated or vacated others.[38] Approving the plats for hundreds of new city and suburban subdivisions, or the siting and design of modern bridges and tunnels, more than preoccupied planners. Other routine tasks occupied the planning staff in the 1920s. These included the long and costly triangulation and topographical survey launched by the city in 1923. This survey employed a corps of surveyors and chainmen. Highly recommended by Frederick Law Olmsted Jr. in his 1911 report, this city survey and another one launched by the county spanned the 1920s and the 1930s and represented a planning tour de force that provided the critical body of data for general planning.[39] These lot plans, zoning ordinances, and survey work comprised the critical triad that, according to Constance Perrin, enabled city planning departments to "keep everything in its place."[40]

BUILDING THE LEGAL EDIFICE

While the CPC's visionary planning for the Crosstown Thoroughfare rivaled in importance its routine business of processing zoning appeals, approving lot plans, and undertaking street surveys, ultimately nothing loomed of greater significance during the 1920s than forging the commission's legitimacy and consolidating its legal and bureaucratic authority over urban land use decisions. Emboldened by its powerful base of support in such organizations as the CCCP, the Civic Club of Allegheny County (CCAC), and the Chamber of

Commerce, and by the resonance of planning generally in the continuing urban conversation, the CPC had embarked in the early 1920s to solidify and
broaden its legal powers, and distinguish itself from other city agencies and
the ACPC. That both mayors Babcock and Magee championed "real" planning
and regularly met with the commission greatly enhanced the agency's stature.
In fact, planning was increasingly viewed as the starting point for any conversation about future city development, a point made clear in 1924 when Magee
conferred with the commission about "preparing a program of city development, emphasizing the importance of making a real city planning study [in
preparation for] a bond issue six or twelve months hence."[41]

Enabling legislation in 1911 for planning had specifically empowered the
commission to approve or disapprove lot plans; but the act had hinted at some
more vague general authority over land use decisions. Seizing the opportunity,
the commission demanded that the city council recognize its broader authority over land use, an authority that between 1919 and 1921 embraced approval
of building permits, especially garage construction. The 1921 court case denying the commission veto power over building permits (*Coyne v. Pritchard*)
stalled, but only temporarily, the commission's momentum.[42]

The CPC sought not only to define and enlarge its powers but also to carefully differentiate itself from the county Department of Public Works, the
agency that in effect owned county planning. Throughout the 1920s, the CPC
zealously, often militantly, guarded its independence from the county Public Works Department. The department, protested Bigger in a discussion of
projected riverfront improvements in 1926, merely constructed the projects
that his commission planned. Commission engineers met regularly with their
counterparts at Public Works, but, implored Bigger, they met as equals, not
as servants.[43] The CPC highly prized both its cherished independence and its
professionalism, and for this reason, despite the work of the JPC, it never regarded the ACPC as an equal partner, a fact that would prove to be a serious
problem for planning in the region.[44]

None of this movement to enlarge the CPC's power and authority happened
accidentally. After 1923 the commission's Legal Procedure and Legislation Committee, aided by the assistant city solicitor, pressed the offensive. Prior to the
widely acclaimed 1926 U.S. Supreme Court decision upholding zoning in the
case of *Village of Euclid (Ohio) v. Ambler Realty Company*, challenges to the city's
1923 zoning ordinance taxed the commission's legal and staff time. However,
creating a zoning Board of Appeals considerably lessened the commission's legal burden while enhancing its power. Likewise, a 1927 supplement to the state's

City Planning Enabling Act officially creating the Department of City Planning both fully legitimized and financially secured the commission's chief arm for carrying out planning. Department personnel, as we have noted, provided the foot soldiers of the planning army. The state legislature had first strengthened the power of the unofficial planning department in 1923 when it ordered that no building parcel could be sold until a lot plan had been approved by the commission and officially recorded. In 1925 a City Planning Enabling Act firmed the department's legal grip by clarifying the commission's jurisdictional powers over lot plans and street openings.[45]

Although private sector organizations, politicians, and corporate elites still joined in the conversation, the CPC commanded a place near the head of the table. Evidence of this broadened public authority to promulgate a vision of orderly urban growth as articulated in the city plan fills the agency's records. The commission, for example, balked when officials of the University of Pittsburgh in 1923 importuned the commission for approval to build a giant athletic stadium in Oakland. In denying the petition, the commission reproached the university for supplying insufficient evidence that the stadium project had been fully studied. University officials, argued Bigger, had failed to site the stadium in careful relationship to the Oakland "Street System," and accordingly, the commission refused to consider any further stadium proposals until the university met planning commission demands for "comprehensiveness." The university revised its plans, and the stadium was finally built in 1925.[46]

In the 1923 stadium case, CPC commissioners had courageously jousted with a prominent city institution; a year later they tilted with one of Pittsburgh's mightiest families, the Heinzes. In 1924 the Heinz family towered in social and civic elite circles. Henry J. Heinz, the scion, had died in 1919, and his heirs, Howard, a member of the ACPC, and siblings, Clifford Heinz and Irene Given, were unwilling to reside at the family's baronial, Olmsted-landscaped Penn Avenue estate, called "Greenlawn." They chose to demolish the mansion and subdivide the block-sized parcel as the "Meade Place Plan of Lots." The plan featured a newly created Meade Street penetrating halfway into the lot and terminating in a cul-de-sac. Again, as in the stadium case, the commission vetoed the plan. In a verdict encapsulating the essence of the planning gospel of the 1920s, Bigger wrote the Heinzes that "the proposed dead-end street called 'Meade Place' . . . is in the line of what must, through the operation of the forces which make for the growth of the city and determine the flow of traffic, become an important traffic thoroughfare and . . . it is the duty of the Planning Commission to foresee such changes . . . to prevent . . . the imposition of any conditions that will make it either impossible or difficult to later effect . . . traffic movement."[47]

The Heinz family protested that, contrary to the commission's assertion, the cul-de-sac constituted a private right-of-way, not a public thoroughfare that was part of the street system. Indeed, cutting Meade Street directly through the Heinz family estate—as the planning commission desired—constituted a legal "taking," and entitled the family to the payment of damages. But these were the early days of public planning when advocates—even the apostolic Bigger—dreaded the monstrous serpents that might rise from the depths of uncharted legal seas. The city's solicitor, Thomas Benner, feared that the Heinz family might make a "test case" out of the Meade Place Plan and advised that "should [the commission's] actions be reversed . . . the commission's power regarding plans [would] be limited if not emasculated." Bigger and the commission reluctantly but tactfully retreated; however, during the two-year legal duel with Heinz family lawyers, the commission aggressively challenged nineteenth-century laissez-faire land use practice by forcefully asserting the primacy of public over private rights in the disposition of land.[48]

The commission won its next battle with the city's elite. Pittsburgh, like Philadelphia, Baltimore, and Charleston, South Carolina, with roots in the eighteenth century, preserved a number of ancient, narrow streets and alleys, artifacts of preindustrialism. However, these dark and narrow pathways, nestled in the heart of the city and bearing delightful names such as Cherry Way and Strawberry Way, were often lined with law offices and wholesaling establishments, quaint taverns and specialty shops. The owners of this valuable real estate—corporations, title companies, estates, banks, and old, prominent families—joined with the city's Better Traffic Committee to promote a "through route from the eastern end suburbs to the North Side" of the city. The project involved widening Strawberry Way and extending it northward via a widened Eighth Street and a new North Side bridge. The new thoroughfare would then run eastward onto either Fifth Avenue or Forbes Avenue. A widened Strawberry Way, proclaimed the project boosters, would expose presently dark, alleylike interior lots to profitable development and enlarge city tax revenues.

The idea of widening Strawberry Way stirred a planning brouhaha, one that unfolded in a classic, albeit occasionally acerbic, conversation about how city form should evolve, and whether public or private interests should prevail. Bigger scorned the idea for its impact on traffic circulation and inveighed against it in several reports. In one lengthy assault, he dissected it intersection by intersection, traffic snarl by traffic snarl. His brutal deconstruction aside, Bigger mainly excoriated the idea's challenge to the commission's newly minted general plan for a Crosstown Thoroughfare, which led from the new Liberty Bridge to Bigelow Boulevard for access to the East End, or for access to the North Side across the Allegheny River. Therefore Bigger viewed the Better Traffic Committee's Strawberry Way design as egregiously intrusive and a wanton assertion of private over pubic interest, the antithesis of good planning.[49]

The CPC's efforts to adhere to principle in the Meade Place case, its demand that the University of Pittsburgh stadium plan conform to the city's general plans, and its assertion that downtown business interests yield to the larger civic good of the Inter-District Traffic Circuit, or for another example, that the city's 1925–1926 Allegheny wharf development plans respect the Flood Commission and the 1924 *Waterways* plans, all attest to the emergence by 1929 of a planning ethos and the Pittsburgh CPC as the arbiter and chief architect of urban form. Guided by Bigger and Hailman (who died in 1930), Pittsburgh planning had matured by 1929, bureaucratically, legally, and politically, from a gangly assortment of civic types closeted in Mayor Babcock's office to mull over a proposed bond issue, to a body of self-assured professionals firmly rooted statutorily and confident that a decade of organization building and experience had conferred respect and authority over urban form. However, despite planning's public and private support, and despite the entrenchment of the planning ethos in Pittsburgh, as the next chapter makes clear, serious obstacles thwarted the planners' goal of replacing drift with mastery in the ordering of urban space.[50]

CHAPTER 6

The Limitations of Planning

FREDERICK BIGGER, the Citizens Committee on the City Plan (CCCP), and the entire planning community in Pittsburgh, took justifiable pride in their accomplishments by 1929. Not only had a legal framework been solidly erected, including city and county planning laws and a city zoning ordinance, but tunnels, bridges, parks and parkways, and plans for a regional highway system and a sophisticated Inter-District Traffic Circuit all attested to the praiseworthy physical achievement of planning in Pittsburgh.

While this planning record, matched in many other cities, attested to the vitality of planning in Pittsburgh during the 1920s, it is often overshadowed historically by another salient fact: despite urban planning's emphasis on solving the horrible conundrum of traffic gridlock, automobile traffic problems worsened rather than improved during the decade, and that failure alone raised troubling questions about the limitations of city planning. In this chapter we explore those limitations: the city's topography-imposed spatial fragmentation, the entrenched legacies of laissez-faire and privatism, the jurisdictional frictions between city and county, public sector versus private sector, and the enormous cost of reshaping an industrial city built for pedestrians and horse-drawn traffic into a modern, machine-age metropolis.[1]

Early-twentieth-century cities like Pittsburgh faced a gigantic dual task of absorbing the high tide of rural and foreign immigration and at the same time dealing with the crush of trolleys, carts, wagons, trucks, automobiles, and pedestrians competing for room on narrow downtown streets designed to accommodate nineteenth-century traffic. Pittsburgh's growing volume of automobile and motor truck traffic merely compounded the problem. Pittsburghers long ago ceased to view the city's tangle of narrow streets and alleyways as quaint social space useful for convivial social intercourse, parades, and protest that had marked the plebeian culture of the nineteenth-century walking city. By 1900 more than 337 miles of streetcar tracks existed in the city. Many occupied the center of downtown streets, leaving barely enough room for automobiles to squeeze between the streetcar and the curb. Unwary passengers exiting or entering transit vehicles risked their lives.[2]

Between 1910 and 1929 automobile registrations rose 8,000 percent in Allegheny County, from 1,601 to 203,866, despite, according to historian Joel Tarr, the greater proclivity of Pittsburghers commuters to ride streetcars. Many other historians have explored the early-twentieth-century growth of automobile use and how the private car eclipsed urban mass transit. Scott Bottles's study of the rise of automobility in Los Angeles, like Paul Barrett's of Chicago and Mark Foster's of Philadelphia, challenges the theory that profit-seeking automobile moguls savaged urban transit systems. By tracing the deep, well-earned animosity of Angelenos for the Los Angeles railway system, Bottles, for example, implicates mass transit in its own downfall.[3]

While Pittsburgh was closer in size to Los Angeles than to broad-shouldered Chicago in the period 1900–1930, Pittsburgh's history of mass transit versus the automobile differed little from either of these larger metropolises. Pittsburgh civic leaders battled an overcapitalized and fiscally handcuffed transit conglomeration that was no less demonized by infuriated half-frozen, strap-hanging Pittsburghers than was Los Angeles's system by warmer but no less choleric Angelenos. Tarr stresses that while Pittsburgh's social and physical topography restrained the kind of massive abandonment of mass transit in favor of the automobile that Los Angeles experienced, automobile usage in Pittsburgh still rose during World War I and, as it did in other cities, soared in the 1920s. Therefore, between 1920 and 1929 Pittsburgh planners, like their colleagues across America, grappled with mounting traffic volumes and automobile-clogged streets.[4]

In an earlier chapter, we hinted that revamping urban-industrial space for automobile use consumed excessive planning time. Approving hundreds of plans for residential garages, automobile showroom palaces, and service stations occupied many harried planners; others worked on planning new bridges, curbs, new and widened streets, and roadway resurfacing, while still others planned parking lots, boulevards, and parkways. All of this planning offered ad hoc solutions to the perceived traffic crisis; by the end of the decade, however, all had failed. Pittsburgh had unflinchingly instituted planning; the planning fraternity had declared victory; yet by 1929 the patently robust planning movement had failed to solve either the signal challenge of the automobile or the bane of sheer urban-industrial ugliness that blemished Pittsburgh's reputation. Indeed, just three years later, Clarence Stein, who had been in Pittsburgh planning Chatham Village for the Buhl Foundation, in a letter to his wife, Aline, assailed the Steel City as "God-forsaken." He described a "barren valley with a few forlorn wooden shacks . . . extravagant bridges [leading] into the smoke of ugly factories and dilapidated slums." He decried "the engineering waste of bridges, highways, tunnels." "And to think that my friend Fred Bigger," he wrote Aline, "has been devoting the best years of his life to making this mess and labeling it *city planning!* Why don't people know when to quit?"[5]

What was wrong here? Clearly, other factors beyond skyrocketing traffic volumes limited the planners' ability to comprehensively and effectively confront congested streets or, for that matter, appreciably improve the city's unsightly urban environment. In truth, the Pittsburgh conversation about planning struggled with historic choices endemic to democracies, between drift versus mastery, spontaneity versus control, freedom versus order. Ironically, planning disciplinarians, backed by civic elites, sought to harness the same exuberant capitalistic forces that had sculpted the urban metropolis and the metropolitan tradition replete with its brand of vibrant civic life that planners coveted. Likewise, housers in the name of public health and "making better citizens" challenged a housing system that, while breeding excrescent slums, had allowed immigrants to survive by taking in boarders and doubling their premises as dram and sweatshops.[6]

Therefore, contrary voices and towering obstacles existed. Indeed, despite Bigger's indefatigable exertions and the toiling of the CCCP, and despite the enthusiastic and unwavering support given planning by the Chamber of Commerce, this was a "New Era" philosophically opposed to the regulatory mood of the Progressive Era. Accordingly, while in praise of planning, businessmen reacted warily to planning schemes perceived as trampling on private property rights. Historian Roy Lubove, in fact, espied an entrenched "tradition of limited government" at work in Pittsburgh, the same tradition that urban historian Sam Bass Warner labeled "privatism" in his seminal study of Philadelphia. Likewise, social and political parochialism still reigned in the 1920s. Small city neighborhoods and suburban township communities, highly particularistic and with deeply seated class and ethnic attachments, distrusted and strenuously resisted the expertise of elites bodies such as the CCCP or the City Planning Commission (CPC) that represented the authority of centralized government.[7]

Pittsburgh's topography posed another obstacle to planning in the 1920s. For Bigger, the city's irregular contours of hills, hollows, and valleys not only increased the cost of building infrastructure but also splintered the region geographically into isolated districts aggravating class and ethnic particularism and fostering local rather than metropolitan or regional political ties. Fragmented urban space spawned fragmented government. In the planning realm itself, the CPC competed for authority with, among others, Allegheny County Planning Commission (ACPC), the Flood Commission, the city Department of Public Works, and the Traffic Commission. Finally, as in New York, Cincinnati, and other cities, Pittsburgh planners confronted an embedded speculative tradition. Real estate interests promoted taller buildings in the downtown and sprawling subdivisions in the suburbs. While city and county planning records speak little about the role of office developers or "community builders" in shaping Pittsburgh planning decisions, nevertheless prominent realtors like L. W. Monteverde sat on city and county planning boards, and in designing downtown streets, particularly the Inter-District Traffic Circuit, planning interests clashed with speculator interests every day. Such limitations, no matter how serious, failed to stifle the planning impulse ignited by Bigger and the CCCP in 1918; however, these limitations impeded the crucial process of updating the city's comprehensive plan (the so-called template by which planners judiciously measured the progress of city development) and obstructed key projects that were under way, many involving traffic circulation, the most vexing problem facing planners in the interwar years.[8]

BIGGER'S PERSPECTIVE

Throughout the 1920s, Pittsburgh's Frederick Bigger, while fully attentive to the details of planning, ardently orchestrated the city's comprehensive plan. Although a true evangelist of planning—and customarily effusive about the discipline's prospects—Bigger occasionally plunged the urban conversation into realms of cynicism, even despair. It was Bigger who bore the main responsibility for conveying the image that planning in Pittsburgh had failed during the Progressive Era. A professional's professional, and as intolerant of dilettantism as he was the messiness of the democratic process, Bigger on numerous occasions vented his frustration—sometimes in written form—about the limitations of the planning process. But he never allowed cynicism or frustration to obfuscate reason. Instead, he articulated a clear, consistent argument about systemic obstacles to effective comprehensive planning. This critique affords a useful theoretical perspective on the limitations of planning in the 1920s.[9]

To begin, Bigger, like many progressive critics of the urban political milieu, especially those in the Regional Planning Association of America (RPAA) such as Benton MacKaye and Fred Ackerman, assailed cities in general for being "primarily dedicated to doing business." Absent a broader "social perspective," reasoned Bigger, private pecuniary interests rather than the commonweal (the so-called public good) guided urban development decisions and forged a pernicious nexus between politicians and land speculators.[10] According to Bigger, opportunistic politicians used public improvement projects such as new streets and playgrounds to appeal to the "narrow local interests" of an unenlightened citizenry. Politically motivated compromises and accommodation, not the expertise of competent planning technicians, governed crucial land use decisions. On the contrary, "competent technicians," argued Bigger, "refuse[d] to remain in public office and withdr[e]w to private professional practice, or, if they remain, they accomplish relatively little because of the strictures placed upon them by their political supervisors—the latter acting for their own interest or on behalf of the special interest of selfish citizens." "Selfishness," added Bigger, "will always resist those restrictions of its privilege . . . [resulting] from the adoption of more orderly and more scientific procedures."[11]

Although engineers formed the inner circle of the planning fraternity, Bigger excluded them from the hallowed sphere of technical and planning competence. He regarded engineers as scientifically trained people, but too narrowly educated and project oriented to comprehend the city organically, to fathom the ecological mosaic of social and economic space connecting workplaces, residences, and recreation. Lacking that organic perspective, engineers perpetuated the haphazard "automatic extension of [piecemeal urban] development block by block."[12]

Topography exacerbated the region's political provincialism and greed, and in Bigger's mind underscored the need for comprehensive planning. Pittsburgh's half a million city dwellers occupied the heart of a complex hill-and-valley-riven metropolitan region embracing over a million people. In the 1920s foreign-born and second-generation ethnic families comprised almost half of the urban population. This immigrant generation, observed Bigger, "tend[ed] to live in groups according to [their] nationality," a tendency, he continued, "which combined with classifications of an economic character [is] intensified by Pittsburgh's serried topography." Superimposed on all this, charged Bigger "is a political system and customs making it possible for the inferior politician to 'play off' one district against another [thus] creat[ing] an insistent demand for simplification and coordination."[13]

The hills and valleys also carved Allegheny County and the larger Pittsburgh region generally into countless townships, boroughs, and other civil jurisdictions, adding to the serious problem of fragmented leadership. At one level, borough and township conceits and rivalries frustrated coordinated city and countywide highway projects; at another—city versus county—issues of professionalism, the division of financial responsibility, and jurisdictional matters kept county and city planners at loggerheads, despite the existence of the Joint Planning Conference (JPC).[14]

Within the city proper, neighborhood and organizational interests collided. In addition to the mayor, the city council, the CPC, and Department of Public Works, a host of other organizations, including the Flood Commission, Chamber of Commerce, and Henry Burchfield's Water Street and Lower Downtown Improvement Association, pressed often narrow and conflicting development plans and programs in the 1920s.[15]

Bigger tirelessly decried political compromisers, along with the eviscerating forces of fragmentation and those who voiced disdain for technical competence. Simultaneously, he nurtured a progressive's inveterate optimism about the ultimate triumph of knowledge and reason over shameful ignorance. However, Bigger harbored less hope for surmounting what he viewed, somewhat cynically, as the fundamental problem confronting the planning profession. Writing in 1925, Bigger observed that his "examination of current city planning indicat[ed] that there are important and determining factors beyond the province of the city planner," which, feared Bigger, meant that *present city planning consists of attempts to contrive results without having any adequate control over causes* [emphasis added]." "Obvious[ly]," contended Bigger, "planning for the future development of any community cannot be done in a permanent way when one part of the community [the private sector] is constantly changing and thereby creating a demand for the changing of another part [the public part] especially when the non-public land retained the function of changing use and of accommodating an ever-increasing number of persons on it." For example, explained Bigger, "street widening encourages an increase of vehicular traffic; more traffic increases property values . . . ; increased property values encourage the owner to erect higher and more bulky buildings; the buildings hold more people and, for this and other reasons, attract more traffic and cause a demand for further street widenings or for subways and thoroughfares; the street widenings or the subway is provided and again property values rise." Bigger averred that city planning would remain futile so long as planners lacked control over the causes of "fluid conditions," so long as they could not control the distribution and density of the population and the shifting and changing and greater intensification of land use, whether it be for homes, businesses, industry, or other purposes.[16] Therefore, as the eternally progressive, but increasingly cynical, Bigger concluded, planners would endlessly produce "form without substance" until public power increased at the expense of private, until cities secured greater control over land than presently afforded by too easily amended zoning laws.[17]

Curiously, Bigger's 1920s sermons on the limitation of planning rarely addressed the soaring capital costs of urban improvements. Yet in addition to the issues of political opportunism, unenlightened engineers, and the agony of an uneducated deluded populace, which, according to Bigger, undermined planning goals, the excessive cost of improvements posed an ever-present constraint. The high price tag for reshaping the nineteenth-century urban landscape, of grappling with what Sam Bass Warner called "the inheritance of the past," and the cost of borrowing forced cities to move circumspectly. Cities historically floated bonds to pay for municipal improvements; keeping bond ratings high, and therefore the cost of borrowing low, forced cities to prudently limit bonded indebtedness.

Pittsburgh's gargantuan $20,000,000 bond issue at the beginning of the decade had stretched the city's borrowing limit. Mayor William Magee in 1922 lamented that Pittsburgh's enfeebled borrowing power compelled the city to delay many necessary street, sewer, and other vital improvements. Undoubtedly, the city's shallow pockets explain the crucial importance of city-county collaboration—no matter how strained—on major highway and bridge projects. Furthermore, widening city streets and clearing away warehouses and rail, ice, and coal yards to make way for a bridge approach, a viaduct, or town hall project involved costly property acquisitions. Cost, rather than the planners' best technical judgment, frequently determined whether a main thoroughfare such as Penn Avenue in the built-up Point Breeze section would be widened to six or eight lanes.[18]

THE BANE OF TRAFFIC CONGESTION

The lawyers, architects, physicians, bankers, and other professionals and businessmen who assembled in Pittsburgh's paneled offices to converse about the city's future exhorted city planners to surmount the limitations of cost, fragmented politics, and privatism especially those that imperiled the downtown. During the 1920s, Pittsburgh, like Chicago, Philadelphia, Los Angeles, and other big cities, faced a traffic problem that threatened to paralyze the specialized modern central business district. Already in the 1920s, the urban "nest egg," the heart of urban finance, insurance, real estate, advertising, marketing, and retail sales, and the vortex of an increasingly complex urban and interurban transportation system, staggered beneath the weight of mushrooming automobile traffic that rendered impassible nineteenth-century streets designed for carts, wagons, and pedestrians.[19]

Pittsburgh's topography confined the city's downtown building to a meager 255-acre parcel, the so-called Golden Triangle formed by the confluence of the Monongahela, Allegheny, and Ohio rivers, from the Hill District to the city's historic Point. Prior to 1910 only one downtown street, the sixty-foot-wide Liberty Avenue, exceeded forty feet in width, and the heavy railroad traffic of the Pennsylvania Railroad on that street made it dirty, deafening, and treacherous.[20] In fact, public streets accounted for fewer than sixty acres of downtown land. Only Bigelow Boulevard served as a main thoroughfare penetrating the populated East End. Congestion was chronic. With street railways crowding the center of most downtown streets, and carriages, drays, carts, and other horse-drawn vehicles battling for the remaining space, scant room existed in 1910 for Allegheny County's 1,601 registered "motor cars."[21]

Although Frederick Law Olmsted Jr. had considered the automobile in his 1911 *Main Thoroughfares* plan, traffic flow on the city's highways and byways remained problematic in the 1920s. In fact, Bion J. Arnold's important 1910 report, *The Pittsburgh Transportation Problem,* ignored the automobile.[22] World War I, however, witnessed automobiles vying with streetcars in the tangle of jammed downtown streets, and the panaceas for solving gridlock—in Pittsburgh and other cities—included widened and double-decked streets, and alternate side and other parking restrictions, in addition to mass transit. Between 1911 and 1919 in the first phase of Pittsburgh's war against traffic congestion, city engineers had widened many downtown streets; the city had hacked sixteen feet off the notoriously steep Grant's Hill and eliminated numerous dangerous grade crossings. Furthermore, it commenced building the Boulevard of the Allies linking the downtown to suburban Oakland.[23]

By the 1920s the traffic problem dominated the civic agenda. Henry Ford's gleaming black Tin Lizzies jockeyed for room on Pittsburgh's narrow, horse-and-buggy-vintage downtown streets. Rising traffic volumes rivaled other disconcerting features of the car culture, including gasoline and service stations (often dangerously situated curbside affairs that in addition obstructed traffic) as well as glitzy automobile showrooms, ugly and obtrusive private garages, and a plague of parked cars, along with a contagion of billboard advertising that, complained the Civic Club of Allegheny County (CCAC), plastered every available

Diamond Street in 1928. Typical traffic congestion in downtown involved a mélange of parked cars, trolleys, moving vehicles, and pedestrians. *Pittsburgh City Photographer Collection, Archives Service Center, University of Pittsburgh.*

inch of street and roadsides with eye-offending broadsides hawking beer, chewing gum, and tobacco. For the CCCP and the Chamber of Commerce, whose new downtown headquarters opened in 1917, and for other downtown-based bodies such as the Ferry Street (now Stanwix) and Downtown Triangle Association, the city's very future hinged on unsnarling the traffic mess and discharging a steady, smooth flow of traffic into and out of the central business district. Businessmen like the Chamber's president, George Wallace, railed against the economic cost of traffic congestion, in lost time and lost business. Cy Hungerford's cartoons, which regularly appeared in the CCCP's *Progress,* lampooned the Golden Triangle as a house packed with incorrigible, bawling brats labeled Fifth Avenue, Fourth Avenue, Liberty Avenue, and Smithfield Street. Another portrayed an able, reliable, hardworking laborer and his family, their car marked "destination Cleveland," packed and poised to escape the Steel City for the modern highways of the City by the Lake.[24]

Pa Pitt: "Gosh! Look What Happened While I Was Asleep!"
From PROGRESS, January, 1921

Cy Hungerford's 1921 cartoon for the CCCP's publication, *Progress*. Hungerford's
cartoon highlights the tangle of traffic that gridlocked Pittsburgh's tightly compacted
downtown. Progress *(January 1921).*

   As the first step in the modernization process, that is, the retrofitting of the
city to accommodate the new automobile technology, businessmen lobbied for
the Boulevard of the Allies to be extended to Schenley Park and the East End
neighborhoods, declaring that the project "afford[ed] the greatly needed relief to traffic." Likewise they promoted the construction of the long-discussed
Liberty Bridge and Tunnel, as well as the Ferry Street Bridge and Tunnel (after
World War II, reincarnated as the Fort Pitt Tunnel). Both projects aspired to
reduce central city traffic congestion while simultaneously ensuring the economic and cultural centrality of the downtown. All of these county projects,

including the West End and McKees Rocks bridges, won ardent support from both city and suburban business interests, but none of these frequently proclaimed solutions to the traffic problem excited greater interest and more vehement support than that of ridding city streets of surface railway cars and building a Pittsburgh subway. Indeed, Mayor Edward Babcock's $10,000,000 subway loop had glittered as the centerpiece of Pittsburgh's gigantic $20,000,000 bond issue in 1919.[25]

THE SUBWAY SAGA

Proposals for rapid transit had rattled around American city halls since the turn of the century. Subway schemes, or, where deemed more cost effective, plans for elevated rapid transit, both classic examples of special purpose planning, fermented amid Pittsburgh's progressive reform. Rapid transit advocates frequently appealed to the republican/egalitarian credo embraced by the disciples of single-taxer Henry George, whose following proved quite sizable in late-nineteenth- and early-twentieth-century Pittsburgh. As opposed to elevated systems, whose infrastructure darkened city streets and whose trains spewed smoke and soot, subways, contended apostles like Bion J. Arnold, promised clean, cheap, rapid transportation that would whisk working-class families to good, affordable housing built on the modestly priced land accessible on the urban periphery. Calls for publicly owned subways fittingly capped crusades for civic virtue, in which reform mayors such as Pittsburgh's George Guthrie overthrew boodling political bosses tied to corrupt machine-controlled traction magnates. Where—as in Pittsburgh—victory over the boodlers played less a role in the subway mania, private traction companies like the Pittsburgh Railways Company (PRC) touted the subway as a means of luring back disgruntled middle-class commuters.[26]

Pittsburgh's transit system differed little from either the Los Angeles shambles that Scott Bottles describes or Philadelphia's early-twentieth-century transit combine. The PRC, whose ownership lay enshrouded within a Philadelphia holding company, had emerged by 1902 as a consolidation of forty previously competing railway companies. Although the merger restored an illusion of sanity to the city's ruinously competitive traction industry, it also burdened the new, heavily overcapitalized company with excessive debt, especially since the merger brought into the traction system hundreds of leaseholders (called "underliers") whose property—railway cars, warehouses, and offices—was rented at guaranteed rates. The need to maintain hundreds of miles of right-of-way, and millions of dollars of infrastructure, and still show a profit sufficient enough to raise additional capital, forced the PRC both to increase fares and to delay improvements. Trolley passengers complained of endless waits and of frigid, overcrowded cars in which hundreds of sullen, indignant, strap-clutching commuters daily stood, crammed tightly together, cold and miserable.[27]

With bossism in retreat in 1909, the Pittsburgh Survey findings in print, and Olmsted Jr.'s planning study under way, the city chose civil engineer and transportation expert Bion J. Arnold to study the Pittsburgh transit situation. Arnold's 1910 report to Mayor William Magee on "the Pittsburgh transportation problem" excoriated the PRC for elevating "profit over service." Arnold's report described mile after mile of bad track, and bad paving "so dilapidated . . . as to be a serious impediment to vehicle traffic"; he found cars and other equipment "so inefficient as compared to more modern types that the continued use cannot be justified." Arnold branded the underliers whose rents formed a first lien against the revenues of the company as the problem, and argued that transit service in Pittsburgh would continue to be unsatisfactory until this leaseholder debt was canceled and the system reorganized and realistically capitalized. In typical progressive parlance, Arnold declared "adequate service . . . [to be] first in importance," and toward that goal recommended "public control" of city transit. His final recommendations seemed modest. To provide more efficient, better service, Pittsburgh should adopt a through-route—as opposed to a loop—surface transit system. Arnold called for greater ease in the use of transfers and, finally, affirmed that, for Pittsburgh, "subways will in the course of time, become desirable and even necessary."[28]

While Arnold's subway endorsement lacked fervor, the idea gained momentum especially after a private New York firm, the Pittsburgh Subway Company, in 1912 successfully lobbied the city council for a franchise. Only Magee's opposition to a private subway proposal that advertised ten-cent fares blocked the New York company's efforts. Four years later, in 1916, the city council created an Office of City Transit Commissioner and appointed Pittsburgh engineer Edwin K. Morse as transit commissioner. The city council gave Morse a year to produce a subway report.[29] Morse's richly detailed 1917 report investigated both the subway and the congestion issues. According to Morse, mounting congestion dictated a publicly owned subway in Pittsburgh, combined with the through-route design suggested by Arnold. Morse emphatically opposed a loop subway system, which he contended would only exacerbate congestion. Like Arnold, he called for a reorganized surface transportation system that included widened downtown streets, strict parking regulations, and a prohibition on downtown automobile parking during rush hours.[30]

Transit Commissioner Morse's enthusiastic endorsement of a Pittsburgh subway joined Arnold's tepid one collecting dust on the city's shelves. A year later, in 1918, with the debt-ridden PRC plunged into receivership, with the guns finally silent in Europe, and with city improvements uppermost on the public agenda, Mayor Babcock unveiled his own $6,000,000 subway plan, one adapted from plans submitted by his Department of Public Works. Except for the subway idea itself, Babcock completely ignored Morse's recommendations. Although Babcock's modest, single-track subway loop would accommodate rapid transit, his Department of Public Works drafted a plan that called for the slower trolley, not trains. Moreover, the proposed downtown loop system featured a single branch serving the city's East End, with only a vague promise of future extensions to the North Hills and South Hills suburbs.[31]

Morse campaigned vigorously against Babcock's $6,000,000 subway bond issue, assailing in particular what he regarded as the flawed idea of a subway loop. Nevertheless, in 1919, endorsed by the Chamber of Commerce and other groups anxious for quick action on transit, and with the public convinced that a flawed subway trumped no subway at all, the bond issue carried. Babcock in 1920 repaid Morse's virulent opposition by firing him as transit commissioner. Despite the positive bond vote, however, Babcock's subway plan never materialized.[32]

During the 1920s, Pittsburgh's business and planning community tried and failed to build the subway approved in the 1919 bond issue. The unhappy saga underscored a weakness of city planning highlighted in Bigger's 1925 "limitations" article. Transit planning in Pittsburgh suffered from urban fragmentation; while the CPC created a subway committee, the city council in 1924 kept the key responsibility for subway planning in the City Traffic Commission, renamed the City Transit Commission in 1926, and later the Department of City Transit.

State court actions proved even more debilitating by blocking both subway funding and the city's freedom to exercise eminent domain powers. A 1919 Pennsylvania State Supreme Court decision empowered Pittsburgh to build a subway, but forbade it from condemning and using the existing property of the PRC. The court's action assured that any subway would be operated by the PRC, not by the public, as both Arnold and Morse recommended and Mayor Magee desired. A second state court decision handed down the same year compelled the city to call a referendum on any subway expenditure exceeding the $6,000,000 voted by Pittsburghers in 1919. These rulings, consistent with the mood of triumphant capitalism and resurgent individualism that infused the 1920s, hobbled Pittsburgh's ability to design a comprehensive transit system. In 1924 the state supreme court terminated the receivership of the PRC. The court ruling bound the PRC to cooperate with the city. A new court-imposed "contract" between the city and the PRC established an advisory board giving Pittsburgh, in Mayor Magee's words, "at least leverage in the court of public opinion." It also opened the way for new subway planning.[33]

A year earlier the CCCP had intensified the subway conversation by launching its own separate transit study as part of its six-part city plan. The CCCP's 1923 *Transit: A Part of the City Plan* reflected optimism and apprehension. While the foreword and introductory remarks to the CCCP *Transit* report exhorted comprehensiveness, the committee's strong engineering composition, which included Arthur Brown, N. S. Sprague, Winters Haydock, and S. L. Tone (of the PRC), accentuated an engineering bias that kept city planning and transit planning in the 1920s neatly compartmentalized and subway plans derailed.[34]

In the same way that Bigger directed the CCCP's street and park plans, Haydock supervised the *Transit* report. Haydock's *Transit* plan began by extolling the 1917 Morse document; he then proceeded by acknowledging the significant metropolitan implications of transit planning. A transportation plan, explained Haydock, "should not be limited by present municipal boundary lines"; moreover, continued Haydock—mimicking Bigger's earlier street and park proposals—transit plans should contribute to the emergence of a more "accessible" urban region. Like earlier Pittsburgh transit studies, Haydock's 1923 report for the CCCP exuded urgency. It bemoaned "the serious and growing traffic congestion of the central business district" identified engineering problems, that is, removing streetcars from downtown streets, and recommended the technology to solve the problem—a subway system. But his generous kudos to Morse notwithstanding, Haydock's 1923 transit study rejected the ex-transit commissioner's main advice, and defiantly resurrected Babcock's and the Chamber's loop system plan, which in effect reinforced the primacy of the downtown. However, rather than Babcock's single loop, Haydock espoused three. He recommended immediate construction of two loops, one serving the East End, the other the North Side. Similarly, he advocated trolley use of the subway tunnels until funds enabled rapid transit. Finally, Haydock imagined a future third subway loop designed to accommodate all transit traffic entering the downtown from Penn Avenue, Second Avenue, and the Smithfield Street Bridge.[35]

Large sections of the Haydock/CCCP *Transit* report addressed traffic relief in the central business district, urging the abolition of trolley tracks on

Second Avenue and Grant Street, and the conversion of principal downtown streets such as Fifth and Sixth avenues to one-way traffic. Consistent with the business orientation of the study, it belittled the notion of banning peak-hour vehicle traffic from the downtown, although it accepted the necessity of imposing some parking restrictions. Likewise, the 1923 plan dismissed Morse's idea for the through-routing of transit, claiming that having streetcars complete their run through the downtown to a specified destination would minimally serve Pittsburgh commuters since passengers would likely transfer in the downtown to other lines. In any case, amid burgeoning suburban growth and fears of decentralization, the tenor of Haydock's report defended the centrality of the downtown and, consistent with urban planning nationwide, safeguarded skyrocketing central city land values. Accordingly, all proposed transit schemes, loops and trunk lines alike, met in the Golden Triangle.[36]

This message proclaiming the primacy of the downtown resounded deafeningly in Edward K. Morse's and Hornes Department Store magnate Albert H. Burchfield's fantastical 1924 transit plan sponsored by Burchfield's Water Street District and Lower Downtown Improvement Association. Situated at the corner of Penn Avenue and Ferry (Stanwix) Street, Hornes Department Store anchored retailing in the lower end of downtown. Morse and Burchfield, however, regarded their grandiose downtown street and transit development plan as eminently practical, and throughout 1924 tirelessly promoted it before the Chamber of Commerce, Rotary, League of Women Voters, Pittsburgh Automobile Dealers Association, and other receptive groups.[37]

In Morse and Burchfield's words, their 1924 plan "solved" all of Pittsburgh's most intractable problems: perennial floods, inadequate parking, traffic congestion, and overcrowded and unreliable public transit. The combined highway, flood control, and transit plan encircled the Golden Triangle with a magnificent floodwall, large enough to accommodate a seventy-foot boulevard and two forty-foot streets. Transit vehicles would speed along six sets of elevated tracks that looped around the Golden Triangle, diving underground through Grant's Hill. Nine roofed stations served commuters and provided access to city theaters, offices, department stores, and shops. A moving sidewalk beneath Fifth Avenue whisked both shoppers and commuters to and from Liberty Avenue and Grant Street connections and the two underground stations on Grant Street. Below the elevated structure sat a six-lane highway plus sheltered parking spaces for 10,000 automobiles.[38] Sardonically, Morse and Burchfield confessed that their plan "destroy[ed] the present beautiful Allegheny [and Monongahela] wharf[s]," but, they observed coyly, "we must destroy occasional beauty for utility." By solving the flood problem and reclaiming wharf space for transportation, that so-called utility meant significantly increasing desirable downtown space for businesses and commercial expansion. Moreover, Morse and Burchfield predicted that the resultant increase in downtown land values would in fifteen years more than pay for the cost of their colossal improvement scheme.[39]

Many Pittsburgh businessmen seriously entertained Morse and Burchfield's futuristic idea for downtown Pittsburgh, and forced the "expert" planning community to seriously consider its fantasia of multileveled highways, transit, and roofed parking. Professional planners and engineers, however, instantly dismissed the plan's closed loop, as well as its overture to higher skyscrapers, and expanded automobile use, as contributing to, not solving, congestion.[40]

Mayor Magee, in fact, still expressed hope for public transit. Magee, like the subway-boosting Chamber of Commerce, believed that the court order discharging the PRC receivers and requiring a new contract establishing cooperation between the city and the PRC lightened the ungainly PRC's onerous financial burden and assured better transit service. He also hoped the new contract achieved greater public sector involvement in transportation planning.[41] Using the contract to advance subway and rapid transit planning, the mayor and city council in 1923 ordered the CPC to prepare a report on the construction of a downtown subway. Toward that end the commission created an awkwardly titled Special Committee on Downtown Congestion and Subway Loop chaired by Gulf Oil executive George Davison. In early 1924 the commission's Subway Committee submitted its findings to Magee and the city council. Aside from Davison's report, which no longer exists, and several other modest studies, the city council's marginalization of the CPC from the ongoing subway conversation had grave implications for true comprehensive planning in the 1920s.[42]

The CPC's lack of enthusiasm for subway transportation evidenced the planners' loss of faith in rapid transit to solve traffic congestion. Their disenchantment in the 1920s with subway and elevated transit systems stemmed in part from the profession's disdain for the narrow technical specialization of traffic and transit engineers, a specialization nurtured at least among traffic experts by the federal Bureau of Public Roads, which cultivated a science of road and highway building. It also derived from what the planners espied as the conundrum of downtown-oriented rapid transit: that spiraling land values and higher office towers equaled escalating congestion. In 1925 Winters Haydock, the chief consultant on the CCCP's 1923 *Transit* report, and traffic engineer Daniel L. Turner collaborated on a study that addressed not only the transit/congestion conundrum but also the paradox embodied in Frederick Bigger's 1925 plaintive cry that planners "attempt to contrive results without having any adequate control over causes."[43] Haydock in 1923 had pressed for a three-loop subway system. Now, in his 1925 coauthored study, he reversed his earlier position to advocate the kind of through transit system that Morse had advanced in 1917. Like Morse, Turner and Haydock asserted that a through subway transit system would liberate Pittsburgh's central business district from its triangular prison and effectively combat congestion.

Turner and Haydock's study, moreover, contained a thorough analysis of the organic relationship between transit, traffic, skyrocketing downtown real estate development, and the imbroglio of congestion. It identified such critical factors as rising automobile usage and a downtown-focused streetcar system, which daily served 355,000 riders commuting into and out of Pittsburgh's central business district. Turner and Haydock linked these facts to a third coefficient in the congestion equation: in 1925 the just over 3 percent of Pittsburgh's downtown office buildings with heights ranging between ten and twenty-six stories contained almost 35 percent of the city's floor area. Increased floor area raised exponentially the size of the daytime office workforce. They calculated that every new twenty-one-story building expanded the city's office floor space by 1.3 percent, thus compounding the futility of managing traffic congestion in a city plagued by a horribly archaic street system.[44]

Significantly, Turner and Haydock spurned the claim that rapid transit supplied a reasonable alternative to the automobile. "What the public wants and rightly so," they wrote in 1925, "is to be able to use the automobile in an automobile age. . . . Consequently, to reduce traffic congestion in Pittsburgh means that additional space must be provided in the triangle to permit . . . [it] to develop to the full economic limit . . . and to conserve the enormous business interest already located there." Like the Chamber of Commerce and other business groups, Turner and Haydock proposed spreading the downtown office and commercial district beyond the Golden Triangle east of Grant Street and across the Allegheny River to the North Side. The subway provided the means. Each weekday morning, surface railways and railroads poured thousands of passengers into the heart of the central business district. Therefore, Turner and Haydock rejected a loop transit system that "isolated . . . surrounding districts," and "localize[d] and crystalize[d] development and thus create[d] congestion." Instead, Turner and Haydock visualized a First and Second Ward subway within a comprehensive rapid transit system that functioned first to spread the boundaries of the business district, and second, to circulate and evenly distribute the city's population.[45]

But while Turner and Haydock's idea of a Metropolitan Rapid Transit System sounded enlightened—a regional network of rapid transit "articulating almost equally well nearly every part of the city and even outside the city"—the plan principally aspired to enlarge the downtown, "to spread the Central Business District beyond the triangle limits." It called for the immediate construction of a subway under Fifth Avenue and Grant Street. As a through system, subway trains in the plan originated in the North Side and carried passengers via neighborhoods such as Bloomfield to a terminus in East Liberty. Ultimately, the authors envisioned the system serving the West End and the South Hills. To fund this system, Turner and Haydock outlined a benefits assessment financing plan that taxed the beneficiaries of the system, owners of adjacent real estate, businessmen positively affected by the system, as well as commuters, all according to how efficiently or how profitably they were served.[46]

The 1925 Turner and Haydock plan spurred activity. The city council enlisted the CPC to study a rapid transit line across the Smithfield Street Bridge to connect with the proposed Grant Street Subway.[47] Still, despite Turner and Haydock's more enlightened rendering, their subway plan failed to overcome the CPC's adamant opposition to what it saw as a piecemeal, technological fix for a complex traffic congestion problem.[48]

The commission's opposition hardly dampened popular interest in subways. In 1926 the subway conversation remained brisk. Turner and Haydock proffered a new financing plan that urged the immediate construction of a regular subway line from Ohio Street on the North Side to Shadyside in the East End. The two engineers affixed a $36,000,000 price tag on the project. Six million dollars (from the 1919 bond issue) sat in hand; to cover the shortfall Turner and Haydock proposed a new $30,000,000 bond issue to be voted on at a 1928 election. Much of the money to pay off this enormous bonded debt, explained the engineers, would come from the lower operating costs of efficient rapid transit. However, Turner and Haydock viewed the city's taxing power as the ultimate source of revenue. Significantly, the city's ability to wield such power hinged on the voters approving an amendment to the state constitution empowering cities to assess property owners for benefits accruing from public improvements—namely, a subway.

Pittsburgh in 1928 secured neither the anticipated financing nor the unified planning and political support for subway development. Fully expecting state and city voters to back the City Transit Commission's "practical" subway scheme, city transit engineers showered the city council with transit designs, including plans for a tube under the Allegheny River connecting the North Side with the proposed downtown subway system. Such premature planning only hardened the CPC's stance that the Transit Commission's subway designs lacked comprehensiveness; specifically, the CPC derided them as "indefinite and indeterminate, in that [they do] not fix the position of the proposed subway in detail so that it could be located on the ground or upon a map." The subway imbroglio illustrates very well Bigger's and the commission's increasing tendency in the 1920s, contrary to Olmsted's warning, to get bogged down in detail, especially where Bigger philosophically was opposed to the project.[49]

A more deadly fate awaited the Transit Commission's financing scheme. Despite the heady optimism of Turner and Haydock's 1927 funding report, and the commission's December 1927 "Annual Report to the Mayor and City Council," which "look[ed] forward with confidence to a favorable decision" on the benefits assessment plan, Pennsylvania voters in November 1928 broadly rejected the idea. Nor did the commission's appeal for a $30,000,000 bond issue fare any better. Politically wary of a subway plan serving initially only East End and North Side neighborhoods, the council simply tabled the bond issue.[50]

Although the CCCP, the Chamber of Commerce, and the planning community in general bewailed the defeat of the benefits assessment legislation, and beseeched the city not to abandon the subway plan, in 1934 that is exactly what happened. A combination of lethal forces—the Great Depression, bankrupt city finances, the planning profession's apathy for engineering fixes such as mass transit, and the political infeasibility of a subway plan that voters increasingly regarded as skewed to the downtown and a few choice neighborhoods—sunk the project.[51]

Pittsburgh's subway debacle occurred despite ardent business support that endured throughout the 1920s. Financing problems, legal obstacles erected by Harrisburg, and the 1919 bond issue itself, which too narrowly earmarked subway funds, seriously limited the city's transit options. But Pittsburgh's fragmented transportation planning also handicapped progress. In progressive fashion, Pittsburgh had compartmentalized its assault on traffic congestion, giving rapid transit to the Traffic Commission and street improvements to the CPC. Engineers, not architects and planners, dominated the transit conversation and monopolized the Transit Commission. Such fragmentation effectively doomed the once ballyhooed subway project, a project that had rarely excited planners to begin with and that by the mid-1920s, in Turner and Haydock's words, lost the enthusiasm of the automobile-crazed public as well.

INTER-DISTRICT TRAFFIC CIRCUIT

If the subway supporters failed, so did those planners and their backers who in the 1920s marketed highway and street-building panaceas for traffic congestion. The compartmentalization of major street planning apart from transit development prevented a realistically comprehensive assault on the so-called traffic problem. Although critics often lumped automobiles together with wagons, drays, and trolleys in the mire of traffic congestion, the most enlightened planners such as Bigger meticulously disconnected traffic and transit for planning purposes. The subway—which tended to foster an out-of-sight, out-of-mind mentality—enabled that wizardry.

If city street planners mingled infrequently with Transit Commission engineers, they interacted just as minimally with the engineers in the county's Department of Public Works, who during the 1920s operated a large-scale, countywide road-building program. However, the county's broad responsibility for major highway and bridge development forced city street planners to arrange some modus vivendi with county highway engineers. The mammoth scale of the county's ambitious 1920s public works agenda, which in addition to roadways included the nationally acclaimed new Point Bridge, the Liberty Bridge and Tunnel, and the rebuilding of the Sixth, Seventh, and Ninth Street bridges over the Allegheny River, in effect helped define the city's major street plans. To abet city and county cooperation, at the urging of the CCCP, the city and the county in 1922 had joined with the CCCP to create the JPC.

Despite the JPC, chronic city-county divisiveness throughout the decade posed a nearly insurmountable obstacle to comprehensive traffic planning, especially progress on the city's and the CCCP's heralded Inter-District Traffic Circuit, the tour de force paraded by the Chamber of Commerce as the centerpiece of its "Pittsburgh Forward" movement. However, hyperprofessional city planners such as Frederick Bigger disdained the ACPC. His contempt stemmed as much from the commission's political complexion as from its obsequiousness to Public Works. Pittsburgh's Republican regime kept a grip on city and county politics during the 1920s, although intraparty rifts battered the Old Guard's once-stalwart ranks. In 1929 a maverick Republican mayor, Charles Klein, won reelection over the opposition of party boss William Larimer Mellon. Meanwhile an independent, Charles McGovern, occupied the

minority seat on the ACPC. These disruptions in the once smoothly functioning Republican machine diminished the political accord that had often helped
foster city and county cooperation.[52]

The CPC's failure to execute the Inter-District Traffic Circuit, or, for that
matter, many of its grandiose schemes for unsnarling traffic congestion, had
deeper roots than the city-county cleavage, despite its seriousness. During the
decade, central city real estate developers made significant additions to several
older office buildings and erected at least half a dozen twenty- to forty-story
office towers in Pittsburgh's already spatially constrained downtown district.
City skyscrapers regularly exceeded the statutory building height limits and
necessitated zoning variances. These developments, as Bigger endlessly bemoaned, intensified traffic congestion and escalated real estate values, all of
which in turn spawned the demand for even higher building heights and even
wider streets, all in defiance of the CPC's yeoman attempts to order and control the patterns of urban growth.[53]

Pittsburgh's CCCP fully believed that its 1921 *Major Streets* plan represented a blueprint for transforming Pittsburgh's narrow, haphazardly planned,
horse-and-buggy-era streets and roadways into a modern system of 130 com-
modious thoroughfares. Bigger, together with Harland Bartholomew, had
served as the chief architect of the plan, which drew heavily upon Olmsted
Jr.'s earlier *Main Thoroughfares*. Indeed, the 1921 plan emphasized Olmsted's
distinction between thoroughfares and streets, and reiterated the Brookline
planner's simple but easily ignored observation that Pittsburgh's hilly topography complicated the construction and terribly escalated the cost of all street
improvements. Like Olmsted's plan, Bigger's 1921 scheme unfolded a system
of main thoroughfares or "main routes of travel . . . between home and workplace, office region and industrial district, residential zone and retail center,
one to another."[54] However, despite strong elements of comprehensiveness (it
charted seventeen major and minor metropolitan district routes—Penn Avenue and West Liberty Avenue, for example, linking the city and suburbs),
this plan, like Olmsted's, focused principally on the downtown triangle. It was
there, stated Bigger, "where congestion had reached a serious point." A 1921
Cy Hungerford cartoon in *Progress* was unambiguous. In the cartoon, a horribly bruised and battered caricature of Benjamin Franklin, familiar to all Pittsburghers as "Pa Pitt," visits his medical specialist, "The Traffic Doctor," aka
the CCCP. "My poor man," observes the physician, "you have every symptom
of auto intoxication, hardening of traffic arteries, congestion of the pedal ex-
tremities, poor circulation and locomotor ataxia." The good doctor prescribed

Take Liberal Doses
From PROGRESS, October, 1921

Cy Hungerford's cartoon emphasizes the importance of planning to cure the traffic-induced illness debilitating poor "Pa Pitt." Progress *(October 1921).*

"liberal doses" of "new" and "wider streets," "better connections," and "improved grades."[55]

The traffic doctor's remedy notwithstanding, Bigger in the *Major Street* plan abjured oversimplifying, either the problem or the solution. Congestion, explained the plan, originated as much from traffic patterns external to the triangle as from within. It was also rooted, as noted, in the reckless overbuilding of the city's physically straitjacketed central business district. Controlling the latter demanded more rigorously policing the use of downtown real property and streets; addressing the former called for the development of an efficient downtown highway loop, an "inter-district bypass" complemented by arteries that would whisk downtown traffic swiftly to and from central city shops and offices.[56]

Working in collaboration with the Flood Commission, whose ongoing quay wall studies were crucial for highway plans based—as most were—on transforming the city's ancient riverbanks into useful thoroughfares, the CCCP physicians labored from 1920 to 1921 on their street plan. In anticipation of heightened floodwalls and a new wharf, the CCCP plan projected Water Street as a six-lane roadway skirting the "embellished" Monongahela waterfront. Likewise, Duquesne Way unfolded as a six-lane route bordering the Allegheny.[57] To connect Water Street and Duquesne Way at the eastern end of the downtown, the planners of this soon-to-be-called Inter-District Traffic Circuit plan proposed removing the Pennsylvania Railroad yards blocking the end of "Old" Grant Street and continuing Grant Street as an eighty-foot-wide thoroughfare out to Liberty Avenue. To further link the Monongahela and Allegheny sides of the city and enlarge the business area and its commercial land values, Bigger and the CCCP proposed making a widened Ross Street a continuation of Bigelow Boulevard, thus making Sixth Avenue a new entrance to the Golden Triangle.[58]

Next to the Flood Commission's wharf recommendations, no other development during the 1920s more challenged and preoccupied city planners than the construction—launched in 1921—of the Liberty Bridge and Tunnel, the main portal to the city's booming suburban South Hills. The massive engineering feat involved spanning the Monongahela River and boring a pair of two-mile-long tunnels through Mt. Washington. It directly linked the downtown and such desirable suburban residential plums—ripe for new, large-scale suburban development—as Greentree, Mt. Lebanon, and Bethel Park. It also relieved the notoriously horrible congestion on the Smithfield Street Bridge that connected the downtown to Carson Street, the South Side, and McKees Rocks. However, unless carefully designed, the downtown-sited northern terminus of the new Liberty Bridge threatened intolerable traffic congestion at the bridge approaches. Therefore, the CCCP favored terminating the bridge near the lower Hill District at Tunnel Street and Wylie Avenue, and it strongly favored a second bridge approach leading from Water Street. It spurned connecting the new bridge to the Boulevard of the Allies.[59]

The CCCP alluded only vaguely to the idea of a crosstown artery. Instead, it stressed the development of main thoroughfares "bypassing" the triangle. The bypass routes, Duquesne Way and Bigelow Boulevard, included widened Ross and Water streets, an extended Grant Street, as well as the new Liberty

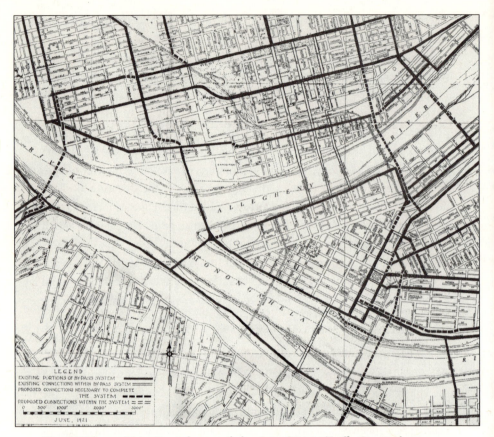

The CCCP's 1921 *Major Street* plan unveiled an Inter-District Traffic Circuit plan.
The plan continued to preoccupy Bigger and the Pittsburgh CPC well into the 1930s.
Citizens Committee on the City Plan, *A Major Street Plan for Pittsburgh: A Part of the
Pittsburgh Plan* (Pittsburgh: Citizens' Committee on City Plan, September 1921). *Archives
Service Center, University of Pittsburgh.*

and Point bridges and the proposed West End Bridge over the Ohio River, all
either under construction or on the drawing board in the 1920s. These routes
won equally overwhelming endorsement from the Chamber of Commerce,
which saw solving the traffic crisis a matter of economic life or death.

The CCCP acknowledged the importance of traffic engineers in producing
its *Major Street* plan. However, in both tone and language the report, liber-
ally punctuated with phrases such as "coordinated systems," exuded a planning, not an engineering, mentality. Although the CCCP tailored the report
for its business-elite constituency, Bigger couched near the end of the report
several highly visionary, RPAA-inspired ideas about "controlling and limiting

the number of persons and vehicles using the central business district" and about the planned decentralizing of business and residences in satellite urban districts. These ideas surely clashed with the Chamber's drumbeat for "Pittsburgh Forward," which spotlighted the Ross Street, Grant Street, and Water Street proposals.[60]

Although long grist for the urban conversation and a font of Chamber boosterism, the 1921 *Major Street* plan sat largely unused, except as a template for CPC approval of street and subdivision plans. Mainly preoccupied between 1921 and 1923 with the creation and passage of the city zoning ordinance, the CPC joined the Chamber and the city council in endorsing the plan. After that, except for perennial conversations about extending the Boulevard of the Allies to Schenley Park and working with the county to develop the Saw Mill Run Parkway, Pittsburgh planners did little about major street planning before 1923.[61]

Allegheny County's spectacular 1924 People's Bond Issue impelled Pittsburgh to take action on major street planning and heightened both the tempo and temper of the city's planning conversation. It likewise bared the cleavage that existed between the engineering-oriented staff of the Allegheny County

Liberty Bridge under construction, with tunnel entrance in distance. *Carnegie Library of Pittsburgh.*

Planning Department and Bigger's team of "planning professionals." The business and the civic elites who joined in the conversation during the 1920s provided mainly applause. In addition to underwriting the construction and improvement of a spectacular array of county roads and highways, the county's 1924 bond issue launched construction of the new Point Bridge, the Liberty Bridge, the Armstrong Tunnel, and a new county office building on the old high school site on Ross Street at Forbes Avenue. Bigger, nonetheless, remained unimpressed. In fact, at a March 1924 meeting of the JPC, he disparaged the county's office, bridge, and Armstrong Tunnel projects for "not show[ing] any relationship to each other or to any general plans which are county-wide in character." Because "the [county's] detailed plan studies thus far exhibited . . . are of debatable merit," charged Bigger, "no wise judgment can be now expressed upon the proposals from the standpoint of sane city planning."[62]

Alarmed by the county bond issue, the CCCP in the fall of 1924 alerted the city council and Mayor Magee concerning the asymmetry between the bond issue projects and the CCCP's *Major Street* plan, especially the implications of the Liberty Bridge and its approaches for the plan's proposed bypass system, or what was now called the Inter-District Traffic Circuit. At a meeting with Magee in early 1925, the CCCP proudly unveiled its "perspective sketch" of this traffic circuit (based on the 1921 plan). Immediately, Magee ordered the CPC to map a major street plan for the city, and using a $50,000 appropriation from the city council, he commissioned a separate study of an "Inter-District Traffic Artery."[63]

A newly salaried city employee, Bigger headed the design team for the traffic circuit, which hewed closely to the CCCP plan. In December 1925 Bigger introduced the main features of his traffic circuit. In Bigger's plan, Water Street and Duquesne Way, transformed into spacious, six-lane thoroughfares, skirted the outer edges of the city's Golden Triangle. Traffic upon reaching the historic Point flowed around a monumental obelisk-graced traffic circle that served to channel buses and automobiles over the new Point Bridge. Likewise, the Water Street ramp afforded south-bound traffic easy access to the Liberty Bridge, while vehicles traveling northbound from the South Hills followed the proposed Ross Street extension over a northbound crosstown viaduct that hastened heavy traffic either across the proposed Eleventh Street Bridge to the North Side or east to Oakland and Shadyside along widened Bigelow Boulevard. In this manner traffic skirted the downtown.[64]

Bigger's 1925 Inter-District Traffic Circuit plan portrayed Liberty Bridge traffic entering the Boulevard of the Allies on grade. A traffic circle at the juncture of the bridge ramp and the boulevard functioned to distribute vehicles east to Oakland, or north above the Panhandle Railroad to Forbes Street and thence downtown or along the viaduct to the North Side and Bigelow Boulevard.[65] County planners—perhaps wary of the impact of the city's Ross Street widening proposal on vaunted county office building plans—espoused an alternate scheme that carried Liberty Bridge traffic northward along old Shingiis Street. Bigger and the CPC roundly condemned the county's Shingiis Street plan as being not only overly extensive but also involving costly property rearrangement. To Bigger's consternation, the city council, lured by the county's irresistible offer to share much of the project's cost, capitulated and accepted the Shingiis Street alignment.[66]

Bigger officially submitted his "Preliminary Report to City Council on the Inter-District Traffic Circuit" on December 28, 1925, "regretting," in his letter of transmittal, that "Council's capitulation made the [CPC's] viaduct impossible of execution," and modestly confessing that the admittedly "flawed" proposal represented only a "suggestion." Pittsburgh's leading professional planner stood by the rest of his design: a widened Water Street, the Duquesne Way thoroughfare, an eighty-foot-wide Penn Avenue, the Water Street ramp, the West End Bridge, the North Side Industrial Highway, and his baroque Point Traffic Circle, the last strenuously backed by Pittsburgh's Better Traffic Committee. Bigger viewed the county's obstruction and the council's shortsightedness as classic examples of political expediency undermining the comprehensive planning process. During the spring of 1927, the CPC designed a "temporary" approach to the Liberty Bridge that terminated at Forbes Avenue. To diffuse the expected crush of traffic at the intersection of Forbes Avenue and the new bridge approach, the commission ordered Sixth Avenue to be opened through to Forbes Avenue.[67]

Meanwhile, the CPC again attempted to salvage what it now more than ever viewed as the vital crosstown viaduct plan to link the Liberty Bridge, Bigelow Boulevard, and the North Side via a new Eleventh Street Bridge over the Allegheny River. The commission delegated the job of drafting plans for this deemed technically feasible crosstown viaduct to the new state-chartered Department of City Planning. The department promptly invited a free flow of planning ideas from the CCCP, the city's Department of Public Works, and other city and county agencies. Simultaneously, it analyzed all past and current plans and produced a new crosstown route aligned along Chatham Street.[68] The route followed Chatham Street and Tunnel Street under Wylie Avenue to an intersection with Bigelow Boulevard. Thence, in the department's plan, traffic moved to a circle at Pennsylvania Station, where northbound vehicles veered onto Eleventh Street and across the proposed new Allegheny River bridge. Eastbound traffic swung onto Bigelow Boulevard.

The level of consensus seemingly assured a department triumph. Commission members, including Gulf Oil's George Davison, applauded the plan, as did the CCCP and the Better Traffic Committee; but not the county. Joined by the Pennsylvania Railroad, whose downtown station and yard properties stood in the path of the crosstown plans, county planners again defied the city. They expressly resented the city's snubbing their design ideas for the crosstown viaduct. "If the County is to have a share of responsibility or liability for this improvement," asserted the ACPC, "the County will expect to be called in."[69]

Progress on the much-ballyhooed Crosstown Thoroughfare, the jewel in Bigger's Inter-District Traffic Circuit crown, soon ended. The county, in fact, ignored the viaduct in its 1928 bond issue, which included funding for the Saw Mill Run Parkway, an airport, a town hall, a new county office building, and the McKees Rocks and West End bridges.[70] Talk about the importance of a traffic circuit and the crosstown link continued into the 1930s, particularly within CCCP and Chamber of Commerce forums, but without conviction. Bigger and the CPC persevered on major street planning throughout 1928, but lethargically. In October Bigger presented what he bemoaned as a still "tentative and still incomplete" traffic circuit plan that differed little from his December 1925 design. When *Progress* in 1929 reported on the status of the "bypass loop," it described the county's, not the city department's, version: traffic in the county plan exited from the South Hills Tubes and headed north across the newly opened Liberty Bridge, "a span," cautioned the CCCP, "point[ing] like a great arrow to the need for [a] cross town artery." This traffic then snaked across the downtown to the North Side unaided by either a viaduct or a new Allegheny River bridge. Once across the Allegheny River, looping traffic steered west on a widened Ohio Street and Western Avenue, then south across the West End Bridge (under construction in 1929), and returned to the South Hills Tubes using the nearly completed Saw Mill Run Parkway.[71] Who or what deserves blame for the debacle of the missing Crosstown Thoroughfare? In short, the two key participants in the urban conversation of the 1920s refused to talk. A deep-seated animosity grew between the ACPC and the CPC, an enmity rooted on the one side in the CPC's disdain for the perceived provincialism, politicization, and engineering bias of the ACPC, and on the other by the city's grudging dependence on but lack of gratitude for the county's largesse.[72]

As during the first decade of the century, Pittsburgh in the 1920s spawned a cornucopia of impressive office towers designed by architects such as Benno Janssen and Henry Hornbostel. Molders of the "modern," urban downtown of the 1920s self-consciously attempted to eradicate what urban historian Sam Bass Warner once referred to as the "inheritance of the past." Modern downtown office architecture, like street widenings, viaducts, interdistrict traffic circuits, and subway plans, comprised a central part of the Chamber of Commerce's "Pittsburgh Forward" movement to expunge the images of Pittsburgh's Stygian past and to redefine the city as a new progressive metropolis. Furthermore, by removing downtown eyesores such as the Pennsylvania and Baltimore and Ohio railroad yards, which blocked through traffic movement on major arteries such as Grant Street, urban face-lifting rendered the downtown and its high-priced real estate not only more attractive and more efficient, but more profitable.

While professional planners such as Frederick Bigger viewed the "Pittsburgh Forward" movement as terribly complex—desirable perhaps, but disturbing—planners constantly espoused urban progress. Widen streets, they preached, and order spaces neatly differentiated by use; clear away old, unsafe tenements and warehouses; salvage open space for parks; and erect safer, more sanitary new buildings. So went the mantra of the progressive planner. However, planners, as Bigger realized, faced a conundrum. Zoning, street widening, rebuilding, and rearranging urban space all involved not only costly takings of previously built urban environment but also the politically explosive tallying of winners and losers. The sheer complexity of earmarking for street widening, bridge approach, or crosstown viaduct development huge swaths of urban land densely built up over 120 years of urban growth presented astounding legal and ethical challenges, and raised the prospect and danger of speculative profiteering. In fact, the CCCP's and the CPC's announcement in 1925 of the alignment for the Crosstown Thoroughfare froze all development activity on the eastern boundary of the Golden Triangle.

Public action operated just as forcefully and often more frequently in the 1920s to spur speculative activity, triggering Bigger's jeremiad against the vicious cycle of wider streets, spiraling land values, higher buildings, and coagulated traffic. Here, then, was the paradox. While the Chamber and civic elites cheered dazzling new additions to the city's soaring skyline, they simultaneously exhorted the city council for wider streets, rotaries, and viaducts to accommodate the growing volume of traffic.

Pittsburgh's postwar downtown building boom began in 1923 and peaked in 1927 when, in addition to Henry Hornbostel's 500-foot-tall new Grant

Building at Third and Grant, construction progressed on the Koppers offices (also on Grant), the Plaza Building, the Keystone Athletic Club, the Law and Finance Building, and several hotels. New rococo and colonial revival movie palaces—Marcus Loew's Penn Theater (1926) on Sixth Street, transformed into the Heinz symphony hall in 1971, and the Stanley Theater (1927) on Seventh, rehabilitated as the Benedum Center for the Performing Arts in the 1980s— added glitz and a touch of modernity to the central city.[73] Even the progrowth Better Traffic Committee balked at the looming traffic difficulties engendered by the frenzy of building. The committee implored the CPC to "use every means in its power to bring owners and designers of new buildings to the realization of the importance of providing adequate loading and short term waiting facilities within the property line."[74]

THE COUNTY OFFICE BUILDING AND TOWN HALL

The odyssey of the County Office Building and town hall projects (the latter, a proposed new exhibition hall) illuminates both the complexity and limitations of professional planning during Pittsburgh's booming 1920s. It also highlights the state of planning in the city on the eve of the Great Depression. Allegheny County's 1928 bond issue enlivened conversation in Pittsburgh, not only about big development projects and planning but also about the perennial topic of metropolitanization—that is, consolidating the hundreds of small rural and suburban townships and boroughs comprising Allegheny County into one political unit called Greater Pittsburgh. Because it focused on projects such as township roads, county parks, and a county airport, the 1928 county bond issue may have strengthened the determination of the city's most ardent apostles of Greater Pittsburgh, namely, the Chamber of Commerce, the CCCP, William Magee, and the West End Board of Trade. Such boosters of a Greater Pittsburgh aspired to restore the city's rightful place among the nation's major population centers, to end expensive and cumbersome dual county/city government, and to streamline city and regional planning. The bond issue actually ignored key city projects such as the Crosstown Thoroughfare while earmarking $1,162,000 for the Saw Mill Run Parkway and the McKees Rocks Bridge and West End Bridge items, projects championed by Henry Tranter's West End Board of Trade and by suburban Mt. Lebanon Township and South Hills real estate interests. Only the $6,000,000 town hall and the $1,500,000 County Office Building—the latter, like the Saw Mill Run project, left over from the 1924 bond issue—directly impacted the city itself.[75]

Significantly, both the County Office Building (involving the potential removal of the county jail, an integral part of Pittsburgh's Richardsonian Allegheny County courthouse) and the town hall project implied that, notwithstanding serious county and city political and professional differences, county planners shared with the city a commitment to the centrality of the downtown as the economic heart of the Pittsburgh region. Unquestionably, the county aggressively pursued a blatantly suburban agenda of road building, regional parks, and connecting bridges, an agenda politically critical to "community builders" engaged in platting large-scale residential subdivisions in the county's already sprawling North Hills and South Hills suburbs.[76] County officials, especially ACPC members such as William Larimer Mellon, Howard Heinz, and James Sansom, differed little in social class and business bias from their colleagues on the CPC. Therefore, although frequently piqued by the city's disdain for the ACPC's lack of technical expertise and unprofessional values, the story of the County Office Building and town hall projects makes clear that during the 1920s, county planners, like their colleagues in the city, kept faith with the downtown.

By 1924 regional population growth, suburbanization, rising automobility, and the concomitant increase in the demand for county services rendered architect Richardson's county courthouse on Grant Street inadequate for housing the county's growing bureaucracy, compelling the commissioners to include a new office building in their bond issue of that year. Toward that end, as mentioned earlier, the county purchased the corner of Ross and Diamond streets, the site of the old South School, a relic of the "walking city," projected to be dwarfed by "big city" office buildings and retail emporiums. The county's decision to expand its government complex at the southeastern corner of the triangle enlisted it not only among the proponents of downtown growth but also among those pressing for the expansion of the downtown eastward along the Fifth and Forbes retail corridor. However, one huge barrier blocked any physical enlargement of the business district: the historic Allegheny County Jail. Surrounded by "forbiddingly" high stone ramparts, the gray, somber Richardsonian pile posed a real as well as a symbolic wall against downtown growth.[77]

Penologists deemed the bastion-like edifice outmoded. Prison experts placed modernization costs at over $500,000, and suggested that the county demolish the aging, dreary structure and construct a modern jail above the new County Office Building. The prospect of replacing the landmark fortress with a blithe parklet or ample space to improve traffic patterns excited Pittsburgh retail merchants, and even for a time intrigued Frederick Bigger. Pursuing the goal of jail demolition, the county commissioners instructed their official architect, Stanley Roush, to develop jail removal plans, including drawings showing a jail addition to the County Office Building. At the same time, the commissioners ordered the ACPC to mobilize public support for the jail removal idea. In the spring of 1925 the commission announced the creation of a Jail Removal Committee, which included representatives of the CCAC, the Pittsburgh Chamber of Commerce, the Retail Merchants Association, the Pittsburgh Real Estate Board, the Uptown Board of Trade, the Engineers Society of Western Pennsylvania, and the Oakland Board of Trade.[78]

Then, in November 1925, marking perhaps the first skirmish in the long battle for the preservation of city historic resources, the Pittsburgh chapter of the American Institute of Architects (AIA) condemned the county's jail demolition plans. The chapter invoked the building's national architectural significance as an integral part of the Richardson courthouse and jail complex, and it secured backing for its position from the national AIA. Rather than destroy an architectural landmark, Pittsburgh architects beseeched the county to reuse the building as a "Hall of Records." The Pittsburgh AIA chapter conceded, however, that the towering stone walls surrounding the century-old keep might be removed. By 1930 the CCCP rallied behind the city architects. The CCCP, however, fought the county's jail plans not on aesthetic grounds but on the practical grounds that rational land use principles, not the jail's forbidding appearance, doomed retail development along the Fifth and Forbes corridor. Furthermore, the CCCP objected to the county's parklet plans for the jail site; the site, insisted the CCCP, was too small and conflicted with the waterfront park scheme proposed in the CCCP's 1923 *Parks* plan.[79] The jail removal controversy underscored a key planning issue of the 1920s, one highlighted by historian Max Page in his *Creative Destruction of Manhattan*. How can a city preserve historic elements of its central city fabric in the face of skyrocketing land values and the perceived imperative of urban growth? This conundrum—still central to city planning at the beginning of the twenty-first century—had infiltrated the urban conversation in the late 1920s. Only the intervention of the esteemed AIA, the CCCP's skepticism about the "practicality" of retail expansion along Fifth and Forbes, and the coming of the Great Depression helped scuttle the jail removal.

More than the jail question, the town hall issue confirmed the primacy of the downtown as the focus of city planning on the eve of the 1930s, and presaged the post–World War II renaissance a decade and a half before its debut. It also highlighted the rivalry between the CPC and ACPC as well as the struggle

between competing public and private visions of the urban future. The resulting political brouhaha undermined the scientific reasoning process that progressives trusted to forge planning decisions. Town halls remained the crown
jewel of progressive city planning long after the "City Practical" had eclipsed
the City Beautiful. Large, classically designed civic centers embodied the progressive faith in the wisdom and virtue of an "enlightened," "informed" public.
Frederick Law Olmsted Jr. crowned his 1911 *Main Thoroughfares* plan with the
rendering of a magnificent civic center fronting a great Beaux-Arts square, an
imperial assemblage that formed a stately entranceway to the city. The CCCP
omitted the town hall idea from its 1920s plans, except for the downsized civic
building that anchored the neighborhood-unit scheme included in Bigger's
park plan. But neither the CCAC nor the Chamber of Commerce fully surrendered the idea of a town hall. The CPC, too, endorsed the town hall idea, but
exhorted the county to employ "the scientific method" in selecting its site. In
fact, Pittsburgh CPC member George Davison chaired the Chamber of Commerce's Town Hall Committee, a body created to sell the town hall idea to the
citizens of Allegheny County.[80]

Beginning in 1928, the Chamber of Commerce, the CPC, and Allegheny
County separately explored numerous proposed sites for a town hall. CPC
members vehemently stressed the importance of locating the hall "in relation
to the City Plan."[81] Proposals for town hall sites flooded in. Realtors, architects, and city and county officials advanced thirty-five sites for the town hall,
including the North Side, Oakland, and, of course, the downtown. Realtor
Franklin Nicola campaigned tirelessly for his Oakland Schenley Farms district, which had continued to accumulate many of the city's cultural and educational institutions and private clubs. Prominent Pittsburgh architect Frederick Osterling, whose studio in Old Allegheny adjoined the Ninth Street Bridge,
championed a North Side location, while under the auspices of the Chamber
of Commerce and the Allegheny Town Hall Association, city businessmen
earnestly lobbied for a downtown site. George Davison of the Chamber's Town
Hall Committee informed the ACPC that his organization desired to fully cooperate with the county in the town hall decision, but "at its own expense" it
had engaged Lincoln C. Dickey, the architect of the Cleveland Auditorium, to
help recommend an ideal site.[82]

Dickey's May 1929 report enumerated site standards for the hall that, among
other things, challenged the ACPC's singular assumption that, because Oakland served as Pittsburgh's cultural center, it rated special consideration as a
site. Monumentality and artistic design ranked high among Dickey's criteria,

but he scored such elements as efficiency of traffic movement, parking, and the centrality of the site even higher. Dickey's report therefore supported the Chamber's and the Town Hall Association's arguments for a town hall located in the downtown, preferably at the eastern, "growth" end of the Golden Triangle, easily accessible by automobile, trolley, and railroad. City businessmen also favored this Grant Street, Second Avenue, and Water Street site, because it abutted the Panhandle Railroad Bridge and the Baltimore and Ohio Railroad terminal and sat convenient to both the Boulevard of the Allies and the proposed Water Street approach to the Liberty Bridge. Perspective plans accompanying Dickey's report displayed a grand (480 foot by 280 foot) neoclassical auditorium complemented by an adjoining huge riverfront recreational pier.[83]

Grandiose as it was, Dickey's plan left county planners unimpressed. In fact, they attributed his report to the "sectional feeling of certain business organizations urging a site in the downtown." On the basis of the ACPC's "scientific" scoring of the thirty-five proposed town hall sites, R. B. Mellon, S. J. Topely, R. H. Watson, S. D. Robison, and the other members of the ACPC dismissed all proposed downtown sites as deficient in parking and too expensive. Instead, they chose Nicola's Schenley Farms site in Oakland, already developed as Pittsburgh's civic center, and where the existing effulgence of Beaux-Arts and neo-Gothic-designed buildings, including the then-under-construction towering Cathedral of Learning, "give a proper setting for a great auditorium."[84]

But it was the county Department of Public Works, not the ACPC or the Chamber of Commerce, that decreed the final verdict on the town hall and ended the conversation. In January 1930 the Department of Public Works systematically debunked the ACPC's case for the Nicola site. By doing so it switched sides and joined the downtown camp in the historic battle between Oakland and the central business district for regional cultural supremacy. The Department of Public Works's "engineering" analysis denounced the Schenley Farms site as too small, too removed from the center of Allegheny County's population, and, contrary to the planning analysis, too lacking in parking and good transit service. The Public Works engineers belittled both the Nicola site's residential character and the CPC's contention that the seating facilities and other amenities missing from a Spartan hall design were available in nearby theaters. "A truly modern town hall," they argued, must be a "comprehensively planned . . . complete auditorium structure." To be a sound public investment, the hall must attract foreign as well as local conventions, exhibitors, and "other attractions," and therefore "be in proximity to hotels, department stores, railroad stations, offices and municipal buildings," that is, the downtown. However, by 1930 the onset of the Great Depression had stalled all plans for reaffirming the eminence and centrality of Pittsburgh's downtown. Visionary plans for building a town hall and encircling the downtown with a complex system of viaducts, six-lane thoroughfares, and dazzling circles remained insubstantial and incomplete.[85]

PLANNING IN THE 1920S

Despite the limitations, the 1920s, as explained in chapter 5, stand in Pittsburgh planning history as a decade of significant accomplishment. First and foremost, led by Frederick Bigger, the city's and county's progressive-minded civic leadership, both in the public and private sectors, collectively forged a solid planning ethos. Fortified by this ethos, Pittsburgh planners bequeathed a substantial legacy. First, they produced a citywide zoning ordinance, and then a six-volume comprehensive plan. Meanwhile, the ACPC drafted and undertook a giant highway and bridge program. In this and other ways, Pittsburgh-region planners, like those elsewhere in urban America, engaged in the heroic task of retrofitting the city and its suburbs for the automobile age. The record is substantial. Moreover, faithful to Fred Bigger's exhortations, the city's and the county's defining palette of planning materials—the town hall, the major highway system, the Inter-District Traffic Circuit, and the Crosstown Thoroughfare—endured and served as a template for future planning in the Pittsburgh region.

However, the planning limitations left an equally significant record of failure. Pittsburgh scuttled its once promising subway plans. Traffic congestion in the 1920s rendered downtown streets snarled and often impassable. Pittsburgh failed to update its comprehensive plan, and the promise of metropolitan government, like the promise of joint city-county planning, proved elusive. Therefore, Pittsburgh in 1929, on the eve of the Great Depression, remained part of a fragmented region, with fragmented politics and a fragmented conversation about the best direction for future city and regional development.

CHAPTER 7

The Depression, the New Deal, and Planning's Survival

THE GREAT DEPRESSION of the 1930s pummeled urban America, especially heavily industrialized cities such as Pittsburgh. The very act of battling economic depression heightened interest in planning nationally. Hitched to the social sciences, economic planning in the 1920s had proclaimed the triumph of technocracy, regularization, and human mastery over the inscrutable business cycle. Now in the 1930s, social, economic, and land use planners hastened to rescue capitalism from the wreckage of collapsing industrialism.

The federal government in the 1930s embraced planning, and New Dealers after 1933, some of them veterans of the Regional Planning Association of America (RPAA), promoted and considerably empowered the city planning movement. The Great Depression had precipitated an urban crisis. Industries failed, banks closed, real estate values plunged, and thousands of the embittered and defeated unemployed wandered city streets. Mass joblessness forced states and localities to find work, any work, for these desperate victims of the cataclysm. These labor-intensive, make-work jobs invariably included roadway, bridge, park, and other city development projects falling within the province of city planning. With the onset in 1933 of the New Deal, the federal government increasingly became the prime source of funding for all city development and the engine propelling the growth of urban and regional planning. However, as explained in this chapter, despite the considerable enhancement of planning's stature nationwide, by early 1936 planning proved a weak instrument for urban development in Pittsburgh despite a wealth of general plans stacked high on planning department drafting tables. Compelled to get things done, but without forceful local political leadership, planners floundered, bogged down in detail, more prone to quibbling than executing exciting new plans for renewing the Depression-weary city. Moreover, the political, jurisdictional, and organizational rivalries that had thwarted Pittsburgh planners in the halcyon 1920s continued to obstruct city planning amid the Great Depression, notwithstanding the gravity of the city's plight. Therefore, despite the federal government's bold leadership in planning and the largesse of desperately needed federal relief dollars, by 1936 the limitations, not the vision, of city planning prevailed in Pittsburgh.

THE GREAT DEPRESSION IN PITTSBURGH

Mercifully, the full impact of the Great Depression arrived somewhat belatedly in Pittsburgh, not until 1931. Sustained by the lingering effects of Pittsburgh's vital 1920s steel-making economy, and by the region's impressive home-building boom, as well as by the surprising resilience of the city's retail and wholesale sectors, Pittsburgh's economy sputtered rather than plunged into the Stygian void of the Great Depression. Unlike Philadelphia, Cleveland, Buffalo, Baltimore, and Cincinnati, where joblessness by the end of 1930 hovered between 15 and 25 percent, unemployment in Pittsburgh barely reached 12 percent, convincing the city's Chamber of Commerce on that Christmas that "Pittsburgh [had] escape[d] the worst of the slump."[1] But not for long. A year later Pittsburgh's steel industry, operating now at less than 40 percent of capacity, faced "one of the most trying periods of its history."[2] Blast furnaces belched out only 18,500,000 tons of pig iron compared with 31,600,000 tons of output in 1930, a 41 percent decline and the lowest level since the recession of 1908. Glass output fell from 105,827,000 square feet in 1930 to 83,000,000 square feet, while soft coal production plunged 47 percent from the 142,350,000 tons mined in 1929 to under 75,000,000 tons in 1932.[3]

The proliferation of soup kitchens and street-corner apple vending, for which tremulous, stiff-collared city leaders required a permit, and a muddle of languorous shantytowns all signaled the onset of the Great Depression in Pittsburgh. The jerry-built shantytowns, called Hoovervilles in the 1930s, sprang up at several locations, the most notorious at Seventeenth and Liberty avenues in the city's "Strip District," adjacent to St. Patrick's Church. Called the "Mayor of Shantytown," St. Patrick's youthful pastor, Father James R. Cox, ministered to the growing ranks of jobless squatters by distributing food and clothing as well as hope. It was from St. Patrick's that Cox in January 1932 organized a hunger march on Washington, D.C., vainly beseeching President Herbert Hoover to extend government aid to the jobless.[4]

As in other cities in America, Pittsburgh's voluntary agencies mobilized to aid the legion of needy. Early in 1930 the city's so-called Welfare Fund raised monies to assist the Red Cross, the Family Welfare Society, Goodwill, and the Travelers Aid agencies to supply clothing, food, and heating fuel for more than 140,000 Pittsburghers. Similarly, ward political clubs, churches, and ethnic benevolent organizations furnished food and coal to neighbors and parishioners. Yet the shoulders of traditional voluntarism bent under a mounting burden of rising caseloads. In October 1931 a group of city philanthropic-minded businessmen founded the Helping Hand Association, headquartered in an abandoned five-story brick mill building on Water Street. Within months the association was nightly housing and feeding between 1,500 and 3,000 men. Helping Hand not only supplied food and lodging to the city's vagrant jobless but medical and dental services as well.[5]

Pittsburgh's business elite, however, never relapsed into softhearted coddlers of the poor. Rain or shine, blizzard or downpour, at 6:30 each morning Helping Hand shoved its lodgers onto the city's mean streets to seek work, even if that meant repairing the worn shoes and threadbare clothing of fellow inmates or peddling apples it supplied to the jobless at $2 a box. This individualistic, "we'll help you take care for yourself" approach characterized Pittsburgh's early 1930s welfare. The Irene Kaufmann Settlement, for example, organized a "thrift garden"—a grow-your-own-food movement—directed by Mary Flinn Lawrence and aided by her equally wealthy neighbors, the aristocratic Witherows and Dalzells.[6]

But the Great Depression battered this individualism unmercifully. Unremitting mass joblessness forced the city in the fall of 1930 to consider supplying more direct aid. By requiring city policemen and firemen to donate a day's wages each week, the city council assembled a puny $100,000 relief fund, which, through the Department of Welfare, it proposed to distribute to the poor for "basic necessities." Major Charles Klein wrote a personal check for $41 to help fatten this patently inadequate relief fund.[7] Pittsburgh civic leaders, however, preferred any stratagem, no matter how anemic, rather than resorting to direct relief; the specter of the European-style dole, even the thin fare offered by the city, terrified city businessmen. Like President Herbert Hoover, they stubbornly held that America's cornucopia remained full and that only "mob fear," exacerbated by a flood of foreign-made goods, prevented the imminent resurgence of prosperity.[8] Pittsburghers such as Howard Heinz observed that the city's $100,000 fund might be better spent not upon the dole, but in underwriting useful, job-creating public improvements. Viewing the city's looming relief rolls as a behemoth, Heinz in February 1931, together with Richard Beatty Mellon, assembled a group of seventy-five city businessmen who forthwith drafted the "Pittsburgh Plan to Stabilize Employment." After conferring with city and county public officials on the desirability of what they called "a more constructive relief program," Heinz and Mellon announced the organization of the Allegheny County Emergency Association (ACEA), chaired by Frank Phillips. Thrilled with Pittsburgh's "voluntary" effort, Hoover instantly recruited Phillips as a member of his President's Organization on Unemployment Relief. The ACEA solicited private monies to cover the labor costs of city and county work relief projects, while the city, together with the 122 other municipalities comprising Allegheny County, furnished the tools, supplies, and engineering and planning costs for the street and road paving, park and sewer projects, and other public improvements funded by the local works relief program.

Taking the lead with its $100,000 jobless relief fund, Pittsburgh launched a "special works program" in February 1931, at which time Mayor Klein, in front of clicking cameras, broke ground for a works project to beautify the plaza fronting the entrance to Schenley Park. By March 1931, 1,400 men, their names taken directly from the city's relief rolls, labored on eleven sewer and street paving projects.[9]

With the savagely harsh winter of 1931 fast approaching, the ACEA hosted a large meeting at the William Penn Hotel, where public officials from 119 county boroughs and townships agreed to expand the relief plan countywide. Plan boosters predicted that township and other local governments would raise about $1,000,000 for tools and materials, a sum to be matched by the $3,000,000 to be raised by the ACEA from private sources. Unfortunately, despite a vigorous fund-raising effort, between February 1931 and November 1932 the association scraped together hardly $1,000,000. With more than 60,000 people jobless, a mere 6,700 men and women toiled in November 1931 on ACEA jobs. The county commissioners shored up the ACEA in 1932 with $500,000 and added another $400,000 in June 1933.[10]

The growing presence of public monies in Pittsburgh-area relief coffers and the increasing significance of public works in job creation greatly enhanced the visibility of planning. Indeed, Pittsburgh's "special" approach to jobless relief boosted city planning at a time when, locally and nationally, private and public planning teetered precariously. Nationwide, planning faced the guillotine. Commissions in thirty of the fifty largest cities ceased operation. Twenty-two official planning commissions disappeared in 1931.

Locally, Pittsburgh's Citizens Committee on the City Plan (CCCP) barely weathered the first years of the Great Depression. Spring 1930 found the organization describing its fiscal prospects as "favorable," but only because Charles Arensburg, Richard Beatty Mellon, and James D. Hailman, who was now quite ill, had freed the CCCP from debt by canceling repayment of their large personal loans to the body.[11] Not that such financial problems were immediately life threatening. On June 5, 1930, the day before Hailman died, Heinz informed Bigger that the board members of the CCCP's parent, the Municipal Planning Association (MPA), had voted to boost Bigger's yearly salary to $10,000.

THE IMPACT OF THE GREAT DEPRESSION ON PITTSBURGH PLANNING

By 1931 the thickening pall enveloping the shabby mill towns and working-class neighborhoods of the Pittsburgh region imperiled even the sanctums of the well-to-do. A battered portfolio convinced Richard Beatty Mellon's son-in-law, Alan M. Scaife, to cancel his long-term contract with the Olmsted firm for landscaping his Shady Avenue estate.[12] Such conditions weakened the civic elites' once steady devotion to the financial and administrative needs of the CCCP. Membership subscriptions declined from well over 25,000 in 1928 to slightly over 23,000 in 1930. Some prominent wealthy board members resigned; board meetings occurred less and less frequently. In late 1931 just $5,702 in cash sat in the CCCP's till, and Bigger warned that normal operating expenses would exhaust that amount in early 1932. Hat in hand, the executive secretary toured the city's corporate offices endeavoring to keep the fourteen-year-old planning vessel afloat. But without success. Despite a $1,000 gift from Howard Heinz, another $500 from his brother Clifford, and a piddling $1,600 in assorted pledges, the campaign miserably failed. The once reliable Buhl and Falk foundations spurned Bigger's pleas.[13]

A few weeks later the CCCP discharged its clerical staff and canceled its office lease. Henceforth, the organization existed in name only, without a base of operation. Howard Heinz, E. W. Mudge, Bigger, and the other members of the MPA met one last time on April 19, 1933; a mere $1,514 now remained in the organization's treasury. The MPA would not reconvene again until October 1936.[14]

Planning's vital signs appeared no stronger in Bigger's other domain, the Pittsburgh City Planning Commission (CPC). Modest budget cutbacks first occurred in 1930. That year Pittsburgh slashed the commission's shade tree staff by 60 percent. As with the MPA, absenteeism among the more and more financially strained volunteer membership of the commission drained the body's effectiveness. Meanwhile, Bigger found the city council more concerned about the city's bleak job outlook and its shredded urban-industrial economy than about managing urban form. Bigger accused the council of making political decisions about zoning and other planning issues, weakening the effectiveness of the commission's work.

Planning fared no better at the county level, where the Allegheny County Planning Commission (ACPC) eliminated its Bureau of Aviation. Worse followed in 1931, when the Great Depression pummeled the Pittsburgh economy full force, and the press demanded tax cuts and government retrenchment.[15] Throughout the Pittsburgh region, budget cuts and other economy measures in 1931 and 1932 diminished the volume of road and street improvement work. Both the CPC and ACPC cut salaries as well as staffs in 1931.

By 1932 Bigger feared for the very existence of the CPC. Mayor Klein's Commission on City Finances threatened to eliminate the body. The city council imposed additional wage cuts on the department planning staff and scheduled employee furloughs. Such slashed appropriation undermined the ongoing topographical and geodetic surveys. Bigger bemoaned that the few plans approved by the city and county reflected such severe "trimmings" that "the effect [was] to prohibit the completion of well-designed projects and the demonstration of their value when so planned."[16] Although the commission budget was pared down radically, planning survived, albeit attenuated. Indeed, Bigger feared that any "further cutting would jeopardize the operation to the point where [it] might not be possible to carry on legally and required duties and services."[17]

The Great Depression not only imperiled planning in Pittsburgh and elsewhere, but it also promised to erode the precious state-legislated authority with which commissions had cloaked themselves during the 1920s. With unrentable downtown commercial property abundant, and tax ratables elsewhere in the city pummeled by the downwardly spiraling real estate market, landlords and politicians alike besieged local planning commissions, seeking zoning variances that would hopefully salvage shattered fortunes. Week after week, desperate owners of large, unoccupied residential property, such as the magnificent Victorian mansion owned by the heirs of the Jennings family at Fifth and Amberson avenues in the Shadyside District, besought the city council for an ordinance requiring the approval of the CPC to change the zoning of their property from "residential" to "commercial" land use. The Jennings heirs wanted to convert the unmarketable mansion into apartments; other beleaguered owners of depressed residentially zoned property clutched at a newly popular fad called "miniature" golf—also known as "baby" or "Tom Thumb" golf—as an alluring escape from bankruptcy. Miniature golf promoters hoped that planning commissions would treat golf not as "commercial" but as a "recreational" and therefore "permissible" land use in residential neighborhoods.[18]

Backed by the Chamber of Commerce and the Allied Boards of Trades, Bigger and the CPC held firm against all political assaults on the planning discipline. Battles raged throughout the decade. Politically sensitive to constituent demands, the city council in the 1930s attacked the bumptious CPC for its uncompromising stand on zoning. In an initial flanking movement, the council succeeded in having the state legislature amend the Zoning Enabling Act to empower the Zoning Board of Adjustment, a body independent of the CPC, to grant permits for miniature golf or "similar playgrounds in residential neighborhoods." The city council next sought passage of state legislation enabling it to override more easily CPC vetoes of its ordinances changing the city zoning map. The council failed, but its actions reinforced Bigger's belief in 1931 that a mere "thin red line" of planners blocked the army of politicians aligned against social order. According to historian of urban planning Mel Scott, under these conditions it was difficult for city planners everywhere in 1931–1932 to sustain faith in the future, "to believe that their expertise would again be in demand."[19]

PLANNING'S INITIAL RESPONSE TO CRISIS

No one denied the seriousness of the challenge faced by Pittsburgh planners in the early 1930s. For years Bigger had railed against evil politicians. But political machinations, budget cuts, and "furloughs" aside, sufficient evidence existed that planning in the Steel City survived the ordeal of the early Great Depression relatively unscathed if not actually invigorated. In fact, many city planning departments, Pittsburgh's included, regarded the economic depression as a unique opportunity to use "relief" labor to carry out the planning mission. Accordingly, the CPC and ACPC actually launched several major planning projects in the early 1930s, before the arrival of the New Deal.[20]

The CPC's proposed Inter-District Traffic Circuit scheme remained central to its mission. Amid all the nagging complaints about staff reductions and undermined programs, the commission pressed forward with its *Major Street* plan, aided by data from its still ongoing topographic survey. Building upon its Inter-District Traffic Circuit and downtown loop plan, a design first unveiled in the 1920s, the CPC's General Plans Committee in 1929 launched a systemwide major street study embracing every important district intersection, all main and secondary arteries, and all tunnel and bridge approaches that posed significant traffic problems. Despite the Great Depression, many traffic problems existed in the downtown. The boom in center city office construction during the late 1920s, including completion of the Gulf Tower and the massive post office and federal building in the early 1930s, greatly intensified the volume of traffic on Pittsburgh's antiquated narrow downtown streets and posed an insurmountable parking problem. A rash of city traffic accidents, topping 1,143 in 1930, underscored the urgency of the problem.[21]

Like downtown real estate and commercial interests, city planners dreaded the loss of business to the suburbs. Indeed, the specter of decentralization, suppressed in the 1920s, loomed amid the declining retail sales, plunging property values, and tax delinquencies that plagued downtown businesses in the 1930s.[22] Frank Duggan of the Better Traffic Committee agreed with Pittsburgh Housing Association head John Ihlder that suburbanization inexorably engendered a new, decentralized "metropolitan" form. Ihlder and Duggan stressed the need for increased downtown accessibility via amplified radial thoroughfares, downtown bypasses, and modern circumferential highways. Simultaneously, state highway engineers, aided by the federal Bureau of Public Roads and automobile clubs, advanced plans to widen the William Penn (U.S. Route 22) and Lincoln (U.S. Route 30) highways as part of a national coast-to-coast "super highway."[23]

One of the signature comprehensive planning activities of the CPC's General Plan Committee during the early 1930s, Pittsburgh's *Major Street* plan encompassed all of these ideas. Under the commission's guidance, the City Planning Department staff, never large enough to suit Bigger, produced giant maps of city areas such as Squirrel Hill, the East Liberty business district, Banksville Avenue, and the north portal of the Liberty Tubes. These exquisite maps were in turn studied, modified, and improved first by the city Department of Public Works, then by the CPC, and finally integrated into the city's master plan. Although staff cuts and furloughs slowed work, the *Major Street* plan moved forward, aided in 1932 by a sizable contingent of relief labor provided by the ACEA.[24]

During the 1930s, Pittsburgh businessmen, especially the Lower Downtown Businessmen's Association (LDBMA), turned again and again to the city's riverfronts, to building high floodwalls and riverfront boulevards, and to commemorating the historic Point. Pittsburgh's sagging Depression-era economy rendered the Point's timeworn rail yards, drab streets, and scabrous warehouses even grimier and more somber. Next to the city's sparkling new Gulf Tower and the impressive post office and federal buildings rising on Grant Street, Pittsburgh's Chamber of Commerce decreed the "unsightly, deplorable condition of the downtown riverfronts . . . wholly incongruous." Chamber president James Rae in 1930 called for "progressive planning for waterfront development as a first step toward downtown beautification," and he urged "co-operation," specifically to have the U.S. War Department accurately define the harbor lines around the Golden Triangle. Cooperation also involved secur-ing agreement for floodwall construction and other riverfront improvements from the so-called river interests—the packet fleet, tugboat operators, and coal barge owners whose livelihoods depended on the ancient Monongahela and Allegheny quays affected by any riverfront plans.[25]

With joblessness climbing, public enthusiasm for riverfront improvements soared in 1930. On the wings of Rae's speech, the Chamber of Commerce cre-ated a Special Activities Committee dedicated to securing a major riverfront project. In Washington, D.C., Senator David Reed introduced a bill into Con-gress for a memorial park at the Point honoring George Rogers Clark. Mayor Klein clambered aboard the Point Park bandwagon. Shortly before taking of-fice Klein had proposed a People's Bond Issue covering the city's cost of flood-walls. In 1930 he charged the city's Department of Public Works to draft such a riverfront study elaborating the improvement. The department promptly as-sured the mayor and the Chamber that it had plans under way to convert Du-quesne Way and Water Street into "boulevards flanked by broad esplanades," but shortly after that assurance it surrendered the project to the CPC. Hob-bled in 1930 by both budget cuts and layoffs, the CPC valiantly completed its "Report on River Front Development" by April 1932 when, with great fanfare, it publicly displayed a model of its recommendations. The model, faithful to the Department of Public Works's promise, showed Duquesne Way and Water Street as grand, tree-lined boulevards adorning the edge of the Golden Tri-angle, now clearly defined by a floodwall and replete with gracefully looping highway approaches to the Duquesne and Manchester bridges at the Point. Bigger incorporated the design into his coveted Inter-District Traffic Cir-cuit project, which included the Crosstown Thoroughfare, also being actively planned in the early 1930s. The 1932 Riverfront Boulevard plan likewise com-plemented the commission's master plan as a constituent part of the *Major Street* plan.[26]

These joint major street and riverfront improvement plans reveal that the Great Depression slowed, but hardly dampened, the ever-resurgent spirit of planning in Pittsburgh. As if to underscore that fact, Pittsburgh in November 1932 hosted the Twenty-fourth National Conference on City Planning, a confer-ence originally scheduled for Seattle. Cosponsored by the Civic Club of Allegh-eny County (CCAC), the Pittsburgh Housing Association, the Chamber of Com-merce, the Allied Boards of Trades, American Institute of Architects (AIA), the

University of Pittsburgh, and both the ACPC and the CPC, among others, the conference met at the Hotel Schenley in Oakland and attracted over 4,000 persons. For Pittsburgh's planning community, the conference had the significance of highlighting the vital role and resilience of planning in the Depression-ridden Steel City. Among the prominent conference speakers, presumably selected by Bigger, were his RPAA colleagues Robert Kohn, Jacob Crane, and Henry Wright. Only days before the conference, Franklin Delano Roosevelt had been elected the new president of the United States, and he had already tapped Kohn, Wright, and Crane to join his New Deal housing team. Bigger's three friends dazzled the Pittsburgh audience with hints of a new day in housing under the escutcheon of the New Deal. The conference also featured a Pittsburgh planning and housing exhibit designed by the famed artist-sculptor Augustus St. Gaudens, plus a tour of the Buhl Foundation's now one-year-old model garden city, Chatham Village, which Wright had designed along with Clarence Stein.[27]

Bigger himself had been involved in the Chatham Village project. It revealed not only his visionary instincts but also his enduring fascination with town planning. In 1930 Buhl proposed to convert the hilly forty-five-acre Bingham property in the Mt. Washington section into a modern, affordable housing community for 300 families. The Great Depression aside, Buhl aimed to demonstrate that by combining fiscally sound investment practice with modern, large-scale construction and community design principles, Pittsburgh's hill terrains could be efficiently and aesthetically utilized for affordable housing.[28]

The challenge to apply garden city principles to a difficult site in an city desperate for good design also attracted Stein and Wright, fresh from their celebrated work on Radburn, New Jersey. It also intrigued Bigger, who had adumbrated interest in housing and modern community design in his 1923 *Parks* report. In April 1931 Bigger, without compensation, produced a "diagrammatic study of the possibilities of community development of the Bingham property."[29] His schema for the Bingham site radiated Clarence Perry's neighborhood-unit social principles, calculated grading and utilities expenses into the development costs, and stressed the economies to be gained by scale and standardization. Charles Lewis, the director of the Buhl Foundation, called Bigger's schema a "splendid study." Like Stein and Wright's in Radburn, Bigger's greenbelt-encircled community plan excluded automobiles while providing automobile-accommodating service lanes and garages on the periphery. Tudor-style row house clusters situated on contoured lots faced beautifully planted interior garden courts. Playground space abounded.[30]

Lewis cheerfully received Bigger's plan, commending "the generous spirit and fine interest of Mr. Bigger in making this material contribution of his time and technical skill."[31] But there is no evidence that the foundation seriously considered the interesting, technically detailed, but rectilinear Bigger plan. For the project design, Buhl chose the better-known Stein and Wright team, whose award-winning curvilinear design for Chatham Village also gracefully accommodated the Pittsburgh hill site. Stein and Wright's elevations and the other central design features, as well as their estimation that the cost of grading and providing durable construction would prohibit rents low enough to house working-class families, closely resembled Bigger's. Indeed, the carefully selected first tenants would be white-collar families battered, but not broken, by the Depression. Eventually, Bigger himself took up residence in Chatham Village and lived there until failing health in the 1960s forced him to locate nearer his doctor and other services.[32]

The ACPC had fully participated in arranging the 1932 National Conference on City Planning that featured the Chatham Village tour. Its involvement announced the epiphany of this oft-maligned agency. During 1931 three vacancies had existed on the ACPC, which, despite CCCP protests, month after month remained unfilled.[33] Before 1932, the Allegheny County Planning Department barely existed, its staff shanghaied by the county Department of Public Works. Charged in 1931 with undertaking the burdensome county survey work for Governor Gifford Pinchot's massive statewide rural highway improvement program, and for planning the county's airport and sundry bridge and highway projects linked to the 1929 People's Bond Issue, the county Department of Public Works had commandeered most of the ACPC's engineering and drafting staff, including the commission's chief engineer, E. L. Schmidt.[34]

Between 1931 and 1932 the ACPC freed itself from the grip of Public Works and asserted its legal authority to approve county land use decisions. Two factors, the Great Depression and the county commissioners' election of November 1931, contributed to this liberation. Signs of imminent change appeared as early as 1930 when state Republican Party stalwart Richard Beatty Mellon retired as chairman of the ACPC and S. J. Topely replaced him. Then in the May 1931 Republican primary, two political independents, Charles "Buck" McGovern and Caldwalder Barr, defeated Republican organization candidates James Coyne and Joseph Armstrong, and both went on to defeat their Democratic rivals (including David Lawrence) in the fall election. The election foretold the demise of the county's Republican political dynasty. In the name of "economy and the taxpayer," McGovern and Barr "reorganized" county government, purged "political dead wood," and in the process freed the ACPC from the Department of Public Works. Hearing that news, ACPC secretary James Sansom rejoiced in language redolent of Bigger's professionalism. Sansom announced that the ACPC was at last "in a position to inaugurate real planning . . . [and] to initiate complete studies looking toward the adoption of a general improvement plan for the county." He envisioned the department's engineering division "preparing charts, maps, and [topographic] data . . . allowing the commission to intelligently consider and develop a systematic plan of improvements."[35]

But Sansom himself succumbed to McGovern's ruthless economic retrenchment ax. In May 1932 the commissioners furloughed the ACPC's entire technical staff, lowered the salaries of the survivors, and placed the whole mission and function of county planning in limbo. With his own salary about to be cut, and convinced that he would be unable to care for his family adequately, Sansom resigned. McGovern and Barr accepted Sansom's resignation and ordered the commission, which now included Secretary Topely and members Mrs. J. O. Miller, General Albert J. Logan, and once-boss William Flinn's daughter, Mrs. William Flinn Lawrence, to find a replacement for Sansom whose credentials coupled engineering skills with knowledge of planning administration. At Mrs. Lawrence's urging, the commission selected for this engineer-secretary position Jo Ray, the junior partner of the distinguished Pittsburgh-based landscape architect Ralph Griswold. A graduate of Texas A&M and the Cornell School of Architecture, Ray had apprenticed under the Olmsted Associates before leaving the Brookline, Massachusetts, firm to join Griswold in Pittsburgh.[36]

But while Ray knew engineering, he lacked engineering credentials, a serious deficiency in the county commissioners' eyes since they conceived the newly restructured ACPC to be chiefly an oversight panel rendering technical and financial judgments about the merits of such public works improvements as roads, bridges, culverts, and sewers. In McGovern's garbled language, planning involved "new projects or re-construction work or what might be called maintenance—changing of grades, changing of re-surfacing of roads, changing of alignments of road[s], or whatever might be."[37] Therefore, while the ACPC in 1932 declared its independence from Public Works, and its "right to pass on all projects," political and economic pressures actually drew it closer toward engineering, not toward Sansom's and Bigger's vision of general planning. Ignoring the ACPC's prerogative to choose its own personnel, the county commissioners, led by McGovern, appointed E. J. Schmidt "temporary" chief engineer, retaining Jo Ray in the secretary's post. Schmidt proceeded to execute the commissioners' reorganization plan. The newly independent, but modestly sized, forty-six-person planning agency conformed perfectly to McGovern's image. It was staffed mainly by draftsmen, road designers, transit men, and roadmen. Jo Ray resigned a year later in 1933. Nevertheless, free of Public Works and headed by Topely and Chief Engineer Schmidt, the commission exuded a pride in expertise and a new-found sense of professionalism.[38]

The reorganization of the ACPC in 1931 invoked a brief era of good feeling among CPC and ACPC ranks. A year earlier the CPC had harshly upbraided the county for undertaking planning and construction projects "without enough regard for the City Planning Commission's recommendations." "It is bad policy," vented an irate Bigger, "to allow the county to disrupt the plans of the city. Some of the county projects may be seriously objected to on the score of inadequate or wrong planning; the county landscape is being needlessly mutilated along the highways."[39] But one year later, with the ACPC fully staffed and independent of Public Works, harmony abounded. The CPC in June 1932 hosted a reception for ACPC commissioners. At the event, also attended by James L. Stuart of the Greater Pittsburgh Parks Commission and Thomas Liggett of the Pennsylvania Parks Association, CPC chair L. W. Monteverde hailed the importance of city-county cooperation. Envisioning the rewards of a coordinated approach to city and regional planning, Monteverde pointed specifically (and perhaps presciently, in view of Robert Moses's work in Pittsburgh in the late 1930s) to the case of New York City, where parks administrator/planner Moses was orchestrating an attractive and majestic bridge and "parkway system" integrating the city's five boroughs with Westchester and Suffolk counties. At the CPC's regular June 17, 1932, meeting, Bigger reported that the CPC and ACPC had established a Temporary Committee on Coordination Procedures, which had agreed to dovetail the city's *Major Street* plan with the county's Major Highway Plan and to cooperate in integrating the county's recreation areas with any parkway or boulevard projects (specifically the Saw Mill Run Parkway) that extended through both the city and the county.[40]

In another example of cooperation, the CPC and ACPC teamed with the Chamber of Commerce to combat the Snodgrass-Brown plan. As flamboyant as it was politically appealing for its job-creating potential, the Snodgrass-Brown plan proposed to transform the Monongahela and Duquesne waterfronts into an all-purpose, urban-transportation extravaganza, featuring a double-decked highway, a subway, parking lots, and riverboat dockage space. The two planning commissions likewise rejected the George Vang Company's $800,000 bid to frame the downtown riverfronts with spacious, elevated boulevards shielding large, quayside parking lots. Consistently opposed to the idea of wharf parking, Bigger blasted both ideas as contrary to the goal of attaining maximum downtown traffic circulation.[41]

Meanwhile, the Chamber disparaged the transit elements of the Snodgrass-Brown plan, especially the subway proposal. The Chamber considered "it exceedingly doubtful whether streetcar subways will prove to be the solution to the traffic problem in large cities." "In any age of rapid transition," quipped a scornful Chamber, "traffic engineers are in doubt as to what will emerge."[42] Thomas Fitzgerald, vice president of the Pittsburgh Railways Company, detected in the Chamber's subway verdict the imminent tolling of the death knell for mass transit in Pittsburgh. Fitzgerald pleaded that streetcars and subways still represented the most economical way of moving large masses of people; but he observed the steady shifting of public attention and resources in 1932 toward major streets, bridges, and tunnels, not public transit. In addition to increasing the public tax burden, asserted Fitzgerald, this heavy investment in automobile infrastructure proved "simultaneously unsound and dangerous economic competition against mass transportation." It entrapped transit companies like his in a death spiral of forced maintenance cuts followed by reduced ridership.[43] Not surprisingly, with the exception of a small federally funded 1934 transit study, this brief skirmish with the Snodgrass-Brown proposal ended further subway discussion in Pittsburgh until the 1940s. Throughout the 1930s, in Pittsburgh and across the nation, the consensus gave primacy to the automobile and motorbus over the trolley and subway.[44]

This dalliance between the CPC and ACPC ended abruptly. The fleeting courtship left the relationship unconsummated. Although independent and cognizant of its newfound professionalism, the ACPC differed substantially from its city counterpart. Schmidt's county agency remained dominated by an engineering mentality and accepted its official, albeit subordinate, role of mainly surveying and approving county commissioner–proposed road and bridge projects. Meanwhile, under Bigger, the CPC operated diurnally as the epitome of textbook professionalism dedicated to data gathering and, as its highest calling, formulating and defending the master plan.

Given their divergent orientations, county and city clashes were inevitable—over the proposed costly Homestead High Level Bridge, for example. The county viewed the bridge as politically desirable; both the three mill towns of the Homestead area and the Carnegie Steel Company desired it as a desperately needed boost for the local economy to be funded under the county's 1928 People's Bond Issue. For the CPC, however, the bridge idea lacked merit. It neither fit into the *Major Street* plan, nor did the hard data on costs associated with the bridge's high elevation and extensive grading requirements justify it. Moreover, Bigger viewed the high-level span as a duplication of existing bridges. It was another politically motivated compromise. From his vantage point, "there [was] more urgent need for the rebuilding of an amplified Smithfield Street Bridge than for the proposed [new] Homestead Bridge, although legally," he added, "the former is not a county structure."[45]

THE NEW DEAL AND PITTSBURGH PLANNING

As Pittsburgh in 1933 entered the fourth year of the Great Depression, the CPC and ACPC represented important, but only two of the participants in the urban conversation. Occasionally shrill and often, but not always, backed by the Chamber of Commerce, the Lower Downtown Businessmen's Association (LDBMA) also voiced its position on street, highway, bridge, and other plans for city development. So did the river interests, along with the U.S. War Department. The Allied Boards of Trades, which represented numerous civic organizations such as the CCAC, as well as many smaller businesses located both within and outside the city, expressed strong opinions about development, especially in the suburban South Hills, where new subdivisions were ripe for residential and commercial building. Finally, under the Roosevelt administration, the federal government would occupy an increasingly prominent place in the urban conversation. Washington had already become engaged in the 1920s as a champion of zoning and a sponsor of the "Own Your Own Home" movement. In the 1930s the New Deal's federally coordinated relief and recovery programs greatly swelled the federal government's voice in urban development.[46]

By forcing cities to coordinate and consolidate their development plans, the federal job-creating programs that arose in the early 1930s exposed deeply divided opinions on the future of urban development. Momentum for federal involvement in undertaking slum clearance, highway building, and other public works built month by month during the early years of the Depression decade. Harold Buttenheim, dynamic editor of *American City* and a vigorous supporter of the Better Homes movement, the home-ownership movement founded by Marie Meloney and nurtured in the 1920s by Secretary of Commerce Herbert Hoover, crusaded in 1931 for federal loans for a massive "deslumming" effort. Indeed, many of the delegates to President Hoover's December 1931 Conference on Home Building and Home Ownership endorsed slum clearance, together with public housing.[47]

A technocrat and an apostle of "scientific management," Hoover saw government as having a leading voice in the Depression-era urban conversation. The federal government, he believed, functioned as a clearinghouse for ideas and information, enabling cities and towns to better navigate the shoals of economic disaster and effectively mobilize local charity and voluntarism. Like Pittsburgh's Chamber of Commerce, which in 1932 spurned suggestions that the city should seek federal assistance for riverfront improvements because government should "never do for us that which we are able and willing to do for ourselves," Hoover scorned the idea of having the federal government directly help the jobless. Government aid, entreated Hoover, must remain voluntary; Washington should merely work to reinforce individual character and initiative. Hoover's flagship depression agency, the Reconstruction Finance Corporation (RFC), created in January 1932, loaned monies to insurance companies, banks, railroads, and limited-dividend housing corporations to stabilize those vital institutions and stimulate the private sector economy. Through his President's Emergency Committee for Employment (like its more sanguine successor, the President's Emergency Committee for Unemployment), Hoover encouraged and applauded local work relief efforts. At last, goaded by Detroit's beleaguered mayor, Frank Murphy, and by the newly formed United States Conference of Mayors, in July 1932 Hoover expanded the RFC by making available $2 billion to assist state and local efforts—such as Pittsburgh's ACEA.[48] Anticipation of RFC funds inflamed the imaginations of Pittsburghers, who fantasized about riverfront boulevards, Point parks, and Homestead and Highland Park bridges. But the Chamber of Commerce, in fact, felt compelled to forcefully deny the general belief "that we are willing to go down to Washington with a tin cup in our hands."[49]

Despite Hoover's technocratic credentials and the fillip his RFC gave to advocates of slum clearance and other public works, it was not Hoover's RFC but Franklin D. Roosevelt's New Deal that hitched wings to the planner's dreams. While Hoover lauded planning, FDR, in Mel Scott's words, "brought to the Presidency a conviction of the need for planning and some ideas so farsighted that they amazed even persons whose business it was to take the long view." As governor of New York, Roosevelt had pursued a vigorous planning and public works agenda, including the type of conservation, highway, and hydroelectric developments dear to the heart of RPAA members such as Lewis Mumford,

Clarence Stein, Benton MacKaye, and Frederick Bigger. FDR's 1932 Commonwealth Club speech in San Francisco adopted the planner's liberal organic view of society, which presumed constant public intervention to compensate for social and economic imbalances.[50]

In the months after November 1932, hundreds of planners and business and agricultural economists such as Alvin Hansen, Gardiner Means, and Rexford Tugwell, enraptured by the idea of a federally interventionist, boldly experimental New Deal, flocked to the nation's capital. RPAA members Clarence Stein, Henry Wright, Robert Kohn, and Fred Ackerman, all friends of Fred Bigger's, who in 1932 now served as vice president of the decade-old regional planning organization, joined others in exhorting FDR and his secretary of the interior, Harold Ickes, for a visionary planning and public works program. Emboldened, Roosevelt in March 1933 launched a bevy of experimental, planning-intensive programs, some blatantly corporatist, some simply microeconomic tinkering, but all imbued with a technocratic faith that a managed economy would engender a more socially responsible capitalism. The more radical New Deal economic planning programs, namely the Agriculture Adjustment Administration, the Tennessee Valley Authority (TVA), the Civilian Conservation Corps, and the National Industrial Recovery Administration (NIRA), departed sharply from any "business as usual" mentality. Title II of the National Industrial Recovery Act established the Public Works Administration (PWA), headed by Ickes.[51]

News of all of these programs swirled through an economically battered Steel City, now experiencing the early stages of a political upheaval. Internal feuding at the local and state Republican Party levels in the early 1930s had left the city's GOP headed by William Larimer Mellon rudderless and vulnerable. Old Guard politicos nervously watched 50,000 Pittsburghers pack the city's Forbes Field baseball stadium in October 1932 to hear FDR lambaste Republican leadership and extol the promise of the New Deal. Shocked Old Guard Pittsburghers watched as such prominent local Republicans as oil wildcatter William Benedum abandoned Hoover for the squire from Hyde Park. Opportunistic Pittsburgh Democrats such as David Lawrence and Joseph Guffey, early champions of Roosevelt, but long accused of servility to the once indomitable Republican machine, mobilized the city's jobless African Americans, Slovaks, Poles, Italians, and other ethnic groups behind FDR. Lawrence's efforts carried Pittsburgh for Roosevelt, and FDR's coattails, plus an avalanche of independent and disaffected Republican voters, helped install for the first time in decades a Democrat, William McNair, in the city's mayor's office.[52]

Roosevelt's victory and his mellifluous rhetoric, laced with a heady optimism about overcoming "fear itself," captivated Pittsburghers in 1933. Even some hardcore Republicans barricaded behind the richly paneled walls of the city's Duquesne Club softened. In July 1933 the Chamber of Commerce adopted a resolution supporting the NIRA, after which the Chamber displayed the Blue Eagle emblem on the masthead of its publication *Greater Pittsburgh*.[53] The NIRA blended 1920s technocracy with government and business cooperation. Through "Codes of Fair Practice," it promised to unite government and business in joint economic planning. Equally alluring to Pittsburgh business, the NIRA promised to employ the multitude of urban jobless on massive self-liquidating public works. It was, in fact, a federally funded ACEA.

The NIRA and the Federal Emergency Relief Administration (FERA), together with the entire New Deal "alphabet soup," represented, moreover, a "New Federalism," whereby the federal government replaced the state as the guarantor of urban-economic well-being, especially in the provision of vital infrastructure. Bridges, highways, schools, waterworks, and tunnels topped PWA administrator Harold Ickes's list, an appetizing menu for employment-famished Pittsburgh. Like the ACEA, Ickes's PWA required city and county governments to share the cost of projects, something extremely difficult for local bodies like Pittsburgh strained by bonded debt and a downwardly spiraling tax base. Therefore, in November 1933, with an expected harsh winter approaching, FDR and his FERA administrator, Harry Hopkins, unveiled the latest in the New Deal goulash, the Civil Works Administration (CWA), which according to Regulation Number 1, "sought to put men to work, [to] create purchasing power, and thus give an impetus to business and employment in general." The CWA endeavored to employ the jobless on "public works that are socially and economically desirable to the community and to the nation."[54] Like the PWA, it asked state and local governments to absorb the costs of materials and equipment such as shovels, bricks, and concrete; most CWA jobs, however, such as cleaning parks, building paths, grading fields, shoveling snow, making mattresses, and copying records, involved minimal nonlabor costs.[55]

In concert with the PWA, the NIRA, the TVA, and other New Deal "alphabet soup" agencies, the CWA exalted planning. In fact, the New Deal mandated evidence of formal planning as a central part of its recovery formula. Toward that end, the New Deal created within Harold Ickes's PWA the National Planning Board (NPB) headed by Frederic Delano, Wesley Mitchell, and Charles Merriam, all veterans of the city planning movement. The NPB counted among its staff and consultants nationally prominent planning figures such as Charles

Eliot, Harland Bartholomew, Russell Van Nest Black, John Nolen, and Alfred Bettman. Although its name changed over the years from the National Planning Board in 1933 to the National Resources Board to, finally, the National Resources Planning Board (NRPB), this body strove to enhance city and regional planning professionalism nationally.[56]

Ickes required sponsors of PWA projects to keep up-to-date six-year comprehensive plans, and, to assure the quality of such comprehensive planning, the NPB in 1933 demanded a steady flow of data on the activities of all city, state, and county planning agencies. An NPB circular, entitled "Securing Results in City Planning," extolled city planning as "the most practical activity in which a city may engage." Ickes, indeed, responded favorably to a resolution from the National Conference on City Planning that "comprehensive city and regional master plans be recognized as an essential public work . . . [and therefore] under conditions and restrictions such as may be imposed by you, be made eligible to receive [PWA] grants and loans."[57]

In an exuberant mood, Pittsburgh planners in 1933 braced for the awaited large-scale federal public works program and savored the challenge posed by the expected flood of development proposals. An NPB survey discovered planning commissions in places such as Pittsburgh euphoric about the New Deal and eager to augment their staffs from the large pool of jobless architects, draftsmen, planning technicians, and engineers.[58] By the summer of 1933, PWA work had compelled planning departments to considerably expand their drafting and surveying staffs.

Housing and slum clearance ranked high among the proposed projects, together with equally labor-intensive highway and bridge work. After an almost two-decades-long divorce, housing and planning reunited again in the 1930s. In fact, housing resonated as an issue between 1931 and 1933. Many delegates had endorsed slum clearance and public housing at Hoover's 1931 Conference on Home Building and Home Ownership. Seizing the moment, housers such as Ernest Bohn in 1931 founded the National Public Housing Conference. Housing topped the agenda of the 1932 meeting of the National Conference on City Planning in Pittsburgh, setting the stage for the 1933 Cleveland Conference on Slum Clearance, where Pittsburgher Fredrick Bigger, together with his Pittsburgh Housing Association ally Joseph Tufts, headed a large Steel City delegation. This conference and others produced congressional resolutions demanding federal aid for slum clearance.[59]

But the nuptials seemed joyless in Pittsburgh. City planners debated clearing slums from the Lower Hill District, and the 1932 National Conference on

City Planning featured a housing agenda; but housing hardly ranked as an urgent issue for Pittsburgh's CPC. True, Fred Bigger's involvement with Buhl's Chatham Village project implied the chairman's personal interest in the garden city idea and in accessible, "moderately priced" housing. In fact, together with Tufts, Bigger in the fall of 1934 attended two important conferences on housing and slum clearance, one in Cleveland and the other in Baltimore. Sponsored by the recently formed National Public Housing Conference, the historic 1934 Baltimore conference declared decent housing to be a government responsibility and set the goal—affirmed by Ickes—of securing a permanent federal public housing program. Ickes earlier in 1933 had established a Housing Division within the PWA headed by Bigger's RPAA colleague Robert Kohn; indeed, Bigger even served as a consultant to the agency. Both the Pittsburgh Housing Association and the city council lobbied Kohn for a PWA "housing demonstration project," identifying and surveying three Hill District areas for potential sites; however, the city's bid for a Housing Division project failed. Significantly, in a still fragmented Pittsburgh, housing, like health and welfare issues, remained compartmentalized beyond the ken of planning. Bigger's personal interest in housing issues notwithstanding, throughout 1933–1937 Pittsburgh's CPC kept silent about housing.[60]

Pittsburgh's failure to secure a PWA housing project in 1934 should not suggest that the PWA, the CWA, or any other New Deal agency ignored the city. Both the city and the county actively pursued federal work relief monies that lifted planning spirits while at the same time engendering problems. In June 1933 the Allegheny County commissioners rushed a stack of proposals to Ickes, including seven bridge projects. Their haste forced chagrined county planners to protest that the commissioners had failed to consult them. Belatedly, they did, and in August the ACPC approved the bridge projects, among them the Homestead High Level, Glenwood, Dravosburg, Rankin, and Highland Park bridges.[61]

By July 1934 the county's list of projects approved by the PWA included not only a bevy of ballyhooed riverfront improvements but also the Saw Mill Run Parkway extension, a widened Banksville Road, and a traffic circle scheme to unsnarl notorious congestion at the south end of the Liberty Tubes. South Hills suburban real estate boosters might have more effusively hailed the package except that both the bridge and Liberty Tubes projects involved toll fees, a funding device historically despised in Pittsburgh, albeit successfully employed by Robert Moses on New York City's 1930s bridge and tunnel projects. Imitating Moses, the county created an Allegheny County Authority to oversee the building and operation of its anticipated bonanza of PWA bridge and other large self-liquidating projects. E. L. Schmidt resigned as the director of the county's Planning Department to head the authority; engineer Park Martin replaced him.[62]

While not a member of the new Allegheny County Authority, department store magnate and influential civic leader Edgar J. Kaufmann promoted Frank Lloyd Wright as the architect to design the riverfront and other improvements to be funded by the much anticipated $24,000,000 PWA grant to the county. Kaufmann included the prospect of PWA work as part of the several other projects he had in mind for Wright in 1934: a design for his office in his store, a parking garage, a planetarium, and a weekend house in the nearby Allegheny Mountains. In return, the architect wanted Kaufmann to fund a three-dimensional model of his Broadacre City plan, Wright's fantastic, though in some ways prescient, vision for new towns on the metropolitan periphery. Kaufmann did underwrite the model, which premiered at Rockefeller Center in April 1935 and then was displayed at his downtown Pittsburgh store. For his part, Wright designed the office for Kaufmann and the weekend retreat that became the world-famous Fallingwater house. But Wright did not receive the public works commission and in his typically superior manner insulted the city. In an article published in the *Pittsburgh Sun-Telegraph*, Wright sneered that "Pittsburgh . . . seems to have ignored all principles in getting itself born as a human asset."[63]

Engineer Park Martin's appointment as director of the Allegheny County Authority in 1935 and his ten-year tenure in that post maintained the strong influence of engineering in the Allegheny County Planning Department. Forty-eight years old at the time of his appointment, Martin had spent his career until then as a transportation engineer and on the fringes of county politics. He grew up in the leafy suburban Ohio River community of Bellevue, just beyond the city boundary. After studying engineering at the Carnegie Institute of Technology (now Carnegie Mellon University), Martin worked briefly for the Pittsburgh and Lake Erie Railroad, the Pittsburgh-Butler Interurban Railway, and his hometown of Bellevue, where he also became its burgess (mayor). He apparently aspired to higher political office, but failed in runs for the Pennsylvania Senate and Allegheny County Commissioner. He devoted most of the years before joining the county payroll to his own small engineering firm. Through his political and engineering activities, Martin undoubtedly developed close contacts with county officials, and in 1933 he became the chief engineer and assistant director of the county's Department of Public Works.

Reportedly quite smart, a good listener, and ever practical, this man operated at the center of the region's planning world for more than twenty years, most notably as Richard King Mellon's handpicked first executive director of the Allegheny Conference on Community Development beginning in 1945.[64]

But in the mid-1930s, Martin's political skills failed to heal the city-county rift. A combination of the unpopular toll scheme plus revelations concerning the high salaries of authority administrative personnel outraged Pittsburghers. Likewise, delays caused by the failure of the Pittsburgh City Council and Mayor William McNair to agree on an ordinance allowing the county to work on city-owned streets and thoroughfares prevented any work on the list of PWA projects until 1935. By late 1935 public anger fueled by exposés featured in the city's virulently anti–New Deal press doomed the Allegheny County Authority, which soon folded. While most of the bridge projects survived the debacle, the brouhaha shrank the Liberty Tubes improvement from an initial sweeping, swooping circle-overpass concept into pallid cosmetic surgery.[65]

The Allegheny County Authority imbroglio overlapped the rise and fall of the CWA. A huge federal "emergency" work relief program launched nationwide in late 1933, CWA operated countywide under the auspices of the County Emergency Relief Board. Over the bitterly cold winter of 1933–1934, it sought to quickly employ thousands of the jobless, including many of the 27,000 sad and despairing men and women who crowded Pittsburgh's relief rolls. Twenty million dollars appropriated from the city's 1932 bond issue helped pay the materials and equipment costs of CWA projects.[66] Most but not all of the region's large-scale CWA construction projects involved improvements to sewerage and drainage systems, parks, and roads, as well as landscaping and building runways at the county's new airport. It was mostly backbreaking toil performed outdoors, dogged and delayed month after month by record cold winter weather. When Harry Hopkins terminated the CWA in May 1934, he not only idled 23,000 relief workers, but he also left many jobs unfinished.

One agency furloughing many disgruntled CWA workers in 1934 was the ACPC. The PWA and CWA together had piled a high volume of survey work onto county planners, which forced the ballooning of the City Planning Department staff. A January 1934 NPB inquiry revealed that the ACPC employed 106 engineers, twenty-seven draftsmen, thirty-three statisticians, and ninety-eight miscellaneous persons. The bulk of those draftsmen and engineers in 1934 worked under the CWA.[67]

While the ACPC used the CWA to staff its greatly expanded bridge and road surveying work, the CPC treated federal work-relief monies as manna.

City planners at first used federal funds to produce traditional surveys for roadway and other public works improvements. But in early 1934 those tasks were dwarfed by the commission's lavish CWA program, one meticulously drafted by Bigger and the commission's General Planning Committee to be a professional planning pièce de résistance. Submitted to Hopkins and CWA staffers in December 1933, Pittsburgh's program counted ten projects, including several "specialized" studies whose management and supervision were subcontracted by the CPC to "qualified public and quasi-public agencies" such as the University of Pittsburgh and the Pittsburgh Housing Association. The ten projects represented the data-gathering process that Fred Bigger considered imperative for comprehensive planning. A few projects, such as the city's geodetic and topographic survey, dated from the 1920s. But most were new, including a "Comprehensive Mapping of City Recreation Sites," a "Platting and Recording of Delinquent City Tax Properties," a "Special Housing Survey" managed by the Pittsburgh Housing Association, a "Physical Inventory of City-Owned Buildings," a "Survey of Sub-Surface Utilities," a "Study of Local Passenger Transportation" overseen by the City Transit Commission, and a study for a proposed subsistence homestead, part of the New Deal's effort to relocate "stranded" urban-industrial populations into more salubrious suburban and quasi-rural locations. The proposed homestead, like the earlier Chatham Village "experiment," enabled Bigger to test ideas brainstormed during cozy RPAA sessions in Clarence Stein's New York apartment during the 1920s. Intrigued as Roosevelt was by the alluring vision of resettling urban jobless on arable land beyond central cities, Ickes in 1933 created a Division of Subsistence Homesteads under the NIRA. Pittsburgh's CPC used CWA workers to plat one such homestead on land located east of the city in Elizabeth Township for the resettlement of "stranded" jobless families.[68]

The new homestead hardly ended Pittsburgh's romance with New Deal–planned communities. Roosevelt's initial experiment with subsistence homesteads abruptly ended in 1935 when the Supreme Court scuttled the National Industrial Recovery Act as unconstitutional. FDR promptly replaced it in 1935 with the Resettlement Administration (RA) headed by brain truster Rexford Tugwell. That year Tracy Augur, a fellow planner, an RPAA associate, and now an RA staffer, invited Bigger to join colleagues Clarence Stein and Henry Wright, who had teamed on the Chatham Village design, in reviewing plans for the RA's first two Greenbelt towns, places where the urban jobless might be "resettled" in wholesome, well-planned communities, which in the spirit of the Greenbelt Town inventor, Ebenezer Howard, would be located on the urban periphery. Soon Edward Lansill, director of the RA's Suburban Division charged with overseeing the Greenbelt Town program, appointed Bigger chief of planning for the first four planned towns. Bigger headed the Greenbelt project until 1937.[69]

The CPC's study of a proposed subsistence homestead in Elizabeth Township represented but one of its CWA-funded planning ventures. By 1934 city planning projects employed 343 engineers, architects, draftsmen, and other skilled personnel, and, as with the county, many of those workers earned CWA wages.[70] Of the city's ten CWA projects, the "Master Plan for Recreation" (a planning venture additionally aided by Buhl Foundation monies) most delighted Bigger and the General Plans Committee. Despite the 1921 *Playgrounds* and the 1923 *Parks* reports, Pittsburgh's recreational facilities in the 1930s languished. The Greater Pittsburgh Parks Association had secured the Buhl grant that enabled the CPC to retain landscape architect Ralph Griswold as a consultant to oversee the project. By 1935, guided by Griswold's landscaping expertise, Bigger's desire for comprehensive planning, and the labor of seventeen architects and three engineers supplied first under CWA and then the Relief Works Division (RWD) of FERA, the CPC hammered out a broad "Master Plan for Recreation." The plan determined the "distribution and development of [all city] play spaces." It "tabulat[ed] existing [recreational] sites and the needs both here and where no city-owned site had yet been provided."[71] CWA labor produced blueprints for the development of Pittsburgh recreation sites well into the post–World War II era, including playground development plans for sites in the Hill District, Polish Hill, Schenley Park, the South Side, and Highland Park. Approved by the CPC and transmitted to the Department of Public Works, the CWA-funded recreation plan provided an arsenal of labor-intensive projects for the new Works Progress Administration (WPA), the massive work relief program launched in 1935 by Harry Hopkins and the New Deal to assure work for all "employable" persons still burdening city relief rolls.[72]

To Bigger's consternation and that of many others in Pittsburgh and the nation, the CWA was terminated in May 1934. However, its legacy served to exhilarate planning professionals. Bigger lauded the CWA's "real significance" and endeavored arduously and with some success to have first the RWD, then the Local Works Division, and finally the WPA continue the topographic survey and other general planning work.[73] Other Pittsburghers were equally impressed. After viewing the whole gamut of CWA planning studies laid before him at the planning department, an enthralled city reporter, Gilbert Love, marveled that he had just beheld "the Pittsburgh of the future, subsistence homesteads and all being planned on gigantic maps by hundreds of engineers, architects and draftsmen."[74]

The CWA tangibly and positively affected city planning in Pittsburgh. In addition to buttressing the city department's staff and facilitating the valuable Buhl-funded services of Ralph Griswold, the CWA triggered a general expansion of the city planning operation. City planning's budget soared from $35,340 in 1932 to $54,375 in 1934, to over $70,000 in 1935. Notably, the 1935 budget included two new $2,120-a-year positions: a city plan designer and a city plan engineer. Indeed, it is safe to say that in light of the severe urban fiscal crisis in Pittsburgh and urban America generally, the New Deal not only preserved city and county planning but elevated their stature.[75]

CHRONIC LIMITATIONS

Regrettably, while planning itself prospered, the city made minimal progress toward realizing any concrete benefits from planning. A few impressive city and county improvements arose on the urban landscape, the Westinghouse Bridge for one and the massive neoclassical federal post office and government building for another. Meanwhile, in 1934–1935, despite all the CWA work, city streets languished in disrepair, playgrounds deteriorated, and dreams of a tree-lined boulevard-ringed waterfront, the Inter-District Traffic Circuit, and the Cross-town Thoroughfare remained ethereal.[76]

Several factors help explain the halting progress of improvements in Great Depression Pittsburgh. First the termination of the CWA in May 1934 and tightened eligibility rules under its successor, the RWD, hobbled both city planning and urban improvements progress. The RWD's hiring rules limited employment to the city's relief rolls, severely restricting not only the use of skilled professionals critically needed on planning projects but also, much to the chagrin of Pittsburgh's Central Labor Union, blocking the use of union labor on federal works projects. Washington's demand that cities absorb the cost of materials and supplies for work projects further handcuffed financially strapped cities such as Pittsburgh. But it was politics that most obstructed progress; first in the form of patronage charges hurled unrelentingly at the CWA and RWD, and then by a barrier erected by the city's bizarre Democratic mayor.[77]

Charges of the politicization of New Deal relief reverberated throughout the Great Depression and were leveled by both political parties. Democratic politico David Lawrence, personally accused of using CWA and later WPA monies to grease his fledgling Lawrence-Guffey political machine, confessed his own belief that political "factions"—Republican and Democratic—manipulated work relief for political gain. Despite Hopkins's personal vigilance and numerous congressional investigations that repeatedly discovered minimal political machinations in the administration of work relief, the charge dogged the programs and sustained in Pittsburgh and other cities a virulent anti–New Deal press.[78]

Roosevelt's honeymoon in Pittsburgh ended in 1935 as Pittsburgh's economy slightly improved. If only briefly, traditionally conservative organizations such as the Chamber of Commerce patriotically had supported the NIRA and CWA. Buffeted by endless strikes, coal mining in the region still tottered in the mid-1930s; but the flagship steel industry, buoyed by a PWA-sparked demand for bridge and other structural steel products, and by new orders for beer cans and a modest boost in automobile demand, staged a small, but cheered, comeback. Expressing a newfound confidence, Jones & Laughlin Steel undertook a $40,000,000 expansion, installing new strip and sheet mills as well as an electrically powered forty-four-inch blooming mill at its Pittsburgh works.[79] The upswing, however, provided little balm for seething Old Guard political temperaments. Although a few Pittsburgh economists forecast a new era of tamed capitalism harnessed by big government, most businessmen, goaded by the city's anti-Roosevelt press, and anticipating Republican victory in the l936 presidential election, excoriated the New Deal. Pittsburgh's Hearst-owned *Sun-Telegraph* in 1935 daily lambasted New Deal spending while newspaper publisher Paul Block of the *Post-Gazette* headlined "The New Deal Failure."[80]

This harshening political mood—one not shared by the swelling ranks of pro-Roosevelt voters recruited from the city's large ethnic, and black, and chronically jobless working class—only emboldened Pittsburgh's maverick Democratic mayor, William McNair, elected in November 1933. McNair's antic-filled mayoralty, soon the bane of New Deal politicians such as David Lawrence and Joseph Guffey, impacted both planning and the course of city improvements. A lawyer and lifelong Democrat, educated at Gettysburg College and the University of Michigan, McNair, under Lawrence's tutelage, had actively campaigned for Roosevelt in 1932. But McNair boasted more than Democrat credentials; he was also an ardent if not fanatical disciple of Henry George. Indeed, McNair rarely missed an opportunity to publicly and exuberantly proselytize for George's single tax panacea, which had a large following in Pittsburgh. Lawrence tapped the perennial Democratic candidate for the 1933 mayoral race, predicting correctly that, unlike himself, a Catholic with suspiciously close Republican connections, McNair would attract both old line Protestant Democrats and independent Republicans such as League of Women Voters head Mrs. R. Templeton Smith and thus clinch the first Democratic Party victory in Pittsburgh since George Guthrie's triumph in 1906.[81]

As mayor, however, McNair's eccentricities verged on the comedic, making him delicious gruel for cartoonists and journalists alike. Being a single-taxer was not by itself inconsistent with New Deal allegiance. RPAA alumni such as Fred Ackerman, Benton MacKaye, and Henry Whitaker espoused variant forms of George's single tax philosophy, and Ackerman occupied a key niche as a New Deal houser. But McNair combined ideological rigidity with theatricality. Believing the single tax a panacea, and federal aid, especially work relief, nothing more than costly, tax-raising fodder for Lawrence and Guffey's monstrous patronage machine, McNair fought all Washington assistance. On his first day in office, McNair planted his desk in the corridor of Pittsburgh's City-County Building and invited the jobless to personally entreat him for aid. One cartoonist portrayed McNair as a giant bestriding a vast but barren, drought-stricken farmland and lecturing a diminutive, half-starved supplicant whose empty dinner plate is outstretched: "We don't need federal or state aid!" bellows McNair. "We can live on what we have right here!" "But mayor," retorts the starveling, "I wouldn't mind [eating] the soil if I had a bit of spinach to go with it!"[82]

Some of McNair's actions were extreme; others were reckless. His austere economy measures involved slashing the city payroll, including his own salary from $15,000 to $10,000. A philosophically consistent Georgian, he abolished all city taxes in lieu of the full collection of "economic rent." He fired department heads gratuitously and made new appointments with impunity. To head Public Works he chose Leslie Johnston, leader of the anti–David Lawrence Citizens League. McNair next eviscerated the city's Traffic Commission, an agency Bigger considered vital. Although he professed faith in planning and spared the CPC the ruthlessness that decimated the Traffic Commission, McNair's slash-and-burn economy measures eventually weakened Bigger's planning operation. McNair's visceral contempt for "high-priced" engineers ultimately translated into funding cutbacks for the CPC's engineer-laden geodetic and topographic survey; it also cost the job of the commission's chief engineer, U. N. Arthur.

Bigger, who by 1935 was preoccupied by his new task managing the RA's Greenbelt Town program, seemed at first nonplussed by the idiosyncrasies of McNair and registered little formal protest, possibly hoping to minimize damage to his Pittsburgh master planning program. But McNair's anti–New Deal behavior eventually proved costly. His vendetta first against Hopkins's RWD, then the WPA, pitted McNair against the city council, impelling the mayor to veto one after another council-approved ordinance seeking to fund the city's share of WPA projects. McNair's actions forced the WPA by August 1935 to suspend all but two of the CPC's ten planning projects. Only the master planning and playground projects survived.[83]

Ravaged by economic depression and numbed by chronic controversy over planning detail, Pittsburgh's cityscape in early 1936 reflected little of the planning energy manifest in the ambitious *Major Street* plan and Crosstown Thoroughfare models, or visible from the host of real estate, topographic, recreation and other CWA studies completed or that had been under way in the CPC. Evidence of county road and bridge development, especially the Westinghouse Bridge with its Frank Vittor–sculpted pylons, dotted the urban edges, but Pittsburgh itself, despite the new federal building, the Gulf Tower, and the Cathedral of Learning, floundered amid a sea of exciting but unexecuted plans. The real estate imbroglio that trapped Depression-era landowners between the rock of terribly devalued central city land and the hard place of high real estate tax assessments produced neither generous city real estate revenues nor the volition for private city development. With city taxes uncollected and the city's bond rating abysmal, conservative Pittsburgh businessmen cheered the low taxes, no-new-costly-development political strategy pushed by McNair. Indeed, the conservative reaction marking the slight crest of Pittsburgh's 1934–1935 steel industry's modest revival heralded the heyday of McNair's political shenanigans, and effectively blunted the impact of a potential CWA-spurred planning and development boom.

In the final assessment, much of the responsibility for the inaction that rendered Pittsburgh's streets traffic-clogged; its riverfronts muddy, debris strewn, and flood prone; and its playgrounds trash-littered lots, resided not only with McNair and city politics but also—as in the 1920s—at the doorstep of the region's political fragmentation. The collapse of the brief harmony between the CPC and ACPC, for example, led to interminable quibbling often over the most minor details. Furthermore, a host of competing Pittsburgh interests— suburban versus downtown, small business versus big business, river interests versus proparks and proparking, prolabor versus antilabor—failed to concur on a single vision for Pittsburgh development.

Evidence of costly fragmentation appeared on the three most visible and contentious of Pittsburgh's planning fronts prior to 1936: the downtown Point

Park improvement, the bridge-tunnel link to the Golden Triangle, and the case of Exposition Hall. Pittsburgh's lower downtown, a dense tangle of rotting railroad yards, aged residential and industrial properties, and a superannuated Exposition Hall, had long posed a problem in an age when civic leaders equated urban health with the vibrancy and attractiveness of the central city. By 1930 the downtown region that planners and boosters regaled as the historic Point had absorbed endless and fruitless planning attention. First the local chapter of the AIA, then Frederick Law Olmsted Jr., then the Art Commission, the CCCP, the CCAC, the CPC, the ACPC, the LDBMA, and the Chamber of Commerce had all showered the Point with ideas for commemorative parks, obelisks, and other monuments—all with little success. Frantic business interests in the 1930s feared that, without downtown revitalization, traffic-clogged streets, plunging property values, and the lure of new suburban stores doomed the historic retail district. Accordingly, business leaders campaigned vigorously in the 1930s for waterfront boulevards, parks, and bypass routes to make the downtown more accessible, to restore its panache, and thus revive economic and social vitality to the commercially shaky district. Pittsburgh's LDBMA actively supported not only the CPC's riverfront boulevard plans but also the idea of transforming the Point into a memorial park, a long-standing proposal that, by 1933, had become a standard feature of downtown improvement schemes. Unlike the CPC, however, downtown businessmen favored using the improved, flood-walled riverfront edges—once built—for automobile parking.[84]

Gnawing philosophical differences about wharf-side parking aside, downtown business interests and city planners shared an abiding passion about the need for free-flowing traffic movement in the Golden Triangle and the importance of bypassing or detouring through traffic around the central business district. Businessmen therefore embraced the city's and the CCCP's Inter-District Traffic Circuit design. But in the early 1930s that signature plan collided with Allegheny County's suburban-based blueprint for a second bridge and tunnel channeling traffic from the downtown across the Monongahela River at Ferry (now Stanwix) Street.

Meant to relieve traffic congestion at the south end of the automobile-jammed Liberty Tunnels, the so-called Wabash Bridge and Tunnel project had actually originated in 1927 when the Pittsburgh and West Virginia Railroad, owners of the Wabash Bridge and the adjoining railroad tunnel through Mt. Washington, slapped a $13,000,000 price tag on the abandoned complex and peddled it to the county commissioners. A few years later the price dropped to

$4,000,000, whetting the interest of county commissioner and ex-Pittsburgh mayor Edward Babcock.[85] Proclaiming the unused railroad infrastructure a "diamond," Babcock pleaded that for a mere $1,200,000, the bridge and tunnel could be revamped to accommodate automobile traffic.[86] The ex-mayor then proceeded to negotiate the price further downward to a "bargain" $3,000,000, corralled his two commissioner colleagues, and, ignoring a skeptical ACPC, sealed the bridge and tunnel deal. Mt. Lebanon, Carnegie, Roslyn Farms, and Pittsburgh's other South Hills suburbs applauded Babcock's action, which they thought was sure to "stabilize" suburban real estate values and increase the attraction of new, upscale residential subdivisions.

Meanwhile, Pittsburgh's Chamber of Commerce, the MPA, and the CPC denounced the Babcock scheme. Bigger and the CPC assailed the ex-mayor's impulsive Wabash deal for violating all the principles of professional planning. Not only did the "costly" project brashly conflict with the city's established plans for an Inter-District Traffic Circuit, but it "would [also] lure traffic into the middle of the triangle before the means [have been made] available to eliminate the 40–50 percent of traffic . . . now in the district only because there are not adequate detours." It would also, blasted the commission, create "intolerable" traffic conditions at the northern downtown terminus of the proposed Wabash vehicular bridge, "burdensome to the businessmen in the locality . . . and costly for the city to handle."[87]

Approved by the ACPC, which prior to 1932 remained the docile captive of county Public Works, and forwarded to the PWA as one of the county's numerous bridge projects, the Wabash package was subsequently quashed in early 1934 by the newly independent ACPC. Under E. L. Schmidt, the ACPC swiftly proposed an alternative PWA project, a new four-lane Fort Duquesne Bridge and Tunnel at the same Ferry Street location. Schmidt's objection to the Wabash improvement was terse: "No matter what you do to convert a railroad bridge into a highway bridge you cannot make it ideal."[88]

However, Schmidt's action hardly achieved harmony between the CPC and ACPC ranks. Despite its heightened professionalism, the ACPC was convinced, perhaps rightly, that the CPC viewed it contemptuously and habitually subordinated county to city designs. When the CPC in 1933 asked the county to include a key part of the city's Inter-District Traffic Circuit (plans for a new Eleventh Street Bridge across the Allegheny River) in its application for an Reconstruction Finance Corporation loan, S. J. Topley, chair of the ACPC, objected that "the County Planning Commission has gone a long way with the City of Pittsburgh and that the planning commission has gone as far as it should go."[89] Like a coiled serpent, the deadly, often irreconcilable tensions between the CPC and ACPC, manifest as much in philosophical disputes over basic planning principles as in seemingly picayune squabbles over whether the Seventh Street connection to Bigelow Boulevard should be aligned twelve feet this way or twelve feet that way, lay poised about to suddenly strike. Bigger and the CPC promptly scorned Schmidt's Fort Duquesne Bridge and Tunnel plans on the same grounds that they had repudiated the Wabash idea.[90] Like the Wabash Bridge and Tunnel, Schmidt's scheme violated the city's inner loop plan, in which the two riverfront boulevards converged in a cloverleaf at the Point and thence coursed south and north over the Point and Manchester bridges. Essentially, the Wabash controversy involved the CPC's objection to any second bridge funneling more traffic into the downtown.

In early 1935 the CCCP responded to Schmidt's Fort Duquesne Bridge and Tunnel plan by unveiling a "shorter route" alternative that eliminated the existing Point Bridge. Reflecting in part Bigger's thinking, the CCCP proposal converted the entire Point area west of Short and Barbeau streets into an urban park centered around the historic Bouquet's blockhouse, the only remains in 1935 of the 1760 Fort Pitt that during the French and Indian War guarded the strategic headwaters of the Ohio River. Attention in 1935 increasingly focused upon how any new bridge crossing the Monongahela at the Point would complement this coalescing vision of a "memorial park." Around that vision, the city and county in 1935 seemed to approach some consensus on a single double-decked, high-level Fort Duquesne Bridge to be located in the vicinity of Short and Barbeau streets, with ramps connecting it to low- and high-level waterfront streets. Any consensus soon vanished in September when the CPC—never fully comfortable with the CCCP plan's incompatibility with the Inter-District Traffic Circuit—suddenly demanded that the county strike the Fort Duquesne Bridge and Tunnel improvement from its list of PWA projects, commanding that "it not be constructed."[91]

Amid the tangle of bridge, park, and riverfront boulevard proposals comprising downtown development in the mid-1930s loomed a third and final explosive issue, Exposition Hall. Like the related bridge controversy, Exposition Hall, owned by the Western Pennsylvania Exposition Society, served to further complicate Point development and helped stall any and all plans for improving the central city. Since 1886 the Victorian, castellated Exposition Hall had occupied the Allegheny riverbank east of the Manchester Bridge. The Exposition Society's original fifty-year lease of the site committed it to hold at least one exposition every year, at which time city schoolchildren were to be admitted free of charge. By the 1920s, with a dwindling membership, the society held fewer and fewer expositions, and under a renegotiated lease the city now paid the society $30,000 a year for the right to store vehicles and other municipal property beneath the cobwebbed ceilings of the aged, scabrous edifice.

When the society's lease surfaced again for renewal in January 1934, a rejuvenated Greater Pittsburgh Exposition Society under the energetic leadership of Peter M. Chamberlain introduced a freshly minted, grandiose plan to demolish the moldering riverside fortress and erect in its place a spectacular multipurpose civic center enclosing a concert hall, convention and exposition facilities, and public meeting rooms. Enthralled by Chamberlain's plan, the city council in 1933 drafted an ordinance approving a new lease and authorizing the society to replace its present sprawling red brick hulk with a building costing no less than $3,000,000. In lieu of taxes, the council ordered the society to return to the city 3 percent of its gross receipts. The council's leasing terms also stated that the proposed expanded Exposition Hall site, which straddled the Duquesne wharf, "would not impede the free movement of traffic at the Point."[92]

Not unexpectedly, Bigger and the CPC dissented, again on traffic grounds, but on others as well. The commission's review of the Exposition Society ordinance charged that such a monumental building represented "an extremely heavy additional traffic burden upon the point district and conflict[ed] with the city's carefully developed riverfront plan in particular the cloverleaf design for articulating traffic from the Water Street Boulevard and Duquesne Way across the bridge."[93]

Challenged to rebut the CPC's charge that the new Exposition Hall threatened traffic congestion at the Point, Chamberlain hired two of the city's most esteemed architects and planners, William York Cocken and Benno Janssen, as well as Harland Bartholomew. Neither Cocken and Janssen's magnificent imperial hall design nor Bartholomew's effort to diffuse the traffic problem satisfied Bigger and the CPC. Whatever the design, argued the commission, a new Exposition Hall "obliterated the Point clover-leaf intersection of the city's approved downtown waterfront plan." Such a grand exposition building posed not only an "extra vehicular burden" but undermined the goal of an "organically planned business district that a great city ought to have." Bigger seized the occasion to proclaim a broad, general planning principle, something he rarely did in a public forum. "City-owned and controlled land," asserted Bigger, "such as that [in the Exposition Hall site case] bordering waterways, should be retained and used for public purposes, and . . . the rights of all the citizens in that land should not be assigned to particular special interests," even for 3 percent of the proceeds he might have added.[94]

Throughout 1934 Bartholomew and the CPC wrestled with the traffic problems raised by the Exposition Hall scheme; by mid-December 1934 the CPC still clung unyieldingly to its verdict opposing the Exposition Society plans.[95] The battle revealed the tenaciousness of Pittsburgh's stubbornly professional CPC in defying politics and even public opinion to uphold the sanctity of its master plan and public land. It also underscored the power of Pittsburgh's New Deal–emboldened planning commission in challenging both the city council and the Exposition Society, the latter armed with a team of illustrious consultants. Yet rather than dying, the Exposition Hall issue simmered for several more years, attesting to the persistence of urban fragmentation and precluding any firm consensus around such vital land use issues as the Point and the future of Pittsburgh's downtown. For this reason, in 1936 civic leaders and planners alike expressed frustration at the absence of solid physical progress in the Depression-wracked Steel City.

CHAPTER 8

Urban Crisis and the Advent of Renaissancemanship

BLOWING SNOW and freezing temperatures made the winter of 1935–1936 one of the city's harshest, a dreaded omen to native Pittsburghers that a sudden spring thaw might trigger flooding. No one, however, predicted the March 17, 1936, St. Patrick's Day disaster when floodwaters of the Allegheny, Monongahela, and Ohio rivers angrily surged over the Point. On March 18, the three rivers crested at 46 feet, 11 feet above the previous calamitous 35.5-foot level of 1907, and muddy, torrential water, loaded with wharf piers, uprooted trees, loosened barges, bridge parts, and other flood-tossed debris, swirled through the darkened office buildings and store-lined streets of downtown Pittsburgh. Rising water buried the heart of the city's business district in 11 feet of water, extinguishing all electrical power and most telegraph and telephone service. Floodwaters engulfed the North Side and the South Side, including city rail yards and steel mills as well as suburban towns along all three rivers. Forty-six people died, and the estimates of monetary damage ranged from the U.S. Army Corps of Engineers' modest estimate of $50,000,000 to the Chamber of Commerce's $250,000,000. Pittsburgh, a city pummeled by economic depression, had now been battered by the equally unmerciful wrath of nature.[1]

The 1936 flood deepened the aura of crisis in a city seemingly rendered helpless by a persistently sluggish economy and a chronic fragmentation of authority. Despite the Great Depression, Pittsburgh clung to its "Steel City" heritage. Although the advent of by-product coke ovens had decades ago yielded the locational edge in steel making to Great Lakes cities such as Gary, Indiana, and Cleveland, the city's Chamber of Commerce stubbornly proclaimed Pittsburgh "America's preeminent steel producer," devilishly feeding the illusion of industrial dominance, which had undergirded the city's conversation about urban growth for a century and a half. But in 1936 few facts supported such a cheery assertion. Although *Greater Pittsburgh,* the organ of the Chamber of Commerce, in January 1936 broadcast "almost incredible gains" in Pittsburgh

Pittsburgh's St. Patrick's Day flood, seen here on March 18, 1936, devastated the downtown, deepened the Great Depression crisis, helped revive the CCCP, and impelled action on city planning projects. *Library and Archives Division, Historical Society of Western Pennsylvania, Pittsburgh.*

steel production, the city's so-called booming steel industry in 1936 operated at a mere 40 percent of capacity.[2] The Chamber's habitual optimism remained somewhat guarded, for despite the modest industrial gains in late 1935, over 50,000 Pittsburgh families collected public assistance, including many who would be forced from their ramshackle riverside shanties the next year by the rising floodwaters of 1936.[3]

Collectively, these crises of the 1930s—the Great Depression, floods, the specter of industrial decline—shifted the terms of the urban conversation. Not only did these cataclysms elevate the role of planning, but they also amplified the voice of the public sector, ensconcing the federal government at the very center of the planning process. As this chapter shows, they forced the city's private planning fraternity to reconsider its historic watchdog/advisory role and to adopt a more actionist posture. With the obstructionist McNair now out of office, replaced upon his resignation by city council president Cornelius Scully, a Democrat and David Lawrence protégé, the path in 1936 was cleared for cooperation with Washington, much-needed federal relief dollars, and action on an urban development agenda. Allied with a new, activist, pro–New Deal and pro–public works city administration, leaders such as Howard Heinz, Richard King Mellon (the son of Richard Beatty Mellon), Arthur Braun, and Wallace Richards renewed the public and private partnership, reinvigorated the urban conversation, and resuscitated the planning program that constituted the foundation of Pittsburgh's post–World War II urban renaissance.

SHAPING A NEW FEDERALISM

The 1936 flood convinced Heinz, Mellon, and Braun to revive the Citizens Committee on the City Plan (CCCP). Like many political and civic leaders in other American cities, they viewed the federal government as a prime source of desperately needed planning and development funds for the upgrading of badly disintegrating municipal infrastructure. Eroded by business failures, high rates of joblessness, and a stagnant real estate market, urban tax bases remained depressed throughout the 1930s, leaving cities without the means to maintain and improve their aging streets, sewers, water mains, schools, libraries, and other public buildings. Therefore Pittsburgh joined cities such as New York, Detroit, and Chicago in acknowledging an emerging new federalism, a growing dependence of municipal and state governments on federal grants-in-aid, long-term loans, and work relief funds for the provision of public welfare and other basic services such as street lighting and road repair, school maintenance, and even the staffing of libraries and symphony orchestras. The 1936 flood crisis underscored the importance of the new urban-federal relationship.

With floodwaters in March 1936 lapping against the rooftops of submerged Pittsburgh trolleys, the Chamber of Commerce (whose offices sat under water) convened a Citizens Flood Committee, which met outside the flood zone in Oakland at the Pittsburgh Athletic Association. The committee demanded flood control and held the federal government responsible for building the necessary dams and containment reservoir.[4] Congress passed the Copeland Omnibus Flood Control Bill, stating that flood control, as distinct from navigation improvements, "came within the scope of federal interest." The state legislature immediately appropriated a piddling $2,461,000 for work relief funds for geological research and other studies preliminary to flood control. However, by August 1936 the federal government had identified sites for nine Ohio River basin reservoirs costing $55,000,000 to be shared by federal and state governments. One year later, in June 1937, after the Pennsylvania legislature had voted a $5,000,000 flood control appropriation, War Department engineers, in consultation with the Pittsburgh City Planning Commission (CPC), drafted a new set of plans for floodwalls protecting Pittsburgh's downtown.[5]

Flood control plans comprised only one aspect of the new federalism that featured Washington, the primary source of funds for executing projects, as a crucial factor in the urban planning process. The Public Works Administration (PWA), like the Civil Works Administration (CWA), mandated planning. In particular, the PWA demanded that city and state sponsors coordinate large-scale road and bridge projects with other improvements, and it gave preference to proposals "integrated with and consistent with state plans." The National Resources Planning Board, after 1935 called the National Resources Committee (NRC), openly promoted the planning discipline and thus inserted Washington boldly into the urban conversation. Through the NRC, Washington actively endeavored to stimulate city and state planning.[6] NRC staff collected data from city and county planning agencies; monitored the state, city, and county planning efforts; and by 1937, through its Urbanism Committee, completed the first government study of the "Role of the Urban Community." Planner Charles W. Eliot headed the Urban Section of the NRC, which produced the report. Lewis Mumford, a consultant on the project, deemed it a "very admirable and effective summary," even if it "overlooked the role of financial monopoly and government in concentrating people in cities."[7]

Data assembled in 1936–1937 revealed the New Deal's general success in stimulating the "planning mentality." The number of official city planning agencies increased from 806 in 1932 to 1,064 at the end of 1936. Nationally, city planning staff sizes and budgets rose, boosted largely, as in Pittsburgh, by federally funded work projects.[8] Pittsburgh's CPC illustrated the impact of this new federalism. During Bigger's absence in Washington, the Department of City Planning's new chief, Carrol Hill, reported to the NRC in July 1936 a staff of over twenty full-time professional planners, designers, draftsmen, and engineers, which in addition to normal general planning, zoning, and lot surveys, supervised seven active Works Progress Administration (WPA) planning projects, including the ongoing geodetic and topographic survey, a master plan for the city's recreation system, the Real Property Inventory and real estate survey, and a master plan study of major and minor streets.[9] By 1937 the Department of City Planning considered its WPA geodetic survey staff so vital that it pleaded to make the staff permanent. A few months later the NRC inadvertently wrote requesting Pittsburgh to confirm that the city had a planning commission. An offended Carrol Hill scribbled back a terse note to the NRC's Harold Merrill: "Dear Merrill: Are you kidding us. I don't know how we could be more active."[10]

THE REEMERGENCE OF THE MUNICIPAL PLANNING ASSOCIATION

Among the civic leaders and planning technicians who comprehended both the gravity of the Pittsburgh crisis and the significance of the unfolding political alliance between city hall and Washington, D.C., were key members of the inactive Municipal Planning Association (MPA). These core MPA members included Howard Heinz, the banker Arthur Braun, E. W. Mudge of National Steel, real estate magnate L. W. Monteverde, advertising executive George Ketchum, and Bigger.

Three years earlier Ketchum and Bigger had padlocked the doors of the association's office; now, on May 5, 1936, a little more than a month after the flood, Heinz summoned the inner circle of planning enthusiasts to lunch within the wood-paneled sanctuary of the Duquesne Club. Heinz urged the revival of the MPA, but insisted that the revitalized organization differ from its predecessor. The old CCCP of the 1920s and early 1930s had sponsored and championed city planning. It policed city development, opposing ill-considered, politically motivated projects, and demanding adherence to the *Pittsburgh Plan*. No longer. Conscious of the great urgency, the new, proactive MPA, while pledging continued fealty to the official city and county planning bodies, would now, exhorted Heinz, assert planning leadership. Shedding its more passive friend-of-planning role, Heinz's new MPA would, in Ketchum's words, identify new improvement projects, actively support "spending money for development," and "aggressively lobby for priorities such as the Inter-District Traffic Circuit, the waterfront floodwalls and boulevards . . . recreation and [now] housing." Heinz charged Bigger to renew publication of *Progress*, and commissioned him to draft a budget for an organization with a board of directors sufficiently expanded to undertake the association's enlarged actionist mission.[11]

The reorganization and refocusing of the city's principal voluntary planning body from a planning watchdog to an agent of planning evolved over a three-year period, 1936–1939. In imitation of New York's Regional Plan Association, the action culminated in a name change from the MPA to the Pittsburgh Regional Planning Association (PRPA). Heinz, Braun, and Ketchum enlarged the

Howard Heinz, circa 1923, a key member of the Municipal Planning Association and the driving force behind Pittsburgh's new "actionist" planning movement. *Library and Archives Division, Historical Society of Western Pennsylvania, Pittsburgh.*

board membership to thirty-five (preferably "younger men"), while eliminating ex-officio members such as the city's director of Public Works, the school board president, and the chairman of the CPC. By May 1938 the resurgent, expanded board, now a politically muscular civic *Who's Who*, included lawyer C. T. Arensberg, Joseph Dilworth of Westinghouse, United States Steel chief Benjamin Fairless, E. T. Weir of National Steel, Joseph Trees, Leon Falk, and James C. Rea of Koppers. Committed to strengthened advocacy, halting the cacophony of discordant voices, and asserting new leadership in the Pittsburgh planning conversation, the PRPA not only pledged to "secure constructive publicity . . . pertaining to municipal planning problems and their solution" but also "to prepare and to publish . . . scientific model municipal studies and plans."[12]

Simultaneously, the bespectacled town planner and planning technician Bigger increasingly withdrew from his previous central position in Pittsburgh's voluntary planning sphere. After helping revitalize and rename the civic planning organization that he was instrumental in founding in 1918, he at first limited his participation to "consultant," then in 1939 terminated his involvement altogether. Bigger in 1937 toiled more in Washington, D.C., where as part of Rexford Tugwell's Suburban Division of the Resettlement Administration, he directed the division's Greenbelt Town program, the New Deal's experiment in decentralizing city populations to wholesome, well-designed model towns on the urban periphery.[13]

Wallace Richards, who replaced Bigger in September 1937 as executive secretary of the MPA, had been introduced to Pittsburgh's planning world by Bigger. Trained in newspaper work, Richards served as a Paris correspondent before shifting to public relations. He first met Bigger while doing public relations in Pittsburgh. In 1937 the bright, indefatigable, chain-smoking Richards was employed with Bigger on the Greenbelt Town project when, probably at Bigger's behest, he took the executive secretary position at the MPA.[14]

Armed with energy and public relations skills, Richards, at the helm of the MPA, promised to advance Pittsburgh's development, complete the downtown waterfront boulevards, construct a crosstown thoroughfare, build better housing, and improve city parks and playgrounds, all by triumphing over fragmentation and forging a regionwide consensus on public works priorities. Pittsburgh's prospects for consensus building suddenly lunged forward in October 1936 when William McNair, then in a life-and-death struggle with the city council and the statewide Lawrence-Guffey organization, suddenly and incredulously fired the city treasurer, James Kirk. The city council seized the opportunity. It refused to approve McNair's choice to replace Kirk. Without a city treasurer, checks went unsigned. The abrupt cessation of city business forced McNair to resign. Immediately, the council approved its president, Democrat and ardent New Dealer Cornelius D. Scully, as mayor. With McNair gone and federal dollars in sight, the city's long-dormant, potentially contentious development agenda sprang to life. Led by an actionist MPA with a dynamic president, Howard Heinz, and a director, Wallace Richards, experienced in public relations, the crusade began to triumph over historic fragmentation, convert city plans into substantial improvements, and revitalize a weary, dirt-encrusted industrial city.[15]

ENDURING OBSTACLES

The MPA, however, continued to encounter overlapping jurisdictions of city and county planning that still entangled all projects for urban improvement in a political fray over regional priorities. County planners, as noted earlier, principally addressed suburban development and the network of parks, roads, highways, and bridges serving the broader metropolitan region. Conversely, despite its legislated responsibility for citywide zoning and the approval of lot plans, Pittsburgh planning historically focused more narrowly on the downtown, where fiercely contested rival plans for an Exposition Hall, the Wabash Bridge and Tunnel, the Inter-District Traffic Circuit, and Point development had stymied progress long before the flood.

Part of the city-county feud stemmed from Pittsburgh's grim financial predicament. While boulevard improvements, crosstown thoroughfares, and Point development topped the city's planning agenda, strapped Pittsburgh coffers forced the city to undertake more studies, surveys, and maps, not concrete projects. As earlier in the Great Depression, zoning and rezoning occupied the CPC's time, as did the shade tree work, which the commission finally shunted to Public Works in 1939. Housing, a personal interest of Bigger's, now also suddenly consumed planners' time. Passage of the 1937 Wagner-Steagall Housing Act created the U.S. Housing Authority (USHA), and soon afterward, in August 1937, the state authorized the Housing Authority of the City of Pittsburgh (HACP). The CPC aided the HACP in building its first three public housing projects, acceding—often grudgingly—to HACP administrator Bryn Hovde's numerous requests for planning assistance in developing sites for Pittsburgh's first Bedford Heights and Aliquippa Terrace housing projects.[16]

Meanwhile, the grand Fiorello La Guardia–inspired, New York City–scale projects that Scully coveted—boulevard systems, parkways, downtown revitalization—lay beyond the city's frail tax base. Pittsburgh in 1938 barely scraped together $15,000 in bond funds for a WPA tree-planting project. A year later tight city finances left Scully and Public Works director Frank M. Roessing "doubtful they can initiate any major improvements during 1939–1940."[17] In addition to the CPC's major topographic and real estate studies, master planning, and studies of "soot fall," finances limited Pittsburgh to WPA projects requiring minimal city contribution. WPA laborers undertook repair work and book cataloging at the Oakland Carnegie Library. They renovated Phipps Conservatory and the county's Soldiers' and Sailors' Memorial, and built curbs, walks, trails, paths, timber bridges, and stone shelters at Schenley Park.[18] Hundreds of WPA workers also graded land, laid out ballparks, and erected grandstands in executing Pittsburgh Park superintendent Ralph Griswold's "Master Plan for Recreation," launched in 1934 by the CWA. Overseen by Bigger and the CPC, and intended to address "the deplorable condition of recreation facilities in the city," work commenced on the "system" in 1938–1939 when WPA labor helped develop playground sites at the Liberty and Franklin schools, at Monterey Street on the North Side, on Herron Hill, in Beechview, and elsewhere.[19]

However, countywide, not citywide, projects employed most of Pittsburgh's many jobless. The ACPC, with its greater resources, sponsored the bulk of PWA-WPA road, bridge, and boulevard programs during the 1930s. Under planning engineer Park Martin, Allegheny County Planning Department staff approved subdivision plans, many after 1937 in burgeoning suburbs such as Mt. Lebanon, which amid the Great Depression opened plush new communities such as Virginia Manor. Between 1935 and 1939 the WPA expended over $81,000,000 in Allegheny County, employing 46,815 workers at its peak during the 1936 flood. While some of those millions of dollars paid WPA white-collar workers, planners, and engineers on the CPC's topographic mapping project as well as city artists, librarians, and Pittsburgh Orchestra members, bridge, highway, and other large county projects consumed much of the money and labor.[20] PWA projects included widening the south end of the Liberty Tubes, erecting the Homestead High Level Bridge, and constructing the control tower, runway, and administration building at the county airport, as well as water lines and a filtration plant at North Park.

Prior to 1937 McNair's opposition to federal work projects had forced the county to transport city relief workers to road and bridge jobs outside Pittsburgh. After McNair's departure, Mayor Scully worked closely with federal, state, and regional WPA administrators and shifted more projects within the city, especially to jobs improving the city's many rutted, almost impassable streets. Two huge countywide road projects employed thousands of workers stone basing, upgrading, and modernizing streets and roadways, many within the city. By 1939 the WPA had paved seventy-two miles of streets in Allegheny County and over thirty miles of sidewalks. A May 1938 memorandum on "Streets and Road and Highways in Allegheny County" revealed the significance of this work for the city. Between 1935 and 1938 the WPA spent over $45,500,000 on street and road projects. County-sponsored street-building and repair projects in Pittsburgh accounted for over a third of the money. WPA workers, constantly vilified in the anti–New Deal press for their presumed slothfulness, built more than thirty-four miles of new city streets and repaired twenty-three miles of what had historically been little more than muddy cow paths, many located on steep Pittsburgh hillsides. This work invariably included laying new sewers and building sidewalks, curbs and gutters, and cribbing with concrete.[21]

As the major sponsor and designer of massive federal public works, county planners, together with county Public Works and the State Department of Highways, imagined themselves at the frontlines of Pittsburgh regional development. Therefore, the Allegheny County Planning Commission (ACPC), while still heavily tilted toward engineering, deeply resented what it viewed as the pompousness and petulance of the CPC, which brashly flaunted its professionalism. Despite numerous efforts to resuscitate the city and county Joint Planning Conference, contentiousness, not cooperation, prevailed; battles raged over design details for the south approach to the Liberty Tunnels, for downtown's Water Street and Duquesne Way boulevards, and for the location of ramps to the proposed Crosstown Thoroughfare.[22]

Nor did politics entirely vanish once McNair disappeared. Bigger in 1937 could still complain that Superintendent of Parks Griswold "seemed to be on the way to complete frustration because of political placement of incompetent employees." Politics turned the WPA into a giant pawn in statewide political struggles. In Pittsburgh, the WPA's massive street- and park-improvement work failed to absolve the federal agency from incessant charges that Democratic bosses used work relief as patronage. Republicans joined bitterly rival Democratic factions in branding the WPA a creature of Democratic machine builders.[23]

CONFLICTING VISIONS OF THE DOWNTOWN

As important as these political and jurisdictional antagonisms were for Pittsburgh, it was the sheer diversity of outlooks and the dissonance in the urban conversation, especially the conflicting visions about the city's downtown, that most thwarted the grand schemes for Pittsburgh development. By 1937 opposing plans for downtown development had produced, in the words of the MPA, a "woeful lack of unity among those who would like to see the community improved. Conflicting points of view as well as the difficulties in the job tend to delay development . . . [and] bring discouragement."[24]

In 1937 it required a stretch of the imagination to conjure up the raw material for beautification of the tangled wreckage called the Golden Triangle. Walking west from Grant Street toward the Point, down track-cluttered Water Street, past moldering Baltimore and Ohio Railroad sheds, along the once-proud Monongahela wharf, pedestrians beheld cars parked askew on the crudely paved quays and a mélange of shed-roofed structures, plus moving and storage warehouses, the Fort Pitt Fish Company, small riverfront lunch counters, and the eyesore elevated ramps leading to the Point and Manchester bridges. In the glory days of the early twentieth century, financial tycoons such

The Monongahela wharf and Water Street in 1932, before construction of the Water Street artery, the first leg of the city's Inter-District Traffic Circuit. *Pittsburgh City Photographer Collection, Archives Service Center, University of Pittsburgh.*

as Henry Clay Frick, Andrew Carnegie, Henry Oliver, and Henry Phipps had jousted, with architecture as weapons. They left behind such gems as the Frick Building; the magnificent, ornate Flemish Gothic Union Trust Arcade building; and the William Penn Hotel, all Frick's. Amid the Great Depression, many of these overassessed monuments burdened a desperately strained city real estate market. New York's Jay Gould's Wabash Railroad terminal lay empty. Seedy hotels, padlocked commercial houses, and unused movie houses typified the downtown scene more than did the then-surviving Jenkins Arcade and Joseph Horne's and Edgar J. Kaufmann's department stores. Even the still regal, albeit grimy, facades of buildings along Fourth Avenue and Grant Street, which included the architectural masterpieces of Henry Hobson Richardson, Daniel Burnham, Frederick J. Osterling, and the firm of Longfellow, Alden and Harlow—failed to dispose of the smoke and despair or untangle the congestion of Pittsburgh's narrow, automobile- and streetcar-clogged streets. In Pittsburgh in 1935 at work on Kaufmann's Fallingwater retreat, Frank Lloyd Wright was asked by the *Pittsburgh Sun-Telegraph* what he would do to help improve the smoky city. Wright snootily quipped, "It's cheaper to abandon it!"[25]

But Pittsburghers such as Edgar J. Kaufmann, Henry Burchfield, Howard Heinz, and Cornelius Scully were ill-disposed to take Wright's advice seriously. After all, four overlapping, yet distinctive, visions existed regarding downtown development. The CPC and the MPA/PRPA shared one. The river interests promulgated another. A third voice belonged to the city's downtown business interests, whose views were expressed by the Lower Downtown Businessmen's Association (LDBMA). Finally, members of the Historical Society of Western Pennsylvania articulated a fourth position.

The ACPC's position on key downtown improvement issues, such as the fate of the Wabash infrastructure and elevating Water Street, coincided with that of the LDBMA, while the Allied Boards of Trades usually sided with the CPC.[26] After March 1936 all factions concurred that the federal government must construct floodwalls to protect the downtown. Most approved riverfront boulevards. They quarreled about the treatment of the historic Point, about the rebuilding of Exposition Hall, and about the location and alignment of a new bridge and tunnel to the South Hills.

Reflecting Frederick Bigger's vision of the good city, the MPA viewed the downtown triangle as an organic whole, to use Bigger's words, as "a central pool primarily devoted to business." As much as it "naturally attracted" business, the downtown, argued Bigger, lured traffic. It was, he claimed, "the 'hub,' or 'focus' of the converging county highways as well as the city's major radial thoroughfares." Therefore Bigger, the MPA, and the CPC made attaining "the freest possible movement of traffic" the first priority of downtown planning. Achieving that goal required building the two-looped Inter-District Traffic Circuit featuring the Water Street and Duquesne Way improvements as attractive and efficient riverfront boulevards. The long-discussed Crosstown Thoroughfare plan would capstone the downtown traffic system. Consequently, both planning bodies, the CPC and the MPA, still condemned the LDBMA's proposed Exposition Hall project as a traffic-congesting obstruction. While they at first opposed a second bridge and tunnel, Bigger and the MPA had by 1937 accepted the necessity for a new southern entrance to the city and favored a bridge located near Ferry (now Stanwix) Street somewhere between Smithfield Street and the Point.[27] The CPC and the MPA, however, spurned the idea popular in New York City, Chicago, and among certain Pittsburghers in the 1930s of increasing traffic flow by "double decking" such key highways as the proposed waterfront boulevards.

Pittsburgh's LDBMA envisioned a revitalized downtown sporting both the

Exposition Hall project and double-decked Water Street and Duquesne Way riverfront boulevards. The LDBMA's plans portrayed a sleek Water Street viaduct linked by ramps, with a bridge and tunnel traffic route over the old Wabash Railroad property, thence south to the Saw Mill Run Parkway. Traffic bound for the city from the South Hills would flow across a rebuilt Wabash Bridge and over the viaduct into the heart of the downtown. The prospect appalled Bigger.

In 1936 the LDBMA formally unveiled its grandiose scheme to refurbish and restore life to the historic business center, to salvage central city property values, and to channel traffic unimpeded into the downtown. Centered on the rebuilt Exposition Hall, the LDBMA's plan had been authored in 1934 by St. Louis's Harland Bartholomew, engineer E. N. Hunting, and architect William York Cocken of the firm Janssen and Cocken. It remained on the table in 1936. Cocken's mammoth, imperial-scale design for the Exposition Hall excited many Pittsburghers, including Mayor Scully and the members of the Chamber of Commerce. As one of his first acts after replacing McNair in October 1936, Scully, as an ecstatic Chamber phrased it, "assured" the Exposition Hall by signing the application for a PWA grant funding 45 percent of the estimated $6,000,000 cost of the project. Together with the Exposition Hall, floodwalls, the elevated Water Street and Duquesne Way boulevards, and a high-level Wabash bridge, viaduct, and tunnel, the Exposition Hall comprised the LDBMA's, the Chamber's, and the county's panacea for Pittsburgh's congested, economically arid downtown. The CPC's objections to the LDBMA's Wabash proposal, Bartholomew's signature notwithstanding, remained unchanged from the early 1930s. Elevated roadways with their "disfiguring access ramps," argued Bigger, "retarded the value of abutting property, and this one deposited traffic directly into the narrow internal streets of an already congested Golden Triangle."[28]

Insomuch as the LDBMA centered its downtown development proposals on floodwalls and riverfront boulevards along the Monongahela and Allegheny sides of the downtown triangle, it complemented the CPC's vision. That hardly softened the rancor of the urban conversation. The CPC strenuously opposed the association's other Exposition Hall and viaduct plans and insisted that the Inter-District Traffic Circuit be completed before launching any new bridge, tunnel, or memorial park projects. Bigger lambasted the goal of the downtown merchants to bring traffic directly into the business district. The whole purpose of the CPC's Inter-District Traffic Circuit, explained the commission, "make[s] it possible for traffic to move around the central district instead of entering it. A very large percentage of the traffic now in the business district has no legitimate reason for being there."[29]

The river interests represented by the Propeller Club also opposed the LDBMA's Wabash and Exposition Hall plans, which they feared detracted from the primary use of the waterfronts for commerce. While the river interests appreciated the importance of flood protection, they clung to the vision of Pittsburgh as a major inland port city boasting a thriving fleet that demanded access to the quays. The October 1929 celebration of completion of the locks and dams along the Ohio River from Pittsburgh to Cairo, Illinois, had witnessed hundreds of richly decorated riverboats jammed together along the Monongahela wharf, reminiscent of the nineteenth century; the scene seemingly confirmed the vision of Pittsburgh as a still vital port city. The CPC balked at the Propeller Club's romantic notion, however, firmly and correctly convinced that the age of Pittsburgh as a major inland port "had passed."[30]

History itself obtruded into the melee by presenting a separate claim on downtown development and vision making. The guardian of Pittsburgh's historical legacy, the Historical Society of Western Pennsylvania, expounded its own plan for reclaiming the flood and financially ravaged Point district. As historian Warren Susman explained, by shattering Americans' faith in science, civilization, and the cornucopia of modern mass production, the Great Depression revived a deep interest in exploring the roots of American culture. WPA-sponsored art and history projects celebrated the American past, and in 1935, through the Historical Sites and Buildings Act, Congress expanded the Department of the Interior's National Park Service to include an Advisory Board on Parks, Historic Sites, and Monuments charged with identifying and overseeing buildings and objects of national historical and archaeological significance.[31]

St. Louis boosters soon convinced the new federal advisory board to designate a swath of thirty-eight riverfront acres occupied by ramshackle slums and warehouses as the Jefferson National Park commemorating the Louisiana Purchase. Watching events in St. Louis unfold, former governor of Pennsylvania, now president of the Historical Society of Western Pennsylvania, John Fisher, in concert with local historian and Chamber of Commerce member Frank C. Harper, seized the opportunity to revive the long-slumbering idea for a "Point Memorial Park," now reborn as "George Washington National Park." Fisher and Harper hailed the Point not only as the site of George Washington's earliest heroics but as the real birthplace of America. Events there in the 1750s determined the nation's future. "It was here that Washington began his glorious career," proclaimed Harper at an April 23, 1937, meeting of the Historical Society, "here in 1758 that the course of history [was] altered, mak[ing] ours an Anglo-Saxon rather than a Latin culture." At that meeting the society bestowed upon Harper full power to appoint a committee to seek federal approval for a George Washington National Park. Harper's Point Park Committee acted aggressively. Calling it the "most practical and least costly solution to the lower downtown problem," Harper's committee proposed a thirty-six-acre park at the Point replete with a rebuilt Fort Duquesne and a rebuilt Fort Pitt. On July 14, 1938, the National Park Service Advisory Committee approved Harper's national park idea. Harper formally announced the favorable report at a 600-person dinner held at the William Penn Hotel. Brimming with enthusiasm at the real prospect for federal dollars to rebuild the Point (St. Louis got $22,500,000 for the Louisiana Purchase Park), Scully, with the blessing of the county commissioners, appointed a blue ribbon Point Park Commission, chaired by Harper, which included several members of the CPC.[32] The commission called for a WPA-funded archaeological excavation of Point sites to search for the remains of the old forts, and, to support this work, Scully ordered the CPC to undertake a special study of land titles and land usage at the Point site to help pinpoint the fort sites.[33]

Into this cauldron broiling with the Exposition Hall, floodwalls, the Wabash Bridge, and the George Washington National Park entered a final contentious ingredient, the Penn-Lincoln Highway. Now made feasible with federal funds, would this long-debated roadway enter or completely bypass the downtown? The controversy over the location for a combined William Penn Highway (U.S. Route 22) and Lincoln Highway (U.S. Route 30) through Pittsburgh engaged all the conflicting parties: the CPC and ACPC, downtown businessmen, and the state and federal governments. It highlighted the persistence of fragmentation as an obstacle to urban progress.

Both the Penn and Lincoln highways represented important east-west automobile and truck routes into Pittsburgh in the 1930s, and both emptied into crowded, congested, commercial main arteries. Founded in 1913 as a lobbying organization pushing for a toll-free highway from New York to San Francisco, the Lincoln Highway Association had long fought for a bypass route through Pittsburgh whereby the Penn and Lincoln highways would be merged at their juncture in suburban Wilkinsburg east of the downtown and, once united, carried through the city as a single four-lane highway.

In 1938 several factors helped propel these plans. First, work commenced on the initial Harrisburg-to-Pittsburgh section of the $61,000,000 PWA-funded "All-Weather Highway" dubbed the Pennsylvania Turnpike.[34] Expected to be completed to Irwin, thirty miles east of Pittsburgh, in 1940, the turnpike portended an avalanche of new traffic on the already congested U.S. Route 30 artery into the city. Second, under the auspices of the U.S. Department of Agriculture's Public Roads Administration (PRA), Congress, as part of the Federal Aid System (FAS) had created in 1937 the Federal Aid Secondary Highway System, which promised to promote federal funding for projects such as the Penn-Lincoln bypass. The PRA approved plans for all FAS highways, and Routes 22 and 30 comprised part of the federal system.[35] The CPC, the Pennsylvania State Highway Department, and Allegheny County agreed on merging the two highways in Wilkinsburg and conveying the Penn-Lincoln bypass via Edgewood and Frick Park and then through a new tunnel under Monitor Street in Squirrel Hill directly into the downtown.[36] However, the CPC, backed by the Allied Boards of Trades, saw equal merit in an alternate route, one completely bypassing downtown Pittsburgh by carrying the new highway across a new Glenwood Bridge near Homestead, connecting to Saw Mill Run Parkway, and then sweeping west through Robinson Township on the route of the old William Penn Highway.[37]

Downtown boosters quickly merged the Penn-Lincoln bypass project with plans for an elevated Water Street link to the South Hills by way of a new bridge and the Wabash Tunnel. With plans under way in 1937 for floodwalls at the Point and PWA funds for the Water Street improvement in sight, cheered by the LDBMA, the ACPC, in concert with State Highway Department engineers, officially aligned the all-important Penn-Lincoln bypass route from the so-called Monitor Street Tunnel under Squirrel Hill, west on Second Avenue along the Monongahela River and via an elevated Water Street downtown, then across the Monongahela on a new bridge, through the Wabash Tunnel to Banksville Road, then westward.[38]

In September 1938 the State Highway Department formally submitted to the PWA plans for the proposed $38,000,000 Penn-Lincoln bypass, for which it sought $14,000,000 in PWA funds. Highway officials expected state "motor funds," plus "substantial assistance from the County of Allegheny and the City of Pittsburgh," to cover the $17,000,000 shortfall. But such agreement on "substantial assistance" seemed remote in 1938. In fact, it was the revived MPA's main objective in 1938 to delay the Penn-Lincoln Highway program if necessary, pending joint analysis of "proposed changes." In the MPA's and the CPC's "proposed changes," the Penn-Lincoln Highway avoided the downtown, either crossing the Monongahela at Tenth Street and cutting through the South Side, or spanning the Monongahela via the Glenwood Bridge, then traveling southward on the Saw Mill Run Parkway route. Like Mayor Scully, the MPA and the CPC remained adamantly opposed to a double-decked highway along downtown Water Street. They cited not only the unsightliness of such a structure but also the great expense and "the heavy damage (in lowered real estate values) to waterfront properties," and furthermore "that it is not absolutely necessary to route a National Highway along Water Street and through downtown Pittsburgh." A June 1938 MPA memorandum charged that "there is evidence that special influence has been exerted on behalf of the County plan." Engineer Hunting of the LDBMA admitted that he had made every effort to have the county and the state fix the route for the national highway along Water Street at the Point "in hope it that would compel the early construction of the new bridge and tunnel to bring South Hills traffic to the merchants of the lower triangle."[39]

Because of industrial Pittsburgh's strategic role in national defense, Scully, the CPC, the federal government, and others in 1939 saw the special importance of the east-west route as war neared in Europe. Moreover, a recently published document by the federal Bureau of Public Roads, *Toll Roads and Free Roads* (1939), underscored the critical importance of traffic flow within and between metropolitan areas. But irreconcilable city and county differences on elevated highways dashed progress. Squabbling and infighting produced impasse and inaction. As a result, the $14,000,000 PWA funds vanished by 1939. "Apparently the possibility of the City and County raising any substantial part of the $17,138,545 is so remote," the Bureau of Public Road's A. E. McClure informed his chief, Thomas McDonald, in July 1939, that "the [Pennsylvania] Department of Highways considers the project a dead issue."[40]

BATTLING OBSTACLES

The MPA had been revived in 1936 to prevent the very debacle that sabotaged the PWA's Penn-Lincoln funding. Indeed, in transforming itself from the MPA to the PRPA in 1938, the private planning body had metamorphosed from a nay-saying, watchdog organization into an action-oriented planning body pledged to forge consensus and surmount the very bickering and backbiting that undermined progress on what was now hailed as the Penn-Lincoln Parkway. Led by Heinz, Braun, and Richards, the PRPA had redefined the focus of Pittsburgh's private planning agency away from one loosely concerned with bringing order, expertise, and comprehensiveness to the city's program of public improvements. In their minds, the existing model, that is Bigger's, adhered too rigidly to codified forms and master plan templates; its restrictive, legislated edifice—meant to dictate conformity—bred controversy over detail and obstructed progress on specific projects. Heinz, Braun, and Richards urged action. These pre–World War II forerunners of the progrowth coalition of businessmen, politicians, and planners who spearheaded the postwar urban renaissance viewed the New Deal as federal largesse, a boon to barren city treasuries. In their minds, private planning bodies like the PRPA, in partnership with public officials, could enlist federal dollars toward large-scale urban reconstruction programs, salvage plummeting downtown real estate values, decongest traffic-clogged central city arteries, and, in general, remake the gritty city into a modern, corporate headquarters and commercial emporium. Toward that end civic leaders, knowing the city's severe financial straits but firmly convinced that a pay-as-you-go budget, not increased taxes, should fund improvements, more greedily than ever eyed the prospect of federal funds. They set aside ideological and political differences with Roosevelt and the New Deal and backed federal efforts to reconstruct Depression-torn urban America, including using War Department funds for floodwall protection, PWA monies for bridge and road building, and the WPA to build streets, sewers, and parks.[41]

With the city so severely handicapped financially—in Wallace Richard's estimation "it was doubtful whether [the city] can initiate any major improvements during 1939 or 1940"—the PRPA actively importuned the federal government for aid in 1938 and 1939. Washington had the money, and, emulating New York City where Mayor Fiorello La Guardia and his Parks commissioner, Robert Moses, were using Washington to rebuild the metropolis, Pittsburgh mayor Cornelius Scully, frequently with Wallace Richards and Frederick Bigger in tow, traveled to Washington to lobby for federal dollars.[42]

The PRPA, the city, and the Chamber of Commerce all listed the Penn-Lincoln Parkway, the riverfront boulevards, the Point, and the Inter-District Traffic Circuit as priority developments. But before federal funds could be secured, Washington compelled the city, the county, the state, and downtown businesses and river interests to reach agreement on the crucial details of those major improvements. In addition, federal cooperation in 1938 required evidence that projects have a wide base of public support.[43]

Heightened anxiety over stalled progress on the city's vital improvement agenda, and evidence of acrimony surrounding the Penn-Lincoln bypass route, unleashed intense if not frantic efforts to forge consensus among warring Pittsburgh groups. By April 1938 the PRPA actively prodded the CPC to wave its objections to a bridge at Ferry Street that would connect to Water Street at a revised higher grade. The commission acceded; but it continued to battle the ACPC's and State Highway Department's elevated roadway design for the Water Street boulevard. Hoping to further advance consensus building, especially on the Penn-Lincoln and Point Park plans, the PRPA and the Chamber of Commerce organized the Council of Organizations (CO). In addition to the Chamber, the PRPA, and the Allied Boards of Trades, the thirteen members of the CO in 1938 included the LDBMA, the Civic Club of Allegheny County, the Pennsylvania Economy League, the Engineers Society, and the Retail Merchants Association. Yet despite the CO's and the PRPA's heroic efforts, compromise on issues such as the Penn-Lincoln bypass proved impossible.[44]

Progress, however, occurred on at least one front, the Water Street improvement, a triumph for Bigger and the CPC. Part of the city's master plan for a major street system in Pittsburgh, the Water Street boulevard formed the initial link in the CPC's beloved Inter-District Traffic Circuit. In mid-August 1938, with a $19,000,000 county-sponsored PWA grant scheduled to expire January 1, 1939, Wallace Richards, the PRPA, and the CO multiplied efforts to force action on the riverfront boulevard plans, for which the PWA's Harold Ickes promised to pay 45 percent of the project's estimated $6,000,000 cost. Using his public relations expertise, the PRPA's Richards, in alliance with Mayor Scully, the county commissioners, and Democratic boss David Lawrence, unleashed the association's elite-laden political clout. Richards's maneuvers to dismantle opposition to urban development and subvert fragmentation established a Pittsburgh model later hailed as renaissancemanship.

Mayor Scully and County Commissioners George Rankin and John Kane in 1938 demanded progress on the riverfront boulevards and toward that end "confidentially" appointed Richards as their agent to wrest agreement from the contending parties.[45] Securing PWA monies for the riverfront project involved filing an application and plans with the State Highway Department, whose approval preceded PWA's nod. In fact, a $5,300,000 PWA application for waterfront improvements already existed in Harrisburg, one unacceptable to the city. At an August 18, 1938, meeting on the waterfront plans with County Director of Public Works John F. Laboon; the city's counterpart, Frank M. Roessing; Bigger; the City Planning Department's chief engineer, Fred Triggs; and the ACPC's Park Martin, Richards successfully wrung agreement from the county to scrap its plans and accept a joint city-county development plan for the riverfront boulevards based upon City Planning's official *Major Street* plan. Water Street would be widened in front of the Baltimore and Ohio terminal from Ross Street to Smithfield Street, and a major boulevard constructed along the Monongahela riverside, with one set of lanes built at street level and another depressed at the proposed flood-wall level from Smithfield Street to Short Street. On the Allegheny side of the Golden Triangle, the projected riverside boulevard would run from Tenth Street to Fancourt along Duquesne Way. Politically astute Richards retained the LDBMA's Hunting to produce cost figures that showed the city's design costing well under the advertised county price tag of $5,350,000 for the Duquesne Way roadway.[46]

Next Richards won consent from a reluctant, overworked county Department of Public Works to develop working drawings of the project and pressed the county to immediately line up engineering firms to bid on the boulevard construction work. More action followed. To expedite the project, Fred Triggs dashed off to Washington, D.C., to lobby both the War Department and the PWA for floodwalls. A month later the first county engineering drawings based on the CPC's design crossed Bigger's desk.

The Water Street artery, 1941, looking east from the Point. Construction on the artery began in 1939. *Pittsburgh City Photographer Collection, Archives Service Center, University of Pittsburgh.*

Then suddenly, amid the euphoria and bustle surrounding the first concrete evidence of progress in Pittsburgh improvements, two rival, albeit ancillary, projects intruded. First, word arrived that drawings for an LDBMA/county-proposed elevated Water Street route for the Penn-Lincoln Highway had been forwarded to Harrisburg. The news alarmed Richards, who feared that the State Highway Department would confuse the two projects. Germany's invasion of Czechoslovakia raised the possibility that this LDBMA/county proposal would gain ascendancy as a "military highway." Immediately, Richards rallied his troops, including PRPA president Heinz, to use their influence to have Scully and the county commissioners lead a delegation to Harrisburg to expunge any confusion and pry loose the waterfront boulevard monies. Richards kept Heinz constantly informed about the status of his progress. On October 10 he called Heinz yet another time, stressing the urgency for drastic action to get final approval from Harrisburg and Washington, and he beseeched the mayor to urge David Lawrence to use the power of the "Democratic machine" on Pittsburgh's behalf.[47]

Just as suddenly, the long-dormant Crosstown Thoroughfare plan, so close to Bigger's heart, reappeared. With the PWA deadline imminent, the city and county Public Works departments resurrected the project, hoping that they might find accord on a plan for this crucial segment of the Inter-District Traffic Circuit. They submitted a plan that bridged Forbes Street and Fifth Avenue and passed under Wylie and Webster avenues, "as proposed by the county," and included a grade separator in the form of a semicloverleaf at Washington Street and Bigelow Boulevard. The plan also included the parallel "distributor streets on each side of the proposed highway" favored by the CPC. Martin opposed the distributor streets, "but in view of the approaching PWA deadline, he agreed to the plan so as not to further delay and possibly lose the project."[48]

Bigger and the CPC considered the Crosstown Thoroughfare the capstone of the Inter-District Traffic Circuit and recalled the long history of frustrated efforts to achieve agreement on the central thoroughfare. The joint committee's composite plan forced both sides to compromise. On October 11 the CPC moved to accept the recommendations of its General Plans Committee, stressing in the motion to be forwarded to the city council the "Commission's conviction that the flanking distributor streets should not be eliminated from the plan but should be included and constructed in the beginning."[49]

Again, however, the Crosstown Thoroughfare plan stalled. In late October Bigger and Triggs reported "the project [again] to be in a dormant state."[50] Allegheny County had resented the tone of the CPC's motion to the city council, and as in many other instances, bristled that "since the County is providing the bulk of the funds for the improvement, the city should be allowed to dictate the plan."[51] Even in the case of the waterfront improvements, when at Richard's behest the city and county cooperated, ACPC members, such as W. D. Mansfield, worried that "in view of the city's attitude and the manner in which these matters are being handled . . . [the] taxpayers will credit the city rather than the Board of County Commissioners with giving these improvements." It would not be until after World War II that the crosstown project was resurrected and finally built.[52]

Richards's public relations skills had wrenched cooperation from city and county officials, and he had navigated the waterfront boulevard proposal through the unseen obstacles posed by both its Penn-Lincoln and the Crosstown Thoroughfare rivals for funding. His final challenges were predictable, if belated; at the proverbial eleventh hour, the river interests and Chamberlain's LDBMA launched a barrage of criticism at the improvement plans. Pittsburgh's Propeller Club had signed on to the riverfront boulevard scheme early, and in fact, meetings on the subject with the coal barge operators represented by the Pittsburgh Coal Exchange had occurred off and on for fifteen years. For months, schematic drawings for the riverfront boulevards hung on the office walls of the county Public Works Department. Now the river men denied they had been consulted. Richards took no chances. Arthur Braun of the PRPA sat on the board of directors of the Pittsburgh Coal Company, and Richards got Braun to intervene by assuring the coal interests that the wharf design would be sufficiently modified to accommodate commercial river traffic. Both river organizations voted, if reluctantly, "not to object" to the plan.[53]

Peter M. Chamberlain, the executive director of the LDBMA, offered more obdurate resistance; in response, Richards discharged the full political might of the PRPA. Unhappy that the waterfront projects ignored the LDBMA's cherished elevated roadway connection to the Wabash properties, Chamberlain in late November staged a pitched battle over what he branded the PRPA's "steamroller tactics." He demanded that all the parties meet with the association's consultant, Harland Bartholomew, to revisit the project. Weakened by declining membership and a barren treasury—by 1938 the Pennsylvania Railroad, the Wabash Railroad, and Jenkins Arcade were its main contributors—the LDBMA lacked the resources for a protracted fight. Dr. James H. Green of the Chamber of Commerce even wondered whether the downtown organization still existed, and if it did, whether Chamberlain spoke for it. At this point Chamberlain mainly sought to have the outer roadway in the plan strengthened so that in the future, an elevated high-speed highway could be constructed over it.[54] Richards, however, accused Chamberlain of fronting for the "Wabash Group," whose property benefited enormously from the elevated route. Richards knew, of course, that two of the PRPA directors, Ernest T. Weir and William Witherow, sat on the Wabash board, and that Heinz, a director of the Pennsylvania Railroad, which owned the Wabash, wielded power in that inner sanctum. The Chamber of Commerce's Green also labored tirelessly to parry Chamberlain's failing thrusts.

Chamberlain lost. The *Sun-Telegraph*'s editorial on December 7, 1938, proclaimed "Cooperation at Last." The *Post-Gazette* cheered that with the opposition gone, the PWA would now contribute $2,355,512 of the estimated $5,890,000 cost of the riverfront boulevard project. "Pittsburgh," wrote the *Post-Gazette*, "needs the waterfront improvement and it needs the jobs which it will create." Moreover, exulted the *Post-Gazette*, this realization of a "50-year dream" shows the capacity of various conflicting groups "to accommodate differences over details," and "promises well for other projected public works."[55]

The "cooperation" reported by the *Sun-Telegraph* proved chimerical, especially when observed against the larger backdrop of events such as stalled progress on the Crosstown Thoroughfare, stumbling advances on park and playground work, and the failure to secure PWA funds for the Penn-Lincoln Parkway. Indeed, the spirit of cooperation sought by Wallace Richards and the PRPA, and evinced in the CO, suffered another setback in the spring of 1939. In a desperate effort to strike fragmentation at its heart, and create a first-class city of over 1,700,000 people, Mayor Scully and the CO, together with the PRPA, the Pennsylvania Economy League, and the League of Women Voters, renewed the now forty-year-old campaign for a Greater Pittsburgh. In 1935 then state senator George Rankin had introduced legislation in Harrisburg for a Pittsburgh Region Metropolitan Charter, which failed to be considered before the state legislature adjourned in 1935. In February 1939 the CO, backed by Howard Heinz and Richard King Mellon, had Scully name a committee headed by Bryn Hovde, executive director of the HACP, which included the PRPA's Arthur Braun and C.F.C. Arensburg as well as the Steel Workers Organizing Committee's (SWOC) Philip Murray and John Robin, secretary to Mayor Scully. Using the charter of 1935 as a model, the Metropolitan Charter Committee in less than a month produced the "Greater Pittsburgh Metropolitan Plan." The initial draft of the "Charter of Greater Pittsburgh," to quote the committee, replaced "the ox-cart county government" with a board of commissioners elected by proportional representation. It abolished minor judiciary posts and created fourteen government departments under a commission-appointed county manager, who was pledged to promote "pay-as-you-go" metropolitan regional development. Finally, the charter established a new Department of Metropolitan Planning headed by a director charged with preparing a master plan and a capital outlay budget.

Despite the appeal to efficiency, modern government, and home rule, and despite assurances that the new Metropolitan Charter Plan left intact the territory and integrity of the 124 boroughs and townships of Allegheny County, the Scully-championed committee's efforts failed badly. Last-minute compromises, especially substituting a board of commissioners chosen at-large for one chosen by proportional representation of districts, invited the potent charge that the Pittsburgh "Democratic machine" had rigged the charter to bail out the bankrupt city. The Metropolitan Charter Committee abandoned the doomed Charter Plan before consigning it to certain defeat at the polls.[56] Founded to forge consensus and overcome obstacles, the PRPA, with federal help, had produced action on the Water Street artery, but not on the Penn-Lincoln Highway, the Crosstown Thoroughfare, the Point, and other key downtown projects. Pittsburgh planning needed much greater momentum.

ROBERT MOSES AND PITTSBURGH'S CRUSADE AGAINST FRAGMENTATION

Months before the denouement of the Metropolitan Charter Plan, Pittsburgh planners expressed disquiet at the scant evidence of progress despite strong PRPA leadership. Planning had broad support nationally and locally, but in Pittsburgh the urban conversation had seemingly reached an impasse. With rumblings of the Metropolitan Charter Plan barely discernible in January 1939, *Progress* pondered perspicaciously the city's future, now that work had begun on one leg of the waterfront parkway. "What Next?" inquired the local planning journal.

Shall it be the improvement of the Saw Mill Run Boulevard, the connection between Duquesne Way and Bigelow Boulevard . . . ? No one knows. There is no recognized sequence of development today. We are just a city and county in which two million people live, who don't know from one year to the next what we are going to do about our expenditure of public funds; what are we going to build, not to build, or tear down; or what we would like to do with our city within the next ten or twenty years. Thus the pleasure of seeing our waterfront boulevard begun is tempered by the knowledge that it was made possible almost by fortuitous circumstances and not as the result of a region-wide official finance and capital improvement program. . . . Isn't it about time for us to attempt to control our environment instead of being subject to it?[57]

Howard Heinz looked elsewhere for help. The belief that outside experts wielded greater authority than homegrown genius and served to forge consensus on city betterment issues, a conviction widely shared in urban America in the early twentieth century, had engendered the 1909 Pittsburgh Survey, as well as Frederick Law Olmsted Jr.'s *Main Thoroughfares* in 1911, and even to some extent the six CCCP reports on which outsider Harland Bartholomew served as adviser in the early 1920s. This time, however, civic leaders turned not to St. Louis or Brookline, Massachusetts, but to New York City—the premier venue for both planning and massive federally funded highway, housing, and other building projects in the 1930s. New York's 1929 Regional Plan, while controversial, had attracted enormous national attention, as did the city's new charter-empowered Metropolitan Planning Commission (MPC), headed by Wallace Richard's old boss, Rexford Tugwell. After visiting Tugwell in New York in October 1938, Richards praised New York's MPC as the "outstanding example of a planning authority in the United States." He hailed it "a model for planning and financing long-range improvements."[58]

Even more than Tugwell's model planning commission, it was the far-reaching highway-building schemes and engineering feats of New York State Parks commissioner, City Park commissioner, and Triborough Bridge Authority chief Robert Moses that stirred Richards's and Pittsburgh's imagination. Ironically, the avowedly conservative, militantly pragmatic Moses detested planners, whom he lumped together with social workers and politicians as "uplifters [and] so-called experts or 'brain trusters.'" Moses, in fact, considered planning just "another form of brain trusting which is this great vogue today." "Planning," continued Moses, "was nothing more or less than forethought applied to any human activity. Pretty nearly every one but a nitwit, a beach comber, or an infant, has a plan. . . . Planning, therefore, is only a new word for an old familiar thing, but how the planners love it. They are in a way the successors to the efficiency experts about whom we heard so much a generation ago. They too had their patter."[59] But the often imperious and irascible Moses knew how to untangle bureaucratic red tape, blast through political obstacles, and "get things done"—a high priority for the actionist planning leadership of Heinz's Pittsburgh planning organization. Moses's achievement in articulating a New York regional parkway, tunnel, and bridge system was legendary, and in 1939 he planned another tour de force, the New York World's Fair, to help flaunt his magnificent system of regional roadways. Not coincidentally, General Motors's "Futurama" exhibit, fashioned by industrial designer Norman Bel Geddes, which featured a ride through a visionary ultramodern city laced with swirling and looping four- and six-lane parkways and superhighways, proved the most popular exhibit at the fair.[60]

Pittsburgh had a sizable corporate representation at the fair, attesting to the city's economic rebound after the slump of 1938. Westinghouse erected a spectacular exhibit at its Electrical Products Building. It was Howard Heinz, however, with his son Rust, who in October 1938 accepted Moses's praise for being the first American corporate leaders to finish an exhibition building, a huge dome towering ninety feet high with 20,000 square feet of space. Rust's sleek Heinz 57 Varieties racing car was one of the main attractions at the food king's exhibit. That September 1938 in New York, Howard Heinz found time to chat privately with Moses about Pittsburgh and what ideas Moses might have for "help[ing] us, and how much [Moses advice] would cost." Heinz afterward periodically reminded Moses about this talk, and in June 1939 Moses wrote Heinz excusing his delay in responding. He was busy in New York, but he also dreaded what he labeled "so-called jack-rabbit surveys." "Nor am I an evangelist," he explained to Heinz. "I feel no call to convert people in other sections." But, added Moses, "there were at present unusual conditions, . . . largely financial, partly due to my absorption in public matters and consequent neglect of my personal affairs, partly to shrinkage of small inherited funds, and partly to working a good deal of time without compensation. The family exchequer is low, and for that reason I have had to consider ways of adding to it." Therefore, he considered writing what he termed a Pittsburgh Preliminary Report "proper." Moses explained that he would have to take a leave of absence from his City Park commissioner job, and he required a "well rounded staff of really competent men of standing and experience" costing no less than $30,000. He personally wanted $15,000. "Possibly these figures seem to be high," he told Heinz, "but I should not care to shade them." Finally, he demanded no publicity, and he barred any luncheon speeches.[61]

Heinz readily acceded to Moses's blunt terms, and he proceeded immediately to raise funds from the Buhl Foundation and from his circle of well-heeled planning-enthusiast friends Arthur Braun, Ernest T. Weir, William L. Mellon, and Richard King Mellon, each of whom contributed from $2,000 to $5,000. Buhl volunteered $25,000, raising the total to $48,750.[62] The PRPA and Buhl envisioned Moses producing a regional highway system modeled on New York City's, with riverside drives, tunnels, and a New York City Triborough-like bridge gracing the Point. Moses, however, balked at that prospect. "That is entirely different from my original conception of [the job] as the result of our talk at the Worlds Fair," expostulated Moses in a letter to Heinz.

I thought . . . what you wanted was a considered opinion on the solution of traffic problems vitally affecting the business district of Pittsburgh. . . . I thought you were in the
position of the family with a sick child. You have had the advice of your family physician and of specialists. [He might—more candidly—have said Bigger and the CPC.] You
may need a surgical operation to prevent the illness from becoming chronic and acute.
You send for a diagnostician [Moses] to get his opinion . . . based on experience, a fairly
quick analysis of what the family and local doctors tell him, and presumably on a certain
gift for reaching correct conclusions on such matters.

The New Yorker apparently beheld such a difference between his own impres-
sion of the Pittsburgh task and what he thought Buhl and Heinz wanted that
he ended by stating that "it is best . . . for you to turn elsewhere."[63]

Moses's concluding sentence stunned Heinz. But he wanted Moses or no one.
He agreed to "leave all the questions of what you [Moses] and your engineers
will do for us to your judgement." "The matter is now in the shape that I think it
should be," wrote Heinz, "left entirely in my hands to handle with you without
any dealings with other donors or the Foundation." This would be a Heinz and
Moses show.[64] Heinz on July 23 was preparing to leave for New York to finalize
matters with Moses when he received the news that his son Rust had been killed
in a car accident. It was not until August 4 that Heinz and Moses reached a "mutual understanding." Within days, Moses's chief parks engineer, Arthur E. Howland, informed Richards about the exact date for the arrival of the team of seven
New York experts. Scully and Richards formally requested Bigger and the CPC
to cooperate with the team, and on August 15 the *Post-Gazette*, using a carefully
prepared text approved by Moses, announced without fanfare that a "Team of
Traffic Experts from New York under Robert Moses [was] Studying Pittsburgh's
Traffic Problem."[65]

Howland and the Moses team arrived in Pittsburgh a full week before news
of what came to be called the *Arterial Plan* appeared in the Pittsburgh papers.
As the "consultant" for the PRPA, Bigger joined Richards at Heinz's home for
a meeting with the Moses team. Indeed, Bigger, like Heinz and Richards, was
intimate with the whole Moses affair, although he must have felt somewhat
discomfited observing outside "experts," agents of a man antipathetic to planning technicians like himself, traversing his turf, rendering judgments about
his city and about his planning. However, Bigger most likely found some comfort in the guiding rationale for Moses's undertaking summed up by Richards
in the wake of the New Yorker's survey. Richards contended that

it is recognized that public agencies and private organizations [in Pittsburgh] experience considerable difficulty in establishing working relationships for the development of
projects and programs that would . . . benefit the Pittsburgh region . . . , that a financial

and capital program for the region is a vital necessity, that such a program automatically implies concentration upon the rehabilitation of the Golden Triangle . . . and that benefits would accrue to the region if some individual with a nation-wide reputation should be commissioned to come to Pittsburgh and make an analysis of some of the basic problems confronting the city and County.[66]

Along with Henry Burchfield of the LDBMA, Bigger and Richards accompanied the Moses team throughout Pittsburgh during their first week of visits. They lunched with steel executives, toured the proposed Penn-Lincoln Parkway route, and cruised the Pittsburgh waterfronts aboard an U.S. Army Corps of Engineers launch. Richards commented that the trip made it "more than evident" to the Moses team that the railroad exercised a "stranglehold" on the Pittsburgh region. "There was not a foot of the waterfront inspected that did not have trackage."[67]

Weeks of assembling traffic and other data, CPC reports, and material on retail sales supplied by the Hornes Department Store, plus meetings with Richard King Mellon in the Heinz Company boardroom and at the Duquesne Club, left the Moses team with several impressions, some, not surprisingly, already shared by most Pittsburghers. First, the city's central business district was blanketed with railroad and trolley tracks; second, and no surprise to Bigger, the New York team found one of Pittsburgh's "messier" problems to be, in Moses's words, "overlapping jurisdictions, not to speak of the personalities involved." Third, Moses concluded that Pittsburgh merchants feared the decentralization of retail business to suburban locations and "in the interest of salvaging their own property in the triangle could be lured into a cooperative program."[68]

The imminence of war in 1939, with the expectation of defense contracts and a revivifying Pittsburgh economy, intensified interest in major improvements. Richard King Mellon, a director of the Baltimore and Ohio Railroad, discussed with Howland and Richards the disposition of that railroad's downtown yards. He stressed that "sacrifices" were imperative. "Immediate steps had to be taken to lift Pittsburgh out of its steady decline." However, Mellon doled out portions of PRPA scripture with a dash of good public relations. It was crucial to "marshal a majority of interests in the region behind an over-all plan," noted Mellon, and if such a plan indicated that "it was necessary to cut away part of the Mellon Bank building that he would not oppose it."[69]

During the course of the Moses survey, the PRPA met frequently to monitor Moses's progress. Heinz kept a day-by-day vigil, meeting periodically with Moses, at least once in Heinz's home. He constantly assuaged the money fears of the Buhl Foundation's Charles F. Lewis, who agonized over the absence of budget figures or receipts from Moses. Heinz assured Lewis that Moses and his crew seemed to be working hard and "doing an efficient piece of work."[70]

Fears about the contents of the report—for example, that Moses possibly favored the Wabash Bridge and Tunnel—peaked during Fiorello La Guardia's fall visit to Pittsburgh to speak at a dinner meeting of the American Public Health Association. At that meeting La Guardia confided to Mayor Scully that Moses had told him that "his Pittsburgh highway report probably will not be acceptable to its sponsors." Richards mused that La Guardia's remarks were deliberate, an effort to pave the way in case Pittsburghers rejected a majority of Moses's recommendations.[71]

But once submitted, Moses's preliminary report raised few eyebrows. Heinz, Braun, Bigger, and Richards scrutinized it line by line, and on the whole found it quite acceptable. They asked him to modify some of his phraseology regarding the Wabash land and structures, to soften his recommendations on trolley lines in the downtown from advocating "immediate" to proposing "gradual removal," and to expunge his kudos to the PRPA for "its cooperation . . . which," they surmised, "might be misconstrued by a critical public." Although Howland doubted that Moses would assent to the changes, after some grumbling and a visit from Richards, Moses rationalized that he was merely simplifying his language and that it was the PRPA that had to live with his recommendations—not himself. He made the changes.[72]

At a Duquesne Club luncheon on November 15, 1939, only three months after initiating the study, Heinz formally announced Moses's much-anticipated findings. The president of the PRPA stressed in his presentation that his organization sought neither applause nor acceptance of the report, but simply "to present it to the Pittsburgh region hoping it would revitalize planning and the improvement program."[73] Moses himself confessed that his treatise contained "little that was new." He admitted in the introduction that he based the report on a "wealth of existing information." He merely assembled and digested all the information on Pittsburgh—the city's past plans (the substance of past urban conversations) and the transportation studies, topographic maps, and retail sales data—identified the malady, and prescribed a cure. He addressed, and indeed dispatched, cherished, albeit controversial, improvement issues. For example, he found the "George Washington Historical Park" idea, with its rebuilt Fort Pitt, as "hard to believe . . . or take seriously." Regarding the Point, he insisted that "traffic science—not emotion or aesthetics should govern improvement decisions" there. Likewise, he rejected the proposal for relocating the existing Point and Manchester bridges. "Our plan," he wrote, "rests on the theory that the two bridges will stay, that free flow of traffic over structures designed according to the highest standards must be provided in place of the present street congestion." Moses saved some of his harshest remarks for the railroads.

The Wabash property is dead; the B&O station and . . . tracks, moribund; and while the Pennsylvania Railroad is an active and going concern, it occupied a grossly disproportionate amount of land in the triangle and is a major cause of traffic difficulties, uneven and haphazard development, and civic ugliness. . . . No proper treatment of the Point is possible which does not look toward the future removal of the Pennsylvania system west of the main freight and passenger stations at Eleventh Street.[74]

To no one's surprise, Moses summoned the wrecking ball for the decrepit Exposition Hall; but he was equally merciless on Pittsburgh's ancient trolley system. Trolleys should be removed from Pittsburgh's crowded downtown streets. He contravened both the CPC's and PRPA's past wisdom by advocating the Wabash Bridge and Tunnel properties as a reasonable alternative route to the South Hills. Finally, in a page from Olmsted Jr.'s 1911 *Main Thoroughfares* report, Moses proposed an esplanade-flanked Duquesne River boulevard, as opposed to the "defect[ive] . . . combined elevated and depressed roadway system set back from the river and without protection from floods, such as is being completed on Water Street."[75]

While opposing the rebuilding of Fort Pitt, Moses favored a Point Park, but a park featuring a shaft of Pennsylvania black granite, steel, glass, and aluminum. He approved Bigger's Crosstown Thoroughfare, but vetoed extending it over the Allegheny River into the North Side. As for the contentious Penn-Lincoln Parkway issue, highlighted in the Moses report as the Pitt Parkway, Moses approved the already-agreed-upon Frick–Schenley Park–Monitor Street Tunnel alignment, and sided with the county and State Highway Department in supporting the downtown Water Street route. Other improvements greenlighted by Moses included widening Manhattan Street in the Manchester area and modernizing the Etna-Sharpsburg highway (now U.S. Route 28).

Moses priced the implementation of his *Arterial Plan* at $38,000,000. Sharing with his Pittsburgh clients his keen knowledge of municipal financing gained from long experience in New York City, Moses proposed that Pittsburgh adopt that city's municipal authority model and fund the new Pitt Parkway, Duquesne Boulevard, and Wabash Tunnel with tolls. Pittsburgh, a city cobwebbed with toll-free bridges and tunnels, naturally totally rebuffed this segment of Moses's report.[76]

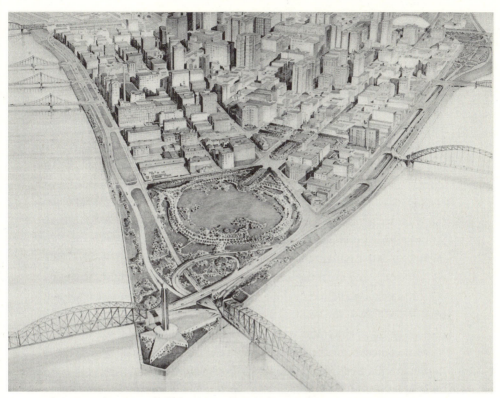

Robert Moses's 1939 *Arterial Plan* for Pittsburgh showing Duquesne Boulevard, the viaduct plan for the Pitt Parkway, and the shaft of black Pennsylvania granite marking the historic Point. Robert Moses, *Arterial Plan for Pittsburgh: Prepared for the Pittsburgh Regional Planning Association* (Pittsburgh: Pittsburgh Regional Planning Association, November 1939). *Archives Service Center, University of Pittsburgh.*

Despite the absence of new ideas, and its challenges to existing proposals, Moses's *Arterial Plan* was generally very well received in Pittsburgh. The city newspapers applauded Moses, the PRPA, and the Buhl Foundation for their contribution to Pittsburgh's well-being.[77] Just months after Moses issued his report, Heinz wrote to Charles Lewis, "I think it is safe to say that we have succeeded in rousing public support to a high pitch."[78] Moses's protestation that his report "represented the honest conclusions of those who have wrestled with similar problems on perhaps more difficult grounds elsewhere," very likely eased the way for its acceptance. Nor did it hurt that the city's civic elite had solicited the report and that Heinz, Scully, and Moses had freely corresponded and shared information.[79]

Only two days after its release, consistent with Heinz's and the PRPA's wishes, Scully importuned the CPC to make a serious study of Moses's *Arterial Plan;* the county commissioners asked Martin and the ACPC to do the same thing. Not surprisingly, the ACPC and the CPC reached much different conclusions from their examinations of the report. Moses had failed to consult with Park Martin, and the ACPC's engineer's pique at the rebuff appeared in his highly detailed, fourteen-page, item-by-item critique. But the rebuff aside, Martin warmed to a study, produced by a New York engineer, that essentially endorsed the county's 1936 long-range plan, including the county's Wabash plans and its alignment for what Moses named the Pitt Parkway. Martin challenged "underestimated" cost figures for sundry projects, but he deemed seven of Moses's eleven recommended improvements to conform beautifully with the county's plans. He emphatically rejected, however, Moses's Manhattan Street widening proposal as "impractical," and, unlike Moses, Martin favored moving the Manchester Street Bridge 600 feet up the Allegheny River. He also thought scrapping all of the city's street railways in favor of buses to be "politically naive." While silent on the New Yorker's proposal to erect a symbolic black stone shaft at the Point, Martin joined his engineering colleague in subordinating history to traffic considerations, and he praised Moses for sharing his own contempt for the CPC's Water Street improvement and for proscribing any similar treatment for Duquesne Boulevard.[80]

As chief consultant for the PRPA, Bigger not only seemingly bore some responsibility for bringing Moses to Pittsburgh, but during the survey months he had lunched with the Triborough Bridge builder and frequently met with Richards, Heinz, and Mellon to review the Moses study's progress and suggest textual revisions. And we can only suspect that the fiftyish "father of professional city planning" in Pittsburgh, the "planning technician" par excellence, anguished over the experience. Bigger plainly occupied a backseat in the Moses venture, while his impatient cohorts, Richards, Heinz, and Braun, in search of "improvements now!" rather than more technical advice, fawned over the actionist New York master builder. Bigger lingered a few more months at the PRPA as a relatively inactive "consultant," then on May 8, 1940, he officially resigned. Ironically, thirty-seven-year-old William Sellew Chapin, one of Moses's "right-hand-men in building New York's Parkway system," replaced him, not as a planning technician but as chief engineer of the PRPA. Chapin, a civil engineer who graduated from Boston's Northeastern University, had worked side by side with Moses since 1929. Privately, Bigger criticized the Moses report as, in the words of journalist Robert Alberts, "a mere rewrite of what he [Bigger] had been saying for twenty years or more."[81]

Bigger's terse, three-page, December 12, 1939, reply to Scully's request for comments on Moses's plan provided a glimpse of the planner's torment. He conceded that the greatest value of the report lay in its "dramatic emphasis on the need to bring together in some reasonable fashion the points of view of those technical men upon whom administration and legislative officials must depend." While excusing Moses for not "cover[ing] fields he was not asked to study," Bigger nevertheless faulted him for ignoring "the demonstrable need of the community for major and minor thoroughfares and recreational develop-ment costing many times the figure cited in the Moses proposal." Bigger de-murred on Moses's slap at the CPC's Water Street improvement, and likewise on his endorsement of the detested Wabash Bridge and Tunnel infrastructure. Nor did Bigger choose to comment on Moses's mass transportation recom-mendations, urging instead, an "early, thorough and constructive study of this important problem." Pittsburgh's patriarch of planning preferred instead to underscore Moses's approval of Duquesne Way, the Crosstown Thoroughfare, and the completion of the Saw Mill Run improvement, all part of the CPC's vi-tal *Major Street* plan and the Inter-District Traffic Circuit. He even conceded that Moses's Pitt Parkway "coincides generally with, or parallels, approved ar-teries of the Major Street Plan."[82]

Like Bigger, PRPA leaders Heinz, Richards, and Mellon hoped that Moses's visit and subsequent report would not only energize the planning process in Pittsburgh but also overcome divisions and force action on a capital improve-ments agenda. In fact, Richard King Mellon and the Chamber of Commerce were so enthralled at the very prospect of Moses's impending report and its implications for stemming the decline of the Golden Triangle as a center of business that, in October 1939, they formed the Golden Triangle Commit-tee, convened 100 businessmen and civic leaders at the Duquesne Club, and drafted a program for face-lifting the downtown. Mellon chaired the commit-tee, whose objectives included eliminating bottlenecks, removing dangerous and unsightly obstructions (meaning railroad yards and the Exposition Hall), readjusting tax assessments for depressed downtown property, and undertak-ing a long-range plan of beautification of the district to include a park at the Point.

Mellon's ardor in 1939, although vital, often proved thoughtlessly impolitic. Missing from those seated for lunch at the October Duquesne Club luncheon were Mayor Scully, Martin, Bigger, and the county commissioners. Informed of the meeting, Scully reacted "icily" that "it was hard to see how . . . [the Chamber] can accomplish [its plans] without the participation of the CPC and other city agencies." Asked about the meeting, another unnamed "public official" observed that "the public money by which such improvements must be made, rest[s] in the hands of Mayor Scully, City Council, Commissioner Kane and I. Lamont Hughes of the State Highway Department. Does the Chamber expect these officers to fit unquestionably into its program after they have read about it in the paper?"[83]

But Mellon's singular political faux pas aside—he would not be guilty of such a lapse again—much of the speech-making at the November Duquesne Club meeting hailed the unity, political accord, and consensus that surrounded the reception of the Moses report. Although the CPC and ACPC still disagreed about some of the plan's details, unity was the key point in Robert Alberts's "postmortem" published in the *Bulletin Index*. Alberts asserted that by "recommending certain projects [and not others], the Moses report tie[d] together [the city's improvement] program into one organic, dramatic entity."[84] Scully in February 1940 sounded the same theme in discussing the Moses plan as part of his newly announced "Program for Pittsburgh," a program that included public health initiatives, public housing, universities, and libraries, as well as main arteries. The mayor saw little dispute over Moses's recommendations, which "closely coincided with previous city and county plans." He also reported "a fair amount of progress . . . in pushing some [of Moses's ideas] into the construction stage." Chapin agreed. Writing Moses in July 1940, he cheerily observed that "we are rapidly shaping up a program based on your report and it appears that we will be able to obtain the endorsement of public bodies. If we can get them to publicly announce it as their own program, we will then be able to get into some detail plans." Out of unity, action. Pittsburgh progress seemed imminent.[85]

FORGING A PITTSBURGH FEDERAL-URBAN LINK

The PRPA deliberately nurtured expectations that from Moses's *Arterial Plan* would flow unity, and from unity action. Moses's report, furthermore, produced an explosion of closely coordinated public and private development activity that fittingly climaxed a half century of similar activity in Pittsburgh. The Chamber's and Mellon's Golden Triangle groups sprang forth from these events, as did Scully's edict in mid-December 1939 commanding the CPC and ACPC to sift through the Moses report and find common ground on five projects to be assigned priority status. The two commissions listed Point Park, the Saw Mill Run Parkway, the Crosstown Thoroughfare, the Pitt Parkway, and the Etna-Sharpsburg highway improvement as their top choices.

Heinz and the PRPA, however, had even bolder plans. The extent of the highly favorable publicity attending the Moses report surprised Heinz and Richards and spurred them to further the transformation of the PRPA, the heir of three decades of civic planning organizations in the city, from traditionally being an adviser and promoter of planning and improvement projects to seizing the leadership of the planning process.[86] They channeled their most strenuous postreport efforts toward building city, county, state, and especially federal consensus around a Metropolitan Improvement Program (MIP). Heinz's efforts here previewed the post–World War II Pittsburgh Renaissance. Indeed, the roots of the MIP lay in the extraordinary prewar planning energy displayed by Howard Heinz. Working closely with local, state, and federal officials, he became a planning dynamo in the months following the release of the Moses report. To mobilize for action, Heinz and the PRPA established five committees, the two most important being the Triangle Committee led by Edgar J. Kaufmann and the Pitt Parkway Committee headed by Mellon. In August 1940 Heinz arranged a meeting involving Scully, County Commissioner Kane, the CPC, the ACPC, and the county Department of Public Works, plus PRPA people, including Richards and William Chapin. Heinz sought to establish a schedule of action to advance several major improvements agreed on by the city and county, including the Seventh Avenue and Bigelow Boulevard grade separation and the widening of Bigelow Boulevard from Tunnel Street to Grant Street (both part of the Crosstown Thoroughfare planning), as well as the Duquesne waterfront and Saw Mill Run Parkway improvements. Two months later Heinz urged establishing a sequence of arterial improvements that would firmly set the city on a desired course of action. Logically, argued the PRPA, the sequence must include the triangle waterfront boulevards, the Crosstown Thoroughfare, the South Side tunnel and bridge improvement (a clear indication of Moses's influence on Pittsburgh planning), and Pitt Parkway. Heinz now packaged these projects as the MIP, a five-year program for which he sought city, county, state, and federal backing, especially from the State Department of Highways and the federal PRA. Locally, he rallied the CPC, the ACPC, the county Department of Public Works, Scully and the county commissioners, the Chamber of Commerce, and the Pennsylvania Economy League.[87]

The PRPA premised its bold vision of urban improvements on an embryonic progrowth psychology, which it observed at work in Chicago and New York City, and which would dominate urban redevelopment after World War II. "The average American city," argued the PRPA, "is not a satisfactory place to live. . . . Public and private planning agencies have as an outstanding objective the eventual betterment of [the] urban environment. The crisis demands nothing less than urban redevelopment enjoining both the public and the private sector." The PRPA called for major improvements to be built where people can see them and benefit from them: "If neglected and decaying central cities are to be restored to health, their citizens prevented from becoming discouraged . . . [and] social and economic values . . . recapture[d]."[88]

Howard Heinz, the planning force who oversaw the budding of the Renaissance in prewar Pittsburgh, never lived to see its postwar flowering. In December 1940, at the age of sixty-three, Heinz was suddenly stricken with severe abdominal pain. Emergency surgery in Philadelphia was initially ruled successful. Then on February 9, 1941, Heinz suffered a cerebral hemorrhage and died minutes later. His legacy of energetic leadership survived, bequeathed to his successor at the PRPA, Richard King Mellon. It endured especially in Mellon's and the PRPA's intense dedication to advancing the MIP, which, with war now raging in Europe, became increasingly entangled with issues of mobilization and defense preparedness.[89]

But while Heinz's energy and the MIP produced tangible signs of progress, they never completely obliterated the lingering obstacles. Some of the PRPA's actions themselves planted seeds of discord, especially its thoughtless and occasionally peremptory dealings with the CPC and ACPC. Despite surface calm, both Bigger and Martin chafed at what they perceived as the Moses report's casual dismissal of the CPC's and ACPC's contributions. Heinz further exacerbated matters. Moses had urged Pittsburgh to undertake a comprehensive mass transit study. Chair of the PRPA's Mass Transit Committee, and convinced that an "impartial" report on the city's mass transit would generate unanimity and action, Heinz in September 1940 commissioned another outsider, W. S. Menden, the retired head of the Brooklyn-Manhattan Transit Company, to direct a Pittsburgh regional transit study. Completed in 1941, Menden's *Pittsburgh Mass Transportation* provided a detailed portrait of the city's present traffic conditions and its mass transit facilities and attempted to correlate the city's mass transportation needs with future arterial highway plans.[90]

The Menden affront aside, and with war and defense issues looming, cooperation and progress, if halting at times, still proceeded. Real evidence of unanimity-driven progress at last appeared on what had earlier been two severely contested improvement issues in Pittsburgh, the Duquesne waterfront and the Penn-Lincoln Parkway. Both projects confirmed not only the prewar energy driving progress on major improvements but also the gnawing difficulties still undermining cooperation despite the vigorous public sector–private sector progrowth initiative launched by Heinz, Mellon, Richards, and Chapin of the PRPA.

Determined to get action on major improvements, the PRPA in early June 1940 met with city and county officials and agreed to give Duquesne Boulevard top billing. The county volunteered to pay the estimated $2,500,000 cost of the waterfront roadway. A week later, after talks with the U.S. Army Corps of Engineers, which policed all design specifications for bridges, wharfs, and flood-walls on inland waterways, county engineers produced "rough sketch plans" for the riverfront highway. But "cooperation be damned" differences over key details in the plans again stymied progress. County planners designed a Duquesne Way complex that featured a widened upper roadway still obstructed by the rude presence of elevated Pittsburgh Railways Company trackage. An outer, lower roadway served through traffic and vehicles requiring access to the Allegheny River wharfs. Despite the scathing in Moses's *Arterial Plan*, the CPC stubbornly clung to its more costly depressed highway design now visible in the nearly completed Water Street improvement. Bigger above all viewed the Duquesne Way improvement as a vital link in the city's Inter-District Traffic Circuit. Therefore Bigger and the CPC insisted that in order to accommodate the turning radius of the largest trucks, the improvement needed to include a seventy-foot separator strip dividing the inner from the outer roadway. Focusing principally on traffic movement, not cost, and desiring to relegate trucks to the margin of the downtown, the CPC's design also contained wharf-side parking terminals for trucks and automobiles arriving over radial highways forced to stop in the triangle area. Ramps gave vehicles access to the parking.[91]

Park Martin and the ACPC favored a narrower fifty-foot strip and only limited wharf parking. For Martin, cost, not aesthetics, governed the design of the improvement. Martin exuberantly defended that position at a critical joint city-county meeting attended by members of both commissions, including Bigger. "We have a proposition," asserted Martin, "where the Board of County Commissioners have [*sic*] offered to do a certain job in the City, and we must approach this subject from the standpoint of the ability of the Commission to finance it, and weigh that against the desired object to be obtained." Martin had discovered that only 13 percent of the trucks manufactured in America were unable to turn on a fifty-foot separator. "At a considerable extra cost," protested Martin, the county was asked to provide for a "very minor movement of traffic."[92]

Throughout 1940 and early 1941 the city and county battled over these details, over the width of separators and over allowing Pittsburgh Railways to share space on such separators with pedestrians. The city in July 1940 approved a "temporary" plan for the construction of a section of the roadway from Ninth Street to Eleventh Street that capitulated on the parking and ramps issues, but not on the sacred seventy-foot separator. Finally, in March 1941, with progress and funding jeopardized by inaction, the CPC yielded. Having surrendered on the parking issue, it now acceded to a sixty-foot separator on the upper roadway. Adding to the chagrin of the CPC—still opposed to tracks on Duquesne Way—the improvement accommodated not only the street railway but also, at least on a short-term-basis, the continued presence of elevated Pennsylvania Railroad tracks. Construction began in 1941.[93]

Pitt Parkway rivaled in importance Bigger's inner loop around the Golden Triangle. It was a gleaming jewel in the PRPA's metropolitan improvement crown, and in early 1940 seemed destined for action. However, here again a handful of lingering, unresolved issues thwarted final agreement—the questions of an elevated highway approach along Water Street into the downtown and Moses's proposed Wabash Bridge and Tunnel route westward. Harrisburg opposed the Wabash route, and Heinz, Braun, and Bigger still shunned building elevated highways in the downtown.

Several events forced a resolution to the impasse and compelled the city to resume civil conversation and present a united front behind the massive improvement. First, the imminent completion of the "Dream Highway," the Pennsylvania Turnpike, in July 1940 sharpened the long-standing fear that thousands of automobiles and trucks would spill onto old Routes 22 and 30, producing a gigantic bottleneck. Second, Hitler's invasion of France in May 1940 elevated the importance of defense considerations, especially the movement of Pittsburgh-produced war matériel as a primary motive for military highway development. By rallying broad-based popular support in the name of patriotism, war, like great fires and other natural disasters, often exerts a profound impact transcending selfish private interest. The war emergency also revealed that the monster of political fragmentation still lurked in Pittsburgh, despite the power of the PRPA. Again, basic intergovernmental rivalries and differences threatened sabotage. While the efforts of Heinz, Mellon, Braun, and Richards to forge unity behind a civic improvements agenda had welded the downtown interests, Scully, and the county commissioners together behind the MIP, the PRPA's funding scheme for these improvements—which hinged on federal participation—stumbled. The obstacle amounted to nothing less than a crisis in federalism. Thomas McDonald of the PRA expressed keen interest in "doing whatever [he] could to assist in the matter of finding a solution to Pittsburgh's regional highway problem." In 1940 he viewed that solution as extending the Pennsylvania Turnpike through Pittsburgh. But following federal protocol, highway aid required an invitation from the Pennsylvania State Department of Highways, headed by I. Lamont Hughes, the former president of Carnegie Steel. Since the Pitt Parkway involved the rerouting of the existing Penn and Lincoln highways. Hughes could not act until Pittsburgh and the county submitted locally endorsed plans to Harrisburg for legislative approval. Thus arose an imbroglio. Calling the City Planning Department "overworked," the CPC refused to act until the PRA issued the funds enabling it to enlarge its staff. Since the parkway lay within the city, the ACPC declared its hands tied. In June 1940, with federal, state, and local funds in limbo, all progress on the Pitt Parkway halted.[94]

Only Hitler's entrance into Paris and the fall of France in June 1940 rescued the Pitt Parkway. Suddenly, in July 1940 the PRPA took a new tack. Word of a "Military Emergency Program" and "National Defense Highway" monies spurred the PRPA to hawk the proposed roadway as a "strategic" defense highway, an idea fully elaborated in an October 1940 document called "Emergency Program—Metropolitan Arteries for the Pittsburgh Region."[95] Excited at the rekindled hopes for the Pitt Parkway, Richards enlisted the State Highway Department in the campaign to make the bypass part of the military highway system. But thinking strategically, Heinz, Mellon, Richards, and Chapin no longer angled for highway construction dollars; aware of the limitations imposed by the war emergency, they were instead "extremely desirous of having an intensive study project set up to develop detailed plans for a metropolitan highway in the Pittsburgh area." War preparedness in 1940 had loosened funds for just such a study. McDonald wrote Hughes on November 18, 1940, that under Section 18 of the Federal Highway Act of 1940, "funds may be used to pay the entire engineering cost of the survey, plans, specifications, estimates, and supervision of construction of projects for such urgent improvements of highways strategically important from the standpoint of national defense . . . and as [a] result of request of the Secretary of War, the Secretary of the Navy, and other authorized defense agencies."[96]

In this battle for funds, the PRPA entrenched itself on the front lines, orchestrating the attack, the role Heinz had envisioned for the organization. Pittsburgh's official planning bodies seemingly sat in the rear while Richards and Chapin convened meetings, often in Scully's office, and dashed off to meetings with Secretary of Highways Hughes in Harrisburg or with McDonald in Washington, D.C. Chapin and his chain-smoking colleague Richards logged countless, arduous hours on the telephone, at the typewriter, assembling information, wheedling, coaxing, soothing ruffled feathers, coordinating meeting after meeting. Knowledge of Section 18 funds, for example, triggered a meeting in Harrisburg between Mellon, Governor Arthur James, and Hughes, one that in Mellon's eyes all but assured state cooperation in matching federal highway funds. At a second meeting on December 18, Governor James committed state support.[97] However, it was not until July 1941, following months of further legwork by Richards and Chapin, including several trips to Harrisburg and Washington, D.C., that Hughes forwarded an application for a $400,000 matching grant. Only months later, on November 26, did the state approve its $200,000 share of the survey grant. But more delays ensued. McDonald withheld the federal government's share until the Bureau of Public Roads confirmed the CPC's and ACPC's "agreement on exactly how to view the problem and the studies necessary to solve Pittsburgh's traffic problem." Finally, on October 1, 1942, the PRA announced its award of $200,000 toward the cost of a study of what the *Pittsburgh Press* called a "transcontinental super highway skirting the edge of Frick Park and entering Pittsburgh along Water Street to be built after the war ends."[98] Apparently, by 1942 the military significance of the highway had waned as the paramount funding consideration.

Progress on another Pittsburgh priority, a Point park, hinged on knowing the alignment of the Pitt Parkway and the grade separation of the Duquesne Way and Water Street improvements at their juncture with the highway approaches to the Point and Manchester bridges. Their other differences aside, Bigger and Moses at least agreed on the primacy of traffic flow as the basis for development decisions at the city's Point. Both also agreed on the importance of a park.[99] Moses in his report highlighted a Point park at the same time he spoofed the idea of rebuilding Fort Pitt. Bigger likewise saw little practicality in rebuilding Fort Pitt.[100] Mayor Scully, however, had emerged as the chief proponent of a national historical park, hailing the Point as the "Gibraltar of the whole colonial defense system." In November 1940, the new Point Park Commission (PPC), appointed by Scully, proposed razing Exposition Hall in order to restore "the frontier status of the Point." The PPC's first task was to research and historically document the location of Fort Pitt. Undeterred by the onset of World War II, and armed with both city and WPA funds, archaeological work began at the Fort Pitt site in January 1942.[101] Supervised by State Archaeologist Wesley L. Bliss, WPA laborers uncovered the red (not white as had been expected) brick curtain walls of Fort Pitt and remnants of the Grenadier Bastion and drawbridge abutments. The excavation disclosed that the city street level in 1942 sat six feet above the level of the fort's old parade grounds. Scully and Dr. A. R. Kelley, the National Park Service's chief of Archaeological Sites who toured the excavations in March 1942, marveled at the discovery, which reinforced plans there for a national park, replete with the fort rebuilt to historical specifications.[102]

PLANNING ON THE EVE OF WAR

On the eve of World War II it was planning's technical role, those pesky details Olmsted Jr. had warned against, that increasingly preoccupied Bigger and the CPC. One of those details included recreation, an issue that after decades ultimately caused housing to be resurrected as a topic for planning. Thanks to Scully's aggressive pursuit of WPA funds, Pittsburgh in 1939 had created a "Special Committee on Parks and Playgrounds," which included Bigger. Between 1938 and 1941 the City Planning Department, in conjunction with Public Works, busied itself developing designs and approving sites for recreation centers and playgrounds as part of a $2,000,000 PWA-WPA-sponsored recreation program launched in 1938.[103] Significantly, some of these playgrounds, such as the Ammon Site, were developed in collaboration with the new HACP headed by University of Pittsburgh history professor Bryn Hovde.

Indeed, in the late 1930s and early 1940s housing nationally suddenly loomed in importance in the urban conversation. Pittsburgh's first public housing projects, Bedford Dwellings and Terrace Village I and II, located in Pittsburgh's Hill District, presented the challenge to configure innovatively a large-scale residential complex on difficult, hilly terrain. It was the kind of neighborhood unit, communitarian planning task that Bigger relished. As a town planner, Bigger had found himself engaged in housing issues during World War I and again in the early 1930s. More recently, in 1937 he directed operations at Greenbelt, Maryland. During 1940, Bigger consulted on housing and redevelopment for the Federal Housing Administration (FHA), and produced the first handbook on urban redevelopment for the FHA in 1941. In his purview of urban redevelopment, Bigger envisioned the possibility of holistically restructuring the fragmented urban environment.[104] Bigger himself was a member of the HACP, and between 1937 and 1942 CPC staff members spent countless hours analyzing HACP site plans and architectural drawings, approving the vacation of streets for the "superblock" designs of the Bedford and Aliquippa Terrace projects. Yet although fully apprised of the need to acknowledge the social implications of planning, especially the crucial relationship of housing and planning, and with Frederick Bigger as its chair, the CPC still complained about its time-consuming housing role, seemingly resentful of the long hours spent poring over blueprints for the new world of public housing. Pittsburgh planners, like those in other cities, failed to integrate the grand low-income housing complexes within the framework of the MIP unfolding for the "new Pittsburgh and its region."[105] Certainly, no evidence existed that the CPC, the ACPC, the HACP, or the county housing authority envisioned the relationship of large-scale public housing to the emerging arterial highway system or park systems, long a primary emphasis in Bigger's cant about housing and "accessibility." In fact, as America entered the war in 1942, and the CPC and ACPC undertook preparations for the postwar world, neither the city's nor the county's plans—whether for Point Park, a new defense airport, or new city and county housing projects—reflected reasoned coordination of the traffic, park, playground, and residential development once contemplated by town planners such as Bigger.

On the eve of World War II, Bigger's CPC grudgingly surrendered much of its leadership of the urban conversation in Pittsburgh. Despite the federal imprimatur, city planning in Pittsburgh lost salience to action-oriented, progrowth planning organizations, such as the PRPA, soon to be eclipsed in importance by the Allegheny Conference on Community Development (ACCD). It was Wallace Richards and Richard King Mellon, not Bigger, who in the immediate prewar era coordinated strategies for the Pitt Parkway and downtown development and who sped by train to Washington, D.C., on frequent lobbying junkets.[106] What radiated from the drawing boards of these Pittsburgh prewar, progrowth planners was the shimmering vision of a restored, economically revitalized downtown, linked regionally and nationally by a modern system of express highways.[107]

The CPC did not surrender easily. The PRPA's vaunted efforts to seize the planning initiative in Pittsburgh and compel action bred resentment. Still indignant over the Moses and Menden snubs, both the CPC and ACPC in 1942 openly resisted the Mellon, Dilworth, and Monteverde overtures to restore harmonious relations between the city's voluntary and official planning bodies. Monteverde as late as January 1942 implored Bigger and the CPC to designate representatives to a joint committee endeavoring to restore harmony between the two groups. Similarly, despite city and county cooperation, which in 1942 culminated in the agreement on Pitt Parkway and Pittsburgh's securing a $400,000 state and federal grant to produce detailed plans for the high-speed roadway, the city and county planning bodies continued to haggle over those details, especially for the Crosstown Thoroughfare.

Nevertheless, in 1943, at the moment key members of the PRPA such as Richard King Mellon and a few other civic leaders spawned a new, even more disciplined and more action-oriented planning organization, the ACCD, a solid basis for postwar city development progress still existed in Pittsburgh. American troops now fought in Asia. In Europe, the Allies marshaled a vast expeditionary force poised for the invasion of the Nazi fortress. At home, the federal government launched a major postwar planning effort that increasingly engendered greater interagency cooperation, especially among the city's public and private planning bodies. Indeed, in light of the impact of the war in further shifting America's steel-making capacity to the Midwest, threatening the viability of Pittsburgh's steel dominance, the young ACCD endeavored to become the central coordinating agency for regionwide planning.[108] Mayor Scully and the county commissioners responded to the federal postwar planning edict by ordering both planning commissions to prepare a City-County Program for the Public Works Reserve. Shortly, the two public commissions shifted from preparing a "post-war reserve (of improvement projects)" to "post-war construction."[109] By 1943 the federal government undertook a coordinated national program of postwar planning that had a strong urban emphasis. In Pittsburgh, postwar planning involved highway projects such as the Pitt Parkway, but also recreation and housing, including plans for the redevelopment of the Hill District.[110] By December 1943 the two official planning organizations unveiled a $90,000,000 postwar planning agenda encompassing 147 projects, including the Crosstown Thoroughfare, the completion of the Saw Mill Run Parkway to the West End, the inauguration of the Crosstown Thoroughfare and the Penn-Lincoln Parkway, and the crucial connection of the Crosstown with the Penn-Lincoln complex.[111]

While fragmentation still gnawed at the fabric of Pittsburgh planning, by 1943, the year the ACCD was founded, the massive prewar effort to battle disharmony, the war, and over half a century of public and private diligence in building an ethos of planning in the city had produced impressive results. Key components of the so-called Pittsburgh Renaissance—Point Park, Duquesne Way, the Pitt Parkway, the Crosstown Thoroughfare—were either nearing completion or awaited detailed plans. More important, the city had struggled against disharmony for decades. It knew the costs and had fashioned mechanisms, albeit still imperfect, to contend against discord. The framework for a postwar, progrowth era of urban rebuilding had solidified.

CHAPTER 9

A Scaffolding for Urban Renaissance

POINT STATE PARK and the Gateway Towers, symbolic of Pittsburgh's Renaissance I, began rising at the confluence of the three rivers in 1950. The celebrated physical rebirth of industrially scarred Pittsburgh had dawned. But this new city neither suddenly sprang, as long suggested, from the economic cataclysm of the Great Depression, nor from the horrendous St. Patrick's Day flooding of 1936 and the environmental degradation of the war years. Like Point Park, which commemorated the historical significance of the confluence of the three rivers during the war between France and Great Britain for continental supremacy in the 1750s, the Pitt Parkway, the Crosstown Thoroughfare, the new Point Bridge, flood protection, and many of the other essential parts of Renaissance I all comprised elements integral to Pittsburgh planning, if not since the turn of the century, then at least since the 1920s.

Indeed, as we have seen, the conversation about Pittsburgh and how urban space there should be more rationally developed took root perhaps as early as the 1880s, when the city's director of Public Works, Edward Bigelow, first proposed parks and carriageways for the city's East End. Pittsburgh bosses, master boodler Christopher Magee and his partner, William Flinn, controlled city councils and orchestrated both the urban conversation and the bond issues that funded the bonanza of nineteenth-century public improvements such as schools, courthouses, city parks, streets, and boulevards. Private philanthropic endeavors, such as Andrew Carnegie's, Henry Phipps's, and Mary Schenley's, and other improvement efforts, often undertaken in concert with the public sector, further enriched the heritage of the late-nineteenth-century city. By World War I city government's cooperation with civic leaders such as Carnegie and Franklin Nicola had produced, for one, the magnificent City Beautiful ensemble of libraries, museums, music halls, and private clubs in Pittsburgh's Oakland section.

Bigelow's role in shaping the "new urban landscape," like Carnegie's and Nicola's place in the City Beautiful movement, underscores the significance of

Pittsburgh in planning history and in the changing nature of the urban conversation about the form and use of urban space. In fact, throughout this history of the Steel City and urban planning, we have argued that Pittsburgh deserves special attention. First, the city reflected key trends in the history of urban planning. Second, and perhaps of greater significance, Pittsburgh on a number of occasions and in several ways was central to the history of modern planning.

Certainly, in the late nineteenth century Pittsburgh's Edward Bigelow exemplified the course of planning history. As the director of city parks, Bigelow endeavored to acquire and shape parklands and make those parks accessible to the city's large immigrant working class. His work, therefore, recapitulated the work of Olmsted Sr. in Boston, Buffalo, Brooklyn, and other cities as described by David Schuyler in *The New Urban Landscape*. Bigelow's park and parkway schemes, not viewed by him as part of a comprehensive vision, fit identically the description of "special purpose planning" that Jon Peterson defined in his *The Birth of City Planning*. Furthermore, gritty Pittsburgh in 1893 responded ecstatically to Chicago's World's Columbian Exposition and the magnificent "White City" that Daniel Burnham, Charles McKim, and Frederick Law Olmsted Sr. erected on the shores of Lake Michigan. The Oakland civic center, that exquisite baroque grouping of hotels, colleges, and monumental buildings adjoining Schenley Park, paid tribute to Pittsburgh's fervent romance with the "White City."[1]

The city exemplified as well the birth of professional city planning in the early twentieth century. It was smoky, uncomely, and turbulent turn-of-the-century Pittsburgh that hosted the nation's most extensive social investigation, the historic Pittsburgh Survey (1907–1909), a scathing indictment of the social and physical costs of untrammeled industrialism, which included Charles Mulford Robinson's charge that "if ever a city needed the definite plan that an outside commission could make for it, it is Pittsburgh."[2] In 1908 Pittsburgh held the "Civic Exhibit," a progressive tour de force cosponsored by the American Civic Association, the Tuberculosis League, and the city's Civic Club of Allegheny County, which not only featured findings from the Survey but also Benjamin Marsh's famous exhibit on congested housing. This effulgence of progressivism culminated in the election of a progressive mayor, George Guthrie. Amid a national wave of City Beautiful planning sparked by the 1902 McMillan Plan for Washington, D.C., Guthrie appointed the Pittsburgh Civic Commission, which in 1909 lured planner Frederick Law Olmsted Jr. to the Steel City under orders to deliver the city's first plan.

In 1911, with the tide of progressivism cresting, and with the city's business community in the vanguard, Pittsburgh joined many American cities in creating an official city planning commission that typically in a few years would be watched over and cheered on by the Citizens Committee on the City Plan (CCCP), a voluntary body comprised of prominent business leaders, professionals, and other civic luminaries. This early close relationship of public planning and the private sector, exemplified in Pittsburgh by the interlocking cooperation between Frederick Bigger and private sector planning boosters such as Henry J. Heinz, Howard Heinz, William Larimer, and Richard King Mellon, paved the way historically for the growth of public-private partnerships in the 1930s.

Accordingly, Pittsburgh continued to be exemplary in the 1920s. During the flapper era, the Pittsburgh City Planning Commission (CPC), led by Bigger, together with the Allegheny County Planning Commission, the CCCP, and private consultants such as Harland Bartholomew, undertook a series of crucial planning tasks. This planning feat, similar to what was occurring in other cities, included enacting a citywide zoning ordinance, publishing with Bartholomew's help a six-volume comprehensive plan, undertaking a countywide bridge and roadway project, and, through education and case law, molding a planning ethos. Moreover, collectively, these planning organizations undertook to retrofit an urban region, built for the horse-and-buggy era, to accommodate the modern age of the automobile.

Pittsburgh also illustrates in similar exemplary fashion the impact of the Great Depression on urban planning. Devastated economically by the collapse nationally and internationally of the capitalistic infrastructure, Pittsburgh, like the rest of urban America, found itself bereft of monies for basic improvements. It was the federal government, through the Public Works Administration (PWA), Civil Works Administration (CWA), Works Progress Administration (WPA), and other New Deal relief and housing agencies, that maintained, upgraded, and modernized urban America's decrepit infrastructure. Washington's new role in funding urban infrastructure and social programs reconfigured the historic urban conversation; it gave federal officials a significant new voice in city planning and narrowed the cast of participants and the scope of the discussion, a shift that lasted well into the 1970s and 1980s. Aimed in the 1930s at maximizing the numbers of jobless people employed on large-scale projects, federal work relief was project oriented. In fact, many city and county streets and roads, bridges, retaining walls, and parks were completed under the auspices of federal agencies. Moreover, with planners such as Fred Ackerman, Robert Kohn, Rexford Tugwell, and John Lansill in key federal positions, the New Deal, as Pittsburgh illustrates, greatly enhanced the prominence of planning. Both the PWA and the National Resources Planning Board not only required city planning but insisted that city planners and public works officials achieve citywide consensus on the location, design, and alignment of city projects, a requirement that, once amplified, would set the stage for the "maximum feasible community participation" rule that governed the federal urban redevelopment and renewal activities of the 1960s and 1970s.[3]

This study also highlights Pittsburgh's key role in urban planning. Historians have too frequently treated Pittsburgh as just another player in the urban planning arena. The Steel City, however, did not merely exemplify how planning in the hands of scientifically minded experts evolved in the early twentieth century from legislating an array of uncoordinated special purpose projects into the professionally led orchestration of something called the "comprehensive plan." Indeed, Pittsburgh helped make planning history. For one example, in its extraordinary embrace of Chicago's "White City" and in its emulation of Burnham's City Beautiful artistry in Oakland, gritty Pittsburgh revealed the extent to which the fair became a model for turn-of-the-century planning.[4]

In the 1909–1910 era, Pittsburgh itself took center stage in the saga of professional planning. Pittsburgh's progressive mayor George Guthrie had sent Allen T. Burns to the 1909 National Conference on City Planning, the meeting assembled in Washington, D.C., by the New York social planner Benjamin Marsh, who hoped to turn the planning agenda from issues of urban beautification to the problems of slum housing and urban congestion. It was there that Pittsburgh discovered Frederick Law Olmsted Jr., the man chosen to act on Robinson's call for the Steel City to make a plan. But it was also there that Olmsted first undertook to challenge Marsh and turn the young planning profession away from Marsh's European-influenced social agenda and toward a planning discipline more nonpolitical, technical, and above all practical. It was at this juncture in planning history that housing as an issue almost disappeared from the palette of city planning. Cities with good comprehensive plans, that made parks and peripheral suburban town sites accessible to working-class families, so the current thinking went, would escape serious slum housing problems. Significantly, immediately following the 1909 conference Olmsted, at the behest of the Pittsburgh Civic Commission, arrived in Pittsburgh, where he tested his new theory of "practical planning," which became the standard for city planning practice. Not surprisingly, Olmsted's *Main Thor-*

oughfares radiated technical expertise. It highlighted the critical role of comprehensive planning, but it also emphasized the importance of planning as a process and of planning details: of rigid attention to bridge, road, and street alignments and widths; quay usage; and the necessity of updated maps, population statistics, and other data. Housing barely entered into this equation; nor, as a result of Olmsted's triumph over Marsh, would housing seriously enter the planner's lexicon again until it reappeared on the horizon in the 1930s.

Pittsburgh again moved center stage in the juxtaposition of planner as "practical," à la Olmsted Jr., versus planner as social visionary, à la Lewis Mumford and the Regional Planning Association of America (RPAA). Frederick Bigger inherited Olmsted's mantle as Pittsburgh's planner-in-chief. As this book has shown, if anyone embodied the tension between the planning mole versus the planning skylark, it was Bigger. On the one hand, he epitomized the mole, the planning technician engrossed in the details of zoning, street widths and alignments, building heights, housing setbacks, and updated topographical maps. On the other hand, Bigger corresponded with fellow RPAA member Clarence Stein and joined Mumford, Stein, Wright, MacKaye, and his other RPAA friends for weekends in New York. Bigger's probable work with the United States Housing Corporation during World War I, his design for Chatham Village, and his work with the Greenbelt Town program in 1937 all suggest that the mind of early professional planners may be more complex than usually fathomed. The Pittsburgh case raises a planning history conundrum: Could the quintessential planning technician, as Bigger was well known to be, double as the quintessential planning skylark? This book suggests that the answer might be yes. In metropolises with older central cities such as Pittsburgh, public planners faced political and economic obstacles that led them to seek incremental adjustments and improvements to established infrastructure and built environments. Those planners working on new communities for the urban periphery had a less-constrained canvas on which to propose more visionary designs. However, even there the commercial goals of developers, limited vision of municipal leaders, and privileged prerogatives of private owners resulted all too often in mundane outcomes.

Bigger's unchallenged leadership of Pittsburgh planning underscores another reason why the history of Pittsburgh's pre-Renaissance planning has deserved special attention. As a realist, Bigger understood full well that city planning, indeed any kind of land use planning, through the use of police proceedings and the powers of eminent domain, implied a veiled threat to property rights. Although he may have cavorted with socialist planners such as Fred

Ackerman and Benton MacKaye, and may have in his own writings expressed
blatantly anticapitalist views, Bigger realized that shaping a planning ethos in
Pittsburgh involved working closely with the city's conservative civic leadership. Therefore, from the very beginning he aggressively and successfully mobilized prominent city businessmen behind planning, making the Chamber of
Commerce and the CCCP "partners" in the urban planning process.

Although the Great Depression forced the business-dominated CCCP to
suspend operations, when the organization revived in 1937 under its corporate
name, the Municipal Planning Association (MPA), and under the personal
leadership of Howard Heinz, it forcefully seized the initiative from the more
plodding direction of city and county planning commissions. In fact, the vigor
with which the MPA assumed planning leadership in the city and forthwith
invited New York's Robert Moses in 1939 to draft an arterial plan, soon mar-
ginalized the CPC, and Bigger with it. Infatuated with Moses, whose contempt
for the docility of planners was palpable, the MPA under Heinz, Wallace Richards, Arthur Braun, and Richard King Mellon aggressively sought consensus
among the planning fraternity and pursued federal dollars for an ambitious
agenda of highway building, Point reconstruction, and other city-rebuilding
ventures that verged on post–World War II "urban renewal."

Indeed, it is fair to say that Pittsburgh became a national model for postwar
urban renewal because the city had in place years before its heralded Renaissance a leadership core and a well-honed instrumentality.[5] Forging an effective public-private partnership with the city's Democratic leadership, the Allegheny Conference on Community Development (ACCD) was poised for the
city-rebuilding task well in advance of the Wagner-Ellender-Taft housing and
urban redevelopment legislation passed by Congress in 1949. In the postwar
years before that date, the Richard King Mellon–David Lawrence–led partnership had obtained legislative authority for redevelopment and lined up private
insurance company funding for the massive Gateway Center complex, one of
the first postwar Renaissance projects nationwide. Thus Pittsburgh began its
Renaissance before Washington underwrote the excessive and hitherto pro-
hibitive costs of downtown slum demolition, land purchase, and infrastructure rebuilding.[6]

However, while pointing out the triumphs, this exploration of the history
of planning in Pittsburgh has not neglected the limitations of planning in the
1890–1943 era. From the very beginning, modern, professional planners, no
matter how scientific and practical, failed to hurdle all the obstacles to achieving orderly development. Indeed, successes aside, by the 1930s Pittsburgh still

confronted horrendous traffic congestion and an unwieldy, inadequate transit system. Cars and trucks poured into the clogged heart of the city, without speedy egress. Many smaller neighborhood streets remained unpaved and without sewers. Annual spring flooding at the Point threatened serious physical and economic damage. To Bigger's chagrin, the existence of a planning ethos left intact the American Lockean tradition of sanctified private property rights; nor had it overcome the social, political, and spatial fragmentation that made achieving consensus difficult on the alignment and other engineering details of bridges, highways, and other key city and county improvement projects. Fragmentation created a host of often unbridgeable cleavages between city and county, city and suburb, and departments of public works "engineers" and departments of planning "professionals," and between and among diverse organizations and agencies, including river interests, downtown businessmen, taxpayers, and rival political parties, all of which intruded upon the planners' objective of scientifically/rationally ordering the use of urban space.

Funding to "carry out the plan" always loomed as another key obstacle to planning progress. In the nineteenth and early twentieth centuries, bond issues funded city improvements and ensconced mayors and other city politicians not only as principals in the urban conversation but, in Frederick Bigger's mind, as obstacles to nonpartisan, scientific planning. When the Great Depression imploded urban credit ratings in the 1930s, the federal government filled the void as the main funding source for urban improvements. New Dealers like Harold Ickes and Rexford Tugwell not only enthroned the planning ethos but, ironically, as this study of Pittsburgh has shown, forced planners to more and more overwhelm city planning departments with a crush of detail. As a result, public planning bodies were compelled to surrender the hallowed general or master planning mission to private voluntary planning organizations, such as the Pittsburgh Regional Planning Association. By 1943, therefore, a prevailing model had appeared for the emergence of a progrowth coalition of private voluntary planning agencies in partnership with progrowth mayors and federal public works officials. It was this coalition that orchestrated the advent of a postwar Pittsburgh Renaissance.

Yet considering the serious obstacles or limitations facing city planning in the prewar era, Pittsburgh planners before the Renaissance, in both the city and the county, compiled an estimable record of achievement. In addition to a host of completed projects and others under construction or nearing final planning, Pittsburgh planners bequeathed the essential scaffolding for the city's historic postwar Renaissance: a planning ethos molded in the 1920s with Bigger's diligent oversight, a close partnership with private sector organizations, a legal and institutional framework, and, with the federal impetus provided in the 1930s, the parkways, crosstown arterials, riverfront improvements, and magnificent Point State Park itself. While Renaissance planners and politicians expanded the planning agenda and accomplished much, Pittsburgh's postwar redevelopment had its roots in an urban conversation, sometimes civil, sometimes contentious, involving the many and the few, and held long before a wrecking ball in the 1950s announced the advent of the Pittsburgh Renaissance.

Notes

PREFACE

1. Greg Hise and William Deverell, *Eden by Design: The 1930 Olmsted-Bartholomew Plan for the Los Angels Region* (Berkeley: University of California Press, 2000).

2. Jon A. Peterson, *The Birth of City Planning in the United States, 1840–1917* (Baltimore: John Hopkins University Press, 2003).

3. Roy Lubove, *Twentieth Century Pittsburgh: Government, Business and Environmental Change* (New York: John Wiley and Sons, 1969).

CHAPTER 1. PLANNING AND THE INDUSTRIAL CITY

1. Richard King Mellon preferred being called "General Mellon," although it appears that he was discharged from the army in 1948 as a colonel. He joined the reserves in 1948 as a brigadier general and retired in 1961 as a lieutenant general. See Robert C. Alberts, *The Shaping of the Point: Pittsburgh's Renaissance Park* (Pittsburgh: University of Pittsburgh Press, 1980), 64.

2. Alberts, *Shaping of the Point;* see also Edward K. Muller, "The Point," in Donald G. Janelle, ed., *Geographical Snapshots of North America,* publication commemorating the Twenty-seventh Congress of the International Geographical Union and Assembly (New York: Guilford Press, 1992), 231–234.

3. For a brilliant historical analysis of Mellon, the Allegheny Conference, and Pittsburgh's postwar development, see Sherie A. Mershon, "Corporate Social Responsibility and Urban Revitalization: The Allegheny Conference on Community Development, 1943–1968" (Ph.D. diss., Carnegie Mellon University, 2000). See also Alberts, *Shaping of the Point;* Lubove, *Twentieth Century Pittsburgh* (Pittsburgh: University of Pittsburgh Press, 1996); John C. Teaford, *The Rough Road to Renaissance: Urban Revitalization in America, 1940–1985* (Baltimore: John Hopkins University Press, 1990), which contains an extensive discussion of the Pittsburgh Renaissance; and Shelby Stewman and Joel A. Tarr, "Four Decades of Public-Private Partnerships in Pittsburgh," in R. Scott Fosler and Renee A. Berger, eds., *Public-Private Partnerships in American Cities* (Lexington, Mass.: D. C. Heath, 1982), 59–124.

4. We discern post–Civil War planning rooted in an "urban conversation" about urban space and its relationship to the urban prospect. So does Robert Fishman in the brilliant introductory essay, "The American Planning Tradition: An Introduction and Interpretation," in Robert Fishman, ed., *The American Planning Tradition: Culture and Policy* (Washington, D.C.: Woodrow Wilson Center Press, 2000), 5.

5. On the ACCD, see Mershon, "Corporate Social Responsibility," 115–221; Joel A. Tarr, "Infrastructure and City-Building in the Nineteenth and Twentieth Centuries," in Samuel P. Hays, ed., *City at the Point: Essays on the Social History of Pittsburgh* (Pittsburgh: University of Pittsburgh Press, 1989), 249–253; and Lubove, *Twentieth Century Pittsburgh;* on postwar planning, see John F. Bauman, "Visions of a Post-War City: A Perspective on Urban Planning in Philadelphia and the Nation, 1942–1945," in Donald A. Krueckeberg, ed., *Introduction to Planning History in the United States* (New Brunswick, N.J.: Center for Urban Policy Research, Rutgers University, 1983), 170–189.

6. Lloyd Rodwin suggests that, rooted as it was in business and a tradition of physical planning, and with only a tenuous link to the social sciences, post–World War II planning was not structured to cope with the serious issues of urban equity that wracked urban America in the 1960s and rendered much of urban renaissance planning inadequate. See Lloyd Rodwin, "Images and Paths of Change in Economics, Political Science, Philosophy, Literature and City Planning: 1950–2000," in Lloyd Rodwin and Bishwapriya Sanyal, eds., *The Profession of City Planning: Changes, Images, and Challenges, 1950–2000* (New Brunswick, N.J.: Center for Urban Policy Research, Rutgers University 2001), 12–23.

7. For a discussion of deliberative nineteenth-century planning in Buffalo, Rochester, and Syracuse, New York, see Diane Shaw, *City-Building on the Eastern Frontier: Sorting the New Nineteenth-Century City* (Baltimore: Johns Hopkins University Press, 2004). On businessmen and reform, see Mansel G. Blackford, *The Lost Dream: Businessmen and City Planning on the Pacific Coast, 1890–1920* (Columbus: Ohio State University Press, 1993); and Christine Rosen, *The Limits of Power: Great Fires and the Process of City Growth in America* (Cambridge: Cambridge University Press, 1986). Both M. Christine Boyer, *Dreaming the Rational City: The Myth of American City Planning* (Cambridge, Mass.: MIT Press, 1983), and Robert M. Fogelson, *The Fragmented Metropolis: Los Angeles, 1850–1930* (Cambridge, Mass.: Harvard University Press, 1967), argue that the rise of professional planning reflected the interest of business and social elites in regaining social control over the unpredictable forces of labor and immigration that threatened disorder in the late-nineteenth- and early-twentieth-century city.

8. See John D. Fairfield, *The Mysteries of the Great City: The Politics of Urban Design, 1877–1937* (Columbus: Ohio State University Press, 1993); and Fishman, "American Planning Tradition," 6–14;

9. Stanley K. Schultz, *Constructing Urban Culture: American Cities and City Planning, 1800–1920* (Philadelphia: Temple University Press, 1987); Clay McShane, "Transforming the Use of Urban Space: A Look at the Revolution in Street Pavements, 1880–1924," *Journal of Urban History* 5 (May 1979): 279–307; Jon A. Peterson, "The Impact of Sanitary Reform upon American Planning, 1840–1890," in Krueckeberg, *Introduction to Planning History*, 13–33. On the "weave of small patterns," see Sam Bass Warner Jr., *Streetcar Suburbs: The Process of Growth in Boston, 1870–1900* (Cambridge, Mass.: Harvard University Press, 1962). On owner/occupants, see Kingston W. Heath, *The Patina of Place: The Cultural Weathering of a New England Landscape* (Knoxville: University of Tennessee Press, 2001).

10. See Fairfield, *Mysteries of the Great City*; Peterson, "Impact of Sanitary Reform," 13–40; David C. Hammack, "Comprehensive Planning before the Comprehensive Plan: A New Look at the Nineteenth-Century City," in Daniel Schaffer, ed., *Two Centuries of American Planning* (Baltimore: Johns Hopkins University Press, 1988), 139–167; and Schultz, *Constructing Urban Culture*. On Downing, Olmsted, and Vaux, see David Schuyler, *The New Urban Landscape: The Redefinition of City Form in Nineteenth-Century America* (Baltimore: Johns Hopkins University Press, 1986).

11. On Olmsted, see Laura Wood Roper, *FLO: A Biography of Frederick Law Olmsted* (Baltimore: Johns Hopkins University Press, 1973); and Schuyler, *New Urban Landscape;* on urban engineers, see Schultz, *Constructing Urban Culture*.

12. On the "fragmented metropolis," see Seymour J. Mandelbaum, *Boss Tweed's New York* (New York: John Wiley, 1965); on the roots of planning, see John C. Teaford, *The Unheralded Triumph: City Government in America, 1870–1900* (Baltimore: Johns Hopkins University Press, 1979); on Olmsted, see Schuyler, *New Urban Landscape;* and Jon A. Peterson, "The City Beautiful Movement: Forgotten Origins and Lost Meanings," in Krueckeberg, *Introduction to Planning History*, 40–57; on Bigelow, see Barbara Judd, "Edward M. Bigelow: Creator of Pittsburgh's Arcadian Parks," *Western Pennsylvania Historical Magazine* 58 (January 1975): 53–67.

13. Fairfield, *Mysteries of the Great City,* 77–82, discusses Henry George's single tax. On the vision of an intensely competitive, capitalistic Boston evolving into a Christian-socialistic utopia, see Edward Bellamy's highly romantic novel, *Looking Backward: 2000–1887* (Boston: St. Martin's Press, 1995). On Bellamy, George, the Social Gospel, and other remedies for industrial unrest and disorder, see Nell Irvin Painter, *Standing at Armageddon: The United States, 1877–1919* (Boston: Norton, 1987); see also Henry F. May, *Protestant Churches and Industrial America* (New York: Octagon Books, 1963).

14. On progressives and efficiency, see Robert H. Wiebe, *The Search for Order: 1877–1920* (New York: Hill and Wang, 1967); and Martin J. Schiesl, *The Politics of Efficiency: Municipal Administration and Reform in America: 1880–1920* (Berkeley: University of California Press, 1977).

15. See Robert H Bremner, *From the Depths: The Discovery of Poverty in the United States* (New York: New York University Press, 1969); Carl Smith, *Urban Disorder and the Shape of Belief: The Great Chicago Fire, the Haymarket Bomb and the Model Town of Pullman* (Chicago: University of Chicago Press, 1995); and Paul Boyer, *Urban Masses and Moral Order in America, 1820–1920* (Cambridge, Mass.: Harvard University Press, 1978).

16. See Mel Scott, *American City Planning since 1890* (Berkeley: University of California Press, 1969). On streets as specialized space, see Peter C. Baldwin, *Domesticating the Street: Reform and Public Space in Hartford, 1850–1930* (Columbus: Ohio State University Press, 2000); and Robert Fishman, *Bourgeoisie Utopias: The Rise and Fall of Suburbia* (New York: Basic Books, 1987).

17. On the Chicago School and planning, see Fairfield, *Mysteries of the Great City,* 158–223; and Fishman, "The Metropolitan Tradition in American Planning," in Fishman, *American Planning Tradition,* 70–73.

18. See Rosen, *The Limits of Power;* Blackford, *Lost Dream;* and Boyer, *Dreaming the Rational City;* see also John Hancock, "Smokestacks and Geraniums; Planning and Politics in San Diego," in Mary Corbin Sies and Christopher Silver, eds., *Planning the Twentieth Century City* (Baltimore: John Hopkins University Press, 1996), 161–187.

19. On isolated ethnic enclaves, see Ira Katznelson, *City Trenches: Urban Politics and the Patterning of Class in the United States* (Chicago: University of Chicago Press, 1981); and Mandelbaum, *Boss Tweed's New York;* on Pittsburgh's ethnic communities, see John Bodnar, Roger Simon, and Michael Weber, *Lives of Their Own: Blacks, Italians, and Poles in Pittsburgh, 1900–1960* (Chicago: University of Illinois Press, 1982).

20. On city transit, see Joel A. Tarr, *Transportation Innovation and Changing Spatial Patterns in Pittsburgh, 1850–1934* (Chicago: Public Works Historical Society, 1978); and Edward K. Muller and Joel A. Tarr, "The Interaction of Natural and Built Environments in the Pittsburgh Landscape," in Joel A. Tarr, ed., *Devastation and Renewal: Perspectives on the Environmental History of Pittsburgh and Its Region* (Pittsburgh: University of Pittsburgh Press, 2003).

21. Wiebe, *Search for Order;* Baldwin, *Domesticating the Street;* see also "What Stirs Up Liberty Street," *Pittsburgh Post,* October 27, 1895.

22. Mandelbaum, *Boss Tweed's New York;* David C. Hammack, *Power and Society: Greater New York at the Turn of the Century* (New York: Columbia University Press, 1987); Samuel P. Hays, "The Politics of Reform in Municipal Government in the Progressive Era," *Pacific Northwest Quarterly* 55 (October 1964): 157–189.

23. Daniel T. Rodgers, *Atlantic Crossings: Social Politics in a Progressive Age* (Cambridge, Mass.: Harvard University Press, 1998), 64; Painter, *Standing at Armageddon.* On the Olmsteds in Buffalo, see Francis R. Kowsky, ed., *The Best Planned City: The Olmsted Legacy in Buffalo* (Buffalo, N.Y.: Burchfield Art Center, 1992); John F. Bauman and Margaret Spratt, "Civic Leaders and Environmental Reform: The Pittsburgh Survey and Urban Planning," in Maurine W. Greenwald and Margo Anderson, eds., *Pittsburgh Surveyed: Social Science and*

Social Reform in the Early Twentieth Century (Pittsburgh: University of Pittsburgh Press, 1996), 153–169; and Wiebe, *Search for Order.*

24. William H. Wilson, *The City Beautiful Movement* (Baltimore: Johns Hopkins University Press, 1989); Peterson, "City Beautiful Movement," 40–57; Blackford, *Lost Dream.*

25. Marilyn Thornton Williams, *Washing "the Great Unwashed": Public Baths in Urban America, 1840–1920* (Columbus: Ohio State University Press, 1991); Greenwald and Anderson, *Pittsburgh Surveyed.*

26. Blackford, *Lost Dream;* Fairfield, *Mysteries of the Great City;* Allen Davis, *Spearheads of Reform: The Social Settlements and the Progressive Movement, 1890–1914* (New York: Oxford University Press, 1967), 60–84; Susan Marie Wirka, "The City Social Movement: Progressive Women Reformers and Early Social Planning," in Sies and Silver, *Planning the Twentieth Century City,* 55–76; Max Page, *The Creative Destruction of Manhattan, 1900–1940* (Chicago: University of Chicago Press, 1999); Boyer, *Dreaming the Rational City.* On the "City as a Whole" concept, see Robert Fairbanks, *For the City as a Whole: Planning, Politics and the Public Interest in Dallas, Texas, 1900–1965* (Columbus: Ohio State University Press, 1999). On the goal of "permanence," see Michael Holleran, *Boston's Changeful Times: Origins of Preservation and Planning in America* (Baltimore: Johns Hopkins University Press, 1998).

27. Peterson, *Birth of City Planning.*

28. Rodgers, *Atlantic Crossings,* 182.

29. William H. Wilson, "Moles and Skylarks," in Krueckeberg, *Introduction to Planning History;* Marc A. Weiss, *The Rise of the Community Builders: The American Real Estate Industry and Urban Land Planning* (New York: Columbia University Press, 1987). Blackford, in *Lost Dream,* stresses that planners focused more on the physical needs of cities than on the needs of people.

CHAPTER 2. RING-LED DEVELOPMENT AND PLANNING

1. "The Substantial Way," *Pittsburgh Post,* September 2, 1887.

2. "The City's Praise," *Commercial Gazette,* November 22, 1895, in the Senator John Dalzell Scrapbook Collection, Historical Society of Western Pennsylvania, Pittsburgh (hereafter cited as Dalzell Collection). In 1886 Dalzell, a lawyer for the firm of Hampton and Dalzell, succeeded James S. Negley as representative in Congress. A conservative Republican, a rabid advocate of laissez-faire and big business, especially the Pennsylvania Railroad, and highly optimistic about Pittsburgh's future, Dalzell vigorously championed a high tariff and freeing the rivers from tolls.

3. J. E. McKirdy, "Pittsburgh as an Industrial and Commercial Center," *American Monthly Review of Reviews* (ca. 1902–1903), in Pennsylvania Room, Carnegie Library, Pittsburgh; Edward K. Muller, "Metropolis and Region: A Framework for Enquiry into Western Pennsylvania," in Hays, *City at the Point,* 181–213. The population figures for the city of Pittsburgh are adjusted to represent the total after the annexation of Allegheny City in 1907. The metropolitan figures include all of Allegheny County, within which Pittsburgh is located. By 1900 this figure total understates the total metropolitan population. See Edward K. Muller, "Industrial Suburbs and the Growth of Metropolitan Pittsburgh, 1870–1920," *Journal of Historical Geography* 27 (2001): 58–73.

4. See Rosen, *Limits of Power,* 68–72. Francis G. Couvares also stresses the segregation and Balkanization of Pittsburgh in the late nineteenth century in *The Remaking of Pittsburgh: Class and Culture in an Industrializing City, 1877–1919* (Albany: State University of New York Press, 1984), 89–91.

5. On late-nineteenth-century city space and the limits of development in Pittsburgh and other cities, see Tarr, "Infrastructure and City-Building," 215; and Stanley Schultz and

Clay McShane, "To Engineer the Metropolis: Sewer, Sanitation, and City Planning in Late 19th Century America," *Journal of American History* 65 (1978): 389–411. Teaford, in *Unheralded Triumph*, 174, argues that despite the "frictions," nineteenth-century professional engineers and civic-minded elites teamed to produce real urban progress. Rosen, in *Limits of Power*, 12–13, sees less progress and stresses the frictions and barriers to progress.

6. *Pittsburgh Post*, September 2 and September 9, 1887; *Pittsburgh Post,* June 14, 1889.

7. Couvares, *Remaking of Pittsburgh*, 83; Robert Jucha, "Anatomy of a Streetcar Suburb: A Development History of Shadyside, 1852–1916," *Western Pennsylvania Historical Magazine* 62 (October 1979): 309–319; Valerie S. Grash, "The Commercial Skyscrapers of Pittsburgh Industrialists and Financiers, 1895–1932" (Ph.D. diss., Pennsylvania State University, 1998); Howard V. Storch Jr., "Changing Functions of the Central-City, Pittsburgh, 1850–1912" (seminar paper, Department of History, University of Pittsburgh, 1966).

8. On the East End and transportation technology, see Jucha, "Anatomy of a Streetcar Suburb"; and Tarr, "Infrastructure and City-Building," 213–253.

9. Robert Fishman, "The Metropolitan Tradition in American Planning," in Fishman, *American Planning Tradition,* 67–68; Jane Jacobs, *The Death and Life of Great American Cities* (New York: Vintage Books, 1961).

10. On this point, see Schuyler, *New Urban Landscape;* and Teaford, *Unheralded Triumph.*

11. Pittsburgh had two councils, the select and common councils, until 1911, when an act of the state legislature replaced them with one council.

12. Allen Humphrey Kerr, "The Mayors and Recorders of Pittsburgh, 1816–1951," mimeographed, 1952, in Pennsylvania Room, Carnegie Library, Pittsburgh; City of Pittsburgh, *Municipal Records and Proceedings of the Councils of the City of Pittsburgh*, No. 57 (December 2, 1916), 643–645; Judd, "Edward M. Bigelow," 57. Richard Bigler's "The Man Who Collected Parks," in *Pittsburgh Press*, April 26, 1981, is useful, but contains errors of fact.

13. City of Pittsburgh, *Municipal Records and Proceedings,* 643–645.

14. Tarr, "Infrastructure and City-Building"; Judd, "Edward M. Bigelow"; Bigler, "Man Who Collected Parks," 4–26, 81.

15. The classic "exposé" of Pittsburgh's machine is Lincoln Steffens's chapter, "Pittsburg: A City Ashamed," in his *The Shame of the Cities* (New York: Hill and Wang, 1969), 101–133; see also Eugene O. Thrasher, "The Magee-Flinn Machine, 1895–1903" (Master's thesis, University of Pittsburgh, 1951); *Pittsburgh Post*, June 15, 1887; Frank C. Harper, *Pittsburgh of Today: Its Resources and People,* vol. 1 (New York: American Historical Society, 1931), 284; Kerr, "Mayors and Recorders," 192; Tarr, "Infrastructure and City-Building," 233; City of Pittsburgh, *Annual Report of the Department of Public Works, 1889* (Pittsburgh, 1889) (hereafter cited as AR, DPW).

16. That Magee in 1892 helped summon the state militia to crush the Amalgamated Association of Iron and Steel Workers in the notorious Homestead lockout only intensified labor's disdain for the ring. See Couvares, *Remaking of Pittsburgh*, 63–74; Kerr, "Mayors and Recorders," 177; and Keith Zahniser, "Popular Religion and Reform in Progressive Era Pittsburgh" (Ph.D. diss., University of California at Santa Barbara, 1997), 52–56, 60.

17. See "Christopher Lyman Magee's Life Story," *Pittsburgh Press*, March 9, 1901, Box 4, Folder 20, Dalzell Collection; AR, DPW (1891); *Pittsburgh Post,* April 23, 1889; and "Chief Bigelow's Break," *Pittsburgh Post*, June 26, 1889; see also Kerr, "Mayors and Recorders," 177–178; Teaford, *Unheralded Triumph,* 179; and Tarr, "Infrastructure and City-Building," 237. On "special purpose planning," see Peterson, *Birth of City Planning,* 21–25.

18. AR, DPW (1897), 2; AR, DPW (1895), 5; *Pittsburgh Post*, September 21, 1891, and September 21, 1895.

19. See AR, DPW (1895).

20. Tarr, "Infrastructure and City-Building," 237; AR, DPW (1899).

21. Susan J. Kleinberg, *In The Shadow of the Mills: Working-Class Families in Pittsburgh, 1870–1907* (Pittsburgh: University of Pittsburgh Press, 1989), 85; Rosen, *Limits of Power,* 58–59; AR, DPW (1890), 130.

22. AR, DPW (1890), 130; Tarr, "Infrastructure and City Building," 237–240.

23. Tarr, "Infrastructure and City-Building," 230–235; see also Jucha, "Anatomy of a Streetcar Suburb."

24. See Tarr, *Transportation Innovation;* Craig Semsel, "The Mechanization of Pittsburgh Street Railways, 1886–1897," *Pittsburgh History* 77, no. 2 (Summer 1994): 54–67; Erasmus Wilson, ed., *Standard History of Pittsburgh, Pennsylvania* (Chicago: H. R. Cornell, 1898), 954; "Street Railways at War," *Pittsburgh Post,* May 10, 1890.

25. AR, DPW (1895), 10–11. On the East End and its amenities, including good transportation, see also Michael P. Weber and Peter N. Stearns, eds., *The Spencers of Amberson: A Turn-of-the-Century Memoir by Ethel Spencer* (Pittsburgh: University of Pittsburgh Press, 1983).

26. AR, DPW (1900), 36.

27. AR, DPW (1891), 160.

28. "A Growing City," *Pittsburgh Post,* May 9, 1890.

29. See Painter, *Standing at Armageddon;* and Wiebe, *Search for Order.*

30. See Schultz, *Constructing Urban Culture,* 184; Teaford, *Unheralded Triumph,* 138; and AR, DPW (1890), 46.

31. See AR, DPW (1889); and AR, DPW (1890), 1.

32. AR, DPW (1890), 47.

33. AR, DPW (1891), 12–13. On McFarland, see Ernest Morrison, *J. Horace McFarland: A Thorn for Beauty* (Harrisburg: Pennsylvania Historical and Museum Commission, 1995).

34. See AR, DPW (1894–1899); Judd, "Edward M. Bigelow," 60–61; Schultz, *Constructing Urban Culture,* 157–158; and Couvares, *Remaking of Pittsburgh,* 107.

35. Judd, "Edward M. Bigelow," 56; Peterson, "City Beautiful Movement," 40–57: Barry Hannegan, "William Falconer and the Landscaping of Schenley Park," *Carnegie Magazine* (May/June 1996): 28–43; Kenneth J. Heineman, "The Changing Face of Schenley Park," *Pittsburgh History* 72 (1989): 112–127.

36. AR, DPW (1895), 316–317.

37. "Flinn Bridge Bills," *Pittsburgh Post,* May 19, 1892; AR, DPW (1891), 11; AR, DPW (1894), 45; Kerr, "Mayors and Recorders," 205.

38. Bigelow's system of parks also included planting green oases in urban neighborhoods, such as the seventeen-acre West End Park, the eighteen-acre Grandview Park, and the sixty-three-acre McKinley Park. He defended these places as "convenient to centers of urban population and *accessible to those whose daily labors rarely give them time to visit our main parks* [emphasis added]." See AR, DPW (1895), 13; AR, DPW (1897), 356; and Judd, "Edward M. Bigelow," 60–63; see also Howard Stewart, coll. and comp., *Historical Data on Pittsburgh Public Parks* (Ann Arbor, Mich.: Edwards Brothers, 1943); and Couvares, *Remaking of Pittsburgh,* 106–108.

39. See AR, DPW (1895), 15–16; AR, DPW (1897), 353; and AR, DPW (1893), 357; see also Stewart, *Historical Data.*

40. AR, DPW (1893), 17.

41. Judd, "Edward M. Bigelow," 16; AR, DPW (1893), 17; AR, DPW (1895), 15; "Pittsburgh: A New Great City," *American Monthly Review of Reviews* (ca. 1902–1903), 73, in Pennsylvania Room, Carnegie Library, Pittsburgh.

42. "Exceeds the Estimate," *Pittsburgh Post,* July 2, 1887; Phillip S. Klein and Ari Higgenboom, *A History of Pennsylvania,* 2nd ed. (University Park: Pennsylvania State University Press, 1980), 87.

43. Kleinberg, *Shadow of the Mills,* 66; Robert A. Woods, "Pittsburgh: An Interpreta-

tion," in Paul U. Kellogg, ed., *The Pittsburgh District: Civic Frontage* (1914; reprint, New York, Arno Press, 1984), 66; AR, DPW (1898), 20.

44. Emily Dinwiddie and F. Elizabeth Crowell, "The Housing of Pittsburgh's Workers Discussed from the Standpoint of Sanitary Regulation and Control," in Kellogg, *Pittsburgh District,* 94–98.

45. "The Seeds of Death," *Pittsburgh Post,* July 20, 1888.

46. "Businesses Are Kicking," *Pittsburgh Post,* June 15, 1888.

47. "People Cannot Drink Water," *Pittsburgh Post,* September 20, 1887.

48. "New Water Company," *Pittsburgh Post,* July 6, 1888; "The Duquesne Water Job," *Pittsburgh Post,* July 20, 1888; "A Wail from the Bluff," *Pittsburgh Post,* June 20, 1888.

49. AR, DPW (1889).

50. Mark J. Tierno, "The Search for Pure Water in Pittsburgh: The Urban Response to Water Pollution, 1893–1914," *Western Pennsylvania Historical Magazine* 60 (January 1977): 24–25; AR, DPW (1909).

51. See *Fifty Years of the Chamber of Commerce of Pittsburgh* (Pittsburgh: Chamber of Commerce, 1924), 33.

52. On the "hump cut," see "The Fifth Avenue Hump," *Pittsburgh Post,* June, 6, 1888; "More about the Hump Cut," *Pittsburgh Post,* June 7, 1888; and *Pittsburgh Post,* June 28, 1888.

53. On the "hump," see "Fifth Avenue Hump"; *Pittsburgh Post,* June 28, 1888; on Diamond Street, see "Diamond Street Widening," *Pittsburgh Post,* April 22, 1893; and *Pittsburgh Post,* June 11, 1889.

54. *Pittsburgh Post,* October 10, 1895.

55. Allen Hazen, "Report of the Filtration Commission of the City of Pittsburgh, Pennsylvania" (Pittsburgh, 1899), 2–85; see also Tarr, "Infrastructure and City-Building," 236.

56. AR, DPW (1898), 19.

57. Tierno, "Search for Pure Water," 28–29; AR, DPW (1902), 6–7.

58. Tierno, "Search for Pure Water," 30–36.

59. Klein and Higgenboom, *History of Pennsylvania.* See Dalzell Collection; Mandelbaum, *Boss Tweed's New York;* and for a more recent interpretation of boss politics in Philadelphia that stresses the palpable corruption of ring regimes as opposed to their "functional" attributes, see Peter McCaffrey, *When Bosses Ruled Philadelphia: The Emergence of the Republican Machine, 1867–1933* (University Park: Pennsylvania State University Press, 1993).

60. See Harper, *Pittsburgh of Today,* 284; Klein and Higgenboom, *History of Pennsylvania;* James Kehl, *Boss Rule in the Gilded Age: Matthew Quay of Pennsylvania* (Pittsburgh: University of Pittsburgh Press, 1980); and *Pittsburgh Post,* July 16, 1888; on the city postmaster issue, see "Out in the West," *Philadelphia Press,* March 16, 1889.

61. "Chris Magee Abdicates," *Philadelphia Press,* May 18, 1889, Folder April 27, 1887–May 1889, Dalzell Collection; "A Breezy Battle," *Pittsburgh Commercial Gazette,* May 16, 1889, Folder April 27, 1887–May 1889, Dalzell Collection; "Anti-Ring Victory," *Pennsylvania Press,* May 1887, Folder June 1889–May 1890, Dalzell Collection.

62. "Harmony in Allegheny," *Philadelphia Press,* August 15, 1889, Folder June 1889–May 1890, Dalzell Collection; see also *Pittsburgh Commercial Gazette,* November 1, 1889, Folder June 1889–May 1890, Dalzell Collection.

63. "Autopsy of a Reformer," *Pittsburgh Post,* September 13, 1897.

64. "Are After Improvements," *Pittsburgh Post,* September 23, 1897; see also Rosen, *Limits of Power,* 52, 262; and Teaford, *Unheralded Triumph,* 21.

65. Teaford, *Unheralded Triumph,* 181.

66. Zahniser, in "Popular Religion and Reform," rightly suggests that evangelical Protestantism helped rally Pittsburgh anti-ring forces in contrast to their view that nineteenth-century Pittsburghers, content with their ring-gained wealth, lacked moral fortitude; see also

Woods, "Pittsburgh"; and Jackson Lears, *No Place of Grace: Anti-Modernism and the Trans-formation of American Culture, 1880–1920* (Chicago: University of Chicago Press, 1994).

67. According to Paul Boyer, progressive Frederick C. Howe described his evangelical upbringing. See Boyer, *Urban Masses and Moral Order*, 176–177.

68. See *Pittsburgh Post,* September 5, 1887, and May 31 and June 19, 1888; Zahniser, "Popular Religion and Reform," 98, 160; Kerr, "Mayors and Recorders," 200; and Boyer *Urban Masses and Moral Order,* 191–192.

69. Zahniser, "Popular Religion and Reform," 102.

70. This interpretation is based on a reading of the *Pittsburgh Post,* 1890–1896; see also Zahniser, "Popular Religion and Reform"; and Couvares, *Remaking of Pittsburgh.*

71. Wilson, *Standard History of Pittsburgh*, 972. On the subject of permanence, see Holleran, *Boston's "Changeful Times."*

72. On the changing culture of Pittsburgh's elite in the late nineteenth century, see Couvares, *Remaking of Pittsburgh,* 96–99; Edward K. Muller and John F. Bauman, "The Olmsteds in Pittsburgh: (Part 1) Landscaping the Private City," *Pittsburgh History* 76 (Fall 1993): 122–141; and John Ingham, *Making Iron and Steel: Independent Mills in Pittsburgh, 1820–1920* (Columbus: Ohio State University Press, 1991), 171.

73. On play, see Beulah Kennard, "The Playground in Pittsburgh," in Kellogg, *Pittsburgh District,* 306–307; and Couvares, *Remaking of Pittsburgh,* 104.

74. Bauman and Muller, "Olmsteds in Pittsburgh (Part 1)."

75. On the transit of progressive ideas from Europe to America, and on the importance of George Hodges, see Rodgers, *Atlantic Crossings;* on environmentalism, see Boyer, *Urban Masses and Moral Order,* 179–187.

76. Zahniser, in "Popular Religion and Reform," 146, makes Calvary the central institution in his study of religion and reform in Pittsburgh.

77. Zahniser, "Popular Religion and Reform," 114.

78. Ronald J. Butera, "A Settlement House and the Urban Challenge: Kingsley House in Pittsburgh, Pennsylvania, 1893–1920," *Western Pennsylvania Historical Magazine* 66 (1983): 31–41.

79. Zahniser, "Popular Religion and Reform," 297; William H. Matthews, *Adventures in Giving* (New York: Dodd, Mead, 1939); Davis, *Spearheads for Reform;* see also Mina Carson, *Settlement Folk: Social Thought and the American Settlement Movement, 1885–1930* (Chicago: University of Chicago Press, 1990).

80. On Graham Taylor, see Boyer, *Urban Masses and Moral Order,* 222; see also Zahniser, "Popular Religion and Reform," 81; and Civic Club of Allegheny County (CCAC), *Fifteen Years of Civic History, 1895–1910* (Pittsburgh: Civic Club of Allegheny County, 1910).

81. On businessmen, reform, and planning, see Robert H. Wiebe, *Businessmen and Reform: A Study of the Progressive Movement* (Cambridge, Mass.: Harvard University Press, 1962); and Blackford, *Lost Dream;* on Pittsburgh, see Pittsburgh Chamber of Commerce and Citizens Municipal League, "For a Better City Government: Addresses Delivered at Pittsburgh Charter Hearings, Harrisburg, April 14, 1897," 9, in Pennsylvania Room, Carnegie Library, Pittsburgh; see also Couvares, *Remaking of Pittsburgh*, 95.

82. Butera, "Settlement House," 37.

83. CCAC, *Fifteen Years of Civic History,* 7.

84. Ibid., 15.

85. See Peterson, *Birth of City Planning,* 98–122; see also CCAC, *Fifteen Years of Civic History*; and Woods, "Pittsburgh."

86. See Citizens Municipal League, "For a Better City Government: Addresses Delivered at Pittsburgh Charter Hearings, Harrisburg, April 14, 1897," 9–105, in Pennsylvania Room, Carnegie Library, Pittsburgh; see also Oliver McClintock and George Guthrie biography files, Historical Society of Western Pennsylvania.

87. Kerr, in "Mayors and Recorders," 203, traces the origins of the Municipal League to 1895. However, two years earlier a meeting took place at M. A. Woodward's house at the corner of Aiken Street and Fifth Avenue, which resulted in the formation of a movement to destroy the ring. See "To Down the Ring," *Pittsburgh Post,* April 7, 1893. Although there were traces of anti-ring sentiment in Pittsburgh's working-class neighborhoods such as the South Side, Bloomfield, and Soho, the roots of reform in the city lay in the East End in Protestant, not Catholic, enclaves. The ring grip remained strongest in the region's ethnic neighborhoods, which may explain why in Pittsburgh an important progressive victory did not occur until 1901.

88. On the reform movement, see Klein and Higgenboom, *History of Pennsylvania,* 418–420; on the Citizens League, see Kerr, "Mayors and Recorders," 206; and "East End in Peril," *Pittsburgh Dispatch,* February 16, 1896, Box 4, Folder 20, Dalzell Collection; also on anti-ring sentiment, see "Bare Ring Methods," *Pittsburgh Post,* October 10, 1897.

89. "In the Way of Reform," *Pittsburgh Post,* October 27, 1895.

90. Zahniser, "Popular Religion and Reform," 150.

91. See Kerr, "Mayors and Recorders," 210–211, 215, 226. On the "ripper" bill and Thomas Bigelow, see Zahniser, "Popular Religion and Reform," 151–153, 187; on Thomas Bigelow, see *Pittsburgh Press,* February 27, 1902, Box 4, Folder 20, Dalzell Collection; and Bigelow Obituary File in Carnegie Library, Pittsburgh, which has clippings on Thomas Bigelow's death, July 21, 1904.

92. "Mr. Carnegie on Art," *Pittsburgh Dispatch,* February 3, 1891, Box 266, Andrew Carnegie Collection, Manuscript Division, Library of Congress, Washington, D.C. (hereafter cited as ACC); Andrew Carnegie, "The Principles of Giving," *Woman's Home Companion,* March 1916, Box 249, ACC.

93. "For the Starving," *Pittsburgh Post,* December 9, 1893, Box 266, ACC; "Carnegie Offers Over $250,000," *Pittsburgh Telegraph,* December 4, 1893, Box 266, ACC.

94. *Presentation of the Carnegie Library to the People of Pittsburgh with a Description of the Dedicatory Exercises, November 5th, 1895* (Pittsburgh: Corporation of the City of Pittsburgh, 1895), 22–43.

95. Franklin Toker, *Pittsburgh: An Urban Portrait* (University Park: Pennsylvania State University Press, 1986), 80, 103.

96. *Pittsburgh Bulletin,* December 2, 1893, Box 266, ACC. For a discussion of Daniel Burnham and the World's Columbian Exposition, see Thomas S. Hines, *Burnham of Chicago, Architect and Planner* (New York: Oxford University Press, 1974).

97. Wilson, *City Beautiful Movement,* 64. Toker also believed that Pittsburghers modeled Oakland on the World's Columbian Exposition. See Toker, *Pittsburgh,* 81.

98. "Rare Plants for Pittsburg," *Indianapolis News,* n.d., Box 266, ACC; Letters from William J. Holland to his parents, Chicago, February 10, 1893, and Pittsburgh, February 15,1893, Box 24, Folder 9, Holland Family Papers, Historical Society of Western Pennsylvania.

99. Andrew Carnegie, "Value of the World's Fair to the American People," *Engineering Magazine* 6 (January 1894): 419, Box 245, ACC.

100. Ibid., 418.

101. Quoted in Joseph Frazier Wall, *Andrew Carnegie* (Pittsburgh: University of Pittsburgh Press, 1970), 817.

102. Letters from William Holland to his parents, Pittsburgh, February 10, March 13, and April 19, 1890, Box 24, Folder 6, Holland Family Papers; letter from H. D. W. English to William Holland, January 22, 1898, Box 27, Holland Family Papers; Tom Rea, *Bone Wars: The Excavation and Celebrity of Andrew Carnegie's Dinosaur* (Pittsburgh: University of Pittsburgh Press, 2001), 42–51.

103. Robert C. Alberts, *Pitt: The Story of the University of Pittsburgh, 1787–1987* (Pittsburgh: University of Pittsburgh Press, 1986), 49–50.

104. Draft, Founders Day Address, Carnegie Institute, November 3, 1898, 12, Box 251, ACC; Founders Day Address, Carnegie Institute, November 3, 1904, Box 249, ACC; Toker, *Pittsburgh,* 105. On the relationship of Henry Hornbostel's design for the Carnegie Technical Schools and the Chicago fair's Court of Honor, see Martin Aurand, *The Spectator and the Topographical City* (Pittsburgh: University of Pittsburgh Press, 2006); for a discussion of Carnegie's unwillingness to fund university requests, see Wall, *Andrew Carnegie,* 865–868.

105. Marilyn Evert and Vernon Gay, *Discovering Pittsburgh's Sculpture* (Pittsburgh: University of Pittsburgh Press, 1983), 184–185.

106. Barry Hannegan, "Pittsburgh's Emerald Necklace," *PHLF* [Pittsburgh History and Landmarks Foundation] *News,* 146 (August 1996): 8–12. By 1898 Andrew Carnegie had already broached the subject with Bigelow, who assured the philanthropist that the city would provide the land. See Draft, Founders Day Address.

107. Alberts, *Pitt,* 57–58; Muller and Bauman, "Olmsteds in Pittsburgh (Part 1)," 132–133.

108. "Dancers Move amid Flowers at Schenley," *Pittsburgh Dispatch,* November 5, 1898, Box 257, ACC; Pittsburgh History and Landmarks Foundation, "National District Nomination Report," 1991, 5.

109. Toker, *Pittsburgh,* 81.

110. Charles Mulford Robinson, "Civic Improvement Possibilities of Pittsburgh," *Charities and the Commons* (February 1906): 818.

111. See Boyer, *Urban Masses and Moral Order,* 225, 241–242.

112. Chamber of Commerce and Citizens Municipal League, "For a Better City Government," 40–55, 137.

113. *Catalogue of the Second Architectural Exhibition 1903* (Pittsburgh: Pittsburgh Architectural Club, 1903).

114. See Muller and Bauman, "Olmsteds in Pittsburgh (Part 1)."

CHAPTER 3. IF EVER A CITY NEEDED THE DEFINITE PLAN

1. *Annual of the Civic Club of Allegheny County: 1897–1921* (Pittsburgh: Civic Club of Allegheny County, 1921), Civic Club of Allegheny County Papers, Carnegie Library, Pittsburgh. In her *Downtown America: A History of the Place and the People Who Made It* (Chicago: University of Chicago Press, 2004), Alison Isenberg stresses the importance of women in civic reform and in the shaping of a planning mentality in the early twentieth century.

2. *Fifty Years of the Chamber of Commerce of Pittsburgh, 1874–1924* (Pittsburgh: Chamber of Commerce, 1925); and the annual reports of the Chamber of Commerce of Pittsburgh, Carnegie Library, Pittsburgh. For an overview of infrastructure development in Progressive Era Pittsburgh, see Tarr, "Infrastructure and City-Building," 228–249.

3. See Peterson, *Birth of City Planning;* see also *Catalogue of the First Annual Exhibition of the Pittsburgh Architectural Club* (Pittsburgh: Pittsburgh Architectural Club, 1900), 91–92; Albert Jay Nock, "What a Few Men Did in Pittsburg," *American Magazine* 70 (1910): 808–818.

4. *Third Exhibition of the Pittsburgh Architectural Club* (Pittsburgh: Pittsburgh Architectural Club, 1905), 5.

5. George Swetnam, "Mayor's Notebook," *Pittsburgh Press,* October 24, 1973; Kerr, "Mayors and Recorders," 239–249. Guthrie was active in Democratic Party politics for years, and in 1913 President Woodrow Wilson appointed Guthrie ambassador to Japan, where he died fours years later.

6. On the origins of the Survey, see Clark A. Chambers, *Paul U. Kellogg and the Survey: Voices of Social Welfare and Social Justice* (Minneapolis: University of Minnesota Press, 1971). See also Lubove, *Twentieth Century Pittsburgh,* 6–19; and Greenwald and Anderson, *Pittsburgh Surveyed.*

7. Ingham, *Making Iron and Steel,* 157–182.

8. Robert W. Jones, "Pittsburgh, a City to Be Proud Of," *Pittsburgh Gazette-Times,* January 16 and January 18, 1910 (this was a four-part series also appearing in December 1909); Bauman and Spratt, "Civic Leaders and Environmental Reform," 153–169.

9. "Municipal League Meeting to Help City," *Pittsburgh Post,* November 3, 1908; *Proceedings of the Pittsburgh Conference for Good Government and the Fourteenth Annual Meeting of the National Municipal League* (Pittsburgh: National Municipal League, 1909). This was a joint conference with the American Civic Association held in Pittsburgh, November 16–19, 1908.

10. Frank E. Wing, "Thirty-Five Years of Typhoid: The Economic Cost to Pittsburgh and the Long Fight for Pure Water," in Kellogg, *Pittsburgh District,* 63–86. Benjamin C. Marsh was secretary of the Committee on Congestion of Population in New York. See Scott, *American City Planning,* 82–88; see also Bauman and Spratt, "Civic Leaders and Environmental Reform," 159–160.

11. *Proceedings of the Pittsburgh Conference for Good City Government,* 30; H. D. W. English, "The Function of Business Bodies in Improving Civic Conditions," in *Proceedings of the Pittsburgh Conference for Good City Government,* 413; "Annual Report of President English to the Chamber of Commerce," Chamber of Commerce of Pittsburgh, 1908, 4. On English, see Ingham, *Making Iron and Steel,* 173.

12. "Roosevelt Praises City for Cleaning Out Graft," *Pittsburgh Post,* September 11, 1920; Theodore Roosevelt, "Civic Responsibility," *Survey* 24 (September 17, 1910): 853, 856–857; Nock, "What a Few Men Did," 808–818; H. V. Blaxter and Allen H. Kerr, "The Aldermen and Their Courts," in Kellogg, *Pittsburgh District,* 139–155. For an overview of vice and corruption reform in Pittsburgh, see Zahniser, "Popular Religion and Reform."

13. *Fifty Years of the Chamber of Commerce of Pittsburgh; Annual of the Civic Club of Allegheny County;* and the annual reports of these two organizations. See also Lubove, *Twentieth Century Pittsburgh,* 41–51. For an overview of environmental reform in Pittsburgh in this period, see Joel A. Tarr, "The Pittsburgh Survey as an Environmental Statement," in Greenwald and Anderson, *Pittsburgh Surveyed,* 170–189.

14. "Giant Group Plans, Wide Thoroughfares, in a New Pittsburgh," *Pittsburgh Dispatch,* November 17, 1907. Frederick C. Howe was a featured speaker at the Third National Conference on City Planning in Philadelphia in 1911, where he extolled the virtues of planning for German cities and lamented the conditions of America's unplanned, haphazardly developed cities. Scott, *American City Planning,* 131–132.

15. *Schenley Farms,* prospectus of the Schenley Farms Company, n.d., Carnegie Library, Pittsburgh; *Oakland Civic District Historic Nomination Report* (Pittsburgh: Pittsburgh History and Landmarks Foundation, 1991), 21; Scott, *American City Planning,* 61–62; Kenneth Kolson, *Big Plans: The Allure and Folly of Urban Design* (Baltimore: Johns Hopkins University Press, 2001), 49–64.

16. James D. Van Trump, "The Angelic Eye: Bellefield from the Air," in *Life and Architecture in Pittsburgh* (Pittsburgh: Pittsburgh History and Landmarks Foundation, 1983), 102. Van Trump lists the year of Nicola's death as 1938.

17. Weiss, *Rise of the Community Builders,* 1.

18. Robinson, "Civic Improvement Possibilities," 819. Nicola was not the region's first community builder. A few of the industrial elite began to consider their business interests on a larger scale and turned to consultants for expertise. The most famous and extensive of these efforts was J. J. Vandergrift's development of a model industrial community bearing his name and designed by the Olmsteds between 1895 and the end of the century. See Anne E. Mosher, *Capital's Utopia: Vandergrift, Pennsylvania, 1855–1916* (Baltimore: Johns Hopkins University Press, 2004).

19. S. Kussart, "One Hundredth Anniversary of the Birth of Mrs. Mary E. Schenley," *Western Pennsylvania Historical Magazine* 9, no. 4 (October 1926): 209–220.

20. *Pittsburgh Dispatch*, April 17, 1906.

21. Alberts, *Shaping of the Point*, 57–62.

22. Toker, *Pittsburgh*, 121–122; *Oakland Civic District Historic Nomination Report*; James D. Van Trump, "Yet Once More O Ye Laurels," in *Life and Architecture in Pittsburgh*, 113.

23. Daniel L. Bonk, "Ballpark Figures: The Story of Forbes Field," *Pittsburgh History* 76, no. 2 (Summer 1994): 55–56. For Oliver P. Nicola, see Harper, *Pittsburgh of Today*, 3:100.

24. Toker, *Pittsburgh*, 109–124; *Oakland Civic District Historic Nomination Report*. Architectural critic Montgomery Schuyler called this part of Oakland "clubland." Montgomery Schuyler, "The Building of Pittsburgh: Part Three, A Real Civic Center," *Architectural Record* 30, no. 3 (September 1911): 231. For a discussion of clubs in this era, see Van Trump, "Yet Once More O Ye Laurels," 112–113.

25. *Schenley Farms*, prospectus.

26. Weiss, *Rise of the Community Builders*, 3–6.

27. Schuyler, "Building of Pittsburgh," 231, 243.

28. Walter C. Kidney, *Henry Hornbostel: An Architect's Master Touch* (Pittsburgh: Pittsburgh History and Landmarks Foundation, in cooperation with Roberts Rinehart Publishers, 2002).

29. The elite did turn, of course, to architects, engineers, and landscape architects to design their individual properties. Aurand, *The Spectator and the Topographical City*; and Kidney, *Henry Hornbostel*.

30. Chamber of Commerce of Pittsburgh, *Annual Report for 1909*, 35–36; "Fix Flood Mark at 36′," *Pittsburgh Post*, March 20, 1907; *Report of the Flood Commission of Pittsburgh, Pennsylvania* (Pittsburgh: Flood Commission of Pittsburgh, 1912), 62–71.

31. Mark David Samber, "Networks of Capital: Creating and Maintaining a Regional Industrial Economy in Pittsburgh, 1856–1919" (Ph.D. diss., Carnegie Mellon University, 1995).

32. *Report of the Flood Commission*, letter of transmittal and 6–8; Roland M. Smith, "The Politics of Pittsburgh Flood Control, Part I, 1908–1936," *Pennsylvania History* 42, no. 1 (1975): 5–24.

33. Stefan Lorant, *Pittsburgh: The Story of an American City* (Lenox, Mass.: Author's Edition, 1977), 554; Alberts, *Pitt*, 61.

34. George W. Guthrie, "Fundamental Municipal Needs in Pennsylvania," *Proceedings of the Pittsburgh Conference for Good Government*, 373–374.

35. H. D. W. English, "Business Bodies Improving Civic Conditions," *Proceedings of the Pittsburgh Conference for Good Government*, 414–416.

36. Robert A. Woods, "Pittsburgh's Civic Problem," *Proceedings of the Pittsburgh Conference for Good Government*, 391.

37. "Dinner Speeches," Mayor George Guthrie, *Proceedings of the Pittsburgh Conference for Good Government*, 466.

38. "The Trend of Things," *Survey* 23 (October 1910): 130; Pittsburgh Civic Commission, *Pittsburgh Civic Commission* (Pittsburgh: Pittsburgh Civic Commission, n.d. [ca. 1910]), a pamphlet found in the Pittsburgh Department of City Planning Library. Robert W. De Forest was president of the Municipal Art Commission of the city of New York and president of the New York Charity Organization Society. See Scott, *American City Planning*, 81.

39. Pittsburgh Civic Commission, *Pittsburgh Civic Commission*; "Pittsburgh Civic Commission: Its Work for City," *Pittsburgh Post*, October 31, 1910.

40. "The Pittsburgh Survey," *Charities and the Common* (January 2, 1909): 515–588; *Charities and the Common* (February 6, 1909): 785–940; *Charities and the Common* (March 6, 1909): 1035–1087.

41. Robinson, "Civic Improvement Possibilities," 826.

42. Ibid., 801–814.

43. Ibid., 814–826.

44. Peter Marcuse, "Housing in Early City Planning," *Journal of Urban History* 6 (February 1980): 105; Rodgers, *Atlantic Crossings,* 160–208.

45. Allen T. Burns, "City Planning in Pittsburgh," *Proceedings of the First National Conference on City Planning, Washington, D.C., May 21–22, 1909* (Washington, D.C.: National Conference on City Planning, 1909), 92.

46. On progressives, planning, and housing issues, see Marcuse, "Housing in Early City Planning," 155; Frederick Law Olmsted Jr., "The Scope and Results of City Planning in Europe," *Proceedings of the First National Conference,* 63–66; and Scott, *American City Planning,* 50–56, 118–120.

47. Olmsted, "Scope and Results," 63–66; Rodgers, *Atlantic Crossings.*

48. Muller and Bauman, "Olmsteds in Pittsburgh (Part 1)," 122–140.

49. Allen T. Burns to Frederick Law Olmsted Jr. (hereafter cited as FLO), June 9, 1909, and FLO to Bion J. Arnold, June 23, 1909, Olmsted Associates Papers, Manuscript Division of the Library of Congress, Washington, D.C. (hereafter cited as OAP). On John Ripley Freeman, see Keith D. Revell, *Building Gotham: Civic Culture and Public Policy in New York City, 1898–1938* (Baltimore: Johns Hopkins University Press, 2003), 119–124.

50. Frederick Law Olmsted Jr., Bion J. Arnold, and John R. Freeman, "Preliminary Report to Pittsburgh Civic Commission upon Methods of Procedure in City Planning," December 13, 1909, in Kellogg, *Pittsburgh District,* Appendix D, 480–491. See also FLO to Burns, June 29, 1909; FLO to Burns, August 2, 1909; FLO to Burns, August 16, 1909; Burns to FLO, September 28, 1909; Burns to Freeman, December 11, 1909; FLO to Burns, December, 15, 1909; and Burns to FLO, December 22, 1909, all in OAP.

51. Scott, *American City Planning,* 72.

52. Olmsted expressed his view of city planning in many different ways--in speeches, letters, essays, and reports. With respect to his Pittsburgh work, some primary examples are: Frederick Law Olmsted Jr., "Draft of Report [on Pittsburgh Main Thoroughfares]," ca. November 1910, OAP; Frederick Law Olmsted Jr., *Pittsburgh Main Thoroughfares and the Down Town District: Improvements Necessary to Meet the City's Present and Future Needs* (Pittsburgh: Pittsburgh Civic Commission, 1911), 1; FLO to Burns, June 29, 1909; FLO to Graham Taylor, June 30, 1909; and FLO to N. S. Sprague [Department of Public Works], Pittsburgh, June 14, 1910, a nine-page draft report on planning, all in OAP. See also Harold F. Howland, "The City Practical: A City Plan to Relieve and Prevent Congestion and to Regulate the Cost of Living," *Outlook* (March 1911), Box 242, File 10, OAP.

53. Edward C. Whiting to FLO, January 4, 1910, OAP; Olmsted, *Main Thoroughfares,* 3–4, 93–100; George W. Lehman to FLO, April 19, 1910; FLO to Lehman, April 25, 1910; N. S. Sprague [Department of Public Works] to Pittsburgh Civic Commission (PCC), July 5, 1910; and FLO, "Final Outline of Report on Surveys for Pittsburgh," October 1910, all in OAP. Olmsted's severe criticism of the city's topographical maps reveals that Edward M. Bigelow's efforts to prepare maps in the 1890s were less than satisfactory. The annual reports of the Department of Public Works do not indicate why his mapping program failed.

54. On data retrieval, see correspondence from Whiting to FLO during 1910, OAP. On the suspicion of city departments, especially the Department of Public Works, see, for example, Freeman to FLO, December 29, 1909; and Fox to FLO, March, 16, 1910, both in OAP.

55. Olmsted, *Main Thoroughfares,* 133–165; John Freeman to FLO, May 31, 1910; and FLO to Burns, February 4, 1910, both in OAP. See, for example, correspondence between FLO and John L. Matthews, secretary of the Mississippi Valley Transportation Company, St. Louis, OAP.

56. Whiting to FLO, January 4, 1910, OAP; *Pittsburgh Post,* April 25, 1910, OAP. Olmsted was in Pittsburgh to meet with various officials and committees on several topics, including the market house proposal. See Olmsted, *Main Thoroughfares,* 18, 123–128.

57. FLO to PCC [report on the hump cut]; FLO to Magee, January 7, 1910; FLO to PCC,

January 17, 1910; FLO to D. H. Burnham and Company [concerning the hump cut effects on the Frick Building, for which Burnham was the architect], January 18, 1910; Whiting to FLO, May 26, 1910; and Whiting to FLO, July 8, 1910, all in OAP. On St. Pierre's Ravine, see Whiting to FLO, January 19, 1910; Whiting to FLO, February 10, 1910; FLO to PCC, February 18, 1910; Whiting to FLO, June 16, 1910; and FLO to Whiting, August 10, 1910, all in OAP.

58. Olmsted, *Main Thoroughfares*, 31–42.

59. Bion Arnold, *Report on the Pittsburgh Transportation Problem Submitted to Honorable William A. Magee* (Pittsburgh: 1910); Tarr, "Infrastructure and City Building," 242–243; Tarr, *Transportation Innovation*, 23–24.

60. Olmsted, *Main Thoroughfares*, 6–11, 17, 20–21, 44–58.

61. Ibid., 1–2, 56–87.

62. Ibid., 49–56; FLO to Magee, July 18, 1910; FLO to Edward M. Bigelow, July 20, 1910; Frank Gosser to FLO, July 25, 1910; FLO to Bigelow, July 30, 1910; FLO to Gosser, August 1, 1910; FLO to Bigelow, October 5, 1910, all in OAP. See also Stephen J. Hoffman, "The Saga of Pittsburgh's Liberty Tubes: Geographical Partisanship on the Urban Fringe," *Pittsburgh History* 75, no. 3 (Fall 1992): 128–141; and Stephen J. Hoffman, "A Plan of Quality: The Development of Mt. Lebanon, a 1920s Automobile Suburb," *Journal of Urban History* 18 (February 1992): 148–154.

63. Olmsted, *Main Thoroughfares*, 11–17.

64. Whiting to FLO, March 11, 1910; FLO to Whiting, March 15, 1910; Whiting to FLO, May 26, 1910; Bernhard to Whiting, May 28, 1910; Bernhard to Whiting, June 28, 1910; Whiting to Bernhard, July 6, 1910; Whiting to FLO, July 28, 1910, all in OAP. On the shift to Arnold W. Brunner, see FLO to Whiting, August 2, 1910; FLO to Whiting, August 17, 1910; Whiting to FLO, August 21, 1910; and from the Olmsted Brothers' office to Brunner, November 30, 1910, all in OAP; and Scott, *American City Planning*, 61, 63, 128.

65. Olmsted, *Main Thoroughfares*, 19–21.

66. Ibid., 22–24.

67. Ibid., 25–28.

68. Ibid., 29.

69. FLO to Whiting, August 17, 1910, OAP.

70. Olmsted, *Main Thoroughfares*, 30.

71. Alberts, *Shaping of the Point*.

72. Olmsted, *Main Thoroughfares*, 101–122.

73. Ibid., 23–24.

74. Ibid., 106–108. For subsequent changes to Bigelow Boulevard, see, for example, M. Graham Netting, *50 Years of the Western Pennsylvania Conservancy* (Pittsburgh: Western Pennsylvania Conservancy, 1982), 67–69.

75. Olmsted, *Main Thoroughfares*, 103–106. See also Robinson, "Civic Improvement Possibilities," 826.

76. Olmsted, *Main Thoroughfares*, 113–122.

77. Charles Mulford Robinson, "The Pittsburgh Street Plan," *Survey* (February 4, 1911): 728–730; Howland, "City Practical."

78. Kerr, "Mayors and Recorders," 250–260.

79. "William A. Magee Scores Mayor Guthrie," *Pittsburgh Post*, February 9, 1909.

80. Chamber of Commerce of Pittsburgh, *Annual Report*, 1910, 18–19; AR, DPW (1910), 5–6.

81. William Magee, "Annual Report of the Mayor," *Annual Reports of the Executive Departments of the City of Pittsburgh for the Year Ending January 31, 1912*; "Big Bond Project Is Laid to Rest by Supreme Court," *Pittsburgh Post*, July 2, 1910; "To Obey Supreme Court Edict with Vengeance," *Pittsburgh Post*, July 9, 1910; "New Issue Of Bonds Outlined," uni-

dentified clipping, September 3, 1910; Whiting to FLO, July 8, 1910; Magee to FLO, July 11, 1910; FLO to Magee, July 18, 1910, all in OAP.

82. Burns to FLO, September 30, 1910; Burns to FLO, November 14, 1910, both in OAP; Allen T. Burns, "What the Civic Commission Engineers Found," unidentified newspaper clipping, November 4, 1910, OAP; "Mayor Jolts the Civic Commission," and "Answer Is Made by Commission," both unidentified newspaper clippings, OAP; "Chamber Endorses Big Loan," *Pittsburgh Post*, November 2, 1910.

83. "Mayor Opens Campaign for Big Bond Issue" *Pittsburgh Post*, October 7, 1910; "Mayor Magee Speaks," *Pittsburgh Post*, October 18, 1910; William A. Magee, "Mayor Magee Outlines Plan of Development," *Pittsburgh Post*, October 31, 1910; "Munch on Issue of Bonds," *Pittsburgh Post*, November 1, 1910; "Mayor Plays Civics," *Pittsburgh Post*, November 3, 1910; "Attacks League Report," unidentified newspaper clipping, November 3, 1910, OAP.

84. For improvements under the Magee administration, see annual reports of both the mayor and the Department of Public Works from 1910 to 1913 in the *Annual Reports of the Executive Departments of the City of Pittsburgh* for the same years. For the Shade Tree Commission, see AR, DPW (1910), 8–9; for example, "Annual Report of the Shade Tree Commission," *Annual Reports of the Executive Departments* (1913), 396, and (1914) (now the Shade Tree Division), 680–684.

85. FLO to PCC, January 17, 1910, OAP.

86. Joseph G. Armstrong, AR, DPW (1912), 6; unidentified author, "City of Pittsburgh and Its Public Works" (Pittsburgh, 1916), 26–28; Olmsted, *Main Thoroughfares*, 128–132; H. C. Frick to D. B. Kinch, November 12, 1910, Helen Clay Frick Foundation Archives, Hump Series, Box 1, Folder 11, Archives Service Center, University of Pittsburgh.

87. John P. Fox to FLO, November 11, 1910, OAP.

88. William A. Magee, "Message to City Planning Commission," December 1, 1911, in "Annual Report of the Mayor" (1911), 65.

89. Magee, "Mayor Magee Outlines Plan of Development"; Magee to FLO, November 25, 1910; FLO to Magee, November 30, 1910; Magee to FLO, December 2, 1910, all in OAP.

90. "Three Meetings on Greater City Plan," *Pittsburgh Dispatch*, January 7, 1911; "Beauty Bodies Hold Big Joint Session," *Pittsburgh Post*, January 10, 1911.

91. Magee to FLO, March 18, 1911; FLO to Magee, March 22, 1911, both in OAP; Magee, "Message to City Planning Commission."

92. Magee, "Message to City Planning Commission." For Allegheny County opposition to Magee's plan to consolidate the city with county suburban communities, see, for example, "Object to Taking in County," *Pittsburgh Post*, October 15, 1910; and Lubove, *Twentieth Century Pittsburgh*, 97–98.

93. William A. Magee, "Annual Report of the Mayor" (1912), 11, 12–13, 20.

94. Lubove, *Twentieth Century Pittsburgh*, 55–58.

95. Magee, "Annual Report of the Mayor" (1912), 10–11; "Annual Report of the Department of City Planning," *Annual Reports of the Executive Departments of the City of Pittsburgh* (1912), 147–151.

96. "Annual Report of the Art Commission," *Annual Reports of the Executive Departments of the City of Pittsburgh* (1913), 3–6.

97. "Annual Report of the Department of City Planning" (1912), for example, see 157–159, 160–162, 164–168; "Annual Report of the Department of City Planning" (1913), for example, see 99–105.

98. James D. Hailman [secretary of the City Planning Commission] to FLO, July 19, 1912; FLO to Hailman (a ten-page report on the meeting with the City Planning Commission), December 10, 1912, both in OAP. See also "Annual Report of the Department of City Planning" (1912), 159–160.

99. "Annual Report of the Department of City Planning" (1912), 142–143, 162–163; "Annual Report of the Department of City Planning" (1913), 106–108.

100. *Pittsburgh Post*, October 31, 1910; Kerr, "Mayors and Recorders," 254–256, 260–266.

101. "Annual Message of the Mayor," *Annual Reports of the Executive Departments of the City of Pittsburgh* (1914), 83–88.

102. See "Annual Report of the Art Commission" (1913–1919); "City Art Board Is Selected," unidentified newspaper clipping, OAP; and John F. Bauman and Edward K. Muller, "The Planning Technician as Urban Visionary: Frederick Bigger and American Planning, 1915–1954," *Journal of Planning History* 1, no. 2 (2002): 124–153.

103. "Report of E. H. Bennett," March 25, 1914, in "Annual Report of the Art Commission" (1914), 11–23. See also "Annual Report of the Art Commission" (1913, 1915).

104. "Annual Report of the Art Commission" (1914, 1915, 1917); see especially the report for 1915, 7–13. Barry Hannegan, "Schenley Plaza: Place of Dreams," *PHLF News* 144 (November 1996): 10–15.

105. "Annual Report of the Art Commission" (1915), 13; "Annual Report of the Art Commission" (1917), 2–6; "Annual Report of the Art Commission" (1918), 4–6.

106. *Comprehensive City Planning for Pittsburgh*, Fifth Special Bulletin of the Municipal Planning Committee, October 10, 1918, in *Annals of the Civic Club of Allegheny County* (Pittsburgh, 1918).

CHAPTER 4. THE REBIRTH OF PLANNING IN POST–WORLD WAR I PITTSBURGH

1. Mel Scott's magisterial *American City Planning* argues that planning in the 1920s consisted mainly of zoning and the development of master plans, neither of which was particularly successful. Caroline Boyer, in *Dreaming the Rational City,* 154, is equally harsh. Boyer, like Marxist historian Richard E. Foglesong in *Planning the Capitalist City: The Colonial Era to the 1920s* (Princeton, N.J.: Princeton University Press, 1986), 229–232, finds "practicalist" planners annihilating the last remnants of urban beauty in the name of urban economy and discipline. "By the end of the 1920s," writes Boyer, "it was evident that American architects and planners had failed. City streets were clogged with traffic." Boyer, *Dreaming the Rational City,* 155. Mark Foster, in *From Streetcars to Superhighways: American City Planners and Urban Transportation, 1900–1940* (Philadelphia: Temple University Press, 1981), 64–67, likewise views the decade despairingly, arguing that zoning and master planning accomplished little. Instead, planners gave up the vision of reconstructing urban cores and turned their efforts toward the suburbs. Finally, Lubove, in *Twentieth Century Pittsburgh,* 91, offers a scathing account of planning in Pittsburgh during the 1920s. He describes planning in Pittsburgh during the decade as "form without substance," and argues that "environmental change was not, to any significant degree, influenced or guided by comprehensive plans; and statutory planning agencies . . . continued to contrive solutions to problems without any control over causes."

2. On zoning, see Seymour I. Toll, *Zoned America* (New York: Grossman, 1964); Patricia Burgess, *Planning for the Private Interest: Land Use Controls and Residential Patterns in Columbus, Ohio, 1900–1970* (Columbus: Ohio State University Press, 1995); and Weiss, *Rise of the Community Builders,* 79–106. See also Boyer, *Dreaming the Rational City,* 139–170.

3. Robert M. Fogelson, *Downtown: Its Rise and Fall, 1880–1950* (New Haven, Conn.: Yale University Press, 2001), 183–217.

4. For a general picture of Pittsburgh's downtown growth, see the publication of the Pittsburgh Chamber of Commerce, *Pittsburgh First,* after 1927 called *Greater Pittsburgh;* on cities and the automobile in the 1920s, see Foster, *From Streetcar to Superhighway;* and Scott Bottles, *Los Angeles and the Automobile: The Making of the Modern City* (Berkeley:

University of California Press, 1987). On the New York case, see Max Page's insightful and eloquent essay on Fifth Avenue in *Creative Destruction of Manhattan*, 21–67.

5. Wilson, "Moles and Skylarks," 88–122; Fairfield, *Mysteries of the Great City*; Boyer, *Dreaming the Rational City*; Foglesong, *Planning the Capitalist City*. See also Page, *Creative Destruction of Manhattan*, 1–67.

6. On the "New Urban Discipline," see Fairfield, *Mysteries of the Great City*, 83–118; on the restructuring of commerce and industrialism in the 1920s and the modern business orientation toward labor and ethnicity, especially the Americanization campaign, see Lizbeth Cohen, *Making a New Deal: Industrial Workers in Chicago, 1919–1939* (Cambridge: Cambridge University Press, 1990), 159–211; see also Lubove, *Twentieth Century Pittsburgh*.

7. See *Chronology of Early Pittsburgh Planning Commission* (n.d.), in the Pittsburgh City Planning Commission Library, Pittsburgh; on Mayor Joseph G. Armstrong, see George Swetnam's brief biography of Armstrong in Melvin G. Holli and Peter d'A. Jones, *Biographical Dictionary of American Mayors, 1820–1980* (Westport, Conn.: Greenwood, 1981); and Pittsburgh City Planning Commission Minutes, April 19, 1918, in the Pittsburgh City Planning Commission offices, Pittsburgh (hereafter cited as PCPC Mins.).

8. On the Bennett plan, see "City's Beauty Pointed Out," *Pittsburgh Leader*, June 20, 1915, and other news clippings in Pittsburgh Planning File, Archives of Industrial Society, University of Pittsburgh, Pittsburgh; on the Art Commission's recruitment of Bigger and the commission's Point project, see Lubove, *Twentieth Century Pittsburgh*, 56–57. The Civic Club of Allegheny County spoke of the new civic spirit infusing the city in 1914 and invited Bigger to address it that year on "Civic Art and City Beautification." Civic Club of Allegheny County (hereafter cited as CCAC), Annual Report (1914), 16, in Carnegie Library, Pittsburgh; also on Bigger, see Joseph Browne, "Bigger Resigns Planning Post," *Pittsburgh Sun Telegraph*, March 9, 1954.

9. *Report of the Voters' League to the Hon. E. V. Babcock, Mayor-Elect of the City of Pittsburgh* (Pittsburgh: Voters' League of Pittsburgh, 1917), 25–31.

10. Frederick Bigger, "Comprehensive City Planning: Fourth and Final Article of a Series for the *Post*," *Pittsburgh Post*, June 24, 1918; see Bauman and Muller, "Planning Technician as Urban Visionary," 124–153.

11. Bigger, "Comprehensive City Planning," *Pittsburgh Post*, June 24, 1918; FLO to James D. Hailman, December 10, 1912, OAP; Bauman and Muller, "Planning Technician as Urban Visionary," 130.

12. See John Hancock, "Planners and Changing American City," *AIP Journal* (September 1967): 293–296. On World War I worker housing communities, see Kristin M. Szylvian, "Industrial Housing Reform and the Emergency Fleet Corporation," *Journal of Urban History* 25 (July 1999): 647–690; Michael H. Lang, "Town Planning and Radicalism in the Progressive Era: The Legacy of F. L. Ackerman," *Planning Perspectives* 16, no. 2 (April 2001): 143–169; and Eric J. Karolak, "'No Idea of Doing Anything Wonderful': The Labor-Crisis Origins of National Housing Policy and the Reconstruction of the Working-Class Community, 1917–1919," in John F. Bauman, Roger Biles, and Kristin Szylvian, eds., *From Tenements to the Taylor Homes: In Search of an Urban Housing Policy in Twentieth Century America* (University Park: Pennsylvania State University Press, 2000), 60–81.

13. *Pittsburgh Post-Gazette*, October 21 and October 24, 1918. On influenza in Pittsburgh, see *Pittsburgh Post-Gazette*, October 22, 1918.

14. On World War I and the Americanism campaign, see Cohen, *Making a New Deal*, 53–97.

15. See *Pittsburgh First*, August 12 and August 26, 1919.

16. On postwar metropolitanization, the "Greater Pittsburgh" campaign, which lasted throughout the decade, see *Pittsburgh First*, August 24, 1920, and April 21, 1923; and *Minutes of the Civic Club Board of Directors*, 1918–1921, in the Civic Club of Allegheny County

Collection, Archives Service Center, University of Pittsburgh, Pittsburgh. On the plea for postwar public works, see *Pittsburgh First,* November 28, 1918.

17. Postwar labor conflict and the efforts of management to deal with it are discussed in several studies. See David Brody, *Labor in Crisis: The Steel Strike of 1919* (Philadelphia: J. B. Lippincott, 1965); and Cohen, *Making a New Deal,* 53–67; see also *Pittsburgh First,* November 8, 1919. On the Americanization campaign in Pittsburgh, see *Pittsburgh First,* September 4, 1920, and January 8, 1921; and the posters and other Americanization campaign materials in the Irene Kaufmann Settlement House Papers, Historical Society of Western Pennsylvania.

18. Cohen, *Making a New Deal,* 162–183.

19. *Pittsburgh First,* January 17, 1920.

20. Citizens Committee on the City Plan Minutes (hereafter cited as CCCP Mins.), June 16, 1919, in Pittsburgh Regional Planning Association Papers, Pennsylvania Room, Carnegie Library, Pittsburgh (hereafter cited as PRPA Papers). For Edward V. Babcock, see *Prominent Men of Pittsburgh and Vicinity* (Pittsburgh: Pittsburgh Press Club, 1912–13), 29; Frank C. Harper, *Men and Women of Wartime Pittsburgh and Environs* (Pittsburgh: Frank C. Harper, 1945), 333; and Kerr, "Mayors and Recorders," 267–273.

21. See Acts of the Legislature of Pennsylvania Creating the Department of City Planning in Cities of the Second Class, Act of 10 June 1911, No. 345, P.L. 872, Amended by Act of 17 May 1921, No. 294 P.L. 841, PCPC Mins.; PCPC Mins., April 19, 1918, and January 15, 1920.

22. See, for example, PCPC Mins., October 27, 1919.

23. "Pittsburgh Begins Great Civic Improvements," *Pittsburgh First,* July 12, 1919.

24. On Babcock's seventeen improvements, especially the Chamber of Commerce's outburst, see *Pittsburgh First,* June 21, 1919; PCPC Mins., December 23, 1918; and U. N. Arthur, "Progress of City Planning in Pittsburgh," *Proceedings of the Twelfth National Conference on City Planning, Cincinnati, Ohio* (Boston: 1920), 27–31.

25. Magee had argued in 1911 that his purpose in having the city planning jurisdiction extend beyond the city limits was "to bring together all the smaller municipalities of the county to work with Pittsburgh in effecting a more comprehensive system of streets and parks, street railway lines and public buildings to the end that all will harmonize and result in greater efficiency for the benefit of the whole county." Untitled and undated article in the *Pittsburgh Post,* OAP.

26. On conflicting city versus county planning visions, see *Pittsburgh First,* June 21, 1919.

27. See Allegheny County Planning Commission, Reports (1928, 1929, 1930, 1931), in the Allegheny Planning Commission Records, Allegheny County Planning Commission Office, Pittsburgh (hereafter cited as ACPC Reports).

28. PCPC Mins., December 4 and December 23, 1918. That the need for metropolitan planning was on the minds of local planners is evident in Morris Knowles, "Engineering Problems of Regional Planning," *Proceedings of the Eleventh National Conference on City Planning, Niagara Falls and Buffalo* (Boston, 1919), 115–138. Knowles identified himself as a consulting engineer from Pittsburgh, but he was soon to be formally involved in the city's planning efforts.

29. On comprehensiveness in city planning, see Frederick Bigger, "Municipal Improvements," *Pittsburgh Post,* July 24, 1915; Bauman and Muller, "Planning Technician as Urban Visionary"; on Olmsted Jr., John Nolen, and the National Conference on City Planning, see Scott, *American City Planning,* 132–149.

30. *Greater Pittsburgh,* February 25, 1928; see Fairfield, *Mysteries of the Great City;* Blackford, *Lost Dream;* and Boyer, *Dreaming the Rational City,* 139–141.

31. George R. Wallace, "Pittsburgh—Its City Planning," *Greater Pittsburgh,* April 15,

1922, 10; Boyer, *Dreaming the Rational City;* Fairfield, *Mysteries of the Great City.* On Bigger, see Bauman and Muller, "Planning Technician as Urban Visionary."

32. See "Unrelated Street Changes Indicate Stupidity; Organized Industry and Organized Business Required an Organized Street System," *Progress* (October 1929); see also Burgess, *Planning for the Private Interest;* and City of Pittsburgh, *Regulations for Motion Picture Theaters, Exhibitions and Demonstrations,* Series of 1923, Ordinance No. 473, in PCPC Library, Pittsburgh.

33. "City Beautiful Is Legislative Bill's Object," *Pittsburgh Dispatch,* November 28, 1918. The best discussion of the City Beautiful movement and its ideological foundations is found in Wilson, *City Beautiful Movement.*

34. See "Citizens Committee for City Planning Here," *Pittsburgh Post-Gazette,* November 28, 1918; Minutes of Citizens Committee on City Plan (CCCP), October 26, 1918, PRPA Papers.

35. See Minutes of Organization Meeting of the CCCP, October 29, 1918, PRPA Papers; and form letter to prospective members of CCCP, ca. October 29, 1918, signed by James D. Hailman, secretary, PRPA Papers. Those Pittsburgh civic luminaries wedded to planning in 1918 unabashedly looked to Chicago for their inspiration. A decade earlier elite members of Chicago's Commercial Club had employed the famed architect Daniel H. Burnham (and his partner Edward H. Bennett) to develop a nationally celebrated and widely emulated "practical" street plan of wide thoroughfares, attractive boulevards, and inviting parks. On Burnham and the Chicago Plan, see Hines, *Burnham of Chicago,* 312–345; Scott, *American City Planning,* 102–109; and Minutes of Organization Meeting of the CCCP, October 29, 1918, PRPA Papers. Like members of the earlier PCC, CCCP members served on various subcommittees concerned mainly, but not exclusively, with the principal portions of the city plan: Playgrounds, Major Streets, Parks, Transit, Railroads, and Waterways. Committees dealing with finances, legal matters, and publicity also existed.

36. CCCP Mins., June 1919, PRPA Papers. For Arbuthnot, see *The Book of Prominent Pennsylvanians* (Pittsburgh: Leader, 1913), 251; and George T. Fleming, *History of Pittsburgh and Environs,* vol. 5 (New York: American Historical Society, 1922), 226.

37. CCCP Mins., December 6, 1918, PRPA Papers; "Citizens' Committee for City Plan Is Organized Here."

38. See Wilson, "Moles and Skylarks," 90, 109.

39. Joseph Arnold, *The New Deal in the Suburbs: A History of the Greenbelt Town Program, 1935–1954* (Columbus: Ohio State University Press, 1970); Roy Lubove, *Community Planning in the 1920s: The Contributions of the Regional Planning Association of America* (Pittsburgh: University of Pittsburgh Press, 1963); John Ormsbee Symonds, interview by authors, January 19, 1995; for the Bigger biography, see Frederick Bigger, American Institute of Planners Membership Questionnaire, February 13, 1939, in Carl A. Krock Library, Cornell University, Ithaca, New York (hereafter cited as Bigger, AIP Vita); and Frederick Bigger, Pittsburgh Chapter American Institute of Architects Membership Data, n.d. (ca. 1962), in Architectural Archives of Carnegie Mellon University Library, Pittsburgh (hereafter cited as Bigger, AIA Vita). See also Bauman and Muller, "Planning Technician as Urban Visionary."

40. See W. H. Robinson, "Report of the Committee on Recreation" (1921), PRPA Papers, where Robinson quotes Bigger on "what is to be done." It is an eloquent statement of Bigger's "accessible city." See also Bigger's vision of Pittsburgh in CCCP, *Parks: A Part of the Pittsburgh Plan, Report No. 4* (Pittsburgh: Citizens Committee on City Plan, 1923).

41. See CCCP, *Playgrounds: A Part of the Pittsburgh Plan, Report No. 1* (Pittsburgh: Citizens Committee on City Plan, 1921); and CCCP, *Parks.*

42. Minutes of "Joint Meeting of Executive and Finance Committee [of CCCP]," December 10, 1918, PRPA Papers.

43. Ibid.

44. CCCP Mins., January 15, 1919, PRPA Papers.

45. For a discussion of cities' legal powers to plan and how that changed over the nineteenth century, see Schultz, *Constructing Urban Culture,* 35–91.

46. PCPC Mins., December 11, 1919, PRPA Papers.

47. *Pittsburgh First,* December 22, 1923.

48. See the list of directors of the Pittsburgh Chamber of Commerce and the Chamber's committee heads in *Pittsburgh First,* May 21, 1919; see also "Chamber Aids Practical Work in City Planning," *Pittsburgh First,* December 20, 1919.

49. See obituary of James D. Hailman in *Progress* (July 1930). On Heinz, see "Committee Chairmanships for 1921–1922 in the Chamber of Commerce," *Pittsburgh First,* July 2, 1921.

50. The Joint Planning Conference (JPC) was formed December 6, 1922, when the by-laws of the JPC were approved. See Meeting of Joint Conference Committee, December 6, 1922, creating Joint Planning Conference, in Allegheny County Planning Commission Minutes, December 7, 1922. The JPC was reconstituted in 1924; see Norman F. Brown, Director of Allegheny County Department of Public Works, to John A. Bell of Allegheny County Planning Commission, March 6, 1924, discussing "Co-ordinated Planning," in Allegheny County Planning Commission Minutes (hereafter cited as ACPC Mins.), March 7, 1924, in Allegheny County Planning Commission offices, Pittsburgh.

51. See PCPC Mins., August 16, 1922; see also "Chamber Aids Practical Work in City Planning," *Pittsburgh First,* December 20, 1919.

52. Frederick Bigger to John Nolen, April 17, 1919, Box 2903, Nolen Papers, Krock Library, Cornell University (hereafter cited as NP).

53. See CCCP Mins., October 13, 1920, PRPA Papers.

54. Bigger to Nolen, March 10, 1919, Box 2903, NP.

55. See Frederick Bigger, "Citizens Committee on City Plan of Pittsburgh: Analytical Report and Estimate of Costs for Preparation of Comprehensive Plan," April 4, 1919, Box 2903, NP.

56. See CCCP, "Minutes of Meeting to Discuss Need to Engage Technical Expert," November 1919, PRPA Papers; see also Bigger to Nolen, April 7, 1919; Nolen, Memorandum of Visit to Pittsburgh, April 21–23, 1919; Nolen to Bigger, August 19, 1919; and Bigger to Nolen, October 7, 1919, all in NP. Bigger also arranged for Nolen to discuss "Industrial Housing" at a CCAC luncheon. Nolen's comments on the report urged the CCCP to pay "adequate attention to publicity and the legal method of carrying out the plan," and he exhorted the committee to work with and not in isolation from county and municipal officials.

57. See Christopher Silver, "Visions of the Modern City," *Journal of Urban History* 22, no. 3 (March 1996): 402.

58. On New York zoning, see Page, *Creative Destruction of Manhattan,* 53–65; Fairfield, *Mysteries of the Great City;* Scott, *American City Planning;* and Boyer, *Dreaming the Rational City.*

59. Page, *Creative Destruction of Manhattan,* 53–65; Fairfield, *Mysteries of the Great City;* Wilson, "Moles and Skylarks," 88–121.

60. Boyer, *Dreaming the Rational City;* Wilson, "Moles and Skylarks"; Ann Lloyd, "Pittsburgh's 1923 Zoning Ordinance," *Western Pennsylvania Historical Magazine* 57, no. 3 (July 1974): 289–305. As early as 1913, the CPC noted the advantage of "the restriction of the heights and character of buildings with . . . the districting of the city," or zoning. In suggesting the need for such enabling legislation, it referred to the experience in Germany and the report of the Heights of Buildings Commission of New York. "Annual Report of the Department of City Planning" (1913), 107.

61. Civic Club of Allegheny County, *Districting and Zoning: What It Is, Why Pittsburgh Should Do It,* Second Special Bulletin Issued by the Civic Club of Allegheny County (Pitts-

burgh: Civic Club of Allegheny County, January 1, 1918), Reel 27, Edward Bassett Papers, Krock Library, Cornell University.

62. Civic Club of Allegheny County, *Districting and Zoning*.

63. See Lloyd, "Pittsburgh's 1923 Zoning Ordinance," 293.

64. Ibid.; CCAC, *Monthly Bulletin* 8 (May 1917), Reel 17, Bassett Papers.

65. PCPC, Minutes, March 10, 1919; Scott, *American City Planning*; City of Pittsburgh, *Zoning Ordinance and Zoning Map* (1923), in Pittsburgh City Planning Commission Library.

66. On importance of zoning to planning profession, see Fairfield, *Mysteries of the Great City*.

67. Janet R. Daly, "Zoning: Its Historical Context and Importance in the Development of Pittsburgh," *Western Pennsylvania Historical Magazine* 71, no. 2 (April 1988): 99–125. For a broader discussion of the attempts to create a metropolitan district or federated city, see Lubove, *Twentieth Century Pittsburgh*, 97–100.

68. Weiss, *Rise of the Community Builders*.

69. See CCCP Mins., January 15, 1919, PRPA Papers; Armstrong quoted in "First Public Announcement of Pittsburgh Plan Heard by Officials, Civic and Business Leaders," *Progress* (July 1923): 5.

70. PCPC Mins., October 13, 1919.

71. PCPC Mins., October 27, 1919, and May 5, 1920.

72. PCPC Mins., May 13, 1920, August 11, and September 20, 1921.

73. PCPC Mins., July 28, 1921.

74. *Progress* (May 1921): 2. On appointments, see PCPC Mins., May 13, 1922.

75. See CCCP Mins., October 20, 1920, PRPA Papers; and Morris Knowles, "Zoning for Pittsburgh," *Pittsburgh First,* January 6, 1923, 2.

76. "Zoning Ordinance Almost Ready for Presentation to Public Preceding Councilmanic Action," *Progress* (October 1922): 1; Department of Commerce, Advisory Committee on Zoning, *A Zoning Primer* (Washington, D.C.: Government Printing Office, 1922); Lloyd, "Pittsburgh's 1923 Zoning Ordinance," 295. Magee's Planning Commission members were James D. Hailman, James W. Clark, W. C. Rice, Frederick Bigger, A. J. Kelly, Morris Knowles, Charles Finley, Dr. J. T. Holdsworth, and James Malone. At the first meeting of this new commission, Magee stated that "the most important duty of this Commission is the completion of the zoning studies and ordinance." PCPC Mins., June 13, 1922.

77. "Zoning Ordinance Completed after Three Years," *Progress* (January 1923): 2. See also James M. Clark, "The Pittsburgh Zoning Ordinance," *Proceedings of the Thirteenth Annual Conference on City Planning, Pittsburgh, May 9–11, 1921* (Boston, 1921), 155–161; and Grash, "Commercial Skyscrapers of Pittsburgh," 165.

78. "Zoning Ordinance Almost Ready for Presentation," *Progress* (October 1922): 1.

79. This was not the first series of meetings on the ordinance. In July 1921 public hearings were conducted on a "tentative" ordinance; see PCPC Mins., July 17, 1921.

80. PCPC Mins., November 28, 1922, and April 25, 1923. On business fears, see PCPC Mins., January 10, 1923.

81. PCPC Mins., July 26, 1922.

82. Lloyd, "Pittsburgh's 1923 Zoning Ordinance," 297–303. According to Janet Daly, some large real estate interests in Pittsburgh did support zoning because, as noted earlier, it diminished risk for their ventures. Daly, "Zoning," 47.

83. "Arguments against Central Feature of the Proposed Pittsburgh Zoning Ordinance," *Pittsburgh First*, February 10, 1923, 2.

84. Lloyd, "Pittsburgh's 1923 Zoning Ordinance," 296–298, 304; Grash, "Commercial Skyscrapers of Pittsburgh," 165. While height restrictions were established, opposition did result in compromises such as the unrestricted height of setback towers and the appointment of a realtor to the Board of Appeals.

85. A good recent discussion of zoning, its philosophical roots, and impact on urban growth can be found in Burgess, *Planning for the Private Interest,* 66–67. The standard study of zoning is Toll, *Zoned America;* see also Scott, *American City Planning.*

86. On the Chicago model, see Minutes of Organizational Meeting [of CCCP], October 29, 1918, PRPA Papers. These committee members contributed their cash as generously as they did their time. On fund-raising among committee members, see Minutes of Joint Meeting of Executive and Finance Committees, October 13, 1920, PRPA Papers.

87. Bigger described the process in the introduction to CCCP, *Parks;* the process was also described by George R. Wallace, "Pittsburgh—Its City Planning," *Pittsburgh First,* April 15, 1922, 10; see also Lubove, *Twentieth Century Pittsburgh.*

88. Bigger to Nolen, April 17, 1919, Box 2903, NP; note that the six reports explicitly credit the person or persons most responsible for the report.

89. See "First Public Announcement of City Plan," *Progress* (July 1923): 1. Indeed, the planning enthusiasts were optimistic that the city had finally embraced planning. For example, James D. Hailman concluded his presentation at the Thirteenth National Conference on City Planning in Pittsburgh by enthusing that "the spirit of city planning is abroad in Pittsburgh as elsewhere and there is every reason to believe that our citizens recognize its importance as the ultimate factor in civic progress." James D. Hailman, "A Major Street Plan for Pittsburgh," *Proceedings of the Thirteenth Annual Conference on City Planning,* 133.

90. See Bert H. Smyers, "Pittsburgh Playgrounds—A Sketch of Their Development," *Pittsburgh First,* April 7, 1923, 2; on the Progressive Era playground movement in Pittsburgh and other cities, see Dominick Cavallo, *Muscle and Morals: Organized Playgrounds and Urban Reform, 1880–1920* (Philadelphia: University of Pennsylvania Press, 1981).

91. "Playgrounds Are Active Agency in Protecting City's Children from Dangers of Street," *Progress* (April 1921): 3.

92. CCCP, *Playgrounds.*

93. Bigger's report deemed playgrounds critical for survival in the complex, congested city "rife with perverse enticements." "Playground activities," stated *Playgrounds,* "furnish opportunity for children and youth to secure invaluable training, cooperative competition taking the place of gang-antagonisms. . . . [Playgrounds served in] upbuilding citizenship which shall be sound physically and morally." See CCCP, *Playgrounds,* 9.

94. See clipping from *Progress,* ca. 1920, Reel 27, File 10, Bassett Papers; and *Progress* (November 1921): 1.

95. CCCP, *Parks;* Ebenezer Howard, *Garden Cities of Tomorrow* (Cambridge, Mass.: MIT Press, 1965); Schuyler, *New Urban Landscape.* On Perry and the neighborhood unit, see Howard Gillette, "The Evolution of Neighborhood Planning: From the Progressive Era to the 1949 Housing Act," *Journal of Urban History* 9 (August 1983): 424–425.

96. In the introduction to the *Parks* report, Bigger was credited with "direct[ing], and develop[ing] . . . and formulat[ing]" the report. See CCCP, *Parks,* 1–15.

97. In his "Report of the CCCP's Committee on Recreation" (1921), Chairman W. H. Robinson quoted a draft of Bigger's *Parks* report, PRPA Papers.

98. CCCP, *Parks,* 41. Several years later, Bigger expanded his concern for the establishment or strengthening of strong neighborhoods or, more precisely in his view, communities through community councils and more accurate definition of community improvement districts by planners. Discussion by Frederick Bigger of the paper of Edwin S. Burdell, "The Social Problem Involved in Securing the Benefits of Slum Elimination," *Planning and National Recovery: Planning Problems Presented at the Twenty-Fifth National Conference on City Planning at Baltimore* (Philadelphia: William F. Fell, 1933), 142–144.

99. CCCP, *Parks,* 57–62.

100. Ibid.; Schuyler, *New Urban Landscape;* Wilson, *City Beautiful Movement.*

101. Fairfield emphasizes the link between planning ideas of the 1920s and Robert Park

and the Chicago School in *Mysteries of the Great City*, 189–224; see also Robert Park and Ernest Burgess, *The City* (Chicago: University of Chicago Press, 1967); and Clay McShane, *Down the Asphalt Path: The Automobile and the American City* (New York: Columbia University Press, 1994).

102. See "Major City Plan Placed before the Public," *Pittsburgh First,* October 1, 1921, 1.

103. *Progress* (June 1921): 2.

104. CCCP, *Transit: A Part of the Pittsburgh Plan* (Pittsburgh: Citizens Committee on City Plan, 1923); E. K. Morse, "Report of the Transit Commissioner to the Mayor" (1917), Carnegie Library, Pittsburgh; Tarr, *Transportation Innovation*, 28, 36.

105. CCCP, *Railroads of the Pittsburgh District: A Part of The Pittsburgh Plan, Report No. 5* (Pittsburgh: Citizens Committee on City Plan, 1923). On union stations in the 1920s, see Bottles, *Los Angeles and the Automobile*, 122–157; see also "Last Phase of Pittsburgh Plan Completed as Two Committees End Railroad Researches," *Progress* (March 1924): 1. In 1925 the Pennsylvania Railroad commenced demolishing its Grant Street freight station as part of a $14,000,000 downtown terminal improvement; see *Pittsburgh First*, June 27 and July 11, 1925.

106. CCCP, *Waterways: A Part of The Pittsburgh Plan, Report No. 6* (Pittsburgh: Citizens Committee on City Plan, 1923), 13–14.

107. *Progress* (July 1923): 1.

108. Arthur Hallam, "Annual Report of the Subcommittee on Major Street Plan," October 30, 1922, in CCCP Mins., PRPA Papers.

109. In truth, the JPC from the beginning worked intimately with the CCCP, even importuning the voluntary planning body to undertake on the commission's behalf a separate study of the downtown approaches to the Boulevard of the Allies. See PCPC Mins., June 1, 1923.

CHAPTER 5. PLANNING AND PROFESSIONALISM IN THE 1920S

1. "President Summarizes World of CCCP," *Progress* (July 1923): 14; *Progress* (July 1928). Four years later, in response to the news that the Allegheny County planned a new bond issue, the CCCP resumed activity.

2. Howard, *Garden Cities of Tomorrow;* Lewis Mumford, "The Fourth Migration," in Clarence Stein, *Toward New Towns for America* (Cambridge, Mass.: MIT Press, 1966); see also Fairfield, *Mysteries of the Great City.* On Patrick Geddes, see Volker M. Welter, *Biopolis: Patrick Geddes and the City of Life* (Cambridge, Mass.: MIT Press, 2002).

3. "Annual Report of the Art Commission" (1918). On "practical" aspects of the City Beautiful movement, see Wilson, *City Beautiful Movement;* and Howland, "City Practical," 394. On World War I and the rise of scientific management and technocracy, see Guy Alchon, *The Invisible Hand of Planning: Capitalism, Social Science, and the State in the 1920s* (Princeton, N.J.: Princeton University Press, 1985).

4. *Frederick Bigger, 1881–1963*, 26, no author or publishing data, in Pittsburgh Planning Department Library, Pittsburgh.

5. See Bigger, AIP Vita; see also Bigger, AIA Vita. On the founding of RPAA, see Stein, *Toward New Towns for America.*

6. Carl Sussman, ed., *Planning the Fourth Migration: The Neglected Vision of the Regional Planning Association of America* (Cambridge, Mass.: MIT Press, 1976), 5.

7. Ibid., 22–23. On Ackerman's more radical politics, see Lang, "Town Planning and Radicalism," 143–169. On MacKaye, see Larry Anderson, *Benton MacKaye: Conservationist, Planner, and Creator of the Appalachian Trail* (Baltimore: John Hopkins University Press, 2002).

8. See Lewis Mumford's introduction to *Toward New Towns for America*, by Clarence

Stein; Roy Lubove, *Community Planning in the 1920s: The Contribution of the Regional Planning Association of America* (Pittsburgh: University of Pittsburgh Press, 1963); and Carl Feiss, telephone interview by Edward K. Muller, November 29, 1995.

9. Frederick Bigger to "My Dear Mumford," June 11, 1924, in Lewis Mumford Papers, Special Collections, Van Pelt Library, University of Pennsylvania, Philadelphia; Bigger to Russell Van Nest Black, n.d., Krock Library, Cornell University; CCCP, *Parks.*

10. On general plan appropriation, see PCPC Mins., September 17 and October 22, 1924; on zoning and other routine matters, see PCPC Mins., January 24, May 21, and November 26, 1924.

11. PCPC, Minutes of Special Meeting, February 13, 1925.

12. Ibid.; PCPC Mins., February 25, 1926, and October 21, 1927; see also "Two Gaps in the Inter-District Traffic Circuit to Be Filled," *Progress* (June 1928): 1.

13. PCPC Mins., January 4, 1928. On the golf course at Nine Mile Run, see PCPC Mins., March 16 and October 14, 1927.

14. PCPC Mins., March 16, October 14, October 30, 1927, and October 30, 1928; see also Department of City Planning, "Report of Shade Tree Commission," PCPC Mins., August 8, 1927.

15. See Appendix II, *An Act Creating the City Planning Commission and the Department of City Planning,* June 10, 1911, in the City Planning Commission Library, Pittsburgh. A good digest of the legal authority for Pittsburgh city planning can be found in the Court Docket *Coyne v. Pritchard*, No. 211, October Term 1921 of Pennsylvania Western District, Reel 27, Folder 10, Bassett Papers.

16. The placement of planning within the Allegheny County Department of Public Works appears regularly in the ACPC's minutes. E. L. Schmidt headed the Engineering Division of Public Works, and Norman F. Brown directed Public Works; see ACPC Mins., 1925.

17. ACPC Mins., March 6, 1924.

18. Minutes of the Joint Planning Commission were included as part of the minutes of the ACPC. On the creation of the Joint Planning Commission, see ACPC Mins., July 5 and August 2, 1922.

19. On the membership, structure, and mission of the county planning commission, see ACPC Mins., March 26 and November 20, 1925, and June 24, 1927. See also Charles D. Armstrong's statement in *Progress* (January 1922): 1. On the philosophical differences between the city and the county commissions over the Liberty Bridge, see PCPC Mins., August 13 and September 24, 1924.

20. Allegheny County had a three-commissioner form of government. One position was reserved for a minority party commissioner, and of the two majority party commissioners, the chair tended to exercise considerable power. Proposed bond issues for highways and bridges failed twice before the successful passage of the 1924 issue. See "Allegheny County Develops Ultimate Highway System Plan," *Engineering New-Record* 99, no. 15 (October 1927): 584; Peter M. Farrington, "The Allegheny County Highway and Bridge Program, 1924–1932" (Master's thesis, Carnegie Mellon University, 1982), 37–57; and Gerald M. Kuncio, "Golden Age in City of Bridges," *Western Pennsylvania History* 82, no. 2 (Summer 1999): 61–63.

21. Fishman, *American Planning Tradition.*

22. "Ultimate Highway System Plan," 581, 584–585; Farrington, "Highway and Bridge Program," 58–62.

23. Farrington, "Highway and Bridge Program," 62–75; Tarr, "Infrastructure and City-Building," 245–247.

24. Farrington, "Highway and Bridge Program," 68, 72; Kuncio, "Golden Age in the City of Bridges," 64–72.

25. On the Chicago School, see Fairfield, *Mysteries of the Great City,* 158–188; and Schultz, *Constructing Urban Culture;* on the culture of planning and scientific management, see Alchon, *Invisible Hand.*

26. Blackford discusses the origins of professional city planning in *Lost Dream;* see also Scott, *American City Planning;* and Peterson, *Birth of City Planning.* On Bigger's background, see Lubove, *Twentieth Century Pittsburgh;* and Bauman and Muller, "Planning Technician as Urban Visionary," 124–153.

27. Mayor Magee first raised the idea for a new bond issue in May 1923; see PCPC Mins., April 4, 1923; for quotation, see PCPC Mins., October 17, 1923.

28. Blackford, *Lost Dream;* on the same subject, see Burgess, *Planning for the Private Interest;* and Weiss, *Rise of the Community Builders.* Information about members of the Pittsburgh CPC was obtained by searching the biographical files of the Carnegie Library, Pittsburgh, and from Alfred Decker Keator, ed., *Encyclopedia of Pennsylvania Biography* (New York: Lewis Historical, 1948); *The Book of Prominent Pennsylvanians* (Pittsburgh: Leader, 1913); and Harper, *Pittsburgh of Today.*

29. See U. N. Arthur to Chairman [of the PCPC], April 24, 1928, PCPC Mins., April 28, 1928; see also PCPC Mins., December 19, 1923, and October 22 and November 12, 1924; on the transfer of shade tree work to the commission, see PCPC Mins., February 23, 1927.

30. U. N. Arthur to Chairman [of PCPC], April 24, 1928, PCPC Mins.; PCPC Mins., April 28, 1928; Planning Commission Budget Committee to Chairman and Members of Planning Commission, August 21, 1926, PCPC Mins., August 21, 1926.

31. See "Exhibit A and B," in letter of U. N. Arthur to Chairman of PCPC, PCPC Mins., August 21, 1926; Arthur to Chairman of PCPC, PCPC Mins., September 22, 1928; and PCPC Mins., August 19, 1926.

32. See PCPC Mins., November 5, 1924, and September 15, 1926.

33. PCPC Mins., January 6, 1921, April 18, 1923, and June 17, 1925. On the May 1921 National Conference on City Planning meeting in Pittsburgh, see "National City Planners to Meet Here in May," *Pittsburgh Dispatch,* December 29, 1920.

34. PCPC Mins., February 24, 1926. On Knowles's talk, see "Report of the Representative of the ACPC at the Pennsylvania Association of Planning Commissions," in ACPC Mins., February 22, 1929.

35. On "mole work," see PCPC Mins., April 19, 1918, and December 6, 1922.

36. PCPC Mins., January 30, 1924, and August 8, 1925.

37. Recall that in December 1912 Olmsted, in a ten-page report to the CPC, had warned the commission against becoming "overwhelmed" in trying to deal with minor plans; see FLO to James D. Hailman, December 10, 1912, OAP. For quote on serving the Board of Appeals to the detriment of the commission, see PCPC Mins., January 9, 1924. At the CPC meeting of August 7, 1926, "the Chief Engineer was directed to advise City Council that the planning commission does not take appeals. The second and third matters were referred to the necessary amendments to the zoning ordinance for introduction to Council at its next regular meeting"; see PCPC Mins., August 7, 1926; see also PCPC Mins., January 30, 1924, and October 14, 1927.

38. See PCPC Mins., March 7, 1923, and September 11, 1928; see also ACPC Mins., February 5, 1926, and May 24, 1927.

39. See PCPC Mins., August 11, 1923; ACPC Mins., May 2, 1924, and July 28, 1926; and Appendix to 1926 Minute Book, "Exhibit C, Department of City Planning Triangulation and Topographic Survey," Budget Cost for 1927, in Pittsburgh Planning Department Library, Pittsburgh.

40. Constance Perrin, *Everything in Its Place: Social Order and Land Use in America* (Princeton, N.J.: Princeton University Press, 1977); see also Burgess, *Planning for the Private Interest;* and PCPC Mins., April 19, 1918, and February 20, 1924.

41. PCPC Mins., October 29, 1924, and June 30, 1926.

42. See *Appendix II, Act Creating City Planning Commission and Department of City Planning* (June 1911). On the city council, see PCPC Mins., June 24 and December 16, 1920. For a discussion of garages and deed restrictions, the CPC's efforts to control garages, and zoning as a strategy, see *Coyne v. Pritchard,* in Bassett Papers; and Burgess, *Planning for the Private Interest.* See also Charles D. Armstrong, "Necessary Legislation to be Presented at 1923 Legislature," *Progress* (January 1923): 1.

43. PCPC Mins., September 15, 1926.

44. See "Effort of CCCP to Give County Commission Greater Legal Authority," *Progress* (January 1922): 3.

45. On *Euclid,* see Scott, *American City Planning,* 238–239; on the commission's growing power and authority, see PCPC Mins., September 9, 1925, and March 16 and June 8, 1927; see also CCCP, "City Planning Accomplishments 1923."

46. On the University of Pittsburgh stadium, see PCPC Mins., November 17 and December 7, 1923.

47. On Meade Place, see PCPC Mins., December 19, 1923, and June 18, July 9, and August 6, 1924.

48. PCPC Mins., November 6, November 12, December 15, and December 31, 1924. For a good discussion of the legal evolution of planning from the nineteenth to the twentieth century, see Schultz, *Constructing Urban Culture.*

49. See Frederick Bigger, "Argument RE: Strawberry Way Widening, Submitted to City Planning Commission by Frederick Bigger on July 13, 1925," PCPC Mins., 1925; PCPC, General Plan Committee, "Report and Negative Recommendation to City Planning Commission Concerning Proposed Strawberry Way Widening," December 1, 1928, PCPC Mins., December 1928; see also PCPC Mins., December 21, 1927, and February 19, April 16, and April 30, 1929.

50. "James D. Hailman," *Progress* (July 1930): 41.

CHAPTER 6. THE LIMITATIONS OF PLANNING

1. See Frederick Bigger, "The City Planning Commission: Its Budget—Its Work," *Progress* (1929): 4; Pittsburgh City Planning Commission, *Report to the City Council of Pittsburgh on the Inter-District Traffic Circuit: A Part of the Major Street Plan Proposed by the Citizens Committee on the City Plan, Submitted in Preliminary Form December 28, 1925 and Issued in Its Present Form March 1926* (Pittsburgh, 1926).

2. On the uses of city streets, in Pittsburgh and elsewhere, and the emergence of automobile and truck traffic as an issue, see McShane, *Down the Asphalt Path;* and Tarr, *Transportation Innovation;* on Pittsburgh's "plebian culture," see Couvares, *Remaking of Pittsburgh.*

3. Tarr, *Transportation Innovation;* Bottles, *Los Angeles and the Automobile.*

4. Tarr, *Transportation Innovation,* 24–25.

5. Clarence Stein to Aline Stein, November 14, 1932, in Kermit C. Parsons, ed., *The Writings of Clarence S. Stein: Architect of the Planned Community* (Baltimore: Johns Hopkins University Press, 1998), 236.

6. See Walter Lippmann, *Drift and Mastery: Spectrum Book, Classics in History* (Madison: University of Wisconsin Press, 1986); Boyer, *Dreaming the Rational City;* Boyer, *Urban Masses and Moral Order;* and Robert B. Fairbanks, *Making Better Citizens: Housing Reform and the Community Development Strategy in Cincinnati, 1890–1960* (Urbana: University of Illinois Press, 1988); on working-class adaptation of housing, see Joseph C. Bigott, *From Cottage to Bungalow: Houses and the Working Class in Metropolitan Chicago: 1869–1929* (Chicago: University of Chicago Press, 2001).

7. See Lubove, *Twentieth Century Pittsburgh;* on privatism, see Sam Bass Warner, *The Private City: Philadelphia in Three Periods of Its Growth* (Philadelphia: University of Penn-

sylvania Press, 1967); on the conservative mood of the 1920s, see Lynn Dumenil, *Modern Temper: American Culture and Society in the 1920s* (New York: Hill and Wang, 1995); on social and political parochialism, see Cohen, *Making a New Deal;* on parochialism and politics, see Katznelson, *City Trenches.*

8. See Page, *Creative Destruction of Manhattan;* Burgess, *Planning for the Private Interest;* Weiss, *Rise of the Community Builders;* PCPC Mins.; and ACPC Mins.; on Bigger, see Bauman and Muller, "Planning Technician as Urban Visionary," 124–153.

9. For an example of Bigger's "occasional" cynicism and despair, see Frederick Bigger, "The Limitations of Urban Planning," *Journal of the American Institute of Planners* 13, no. 6 (June 1925): 139, 200.

10. Bigger, "Limitations of Urban Planning," 200; see also Lang's study of Frederick Ackerman, "Town Planning and Radicalism," 143–169.

11. Frederick Bigger, "Obstacles to the Development of a Recreation System," *American City* 36 (June 1927): 813–815.

12. Frederick Bigger, "The Limitations of City Planning," *Journal of the American Institute of Architects* 8, no. 6 (June 1925): 199.

13. Frederick Bigger, "Regional Planning as Seen through the Pittsburgh Experience," *Progress* (January 1929): 7.

14. Bigger, "Obstacles to the Development of a Recreation System," 813.

15. See various communications to Pittsburgh Department of City Planning, 1924–1929; for example, F. R. Babcock, General Planning Committee of Chamber of Commerce, to Chairman and Members of City Planning Commission, July 20, 1926, PCPC Mins., August 7, 1926; and "The CCCP Does Not Approve County Bond Issue," *Progress* (April 1924): 1.

16. Bigger, "Limitations of Urban Planning," 200–202.

17. Roy Lubove made Bigger's 1925 observations a major theme in his *Twentieth Century Pittsburgh.*

18. On "cost" limitations, see Magee's remarks in *Progress* (May 1922): 1; and PCPC Mins., November 3, 1921, and May 20, 1925; Teaford discusses the vital role of city borrowing capacity in *Unheralded Triumph.*

19. See two recent excellent studies of the downtown, Fogelson, *Downtown,* 183–193; and Isenberg, *Downtown America.*

20. Tarr, *Transportation Innovation,* 26.

21. See E. K. Morse, *Report of Transit Commission* (Pittsburgh 1918); and Tarr, *Transportation Innovation,* 24.

22. Olmsted, *Main Thoroughfares.* In fact, Bion J. Arnold, in his *Report on the Pittsburgh Transportation Problem,* ignored the automobile; for a discussion of the automobile and the hierarchy of street uses, see McShane, *Down the Asphalt Path.*

23. Morse, *Report of Transit Commission;* for the problem in other cities, see Foster, *From Streetcar to Superhighway.*

24. See James J. Flink, *The Car Culture* (Cambridge, Mass.: MIT Press, 1975), 42–65; and "Boulevard of the Allies," *Pittsburgh First,* June 25, 1921, 14; see also Hungerford cartoons in special anniversary issue of *Progress* (January 1929).

25. See "Boulevard of the Allies"; "Map of the Proposed Subway for Downtown Section of Pittsburgh," *Pittsburgh First,* June 28, 1919, 5; and "The Street Railway Situation Is Subject of National Chamber Referendum," *Pittsburgh First,* November 27, 1920, 5. Many bridge and tunnel projects, although located in the city, were agreed to be under the authority of the county. Fogelson examines Pittsburgh's subway saga in *Downtown,* 44–111.

26. See Fairfield, *Mysteries of the Great City,* 77–85; Fogelson, *Downtown,* 56–67; and Foster, *From Streetcar to Superhighway;* on the "affordable housing" movement, see Carolyn S. Loeb, *Entrepreneurial Vernacular: Developers' Subdivisions in the 1920s* (Baltimore: Johns Hopkins University Press, 2001).

27. For an excellent discussion of the Byzantine ownership of the PRC, see Arnold, *Report on the Pittsburgh Transportation Problem;* see also Tarr, *Transportation Innovation;* and James Judson Gillespie, "Going Nowhere: Pittsburgh's Attempt to Build A Subway, 1910–1935" (Seminar paper, Department of Humanities, MIT, 1990).

28. Through-route systems routed transit vehicles from point A in the city to point B. Loop systems operated vehicles in a continuous "loop"; Arnold, *Report on the Pittsburgh Transportation Problem*; Fogelson, *Downtown*, 75–79.

29. Gillespie, "Going Nowhere," 21–25. The Pittsburgh Subway Company and Morse are also discussed in Fogelson, *Downtown*, 76.

30. Morse, *Report of the Transit Commission;* see also Pittsburgh Transit Commission, *Synopsis of Report of Transit Commissioner* (Pittsburgh, 1918), in Pittsburgh Department of City Planning Library, Pittsburgh; and Gillespie, "Going Nowhere," 25–28.

31. On receivership of the PRC, see A. W. Thompson, "Problems of the Pittsburgh Railways," *Pittsburgh First*, March 11, 1922, 2; and Tarr, *Transportation Innovation*, 23; on Babcock's plan, see, "Map of Proposed Subway"; and Gillespie, "Going Nowhere," 29–30.

32. Tarr, *Transportation Innovation*. On opposition to Babcock's plan and Morse's role in that opposition, see Gillespie, "Going Nowhere," 31–40; and Fogelson, *Downtown*, 79.

33. "Subway," *Progress* (January 1929).

34. On derailed subway plans, see Fogelson, *Downtown*, 75–79; Gillespie, "Going Nowhere"; and Stanley Mallach, "The Origin and Decline of Urban Mass Transportation in the United States, 1890–1930," *Urbanism Past and Present* No. 8 (Summer 1979): 1–18; on the CCCP and Bigger's role, see Bauman and Muller, "Planning Technician as Urban Visionary"; and CCCP, *Transit*, 11, 15–17.

35. CCCP, *Transit*, 13–14.

36. Ibid.

37. See "Transportation, Auto Parking, and Flood: E. K. Morse and A. H. Burchfield Address the Chamber at Its Monthly Meeting and Set Forth a Plan of Solving Above Problems," *Pittsburgh First,* February 23, 1924, 5; and Edward Morse and Henry Burchfield, "Pittsburgh Water Street District and Lower Downtown Triangle Improvement Association/The Morse-Burchfield Plan" (Pittsburgh, 1924), 2–3, in Pittsburgh Planning Department Library (hereafter cited as Morse-Burchfield Plan).

38. See "Transportation, Auto Parking and Flood," 5; and Morse-Burchfield Plan, 11–36.

39. Morse-Burchfield Plan, 13.

40. On the Morse-Burchfield Plan and how it compelled planners to take Morse and Burchfield's subway ideas seriously, see PCPC Mins., January 23 and February 6, 1924; see also "Transportation, Auto Parking and Floods," 5.

41. See "Mayor Magee Discusses Rapid Transit," *Pittsburgh First,* February 2, 1924, 11.

42. PCPC Mins., August 16, 1924. Davison's report was submitted and adopted by the CPC in January 1924; it was then transmitted to the city council. See PCPC Mins., January 16 and January 30, 1924.

43. Bigger, " Limitations of City Planning," 201.

44. Daniel L. Turner and Winters Haydock, Traffic Commission, Bureau of Traffic Relief, *Report on a Recommended Subway in the First and Second Wards of Pittsburgh, Proposed First Step in a Rapid Transit Program* (Pittsburgh, 1925), in Pittsburgh Department of City Planning Library (hereafter cited as Turner and Haydock Study).

45. The downtown did not expand as Turner and Haydock had imagined until the 1980s. See Turner and Haydock Study.

46. Daniel L. Turner and Winters Haydock of the Department of City Transit, *Communication from the City Transit Commission of Pittsburgh to the Mayor and City Council Containing a Report on a Plan for Financing Initial Subway Construction in Pittsburgh* (Pittsburgh, March 1926).

47. PCPC Mins., August 26, 1925.

48. Note the skeptical tone of the letter from the City Planning Department to the chairman of the CPC, November 9, 1926, disapproving proposed Council Ordinance 2174 for location of proposed subway. See PCPC Mins., November 10, 1926.

49. The PCPC's Committee on Public Works "disapproved" the Transit Commission's plans in a letter to the chairman of the PCPC, November 9, 1926; see PCPC Mins., November 10, 1926.

50. City Transit Commission, *Annual Report of the City Transit Commission to the Mayor and City Council* (Pittsburgh: December 22, 1927), 24. On the council's rejection, see Gillespie, "Going Nowhere," 48.

51. On the subway lament, see *Progress* (January 1929): 8; on the subway's demise in 1934, see Gillespie, "Going Nowhere," 48.

52. On the ACPC, see ACPC Mins., March 28, 1924; on politics, see, Michael P. Weber, *Don't Call Me Boss: David L. Lawrence, Pittsburgh's Renaissance Mayor* (Pittsburgh: University of Pittsburgh Press, 1988); Lubove, *Twentieth Century Pittsburgh*; and Bruce Stave, *The New Deal and the Last Hurrah: Pittsburgh Machine Politics* (Pittsburgh: University of Pittsburgh Press, 1970).

53. The last of these skyscrapers, the Gulf Building, was begun in 1930 and completed two years later. See Valerie S. Gash, "The Commercial Skyscraper of Pittsburgh Industrialists and Financiers, 1885–1932" (Ph.D. diss., Pennsylvania State University, 1998), ch. 6; see also Bigger, "Limitations of City Planning," 201.

54. See CCCP, *A Major Street Plan for Pittsburgh: A Part of the Pittsburgh Plan* (Pittsburgh: Citizens Committee on City Plan, September 1921); see also *Progress* (June 1921): 2.

55. *Progress* (October 1921): 1.

56. CCCP, *Major Street Plan,* 28–39.

57. "Development of Major Street Plan Promises Relief from Congestion," *Progress* (January 1921): 1.

58. CCCP, *Major Street Plan,* 28–34.

59. Ibid.; "Major City Plan Placed before the Public," *Pittsburgh First,* October 1, 1921, 6.

60. CCCP, *Major Street Plan,* 34. The CCCP's John D. Hailman described the CCCP street plan in the *Proceedings of the National Conference on City Planning* (1921), 120–143. On the Chamber of Commerce's views, see "Major City Plan Placed before the Public," 1; see also W. G. Campbell, "Tunnels for Traffic—Pittsburgh's New Auto Tubes of Widespread Interest," in *Greater Pittsburgh* [the new name for *Pittsburgh First*], October 2, 1926, 23.

61. See PCPC Mins., November 13 and November 27, 1922. See also *Progress* (April 1922): 4. Suddenly in early 1923, Pittsburgh planners, aided by the Department of Public Works and the Department of Safety, undertook a series of traffic counts in the downtown. This was probably in response to plans for both subway and highway development, but it also reflected the increasingly important role of the highway engineering–oriented federal Bureau of Public Roads, whose head, Thomas McDonald, pressed for such counts. See Bruce Seely, *Building the American Highway System: Engineers as Policy Makers* (Philadelphia: Temple University Press, 1987).

62. See Minutes of Joint Planning Conference, in ACPC Mins., March 1924.

63. See PCPC Mins., December 26, 1924, and January 28 and February 25, 1925.

64. PCPC Mins., May 27, July 10, and July 13, 1925.

65. PCPC Mins. contain a massive amount of material on the Inter-District Traffic Circuit; see, for example, PCPC Mins., December 16, 1925.

66. On the "rectangular traffic circuit scheme," see PCPC, Minutes of Special Meeting, August 7, 1925; for Bigger's vigorous attack of the county plan, see PCPC Mins., August 5, 1925; on Ross Street, see PCPC Mins., June 12 and December 16, 1925.

67. City Planning Commission, *Inter-District Traffic Circuit*; see "City Plan Presented to Council," *Pittsburgh First*, January 2, 1926; and PCPC Mins., June 16, 1926.

68. PCPC Mins., August 11, 1926; U. N. Arthur, Department of City Planning, to Chairman and Members of CPC, September 28, 1926, PCPC Mins., September 29, 1926.

69. ACPC Mins., October 25, 1927.

70. ACPC Mins., May 1, 1928.

71. "Liberty Cross-Town Artery Deemed Imperative to Pittsburgh's Future," *Progress* (May 1929): 1.

72. "A Day Discloses over a Ten Year Record of Progress," *Progress* (January 1929): 1.

73. "Building Boom in Pittsburgh and Elsewhere," *Pittsburgh First*, June 20, 1925; "Plaza Building," *Greater Pittsburgh*, September 9, 1927; "New Building Will Be Miniature City," *Pittsburgh First*, March 1, 1924; "Pittsburgh's Building Boom the Most Remarkable in City History," *Greater Pittsburgh*, September 24, 1927.

74. For Better Traffic Committee quote, see PCPC Mins., May 2, 1928.

75. For bond issue, see ACPC Mins., June 1, 1928.

76. On the important city-development role of "community builders" in this period, see Weiss, *Rise of the Community Builders*; on 1920s suburbanization, see Kenneth Jackson, *The Crabgrass Frontier: The Suburbanization of the United States* (New York: Oxford University, 1985), 157–172.

77. The linking of the jail removal to the new County Office Building was broached as early as May 1924 in ACPC Mins., at which time the jail was referred to as "an admitted impediment to the eastwardly extension of the business district of the city." See ACPC Mins., May 2, 1924; see also brief history of jail removal issue in a communication from James Armstrong, Chair, and A. C. Gumbert and James Houlahan, members of Board of County Commissioners, to the Allegheny County Department of Planning, ACPC Mins., August 22, 1924.

78. Bigger in May 1925 favored the jail removal; see PCPC Mins., May 1, 1925, where Bigger expressed just such an opinion. On design issues, see ACPC Mins., October 8, 1926; on Roush, see ACPC Mins., March 6, 1925; and on the Jail Removal Committee, see "Report of Secretary of Allegheny County Planning Commission," June 1925, in ACPC Mins., June 30, 1925; see also ACPC Mins., May 6, 1925.

79. On the Pittsburgh chapter of the AIA's opposition to the jail removal, see ACPC Mins., November 20, 1925, and December 2, 1927; and PCPC Mins., November 18, 1925.

80. Town hall discussed in "Wharf Repairs and Flood Wall Approved," *Pittsburgh First*, March 27, 1926, 7; on PCPC views, see PCPC Mins., October 9, 1928; on Davison, see ACPC Mins., November 30, 1928.

81. See PCPC Mins., August 26, September 4, and October 9, 1928.

82. ACPC, Minutes of Special Meeting, November 30, 1929; sites discussed in detail at Special Meeting of ACPC, December 23, 1929, see ACPC Mins., December 23, 1929.

83. For the Dickey report, see "Arguments and Exhibits in Support of Locating Allegheny County Town Hall at Grant Street, 2nd Ave., Water Street, and P.R.R., Pittsburgh. Presented to the Planning Commission of Allegheny County by W. J. Strassburger representing Allegheny Town Hall Association," December 9, 1929, in ACPC Mins.; and "Report of Allegheny County Planning Commission, 1929," in ACPC Mins., December 23, 1929.

84. On the town hall issue and "sectional feeling," see Report of Allegheny County Planning Commission, 1929; on the town hall decision, see ACPC Mins., December 23, 1929. The ACPC also believed that the Nicola site, being close to Carnegie Hall and the Syria Mosque, reduced the needed seating capacity for a town hall. See ACPC Mins., December 27, 1929.

85. Director of Public Works, "An Analysis Based on Economic and Engineering Facts Concerning the Proposed New Town Hall of Allegheny County," January 17, 1930, in ACPC Mins., January 17, 1930.

CHAPTER 7. THE DEPRESSION, THE NEW DEAL,
AND PLANNING'S SURVIVAL

1. See "Pittsburgh Escapes Worst of Slump," *Greater Pittsburgh,* November 22, 1930, 1; and "Chamber and University Survey of Employment Conditions in Pittsburgh District," *Greater Pittsburgh,* December 27, 1930, 1.

2. "Steel Industry Meetings Adversity," *Greater Pittsburgh,* January 1932, 9. On the Great Depression, see, among other works, Jo Ann E. Argersinger, *Toward a New Deal in Baltimore: People and Government in the Great Depression* (Chapel Hill: University of North Carolina Press, 1988); Mark I. Gelfand, *A Nation of Cities: The Federal Government and Urban America, 1933–1965* (New York: Oxford University Press, 1975); and Robert S. McElvaine, *The Great Depression: America, 1929–1941* (New York: Times Books, 1993).

3. See data in *Greater Pittsburgh,* February 1933, 20.

4. On the Great Depression, breadlines, soup kitchens, and Father Cox, see Weber, *Don't Call Me Boss,* 47; and Stave, *New Deal and the Last Hurrah;* on Cox in particular, see Thomas H. Coode and John D. Petrarulo, "The Odyssey of Pittsburgh's Father Cox," *Western Pennsylvania Historical Magazine* 55 (July 1972): 217–38; and Sally Witt, "Father Cox and Pittsburgh in the 1940s," *Pittsburgh History* 80 (Summer 1997): 52–60.

5. See Stave, *New Deal and the Last Hurrah;* and Bodnar, Simon, and Weber, *Lives of Their Own,* 212–220; on the Welfare Fund, see *Greater Pittsburgh,* November 8, 1930, 2; on the Helping Hand Association, see *Pittsburgh Sun-Telegraph*, December 1 and December 3, 1930. See also Kenneth J. Heineman, *A Catholic New Deal: Religion and Reform in Depression Pittsburgh* (University Park: Pennsylvania State University Press, 1999).

6. See Angus O'Shea, "Pittsburgh's Helping Hand," *Greater Pittsburgh,* October 1931, 15; on "thrift gardens," see William P. Witherow, "The Thrift Garden Movement," *Greater Pittsburgh,* April 1932, 21.

7. *Pittsburgh Post-Gazette*, November 21, 1930; *Pittsburgh Sun-Telegraph*, December 1, 1930; *Greater Pittsburgh,* November 22, 1930, 3.

8. Charles Westerfield, Oakland Board of Trade, to C. V. Sharp, Secretary of Allied Boards of Trades, October 27, 1930, in Allied Boards of Trades Papers, Historical Society of Western Pennsylvania.

9. See Ralph Carr Fletcher and Katherine A. Biehl, "Trends in Direct Relief Expenditures in Allegheny County, 1920–1937," *Federato* 13, no. 5 (May 1938): 121; Frank Phillips, "$3,000,000 to Provide Jobs," *Greater Pittsburgh,* October 1931, 5; "The Pittsburgh Plan," *Greater Pittsburgh,* March 14, 1931, 1; "Back to Work Movement Starts," *Greater Pittsburgh,* February 28, 1931, 3. See also Joanna C. Colcord, *Emergency Work Relief: As Carried Out in Twenty-six American Communities, 1930–1931* (New York: Russell Sage, 1932).

10. See Stave, *New Deal and the Last Hurrah,* 110.

11. Municipal Planning Association Minutes, May 16, 1930, in Municipal Planning Association Papers, Carnegie Library, Pittsburgh (hereafter cited as MPA Mins.); Scott, *American City Planning,* 28.

12. See Muller and Bauman, "Olmsteds in Pittsburgh," 137.

13. See MPA Mins., May 16 and June 6, 1930, and February 1, November 29, April 11, and May 16, 1932.

14. MPA Mins., December 20, 1932, and April 19, 1933.

15. In response, Mayor Charles Klein included a tax cut in his 1931 budget; see *Pittsburgh Sun-Telegraph*, December 1, 1930.

16. See MPA Mins., May 16, 1930; on the topographic survey, see PCPC Mins., November 24, 1931.

17. Frederick Bigger, "Report to Board of Directors of Municipal Planning Association," November 29, 1932, in MPA Mins., November 29, 1932.

18. On "baby" golf, see *Pittsburgh Post-Gazette*, October 18, 1930; and Scott, *American City Planning*, 278; on zoning issues, including golf, see PCPC Mins., October 21, 1930, March 3, May 19, and November 24, 1931, and March 29, 1932.

19. Scott, *American City Planning*, 288. On the city council versus the CPC, see Board of Directors Minutes, Municipal Planning Association, June 2, 1931; PCPC Mins., March 17, 1931; Allied Boards of Trades Minutes (hereafter cited as ABT Mins.), April 29, 1931, in Allied Boards of Trades Records, 1922–1940 (hereafter cited as ABT Records), Historical Society of Western Pennsylvania; *Pittsburgh Post-Gazette*, October 18, 1930; and Bigger, "Report to Board of Directors."

20. PCPC Mins., February 23, 1932; see also John Ihlder, "What Census Shows in Pittsburgh," *Greater Pittsburgh*, June 14, 1930, 3.

21. Frank Duggan, "Traffic Here Takes 1,142 Lives," *Greater Pittsburgh*, March 24, 1930, 5; "Issue of Street and Highway Safety," *Greater Pittsburgh*, July 12, 1930, 2. On the *Major Street* plan, see PCPC Mins., April 27, 1930; see also "Plan of Saline, Monitor and Forward Avenue Connection: A Part of Major Street Plan," PCPC Mins., August 29, 1930. The Koppers, Grant, and the City-County Office buildings were completed in the closing years of the 1920s.

22. For an excellent discussion of the problems of downtown business in the 1930s, see Fogelson, *Downtown*, 218–248.

23. See Ihlder, "What Census Shows in Pittsburgh," 3; and Carroll Hill, "The Business District: The Major Street Plan, 1931, Department of City Planning Study Commissioned by City Council," PCPC Mins., August 7, 1932. On the important role of the Bureau of Public Works nationally, see Bruce B. Seely, *Building the American Highway System: Engineers as Policymakers* (Philadelphia: Temple University Press, 1987).

24. See "Issue of Street and Highway Safety," 5; Board of Directors Minutes, Municipal Planning Association, May 16, 1930; on ACEA labor, see PCPC Mins., February 23, 1932.

25. "Chamber Aids Waterfront Plans," *Greater Pittsburgh*, July 26 1930, 10; James Rae, "Improving Pittsburgh's Waterfronts," *Greater Pittsburgh*, August 28, 1930, 11.

26. ABT Mins., October 14, 1930. On Senator David Aiken Reed's bid to make the Point a national park, see Alberts, *Shaping of the Point*, 43; see also PCPC Mins., May 17, 1932; and PCPC, "Preliminary Analysis of the Present Problem of Street and Wharf Development on Downtown Waterfront (To General Plans Committee of City Planning Commission)," June 25, 1932, PCPC Mins., June 1932; on the model, see PCPC Mins., March 21, 1933.

27. See *Pittsburgh Post-Gazette*, November 11, 1932; and PCPC Mins., November 29, 1932.

28. Charles Lewis, "Housing: A Program for Administration," November 18, 1931, in Buhl Foundation Papers, Historical Society of Western Pennsylvania (hereafter cited as Buhl Papers).

29. Lewis, "Housing." On Stein, Wright, and Radburn, see Daniel Schaffer, *Garden Cities for America: The Radburn Experience* (Philadelphia: Temple University Press, 1982).

30. Frederick Bigger, "Project No. 1: Development of the Bingham Tract, Mt. Washington," October 15, 1931, Buhl Papers.

31. Lewis to Board of Managers of the Buhl Foundation, April 17, 1931, Buhl Papers.

32. Bigger to Holden, November 13, 1962, in correspondence between Arthur C. Holden and Frederick Bigger, 1960–1963, Holden Letters, Historical Society of Western Pennsylvania.

33. In May 1931 Bigger berated the ineffectiveness of the ACPC. He urged the county "to fill the three vacancies with men of our [CCCP] own of whom I should be one." See Bigger to Directors of the Municipal Planning Association," MPA Mins., May 2, 1931.

34. On the county rural highway work, see ACPC, "On the Proposed Rural Road System of the State," n.d., in ACPC Mins., April 2, 1931; and H. E. Kloss, "Traffic Problems in Pitts-

burgh," *Greater Pittsburgh,* February 1932, 23. One of the county highway projects in 1931 was the development a preliminary plan for a Penn-Lincoln, that is, Route 22/30, bypass of the city.

35. On the election of November 1932, see Weber, *Don't Call Me Boss,* 38–45; on Sansom's professionalism, see James B. Sansom, "Report of the Secretary, 1931," in ACPC Mins., 1930–1938.

36. See ACPC Reports, July 15, 1932.

37. "Transcript of Meeting," in ACPC Mins., August 14, 1932.

38. ACPC Mins., July 19 and July 20, 1932.

39. Bigger to Directors of MPA, in MPA Mins., May 2, 1931.

40. See PCPC Mins., May 7, May 17, and November 8, 1932.

41. "Subway Plan Untimely," *Greater Pittsburgh,* May 1932, 15.

42. On Vang and Snodgrass-Brown, see PCPC Mins., February 7, 1933; and ACPC Mins., December 1, 1932.

43. Thomas Fitzgerald, "Mass Transportation," *Greater Pittsburgh,* May 1932, 19–20; Thomas Fitzgerald, "Street Railway Transportation Future," *Greater Pittsburgh,* May 1934, 12.

44. For the last discussion of transit in the 1930s, and particularly the 1934 CWA transit study, see Winters Haydock to Harold Merrill, March 27, 1934, Box 846, Records of the National Resources Planning Board (hereafter cited as NRPB Records), Record Group (RG) 187, National Archives and Record Service (NARS), College Park, Md.

45. "Preliminary Analysis of Proposed High Level Bridge at Homestead," February 2, 1932, PCPC Mins.

46. On suburban development in the 1920s and 1930s, see Hoffman, "Plan of Quality," 141–181; see also "Memorandum of Hearing Held by U.S. Corps of Engineers in Council Chambers, November 1, 1932, RE: Proposed Improvement of Allegheny Wharf between Ninth and Stanwix Streets," PCPC Mins., November 2, 1932; on the expanding urban role of the federal government during the 1920s and 1930s, see Gelfand, *Nation of Cities;* and Janet Hutchinson, "Shaping Housing and Enhancing Consumption: Hoover's Interwar Housing Policy," in Bauman, Biles, and Szylvian, *From Tenements to the Taylor Homes,* 81–102.

47. On deslumming and the Better Homes movement, see John F. Bauman, *Public Housing, Race, and Renewal: Urban Planning in Philadelphia, 1920–1974* (Philadelphia: Temple University Press, 1987), 20–21; and Hutchinson, "Shaping Housing and Enhancing Consumption."

48. John Hancock, "The New Deal and American Planning: the 1930s," in Schaffer, *Two Centuries of American Planning,* 198; Scott, *American City Planning,* 295. On Hoover and the Great Depression, see Albert Romasco, *The Poverty of Abundance: Hoover, the Nation, the Depression* (New York: Oxford University Press, 1965); on Hoover and technocracy, see Alchon, *Invisible Hand,* 33; on Hoover and promoting local public works, see *Pittsburgh Sun-Telegraph,* December 2, 1930.

49. "Federal Wharf Plan Opposed," *Greater Pittsburgh,* August 1932, 14; see also ACPC Mins., May 4, 1933.

50. See Scott, *American City Planning;* Otis L. Graham, *Toward a Planned Society: From Roosevelt to Nixon* (New York: Oxford University Press, 1976), 20; and Edward K. Spann, *Designing Modern America: The Regional Planning Association of America and Its Members* (Columbus: Ohio State University Press, 1997), 130–174.

51. Scott, *American City Planning,* 300; Hancock, "New Deal and American City Planning," 190; Spann, *Designing Modern America,* 142; Graham, *Toward a Planned Society,* 52; Arthur M. Schlesinger Jr., *The Coming of the New Deal* (Boston: Houghton Mifflin, 1958).

52. Weber, *Don't Call Me Boss,* 51; Stave, *New Deal and the Last Hurrah,* 56–57.

53. See *Greater Pittsburgh,* July 1933, 1, 3; and *Greater Pittsburgh,* May 1933, 1.

54. "Federal Civil Works Administration of Pennsylvania: General Rules and Regula-

tions No. 1," November 20, 1933, in Civil Works Administration (CWA) State Series, Pa. Office Files, Box 43, November–December 1933, WPA Records, RG 69, NARS.

55. See Bonnie Fox Schwartz, *The Civil Works Administration, 1933–1934: The Business of Emergency Employment in the New Deal* (Princeton, N.J.: Princeton University Press, 1984); and Thomas Coode and John F. Bauman, *People, Poverty and Politics: Pennsylvania during the Great Depression* (Lewisburg, Pa.: Bucknell University Press, 1981).

56. Charles W. Eliot to Research Staff of National Planning Boards, February 3, 1934, in Central Office Files, 203.11, Box 880, NRPB Records, RG 187, NARS; Graham, *Toward a Planned Society,* 56.

57. On planning "as most practical activity," see National Planning Board (NPB) Circular, "Securing Results in City Planning," n.d. (ca. 1935), File 410, Box 840, NRPB Records, RG 187, NARS; and Charles Eliot to Robert Whitten, December 11, 1935, in Central Office Files, 203.11, Box 880, NRPB Records, RG 187, NARS; and Bettman to Ickes, October 23, 1933, in Central Office Files, 203.11, Box 880, NRPB Records, RG 187, NARS.

58. Scott, *American City Planning*, 304–308; PCPC Mins., April 19, 1933.

59. Scott, *American City Planning*, 283; John Millar to Joseph F. Tufts, June 24, 1933, in General Files, Ernest J. Bohn Papers, Ernest J. Bohn Collection, Department of Special Collections, Case Western Reserve University Library, Case Western Reserve University, Cleveland.

60. See "Planning and National Recovery: Planning Problems Presented at the 25th National Conference on City Planning," October 9–11, 1933, PCPC Mins.; Scott, *American City Planning,* 316; on Cleveland, see J. H. Millar to B. J. Newman, August 29, 1933, Box 7, General Files, National Conference on Slum Clearance, Bohn Papers. Bigger clearly accepted the distinction between social planning such as for housing and what he termed "city and regional planning," when he said, "the term 'community planning' appears to be a better term . . . when we are dealing with living parts of cities, with problems of community housing, and the like." Bigger, discussion of the paper by Burdell, "Securing the Benefits of Slum Elimination," 144.

61. See PCPC Mins., May 9, 1933; "Allegheny County Planning Commission Report for 1933," in ACPC Mins.; ACPC Mins., August 3 and September 6, 1933.

62. See ACPC Mins., August 2, 1934. Ickes ordained that PWA projects should be large-scale, costing over $25,000, and "self-liquidating." Self-liquidating meant that while the federal government contributed 60 percent or more of the capital costs of the project, communities had to fund the shortfall through taxes or fees, tolls being a logical choice for bridges and highways. Cities such as Pittsburgh found that provision onerous, and Ickes dropped it in 1934; see Gelfand, *Nation of Cities,* 46; and Argersinger, *New Deal in Baltimore*, 60–61. On Park Martin, see ACPC Mins., February 7, 1935.

63. Franklin Toker, *Fallingwater Rising: Frank Lloyd Wright, E. J. Kaufmann, and America's Most Extraordinary House* (New York: Alfred A. Knopf, 2003), 103–157; Frank Lloyd Wright, "Broadacres to Pittsburgh," *Pittsburgh Sun-Telegraph,* June 24, 1935; Scott, *American City Planning,* 336.

64. Park Martin file, Pennsylvania Room, Carnegie Library, Pittsburgh; see also Alberts, *Shaping of the Point,* 139–141.

65. See "PWA Grants $25,000,000 to County," *Greater Pittsburgh,* July 1934; on the tolls protest, see ABT Mins., June 27, 1934; and *Pittsburgh Post-Gazette,* October 9–10, 1934; on the Allegheny County Authority, see "Move to End Delay Is Made by Authority," *Pittsburgh Sun-Telegraph*, October 16, 1934; *Pittsburgh Press,* March 3, March 5, July 10, and July 11, 1935; *Pittsburgh Post-Gazette,* July 17, 1935; and ACPC Mins., August 2, 1934, and February 7, 1935.

66. See Eric Biddle, State CWA Administrator, to Harry Hopkins, December 12, 1933, CWA State Series, Pa. Office Files, Box 43, WPA Records, RG 69, NARS.

67. ACPC, "Response to National Planning Board Questions on CWA Assistance for Planning," January 8, 1934, File 412.11, Box 852, NRPB Records, RG 187, NARS.

68. During the 1930s, many New Dealers concluded that the age of industrialism had ended and that much of America's workforce of miners and steelworkers had become superfluous and therefore stranded in economic backwaters. This idea motivated the Greenbelt Town idea. On the idea of a "stranded" workforce in the Pittsburgh District, see John F. Bauman, "Orwell's Wigan Pier and Daisytown: The Mine Town as a Stranded Landscape," *Western Pennsylvania Historical Magazine* 67 (April 1984): 93–106.

69. On Pittsburgh and subsistence homesteads, see PCPC Mins., January 19, 1934; see also Scott, *American City Planning,* 336; Arnold, *New Deal in the Suburbs,* 47–49, 87; and Bauman and Muller, "Planning Technician and Urban Visionary," 124–153.

70. National Planning Board, Federal Emergency Administration of Public Works, "Questions on CWA, Department of City Planning," January 26, 1934, File 412.11, Box 852, RG 187, NARS.

71. Netting, *50 Years of the Western Pennsylvania Conservancy,* 65; Frederick Bigger, "City Planning Commission Progress Report, RE: CWA Program," December 18, 1933, in PCPC Mins; Pittsburgh Department of City Planning, "Report on the Master Plan for Recreation Sites and Service Areas," June, 11, 1935, Planning Department Library; see also PCPC Mins., March 5, 1935.

72. PCPC Mins., April 3, 1934. On the CWA and the WPA, see Schwartz, *Civil Works Administration, 1933–1934;* Argersinger, *New Deal in Baltimore;* and Roger Biles, *A New Deal for the American People* (De Kalb: Northern Illinois University Press, 1991); on Pittsburgh, see Charles M. Reppert, "The Federal Work Relief Program," *Greater Pittsburgh,* August 1935, 2.

73. PCPC Mins., August 30, 1935; Henry Hornbostel to James Griffen, January 22, 1934, in CWA State Series, Pa. M-Z, Box 45, WPA Records, RG 69, NARS. CWA Pittsburgh white-collar work projects (which required modest materials and equipment costs) extended well beyond the planning department projects. Under the umbrella of the Department of Health and the Mellon Institute, for example, CWA workers undertook a major air pollution study that had importance for post–World War II efforts to clean up the city's air. See Office of the Division of Federal Programs to D. L. Thompson, U.S. Public Health Service, February 12, 1934, CWA State Series, Pa. M-Z, Box 45, WPA Records, RG 69, NARS.

74. *Pittsburgh Press,* June 6, 1935, 21.

75. See Special Budget Committee to Chair and Members of City Planning Commission, August 21, 1933, PCPC Mins., August 21, 1933; and Special Budget Committee to Frederick Bigger, September 10, 1935, PCPC Mins.

76. *Greater Pittsburgh,* October 1934, 5.

77. Weber, *Don't Call Me Boss,* 113.

78. On the charge of Republicans getting jobs, see Katherine Godwin, Secretary, to Eric Biddle, Pennsylvania Relief Director, enclosing report to Harry Hopkins, January 1, 1934, CWA State Series, Pa., Box 43, WPA Records, RG 69, NARS; Memorandum, Arch Mandel to Aubrey Williams, March 19, 1934, concerning "Inquiry Regarding Partisan Politics in Pennsylvania," FERA Administrative Central Files, Pa. 401.3, Box 251, WPA Records, RG 69, NARS; Lorena Hickock to Harry Hopkins, August 24, 1935, Box 68, Harry L. Hopkins Papers, Franklin D. Roosevelt Library, Hyde Park, New York; Stave, *New Deal and the Last Hurrah,* 11; Weber, *Don't Call Me Boss,* 68

79. R. Templeton Smith, "Conditions in Coal Industry," *Greater Pittsburgh,* January 1934, 7; see also "$40,000,000 Expansion at J&L," *Greater Pittsburgh,* December 1935.

80. See "Spendthrift Congress Sets a $10 Billion Dollar Record," *Pittsburgh Sun-Telegraph,* August 23, 1935; and Paul Block, "The New Deal Failure: A Caustic Review of the Sins of Omission, and Commission, and Their Destructive Effects on Business Enterprise Throughout the County," *Greater Pittsburgh,* December 1935, 5.

81. Weber, *Don't Call Me Boss*, 41–43; Stave, *New Deal and the Last Hurrah.*

82. On McNair's eccentricities, see file of undated political cartoons, especially "Mother Earth" (ca. 1935–1936) by Cy Hungerford, and cartoons by Quin Hall and others in the *Pittsburgh Sun-Telegraph* and *Post-Gazette,* in Archives of Industrial Society, University of Pittsburgh. There was one exception to McNair's obstructionism. Reflecting his single-taxer's affinity for land reform, McNair repressed his antipathy for the New Deal just long enough to embrace federal slum clearance and housing programs. He endorsed council-man George Evans's campaign—in vain until 1938—to secure federal aid for Hill District renewal. For McNair and the slum clearance issue, see George Evans to John M. Carmody, April 18, 1934, CWA State Series, Pa., Box 44, Projects, WPA Records, RG 69, NARS.

83. On McNair and his adverse impact on planning, see "Life of William Nisely Mc-Nair," n.d., McNair Papers, Archives of Industrial Society, University of Pittsburgh; on Mc-Nair's affinity for the single tax, see Walter Davenport, "Mayor's Day In," *Collier's,* April 21, 1934, 12; and "Mayor McNair's Budget," *Pittsburgh Post-Gazette,* October 12, 1934; on the single tax sympathies of the RPAA (Bigger himself may have had Georgian tendencies), see Spann, *Designing Modern America,* 24–36; on Lawrence and McNair, see Weber, *Don't Call Me Boss,* 89–125; on McNair and the WPA, see Eric Biddle to Hopkins, March 11, 1935, CWA State Series, Pa., Box 45, Work Relief, WPA Records, RG 69, NARS; on planning, see PCPC Mins., August 23, 1935; on terminating the Traffic Bureau, see "Firing Spree Is Started by Mayor McNair," *Pittsburgh Post-Gazette,* October 10, 1934; on suspended WPA projects, see PCPC Mins., July 30 and February 19, 1935; on the city council's battle with McNair, see City of Pittsburgh, *Municipal Records* (August 14, 1935–November 18, 1935); and "Jones Out-wits McNair on WPA Funds," *Pittsburgh Sun-Telegraph,* September 3, 1935.

84. On waterfront problems and planning, see "Needs of Waterfront Project Empha-sized," *Greater Pittsburgh,* December 1935, 7; PCPC Mins., September 26, 1933; and ACPC Mins., November 5, 1931.

85. The Allegheny County commissioners sent the ACPC a notification of their purchase of the Wabash properties. The ACPC then forwarded a "resolution" to the commissioners opposing the idea; see ACPC Mins., December 31, 1931. This narrative of the Wabash deal is based on the "Report of Discussion on Communication of the Board of County Commis-sioners Relative to the Wabash Bridge and Tunnel Project," November 1931, in ACPC Mins., 1930–1938. Finally, in 2003 the conversion of the Wabash Tunnel into a vehicular artery, this time for buses and HOVs (high-occupancy vehicles), was nearing completion.

86. ACPC, Minutes of Special Meeting, December 24, 1931.

87. W. C. Rice to County Planning Commission, December 22, 1931; a complete outline of city planning's objections to the Wabash project is found in ACPC Mins., December 22, 1931; see also PCPC Mins., December 22, 1931. The MPA opposed the Wabash project, see MPA Mins., February 1, 1934; and "Wabash Project Opposed," *Progress* (December 1931): 1. On suburban backing for the Wabash plan, see ACPC Mins., December 31, 1931. Babcock especially emphasized the Liberty Tubes congestion, arguing that if the tubes were con-gested now, amid the Great Depression, what would they be like in prosperity? See ACPC Mins., December 24, 1931.

88. ACPC Mins., January 4 and June 7, 1934.

89. ACPC Mins., May 1, 1933.

90. ACPC Mins., January 4, 1934.

91. *Pittsburgh Sun-Telegraph,* February 1, 1935; PCPC Mins., June 11 and August 23, 1935. On the CPC's order not to build the Fort Duquesne Bridge, see PCPC Mins., Sep-tember 10, 1935. The Bouquet's blockhouse had long been the center of historical interest. In the 1890s the Pennsylvania Railroad attempted to raze the eighteenth-century bastion. The Pittsburgh Chapter of the Daughters of the American Revolution (DAR) protested the planned demolition, and in 1894 Mary Schenley, a DAR member, purchased the structure

and deeded it to the Fort Pitt Society, a division of the Pittsburgh Chapter; see Alberts, *Shaping of the Point,* 168

92. The history of the Exposition Society is laid out in "Preliminary Memorandum 8–30–33—Information Requested Re Exposition Building at Point, Legal Status," PCPC Mins., August 30, 1933; see also PCPC Mins., April 20, 1932, and January 19, 1934.

93. The CPC investigated the Exposition Society's proposal before 1934 and made its objections known; see "Staff Report to the City Planning Commission, RE: Suggestions Affecting 'The Point,' An Exposition and Recreation Building," October 25, 1933, PCPC Mins.

94. See PCPC Mins., February 20, 1934, which contain "Staff Report RE: Proposed Ordinance February 18, 1934, for Exposition Hall."

95. PCPC Mins., December 4, 1934.

CHAPTER 8. URBAN CRISIS AND THE ADVENT OF RENAISSANCEMANSHIP

1. See "The Great Flood," *Greater Pittsburgh,* March 1936, 3; and Weber, *Don't Call Me Boss,* 199–201.

2. "Almost Incredible Gain," *Greater Pittsburgh,* January 1936, 39; "Steel Stages Remarkable Comeback," *Greater Pittsburgh,* January 1937, 11–13; "Irwin Optimistic on Steel: Huge New Plant Here,' *Greater Pittsburgh,* January 1937, 1; "Geography of Steel's Pittsburgh Comeback," *Greater Pittsburgh,* May 1937.

3. Weber, *Don't Call Me Boss,* 201; Oliver Kiely and Brian Kissler, "Industrial Recovery and Social Consequence: Pittsburgh, 1939–1941" (Senior seminar paper, California University of Pennsylvania, April 1996), 12.

4. John M. Barry, *Rising Tide: The Great Mississippi Flood of 1927 and How It Changed America* (New York: Simon and Schuster, 1997), observes that Pittsburgh suffered from the 1927 flood, but hardly as seriously as it would in 1936. The 1927 flood, according to Barry, helped established the federal government's responsibility for flood control. Jeanne R. Lowe, in *Cities in a Race with Time: Progress and Poverty in America's Renewing Cities* (New York: Random House, 1967), contends that the 1936 flood engendered the Pittsburgh Renaissance.

5. See "$50,000,000 Bond Issued," *Greater Pittsburgh,* August 1937; PCPC Mins., June 8, 1937; William T. Rogers, "Flood Control Is on the Way," *Greater Pittsburgh,* August 1936, 17; William T. Rogers, "Flood Control Ready to Start," *Greater Pittsburgh,* July 1937, 17; Smith, "Politics of Pittsburgh Flood Control: Part I," 5–24; and Roland M. Smith, "The Politics of Pittsburgh Flood Control: Part II, 1936–1960," *Pennsylvania History* 44, no. 1 (1977): 3–24.

6. Scott, *American City Planning,* 342–359.

7. Lewis Mumford to Charles Eliot, July 18, 1937, Box 840, Folder 410, National Resources Planning Board (NRPB) Records, RG 187, National Archives and Records Administration, Silver Spring, Md. (hereafter cited as NRPB Records, RG 187, NARS).

8. NRC studies also lamented the "continued passivity and purely nominal existence of many commissions. . . . Many city and county planning commissions are run by a busy engineer or manager who . . . cannot give planning the attention which is necessary." See NRC Circular X (May 15, 1937) on "Status of City and County Planning in the United States," Box 840, Folder 410, NRPB Records, RG 187, NARS.

9. NRC, "Survey of City and County Planning and Zoning, Pittsburgh, Pennsylvania," July 17, 1936, Box 862, Folder Pa. 412.21, NRPB Records, RG 187, NARS.

10. Harold Merrill to Carrol V. Hill August 14, 1937; Merrill to Cornell V. Scully, June 19, 1937, Box 846, Folder 8, NRPB Records, RG 187, NARS.

11. Frederick Bigger, "personal record memorandum," May 5, 1936, Pittsburgh Regional Planning Association Minutes (hereafter cited as PRPA Mins.), Folder 83, in Pittsburgh

Regional Planning Association Records, Carnegie Library, Pittsburgh (hereafter cited as PRPA Records).

12. Pittsburgh Regional Planning Association By-Laws, PRPA Mins., February 1, 1938, Folder 83, PRPA Records; see also "Record of Interim Action of Board of Directors of MPA," October 13, 1936, Box 83, PRPA Records; and MPA Director's Meeting Minutes, April 27, 1937, Folder 83, PRPA Records.

13. See Arnold, *New Deal in the Suburbs;* Bauman and Muller, "Planning Technician as Urban Visionary," 124–153; and MPA Mins., January 12, 1937, Folder 83, PRPA Papers.

14. MPA Mins., January 12, 1937, Folder 83, PRPA Records; "Pittsburgh, State and National Planning Progress," *Bulletin Index,* August 11, 1940.

15. Weber, *Don't Call Me Boss;* see also Newspaper Clipping File, McNair, Carnegie Library, Pittsburgh.

16. Carrol V. Hill left the CPC in 1939 to join the HACP as a technical assistant; see Frederick Bigger, Special Committee on 1939 Budget, PCPC Mins., December 20, 1938. See also Housing Authority of the City of Pittsburgh, *The First Seven Years: A Report of the Housing Authority of the City of Pittsburgh for the Years 1937–1944* (Pittsburgh: Housing Authority of the City of Pittsburgh, 1944). On housing and planning, see also Scott, *American City Planning,* 346–347.

17. PRPA Mins., January 13, 1939, PRPA Records; Peter J. DeMuth, Member of Congress, to Captain G. E. Textor, WPA, January 13, 1938, Central Files, SS 651.221, Box 2434, WPA Records, RG 69, NARS. On the New York "approach," see Joel Schwartz, *The New York Approach: Robert Moses, Urban Liberals, and Redevelopment in the Inner City* (Columbus: Ohio State University Press, 1993). On emulating New York, see Alexander Hoffman, "Why They Built Pruitt-Igoe," in Bauman, Biles, and Szylvian, *From Tenements to the Taylor Homes,* 180–206.

18. Director of Public Works Roessing tried to find projects that fit into the city budget, such as storm water and drainage improvements. See John Croak to F. C. Harrington, WPA Administrator, February 5, 1938, WPA Central Files, PA 651.106, Box 2432, WPA Records, RG 69, NARS. On air pollution studies, see reference to WPA "Study of Sootfall and Air Pollution," in ABT Circular October 25, 1939, ABT Mins., Box 1, Folder 4, ABT Records.

19. Many cities jealously emulated New York City's success in securing public works; see Hoffman, "Why They Built Pruitt-Igoe." On Griswold and the importance of the WPA in developing Pittsburgh recreation, see Griswold's talk before the ABT, where he called the city "last among cities of the same population in acreage of parks"; ABT Mins., October 10, 1937, Box 1, Folder 3, ABT Records; and "Department of City Planning Conference with Special Committee of Pittsburgh Board of Education re: Playground Development," PCPC Mins., May 5, 1936; on the WPA and recreation sites, see Wallace Richards Log, July 7, 1938, PRPA Mins., Folder 83, PRPA Records (hereafter cited as WR Log); "400 Jobs Begin at Schenley Park," *Pittsburgh Post-Gazette,* February 21, 1938; "Park Project to Make Work for 1000s," *Pittsburgh Press,* March 4, 1938, News Clip File, Division of Information (DOI), Box 149, WPA Records, RG 69, NARS.

20. See "The WPA in Allegheny County from the Beginning of the Program to June 1938. Report of the Community Improvement Appraisal" (1938), DOI, Box 35, WPA Records, RG 69, NARS.

21. Ibid.; ACPC, "Annual Report" (1936–1937) in Allegheny County Planning Commission Library; F. B. Maltby to E. C. Smith, Chief Regional Engineer, memorandum on "Street Work in Allegheny County," May 14, 1938, WPA Central Files, State Series, Pa. 651.104, Box 2430, WPA Records, RG 69, NARS. See also WPA Photographs, in Photo Archives of the Archives of Industrial Society, University of Pittsburgh.

22. See PCPC Mins., May 18, 1937, and May 10, 1938.

23. "'Give or Else' Guffey Edict to Officeholders," *Philadelphia Inquirer,* August 10, 1938,

DOI, Box 149, WPA Records, RG 69, NARS; see David Lawrence to Hon. William C. Bullitt, May 13, 1938, about the WPA being used by J. Banks Hudson and the Wilson-Kennedy ticket to "beat the [pro-FDR-Earle-Guffey] ticket to a pulp in Pennsylvania," in Box 36, Hopkins Papers; and George H. Earle, Governor, to Hon. Harry Hopkins, April 9, 1938, telegram, relative to WPA being used "more actively than ever to harm Democratic organization," CWA State Series, Pa., Box 610, WPA Records, RG 69, NARS.

24. "The Golden Triangle: Will It Be Allowed to Deteriorate before a Correct Plan Is Adopted?" *Progress* (November 1937): 4.

25. Alberts, *Shaping of the Point;* "City Target of Architect," *Pittsburgh Post-Gazette,* July 1, 1935, quoted in Richard L. Cleary, *Merchant Prince and Master Builder: Edgar J. Kaufmann and Frank Lloyd Wright* (Seattle: University of Washington Press, 1999), 54. For an interesting interpretation linking Carnegie, Frick, and Gould to the history of downtown real estate, see the provocative ideas of "a Pittsburgh Real Estate man," in John H. O'Donnell, "A Golden-Triangle Plan," *Greater Pittsburgh,* August 1938, 4.

26. See ABT Mins., June 29, 1938, Box 1, Folder 3, ABT Records.

27. This is the present site of the Point Bridge. On the Ferry (Stanwix) Street site, see PCPC Mins., October 20, 1936; on Bigger and the PCPC position on downtown, see Bigger to Heinz, Braun, Mudge, Arensburg, Ketchum, Memorandum, November 19, 1936, PRPA Mins., Box 83, PRPA Records; most important, see also "General Statement RE: Downtown District and Its Planning Problems," May 6, 1937, PCPC Mins., May 6, 1937. On PRPA views, especially those articulated by the organization's president Howard Heinz, see "Master Regional Plan," *Greater Pittsburgh,* June 1938, 19. On the centrality of the downtown, see Fogelson, *Downtown;* and Isenberg, *Downtown America.*

28. On the Exposition Hall seeming to be "assured," see P. M. Chamberlain, "Downtown Businessmen's Association's Program," *Greater Pittsburgh,* March 1937, 4; Staff of Planning Commission, "Report RE: Proposed Plans for the Development of the Wabash Properties for Vehicular Traffic and the Improvement of the Riverfront Roadways as Submitted by the LDBMA," PCPC Mins., November 17, 1936; and Frederick Bigger's personal memorandum, February 1, 1937, PCPC Mins., February 1, 1937.

29. Bigger to Heinz, Braun, Mudge, Arensburg, and Ketchum, Memorandum, November 19, 1936; PCPC Mins., November 19, 1936.

30. In tonnage, the Pittsburgh District was, by the 1920s, and so remains today, a port for bulk goods such as coal, sand, and gravel; the day of the Monongahela wharf as a transfer point for merchandise had long passed by 1930 and never returned. See Edward K. Muller, "River City," in Tarr, *Devastation and Renewal.*

31. See Warren Susman, *Culture as History: The Transformation of American Society in the Twentieth Century* (Washington, D.C.: Smithsonian Institution Press, 2003); William J. Murtagh, *Keeping Time: The History and Theory of Historic Preservation in America,* rev. ed. (New York: John Wiley, 1997); and Michael Kamen, *Mystic Chords of Memory: The Transformation of Tradition in American Culture* (New York: Alfred A. Knopf, 1991).

32. "Historic Park Plans at Point Move Ahead," *Pittsburgh Post-Gazette,* January 28, 1938, clipping, Box 124, PRPA Records.

33. Frank Harper, "Finding Fort Pitt for Point Park," *Greater Pittsburgh,* February 1939, 12; "Point Park Project Makes Definite Progress," *Pittsburgh Post-Gazette,* March 30, 1938, clipping, Folder 83, PRPA Records.

34. "Expect Completion Turnpike Financing within Ten Days," *Pennsylvania Construction Digest,* August 31, 1938, Box 153, PRPA Records.

35. On the FAS, see Seely, *Building the American Highway System.* Funding for the Penn-Lincoln bypass project was also available because of the 1936 flood; see R. R. Tomes, Bureau of Public Roads, to C. T. Swain, District Engineer of Bureau of Public Roads, March 21, 1938, Federal Aid System (FAS) 481 Correspondence, Pennsylvania, January–July, Folder

2858, RG 30, Bureau of Public Roads Papers, National Archives and Records Administration (hereafter cited as BPR Papers, NARS). From 1919 into the 1950s Thomas H. McDonald, who headed the federal Bureau of Public Roads, was an ardent supporter of planning. See Raymond Mohl, "Ike and the Interstates: Creeping toward Comprehensive Planning," *Journal of Planning History* 2, no. 3 (August 2003): 237–263. On the Lincoln Highway, see also Brian Butko, "Still a Grand View: The Ship Hotel and the Lincoln Highway," *Pittsburgh History* 72 (Fall 1989): 140–147.

36. ACPC, Annual Report (1937), Allegheny County Planning Commission Library.

37. This alternate route was very similar to the route touted by Mrs. Corey Yost, who wrote countless letters to the BPR pressing her case for a Penn-Lincoln bypass that would run south of Pittsburgh through Braddock and Homestead and thus serve as a critical defense highway route in time of war. See the extensive Corey Yost correspondence in FAS Pa., RG 30, BPR Papers, NARS.

38. ACPC, Annual Report (1937). This is almost the present alignment of the Penn-Lincoln bypass, now called Parkway East. On routes, see William Penn Highway/Pitt Parkway, WR Log, June 11, 1938, Folder 263, PRPA Papers; see also Pennsylvania Highway Department Map, 481 Correspondence, FAS Pa, Folder 2858, RG 30, BPR Papers, NARS.

39. See A. E. McClure, Senior Highway Engineer, to Thomas McDonald, August 24, 1939, 481 Correspondence, FAS Pa., Folder 2858, RG 30, BPR Papers, NARS; see also PRPA, Bulletin No. 2, "William Penn Highway Route," March 23, 1938, Folder 263, PRPA Papers; and Memorandum for PRPA [probably by Frederick Bigger] to Howard Heinz, Arthur Braun, and Joseph Dilworth, summarizing report of conference held June 21, 1938, between county commissioners and the PRPA, Folder 263, PRPA Papers. Park Martin's absence from the meeting became an issue. On opposition to elevated structures, see PCPC Mins., May 24 and May 25, 1938.

40. On Scully, the CPC, and Pittsburgh as a critical city, see Scully to PCPC, July 13, 1939, PCPC Mins., July 13, 1939; and A. E. McClure to "My Dear McDonald," August 24, 1939, 481 Correspondence, FAS Pa., Box 2858, RG 30, BPR Papers, NARS.

41. Frank L. Duggan, "Pittsburgh's Tax Situation," *Greater Pittsburgh,* December 1938, 4. On the progrowth coalition, see John Mollenkopf, *The Contested City* (Princeton, N.J.: Princeton University Press, 1983).

42. WR Log, June 9, 1938, Folder 83, PRPA Records.

43. Bigger to President and Members of Council, January 29, 1938, in MPA Board Mins., Folder 83, PRPA Records; "East-West By-Pass," PRPA Mins., April 25, 1938, Folder 83, PRPA Records; PRPA Mins., January 13, 1939; see also WR Log, 1938 passim, Folder 83, PRPA Records.

44. See Fred Triggs, "City Planning Progress, 1939," *Greater Pittsburgh,* January 1939, 14; on the Council of Organization, see WR Log, April 4, 1938, PRPA Records; PRPA Mins., February 1, 1938; and MPA Executive Mins., May 5, 1938, all in Folder 83, PRPA Records.

45. WR Log, August 18, 1938, Folder 83, PRPA Records; PCPC Mins., June 28, 1938.

46. PCPC Mins., September 13, 1938.

47. WR Log, September 17, 1938, Folder 83, PRPA Records. On the war scare, see WR Log, September 21, 1938, Folder 83, PRPA Records; on Scully and Lawrence, see WR Log, October 10, 1938, Folder 83, PRPA Records.

48. ACPC Mins., October 6, 1938.

49. PCPC Mins., October 4 and October 25, 1938; for quote, see PCPC Mins., October 11, 1938.

50. PCPC Mins., October 4, 1938.

51. ACPC Mins., November 3, 1938.

52. Ibid.

53. WR Log, December 1, 1938, Folder 83, PRPA Records.

54. Indeed, it was after World War II. See WR Log, December 7, 1938, Folder 83, PRPA Records.

55. "Way Cleared for Wharf Boulevard," *Pittsburgh Post-Gazette,* December 2, 1938; "Cooperation at Last," *Pittsburgh Sun-Telegraph,* December 2, 1938.

56. On the charter, see Robert Olsen in *Bulletin Index,* March 16, 1939; see also "A Beneficial Plan," *Pittsburgh Sun-Telegraph,* March 23, 1939; "New Metropolitan Charter Is Submitted," *Pittsburgh Post-Gazette,* March 22, 1939; "Metropolitan Plan Has Joker Concealed in Deck," *Hilltown Record,* March 31, 1939; and "Plan to Submit Metro Plan to Session Dropped," *Pittsburgh Post-Gazette,* April 19, 1939.

57. "Pittsburgh Begins to Re-Build," *Progress* (January 1939): 1.

58. WR Log, October 28, 1938, Folder 83, PRPA Records.

59. Robert Moses, typescript essay, ca. 1938–1939, in Robert Moses Papers, New York Public Library Special Collections, New York (hereafter cited as RMP). On Moses, see Schwartz, *New York Approach;* and Robert Caro, *The Power Broker: Robert Moses and the Fall of New York* (New York: Alfred A. Knopf, 1974).

60. Seely, *Building the American Highway System,* 170–171.

61. Robert Moses to Howard Heinz, May 6, 1939, RMP.

62. "Planning for a Greater Pittsburgh," *Bulletin Index,* November 2, 1939.

63. Robert Moses to Howard Heinz, August 13, 1939, RMP.

64. Howard Heinz to Robert Moses, August 17, 1939, RMP.

65. Moses informed his boss, Fiorello La Guardia, on August 2 that he had arranged to "review findings on traffic arterial improvements in Pittsburgh and shall take a ten day leave without pay." See Robert Moses to Fiorello La Guardia, August 2, 1939, RMP; Howard Heinz to Robert Moses, August 4, 1939, RMP; see also WR Log, August 15 and August 16, 1939, Folder 83, PRPA Records; "Pittsburgh City Traffic Survey Gets Under Way," *Pittsburgh Post-Gazette*, August 16, 1939.

66. WR Log, "Moses Survey Excerpts," November 16, 1939, PRPA Records.

67. WR Log, "Moses Survey Excerpts," September 9, 1939, PRPA Records. Pittsburgh shared the concern about suburban retail competition with most other large cities. See Fogelson, *Downtown,* 218–248.

68. See Robert Moses to Howard Heinz, September 5, 1939, RMP; Wallace Richards, "Moses Survey Excerpts," September 22, 1939, PRPA Records.

69. Wallace Richards, "Moses Survey Excerpts," September 21, 1939, PRPA Records.

70. Wallace Richards, "Moses Survey Excerpts," September 28, 1939, PRPA Records.

71. Wallace Richards, "Moses Survey Excerpts," October 19, 1939, PRPA Records.

72. Moses was upset with Heinz in November 1939 because Heinz had not personally acknowledged receipt of an advance copy of his report. Moses stated that he would not have made the changes if Heinz had asked; see WR Log, "Moses Survey Excerpts," October 30 and November 2, 1939, PRPA Records.

73. Wallace Richards, "Moses Survey Excerpts," November 15, 1939, PRPA Records.

74. Robert Moses, *Arterial Plan for Pittsburgh: Prepared for the Pittsburgh Regional Planning Association* (Pittsburgh: Pittsburgh Regional Planning Association, November 1939), 1–8.

75. Ibid., 13.

76. On tolls, see ABT Mins., January 3, 1940, Box 1, Folder 4, ABT Records.

77. "Well Received," *Pittsburgh Press,* November 20, 1939.

78. Howard Heinz to Charles Lewis, January 16, 1940, "Moses Survey," Folder 78, PRPA Records. The Allied Boards of Trades found Moses's report similar to other surveys; however, as noted, it rejected the use of tolls and his call to remove trolleys from the city streets. See "Resolution on a Recent Traffic Survey of Pittsburgh by New York City Traffic Experts

and Park Commissioner Robert Moses," n.d. (ca. 1940), ABT Mins., Box 1, Folder 4, ABT Records.

79. See PCPC Mins., November 21, 1939; "Planning for a Greater Pittsburgh"; "Pittsburgh's Birthday," *Pittsburgh Sun-Telegraph*, November 28, 1939; and Howard Heinz to Robert Moses, November 14, 1939, RMP.

80. Park H. Martin, Planning Engineer, "Review of Robert Moses' *Arterial Plan for Pittsburgh*," December 7, 1939, ACPC Mins.; see also "Report of Allegheny County Planning Commission, 1939," in ACPC Mins. Moses received and filed all of the Pittsburgh reactions to his report. See A. E. Howland to Moses, December 11, 1939, conveying news clipping from the *Pittsburgh Press*, December 8, 1939, RMP. See "Planning Commission Backs Traffic Plan," *Pittsburgh Press*, December 8, 1939; and *Pittsburgh Post-Gazette*, December 9, 1939.

81. "Expert Heads City Planning," *Pittsburgh Post-Gazette*, July 10, 1940; "Former Aide of Moses Named to Planning Post," *Pittsburgh Sun-Telegraph*, July 9, 1940. On Bigger's resignation, see PRPA Mins., May 31, 1940, PRPA Records; "Fred Bigger Resigns as Planning Consultant," *Pittsburgh Sun-Telegraph*, May 8, 1940; and "Planning Progress," *Bulletin Index*, July 11, 1940. See also Alberts, *Shaping of the Point*, 55.

82. Frederick Bigger to Cornelius Scully, December 12, 1939, in PCPC Mins; "City Planning Board's Report to Mayor Scully on Moses Traffic Survey," *Pittsburgh Sun-Telegraph*, December 17, 1939.

83. "Face Lifting," *Bulletin Index*, October 26, 1939; "Important Move to Solve Triangle Problem," *Pittsburgh Post-Gazette*, October 26, 1939; Alberts, *Shaping of the Point*, 55.

84. "Planning for a Greater Pittsburgh."

85. William S. Chapin to Robert Moses, July 19, 1940, RMP; Cornelius Scully, "A Program for Pittsburgh," *Greater Pittsburgh*, February 1940, 16.

86. Evidence of the relationship between the Moses report and an "action agenda" can be discerned from the following: PRPA Mins., November 29, 1939, PRPA Records; Howard Heinz to Robert Moses, November 14, 1939, RMP; and WR Log, "Moses Survey Excerpts," November 16–November 20, 1939, PRPA Records.

87. William Chapin, "Talk at William Penn Hotel," ca. October 8, 1940, PRPA Mins., October 8, 1940, PRPA Records. Chapin constantly emphasized the importance of "converting programs into construction contracts"; see William Chapin to Thomas McDonald of PRA, June 7, 1941, RG 30, 481 Correspondence, FAS Pa. 1941, Box 2856, PBR Papers.

88. "Cities in Crisis," *Progress* (November 1941): 1.

89. See Wallace Richards to Ralph Watkins of the NRPB, September 8, 1941, RG 30, 481 Correspondence, FAS Pa., Box 2856; and "Metropolitan Program: Progress and Activity, 1941–1945," RG 187, Box 846, E8, P150, NRPB. On Heinz's death, see "Howard Heinz 63, Food Firm Head, Civic Leader, Dies," *Pittsburgh Press*, February 11, 1941; and PRPA Mins., March 3, 1941, PRPA Records.

90. Details of the Menden study and Heinz's role can be found in WR Log and the PRPA Mins. covering the period June 5, 1940, to September 1941, in PRPA Records. On affronted planning commissions, see Executive Committee Meeting Minutes, PRPA Mins., January 12, 1942, PRPA Records. Funds for the study came from Buhl ($15,000), Edgar J. Kaufmann's Retail Merchants Association ($10,000), and the Philadelphia Company, the holding company for Pittsburgh Railways, which expressed "perfect willingness to turn over all its streetcar business to one well-organized independent company" ($10,000). Menden's fee was $15,000, and the cost of the study was $35,000. See "City-County Traffic Flow to Be Studied," *Pittsburgh Post-Gazette*, September 19, 1940; Howard Heinz to W. S. Menden, December 12, 1939, and September 23, 1940, Folder 83, PRPA Papers; "Memorandum on Conversation with Mr. Wallace Richards Concerning Menden Traffic Survey," October 2, 1940, General Files, Transportation and Zoning, Buhl Papers; see also the Allegheny Conference

of Community Development, "Report of Committee on Mass Transit," April 1947, in Pittsburgh Planning Department Library.

91. ACPC Mins., February 1 and February 21, 1940; "Plan Studied for Duquesne Way Project," *Pittsburgh Post-Gazette*, January 15, 1940.

92. ACPC Mins., March 7, 1940.

93. "Project Progress," *Progress* (November 1941): 3; ACPC Mins., April 3, 1941; PCPC Mins., February 25, 1941.

94. See "Misunderstandings Relative to Immediate Steps Which Should be Taken to Advance Design and Construction of Pitt Parkway (22–30 Relocation)," WR Log, June 21, 1941, Folder 264, PRPA Records; see also WR Log, April 25, 1940, Folder 263, PRPA Records.

95. See Willard Buente to War Department, Adjutant General's Office, July 1, 1940, 481 Correspondence, FAS Pa., March–December 1940, Box 2857, RG 30, BPR Papers, NARS. Wallace Richards and William Chapin took Moses and Howland on a tour of the new Pennsylvania Turnpike. According to Richards, Moses called the "Military Highway idea a little heavy." WR Log, August 15, 1940, Folder 265, PRPA Records.

96. See T. C. Frame, Chief Engineer, PRA, to H. R. Leland, Senior Highway Engineer, PRPA, in Harrisburg, December 18, 1940, WR Log, Folder 263, PRPA Records; and MacDonald to Hughes, November 18, 1940, 481 Correspondence, FAS Pa. March–December 1940, Box 2857, RG 30, BPR Papers, NARS.

97. PRPA Mins., December 3, 1941, PRPA Records; see also WR Log, August 20, 1940, Folder 187, PRPA Records; and Mr. Toms to Commissioner Thomas McDonald, October 24, 1940, 481 Correspondence, FAS Pa., March–December 1940, Box 2857, RG 30, BPR Papers, NARS. In support of the Federal Aid System, the BPR made federal grants to state highway departments.

98. See "Super Parkway Gets Approval as Post-War Project," *Pittsburgh Press,* October 1,1942; and "Minutes of Pitt Parkway Meeting, April 12, 1942," WR Log, Folder 264, PRPA Records; see also PRPA Mins., May 26, 1942, PRPA Records; and Wallace Richards to R. K. Mellon, October 2, 1942, WR Log, Folder 264, PRPA Records.

99. *Progress* in 1939 was edited by Bigger and reflected his ideas. In an editorial, "The Point Problem," *Progress* (January 1939): 1, Bigger stressed the primacy of traffic, but also the importance of a park.

100. Moses tried to use his influence to get the Andrew Mellon Trust to fund the building of a memorial park. He believed that this was an appropriate use of the Mellon funds. This was the basis for what would be Mellon Square. See R. P. McNulty to Mrs David K. E. Bruce, September 19, 1939, RMP.

101. "WPA Workers to Dig the Fort Pitt Foundations," *Pittsburgh Post-Gazette*, December 11, 1941. See Wesley L. Bliss, "Report of the Point Park Commission" (1942), Historical Society of Western Pennsylvania. The Point Park Commission consisted of City Councilman Fred W. Weir, who chaired the commission; Willard Buente, chief engineer of the City Planning Department; Congressman Herman Eberharter; County Commissioner John Kane; Frank Roessing of Public Works; Herbert L. Spencer, president of the Pennsylvania College of Women; and Mayor Cornelius Scully.

102. "Excavations at Fort Pitt Blast Popular Traditions." *Pittsburgh Post-Gazette*, n.d., Folder 124, PRPA Records; "Point Park Hailed by U.S. Official," *Pittsburgh Sun-Telegraph*, March 19, 1942; W. D. Bliss, "Report of the Point Park Commission," 1942; Alberts, *Shaping of the Point*, 44.

103. "Pittsburgh to Spend $2,000,000 to Improve Playgrounds and Parks," *Progress* (October 1938): 1; PCPC Mins., November 15, 1938, and November 19, 1940; "City's Efficient Director of Public Works Gives Children Better Play Sites," *Pittsburgh Post-Gazette*, July 15, 1939.

104. See Frederick Bigger to Ernest J. Bohn, January 6, 1942, Bohn Papers.

105. On housing and planning, 1937–1942, see PCPC Mins., October 1, 1940, July 8 and December 2, 1941, and January 27, 1942. Carroll Hill, chief engineer of City Planning, became technical director of the HACP; see PCPC Mins., October 3, 1939; see also "Slum Housing Falls before Federal Units," *Pittsburgh Post-Gazette,* October 25, 1940. On Bigger and housing, see "Man of the Year," *Bulletin Index,* January 4, 1940; on early housing projects, see John F. Bauman, "History and Significance of Housing Authority Projects: PA–1–2 and PA–1–8, and PA–1–3," submitted to Housing Authority of City of Pittsburgh, February 1997.

106. The PRPA reflected the CPC's pique in its Executive Committee Meeting Minutes of January 12, 1942. In a section of the minutes titled "Star Chamber Policy," it stated that "the Planning Commission has adopted a policy that 'any outside agency' should not be permitted to study a problem in cooperation with the Planning Commission Staff prior to the time that the staff has submitted a recommendation to the Commission and the Commission has formally accepted such recommendation as an official plan. This has resulted in creating a situation best exemplified in the studies for the Duquesne-Crosstown connection." See Folder 83, PRPA Records. Fogelson makes the same point about the salience of the downtown in his *Downtown.*

107. Ralph Griswold noted the lack of integration of landscape into highway planning; see "Talk by Ralph Griswold at Joint Meeting of Board of Directors of PRPA," October 8, 1940, PRPA Mins., Folder 83, PRPA Records.

108. Mershon, "Corporate Social Responsibility," 153–221. Mershon, as we do, argues that the founding of the Allegheny Conference grew out of both the long prewar experience in Pittsburgh of private planning organizations and the impetus by the federal government to energize planning for postwar urban America at the local level. She also points out that, in Pittsburgh, elites embraced planning at this time to make the city a more efficient place within which to conduct business and to improve the quality of life by effecting environmental reforms. Rather than being framed, as so often was the case, as an issue of environmental quality versus growth in jobs, Pittsburgh leaders saw environmental reform as crucial for sustaining economic growth after the war.

109. PCPC Mins., March 31, 1942; ACPC Mins., September 30, 1943. On postwar planning, see Bauman, "Visions of a Post-War City," 152–170.

110. See Housing Authority of the City of Pittsburgh Minutes, March 26, 1943, in Housing Authority of City of Pittsburgh office, Pittsburgh; and J. L. Shotwell to Mrs. Joseph Barnett, Chief of the Urban Division, September 7, 1948, FAS Pa., RG 30, BPR Papers, NARS.

111. "Report of the City Planning Commission, 1943," in Pittsburgh City Planning Commission Library.

CHAPTER 9. A SCAFFOLDING FOR URBAN RENAISSANCE

1. Schuyler, *New Urban Landscape;* Peterson, *Birth of City Planning;* Wilson, *City Beautiful Movement.*

2. Robinson, "Civic Improvement Possibilities," 826.

3. On postwar urban redevelopment and renewal, see James Q. Wilson, ed., *Urban Renewal: The Record and the Controversy* (Cambridge, Mass.: MIT Press, 1967); and Bernard J. Frieden and Lynne B. Sagalyn, *Downtown, Inc.: How America Rebuilds Cities* (Cambridge, Mass.: MIT Press, 1992).

4. On the term "special purpose," see Peterson, *Birth of City Planning,* 6, 88.

5. On Pittsburgh as a postwar model of urban renaissance, see Teaford, *Rough Road,* 47; John Guinther, *Direction of Cities* (New York: Penguin, 1997), 207–208; and Lowe, *Cities in a Race with Time,* 110–111.

6. Wilson, *Urban Renewal;* Alberts, *Shaping of the Point;* Teaford, *Rough Road.*

Index